Using ACCPAC® Plus

Second Edition

Erik Genzer and John McMurray
Sheridan College

Addison-Wesley Publishers

Don Mills, Ontario • Reading, Massachusetts • Menlo Park, California
New York • Wokingham, England • Amsterdam • Bonn
Sydney • Singapore • Tokyo • Madrid • San Juan

DESIGN:	Steve Rimmer/Alchemy Mindworks Inc.
COVER DESIGN:	Anthony Leung
SPONSORING EDITOR:	Shirley Tessier
COPY EDITOR:	Edie Franks
COORDINATING EDITOR:	Kateri Lanthier
TEXT FORMATTING:	Judy Petersiel

Canadian Cataloguing in Publication Data

```
Genzer, Erik
    Using ACCPAC®Plus
2nd ed.
''Version 6''.
ISBN 0-201-60165-6

1. ACCPAC Plus (Computer program).  2. Accounting -
Computer programs.  I. McMurray, John, 1942-     .
II. Title.

HF5679.G46 1992      657'.0285'5369   C92-094417-5
```

MS-DOS® is a registered trademark of Microsoft Corporation.

ACCPAC® Plus is a registered trademark of Computer Associates International, Inc.

Copyright © 1993 Addison-Wesley Publishers Limited

ISBN 0–201–60165–6

D E F - WC - 96 95 94

Table of Contents

UNIT II *GENERAL LEDGER & FINANCIAL REPORTER* *25*

Chapter 6   More Batch Processing   85

Chapter 7   Period End   103

Chapter 8   Financial Reports   121

PREFACE

ACCPAC Plus V.6 is the most recent version of the ACCPAC Plus series, which is recognized as an industry leader among microcomputer accounting software packages. Because of this, a working knowledge of ACCPAC Plus V.6 is a real asset to accounting students. *Using ACCPAC Plus Second Edition* provides one of the easiest and most effective ways to acquire this knowledge. The book presents practical, hands-on experience organized for individual learning.

Using ACCPAC Plus is a modular, skills-oriented, individual learning package designed for students with a fundamental knowledge of accounting principles and terminology. It applies the concepts and practices learned in an introductory accounting course to the real world of computerized accounting through the use of a simulation (E. & J. Enterprises). Over a five-year period, the concepts and principles used in *Using ACCPAC Plus* have been tested with over 2000 post-secondary students at Sheridan College and over 600 mature students in professional development workshops.

The book focuses on the most frequently used ACCPAC Plus Accounting software modules. The first unit, Introduction, details the installation of the ACCPAC Plus System Manager and introduces you to basic keystroke functions. The three remaining units, listed below, may be used independently, or data may be exchanged between modules as you complete the three units:

General Ledger and Financial Reporter

Accounts Receivable

Accounts Payable

Within each unit, each chapter is designed as a learning module covering related functions. Each chapter provides step-by-step instructions so that students can perform actual accounting tasks. The tables throughout the book provide students with printouts to compare with their own results so that data entry errors can be corrected before proceeding. Chapters should be covered in the order presented since the material introduced and the data entered in one chapter is then used in the following chapters.

At the end of each chapter, we present both review questions and an exercise based on the content of the chapter. The review questions should be used by students to test their knowledge of the material introduced in the chapter. The exercise gives students a chance to review the instructions in the chapter using a simulation parallel to that of E. & J. Enterprises but based on a company named after themselves. Again, transaction data is provided, but detailed instructions are not. Completing these exercises will reinforce the student's understanding of how to use ACCPAC Plus.

At the end of three units of *Using ACCPAC Plus* is a Macavity & Co. case. These cases provide a further opportunity to practice and reinforce the skills learned in each unit.

A NOTE TO STUDENTS

As you work through each chapter, make sure you understand what you are doing in each step: do not simply follow the instructions. Try to understand the system of menus, messages, and data entry screens. Too often people simply press keys as instructed rather than really observing what each keystroke does.

Read the descriptions and instructions carefully. If you miss an instruction it can cause the program to appear as though it is not working properly. When you do make an error, do not get discouraged – making mistakes often provides the best opportunity for learning about a software package. Try to trace the error to its source and then correct or adjust it. If you need help, ask! Remember that education is not only learning the *right* answers, but learning to recognize errors and to correct them.

Near the end of each chapter, you will be asked to make a back up of your data files. Make sure that you follow this instruction! If the unthinkable happens and you lose your working data files, you can recover by copying the back-up files onto your working disk and then doing the chapter again.

Computer Associates has greatly increased the sorting ability for the reports in ACCPAC Plus V.6. As a result of this increased power, the number of files and the required amount of floppy disk space has increased greatly. If you are using a computer system with high density disk drives of either 1.2 or 1.4 megabytes capacity, you will require only one disk for the working data and one for a back up for all of the companies in this book. If you are using double density disks, by the time you start the last section, Accounts Payable, there will be insufficient space remaining on a disk to hold more than one company. In this situation you will have to keep a live data disk and a corresponding back-up disk for each company.

WORKING WITH DOS

Before starting to use application software you should have some understanding of how microcomputer system software works. The best way to obtain this understanding is through a short tutorial. We suggest that you review the DOS commands that you must know before working with ACCPAC Plus by reading the Back-up Procedures appendix.

A NOTE TO INSTRUCTORS

Students will require over 35 hours to work through *Using ACCPAC Plus*. The workbook is an effective tool for teaching students in three different contexts:

1. as a complement to your textbook in an introductory accounting course
2. as training in computer skills after the completion of an introductory accounting course
3. as a series of three workshops in a professional development or skills retraining program.

The cases at the end of the last three units allow students to gain extra practice, but they can also be used to evaluate students' progress.

Teaching students to use ACCPAC Plus V.6 may look easy, but it actually requires extensive preparation. To assist the instructor, Addison-Wesley has published an Instructor's Manual. Request this upon adoption of the text.

ACKNOWLEDGEMENTS

We would like to extend our appreciation to our many students and colleagues at Sheridan College who have contributed to the evolution of our instructional materials over the last seven years. We would also like to thank Ron Doleman, Kateri Lanthier, Shirley Tessier, and Judy Petersiel at Addison-Wesley for their suggestions, patience, and encouragement.

E. Genzer
J. McMurray
May, 1992

UNIT

I Introduction

CHAPTER

1 Using ACCPAC Plus

The ACCPAC Plus accounting system offers the following modules:

General Ledger & Financial Reporter
Accounts Receivable
Accounts Payable
Retail Invoicing
Payroll
Order Entry
Inventory Control & Analysis
Job Costing
Sales Analysis

ACCPAC Plus software is designed so that each module may be used as an individual unit or several modules may be integrated to work together. This flexibility and the comprehensive capabilities of each module have made ACCPAC Plus one of the most popular accounting systems available for microcomputers. The addition of the System Manager, extensive Help screens, the Finder, and a pop-up menu system have made the ACCPAC Plus system even easier to operate.

ACCESS Companion Products are available to supplement ACCPAC Plus. These products, available from Companion Developers, certify that the programs are compatible with ACCPAC Plus (version 6.0) modules.

This book will show you how to install and operate the ACCPAC Plus (version 6.0) standard System Manager, General Ledger and Financial Reporter, Accounts Receivable, and Accounts Payable modules.

SYSTEM MANAGER

The System Manager makes it easier for the user to work with the microcomputer's operating system. In this book, we will use it to install the ACCPAC Plus accounting modules and to use DOS commands from within an operating accounting module.

In addition, the System Manager enables the user to control some aspects of the screen display, organize system security with password protection, and select printers.

GENERAL LEDGER & FINANCIAL REPORTER

The General Ledger and Financial Reporter module is central to the operation of an integrated ACCPAC Plus accounting system, so install this module first and add other modules later. Once you learn to operate the General Ledger and Financial Reporter module, you can quickly learn to operate the other modules.

The General Ledger is a batch-oriented system. This means that transactions entered into the General Ledger are saved in groups called transaction batches. Each of these batches can be printed so that entries can be checked against source documents and corrections made before posting the transactions to the General Ledger accounts. Several unposted batches may be in use at any time. Batches of transactions from other ACCPAC Plus modules can be transferred to the General Ledger, printed, and then posted.

The Financial Reporter uses the data posted to the General Ledger to print financial statements.

ACCOUNTS RECEIVABLE

ACCPAC Plus Accounts Receivable can be adapted to meet the specific requirements of a particular business. You can enter and process transactions in several ways. Printing the Posting Journals provides a complete audit trail. Customer account information can be displayed on the screen or used to print customized statements and comprehensive reports. You can distribute Accounts Receivable data to General Ledger accounts.

ACCOUNTS PAYABLE

ACCPAC Plus Accounts Payable performs all the record-keeping functions of an organization's purchasing and bill-paying processes. You can enter and process transactions in several ways. Payment controls can be set at both the vendor and invoice level. Check processing can be controlled in all phases. Printing Posting Journals and Check Registers provides a complete audit trail. Comprehensive management reports can also be printed. Accounts Payable data can be distributed to General Ledger accounts.

SPECIAL KEYS

Your computer keyboard has keys that tell the computer to perform special tasks. The tasks change, depending on what software you are running. The following paragraphs present a description of the special keys that you will use most often with ACCPAC Plus.

The Escape Key [Esc]

Pressing the escape key **Esc** will return the display to the previous menu or data entry screen. Although the escape key provides a useful way to move backwards through the menu system, this key should be used carefully because you can lose data if you don't complete a procedure before you press **Esc**.

The Return or Enter Key [Enter]

Pressing **Enter** accepts a default in the data entry field, selects a highlighted menu option, or signifies that data entry is complete. The Enter or Return Key is also pressed in response to prompts that ACCPAC Plus displays in the lower part of the screen. Read these prompts or messages carefully before pressing any key.

The Help Key [F1]

Pressing the help key, **F1**, allows you access to Information screens about ACCPAC Plus. The System Manager and the accounting modules each provide many screens that can help you use the module. When you press **F1**, ACCPAC Plus searches for the Help screen related to the function that you are working with and displays it in a window on the right side of the screen. Press **Esc** to return to the program that you were working on.

Error Message Release Key [F2]

When ACCPAC Plus receives an instruction it cannot follow, an error message will appear on the screen and operations will be interrupted. You will be instructed to press **F2**. When possible, ACCPAC Plus will return to the program. Otherwise, you will be returned to DOS and you will have to restart ACCPAC Plus.

System Manager [F3]

Press **F3** to gain access to the System Manager. After the initial set up, you will use the System Manager to enter DOS commands and install ACCPAC Plus accounting modules.

Finder F5

Press **F5** to activate a scanning feature that displays data such as General Ledger account codes, customer numbers, or vendor numbers in a window on the screen. You can select the information you wish to use and it will be automatically inserted into a data entry field.

MENU SELECTION

Options can be selected from a menu in several ways:

If the options are preceded by a number, press the number for the option you wish to select.

If the options are not numbered, press the first letter of your selection.

Any menu option can be selected by highlighting it with the selector bar and pressing **Enter**.

DATA ENTRY

ACCPAC Plus displays data entry fields on the screen. You enter information in one of these fields by moving the cursor to the field, typing the information, and then pressing **Enter**. The cursor will then move to the next data entry field or to the message line at the bottom of the screen.

HOW TO USE THIS BOOK

This book follows the accounting cycle of the E. & J. Enterprises company, a small but rapidly expanding business that provides accounting services and markets software. Each chapter in the text is designed as a learning module and covers a specific set of related functions using transactions involving E. & J. Enterprises. You should work through the chapters in order, as concepts and data from one chapter are used in subsequent chapters.

Each chapter provides step-by-step instructions and keystrokes for completing each task. Your understanding of how the software package works can be reviewed by answering the review questions at the end of each chapter. The exercises, which follow the review questions, offer an additional simulation that parallels the work you are doing with E. & J. Enterprises. These exercises allow you to practice the skills that you learn as you proceed through the E. & J. Enterprises simulation, without endangering your main data files.

As you work through each chapter, read the descriptions and instructions carefully. If you miss an instruction, the program may appear to be working improperly. Watch the computer display as you enter data or menu selections. Try to understand the system of menus, messages, and data entry screens. Too often people using a learning package just press the keys as instructed without really paying attention to what each keystroke does.

Near the end of each chapter you will be asked to back up your data files to another data disk. Do this conscientiously. If the unthinkable happens and you lose your working data files, you can then start the chapter over after you have copied the backup data files to your working disk. If you do not know how to back up your data files refer to the Back Up Procedures Appendix or consult your computer resource person or network manager.

E. & J. ENTERPRISES

E. & J. Enterprises was started by two successful and dynamic friends, Erin Gogetter and Joan Ambitious, shortly after they graduated from college. The two friends had observed that there was a need within Georgetown for a business providing accounting services and selling accounting-related software and hardware. The company was founded at the beginning of November 1997 but did not start operating until the first of July 1998. Their fiscal year ends on October 31. The books were kept manually for the first three months. The business has been successful and at the end of September 1998, Erin and Joan decided to computerize the accounts using ACCPAC Plus General Ledger, Accounts Receivable, and Accounts Payable software.

You have been hired to operate the ACCPAC Plus accounting system and to create a second set of records for an office in a nearby town. Erin and Joan want the two companies to have different names and to operate separately. They are really enthusiastic about your potential, and they offer to name the second company after you. You will work for the company as you work through this book. Each chapter will lead you through one phase of converting E. & J. Enterprises' manual accounting system to ACCPAC Plus. The exercise at the end of each chapter will apply the information in that chapter to the new company created using your name. The books will be closed on October 31, 1998, the end of the company's fiscal year. This will allow you to go through the full accounting cycle without having to enter twelve months' work.

DISKS REQUIRED

If your computer has high density disk drives you can store the data for E. & J. Enterprises, the company used in the exercises, and the Macavity Case data on one high density disk using subdirectories. You would then back up your data to a second high density disk.

If your computer uses only double sided double density disks, you will require three working disks. A separate disk would be used for each of E. & J. Enterprises, the exercises, and the Macavity Case. Three more double sided double density disks would be required for back ups.

In all cases you should use subdirectories for each set of data files.

CHAPTER

2 The System Manager

In this chapter you will install the ACCPAC Plus (version 6) standard System Manager. You will then use the System Manager to install an ACCPAC Plus accounting module, select your printer, and add to or modify the Start Menu. You will need two blank formatted disks. Label one "WORKING" and the other "BACKUP".

INSTALLING THE SYSTEM MANAGER

If the ACCPAC Plus (Version 6) standard System Manager has been installed on your hard disk, skip this section and turn to the section on Installing an Accounting Module. If you are installing either the Windowing System Manager or System Manager/2 for OS/2, follow the instructions provided with your software. If you are installing ACCPAC Plus on a network, refer to the LanPak Network Administrator's Manual and the manual provided with your network software, and ask your network manager for help.

Display the DOS C > prompt on the screen by entering the commands or menu selections required by your computer system. Switch the default directory to the root directory of the hard drive where you want to install ACCPAC Plus. If necessary, consult your DOS manual or the Back-up Procedures Appendix.

Write protect the original ACCPAC Plus System Manager disks. Then insert the ACCPAC Plus System 1 disk in drive A. You should have a prompt on the screen that shows the drive where you want to install the ACCPAC Plus System Manager.

❏ Type: A:Install

❑ Press: [Enter]

If a prompt appears on your screen saying that the "config.sys" file has been adjusted, you will have to open the gate on drive A and reboot the computer. Then close the gate on drive A and enter the install command again.

Follow the instructions displayed on the screen to continue installation. Do not press any keys while the disk drive lights are on. If requested, insert each additional ACCPAC Plus System disk in drive A and press any key to continue installation.

When installation is complete, remove the System disk from drive A and press any key. The ACCPAC Plus System Manager will start and in a few seconds will display the Install screen (Figure 2–1).

Figure 2–1

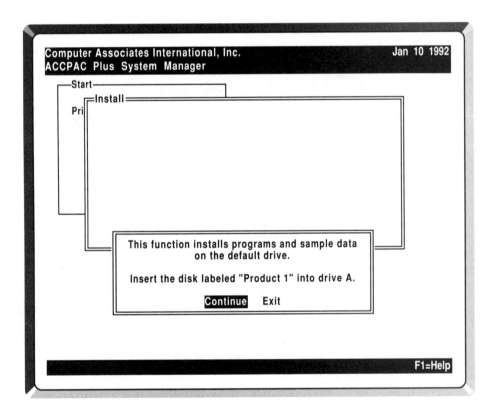

If you wished to install an ACCPAC Plus accounting module, you would select Continue.

❑ Move the selector bar to Exit.

❑ Press: [Enter] to display the Start Menu.

The Start Menu is used to tell ACCPAC Plus which accounting module to use and the location of the data files. In this chapter you will see how to add lines to, or modify lines on, the Start Menu. If you are not ready to install an ACCPAC Plus accounting module, turn to the section on Exiting ACCPAC Plus at the end of this chapter.

INSTALLING AN ACCOUNTING MODULE

If the ACCPAC Plus accounting module that you wish to use has been installed on the hard disk of your computer, turn to the section on Selecting Your Printer. Each ACCPAC Plus accounting module that you use must be installed separately; however, the installation procedure is basically the same for all modules. The General Ledger and Financial Reporter will be installed in this example.

❑ Press: [F3] to display the System Manager Menu (Figure 2–2).

Figure 2–2

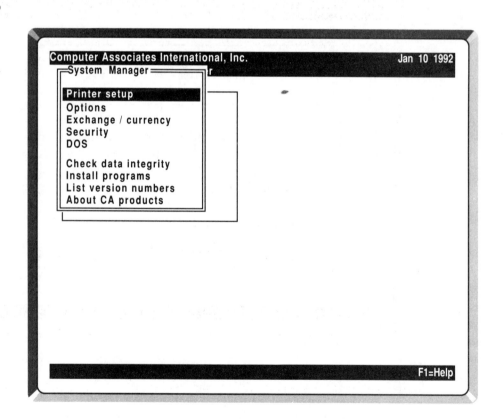

❑ Press: I to select Install programs.

The program will display the Install Menu (Figure 2–1) again with the first set of instructions on screen.

❑ Write protect the original ACCPAC General Ledger and Financial Reporter disks.

❑ Insert the write protected Product 1 disk in drive A.

❑ Select: `Continue`

The program will display the following prompt.

```
Do you want to install sample data?

         Yes        No
```

❑ Press: `N` for `No`.

Installation will then begin, but no sample data will be installed. After a minute or two, the disk drives will stop and the display will change again. If requested, insert the next ACCPAC Plus Product disk in drive A and follow the new instructions. When installation is complete the following prompt will appear at the bottom of the screen.

```
For documentation changes insert Product 1 disk
         in drive A & type A:README
                  Continue
```

To inform users of changes to their printed manuals most software manufacturers include a "README" file on disk. The command to display or print this "README" file should be entered at the DOS C > prompt.

❑ Press: Enter to Continue.

You will then be asked,

```
Do you want to install another program?

         Yes        No
```

❑ Press: `N` for `No`.

The System Manager Menu (Figure 2–2) will reappear.

❑ Press: Esc

This returns you to the Start Menu (Figure 2–3), which now has a new line for the ACCPAC Plus accounting module that you have installed. This screen shows that the System Manager and the General Ledger and Financial Reporter modules have been installed.

Figure 2–3

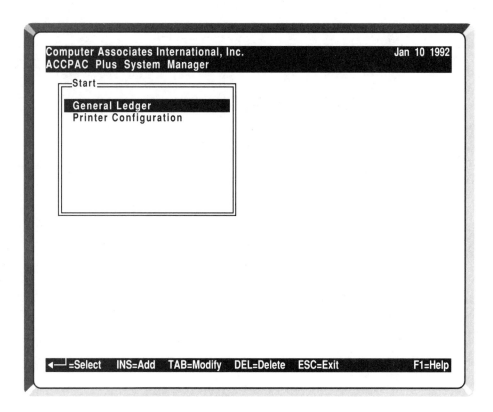

```
┌─────────────────────────────────────────────────────────────┐
│ Computer Associates International, Inc.          Jan 10 1992  │
│ ACCPAC  Plus  System  Manager                                 │
│  ┌─Start──────────────────────────────┐                       │
│  │ General Ledger                     │                       │
│  │ Printer Configuration              │                       │
│  │                                    │                       │
│  │                                    │                       │
│  │                                    │                       │
│  └────────────────────────────────────┘                      │
│                                                               │
│                                                               │
│  ◄──┘=Select   INS=Add   TAB=Modify   DEL=Delete   ESC=Exit      F1=Help │
└─────────────────────────────────────────────────────────────┘
```

SELECTING YOUR PRINTER

If your printer has been installed, turn to the section on Exiting From ACCPAC Plus.

When you install ACCPAC Plus you should select your printer to ensure that reports and financial statements are printed properly. If you change printers, the new printer should be selected from the list of printers supported by ACCPAC Plus. Your printer manual should tell you which printer to select.

❑ Press: F3 to display the System Manager Menu (Figure 2–2).

❑ Press: P to display the Printer Setup Menu, Figure 2–4.

Figure 2–4

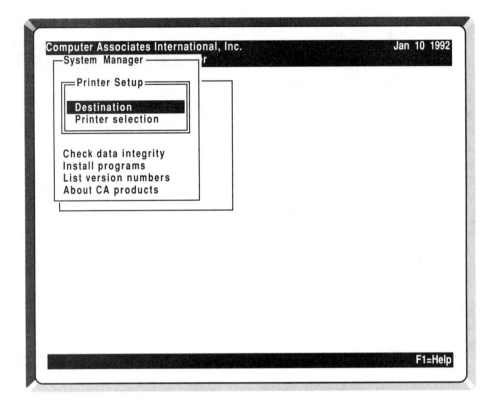

❑ Press: D to display the Destination Menu.

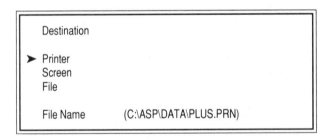

The choices on this menu allow you to control where the computer output is sent to when you print a report or a financial statement. In most cases, you will want a printed report as indicated by the mark beside Printer on this menu. The Screen option displays the report on the screen. You would use the File option and then assign a unique File name if you wished to save the report on disk for use with a word processing package.

❑ Press: [Esc] to return to the Printer Setup Menu.

❑ Press: P to display the Printer Selection Menu, Figure 2–5.

Figure 2–5

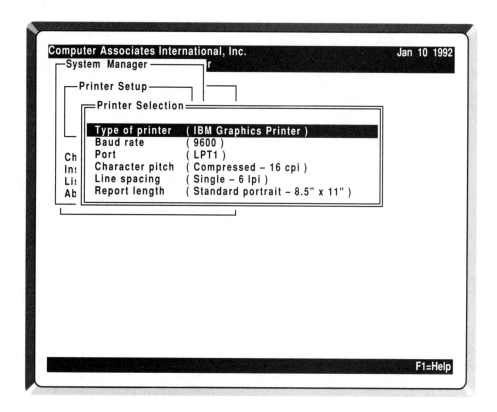

□ Press: T for Type of printer

□ Move the selector bar to the printer recommended in your printer manual.

□ Press: [Enter]

The Baud rate option only applies to serial printers. If you are using a serial printer refer to your printer manual for the correct Baud rate.

The Character pitch option controls the number of characters (letters or numbers) printed across one inch of a line. As many of the reports produced by ACCPAC Plus require more than 80 characters per line, you should select Compressed – 16 cpi for Character Pitch and a Line spacing of Single - 6 lpi or six lines per inch. The Report length should be Standard portrait - 8.5" x 11".

□ Press: [Esc] until you return to the Start Menu.

EXITING FROM ACCPAC PLUS

To quit ACCPAC Plus from the Start Menu,

□ Press: [Esc]

The program will request confirmation by showing the message,

```
┌─────────────────────────────────────────────────────┐
│┌───────────────────────────────────────────────────┐│
││         Do you really want to exit the system?     ││
││                                                     ││
││                    Yes       No                    ││
│└───────────────────────────────────────────────────┘│
└─────────────────────────────────────────────────────┘
```

❏ Move the cursor to Yes.

❏ Press: [Enter]

The screen will again display the DOS C > prompt.

Every time you are finished working with ACCPAC Plus, you must quit using this method. If you do not exit properly, the data files that you are using may be damaged.

STARTING THE SYSTEM MANAGER

If your computer system is part of a network or has a menu, ask a resource person how to access ACCPAC Plus.

To begin working with the ACCPAC Plus accounting system, insert your blank, formatted, working data disk in drive A and close the gate. At the DOS C > prompt,

❏ Type: Plus

❏ Press: [Enter]

A few seconds later, the Start Menu (Figure 2–3) will appear on the screen. If you have installed other ACCPAC Plus modules on your computer, the listing will be different from that shown in Figure 2–3. If "General Ledger" is displayed in the Start Menu, the General Ledger and Financial Reporter module has been installed on your system's hard disk. You should confirm that the correct versions of both the ACCPAC Plus System Manager and the General Ledger and Financial Reporter module have been installed.

❏ Press: [F3] to display the System Manager Menu (Figure 2–2) again.

The Printer setup and Install options were used earlier in this chapter to install the General Ledger and Financial Reporter module, and to select your printer settings. The DOS option will be used when you back up your data files as explained in Appendix A.

❏ Select: List version numbers

A list of the version numbers of the ACCPAC Plus software installed on your computer similar to Figure 2–6 will be displayed on your screen.

The ACCPAC Plus System Manager should be version 6.0B or higher. The General Ledger and Financial Reporter should be version 6.0A or higher. If necessary, install current versions of your software.

❏ Press: [Esc] twice to return to the Start Menu.

Figure 2–6

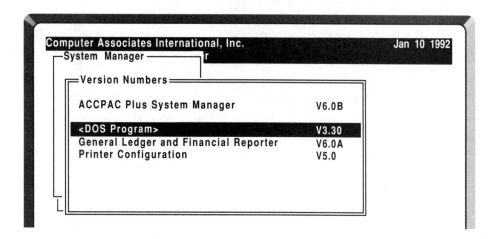

```
Computer Associates International, Inc.                    Jan 10 1992
 ┌─System  Manager ──────────┐r
 │                           │
 │ ┌─Version Numbers ═══════════════════════════════════════════
 │ │
 │ │ ACCPAC Plus System Manager              V6.0B
 │ │
 │ │ <DOS Program>                           V3.30
 │ │ General Ledger and Financial Reporter   V6.0A
 │ │ Printer Configuration                   V5.0
 │ │
 │ │
 │ │
 L─┘
```

THE START MENU

The Start Menu is used to specify the ACCPAC Plus accounting module that you wish to use and the location of the data files you wish to work with. You must make a separate entry, or line, on the Start Menu for each program module and each company for which you enter data.

The Start Menu information will be stored in the ACCPAC Plus System Manager files on your hard disk, not on your data disk. If you use another computer or if your start line information is deleted, you will have to enter it again.

Before adding to a start list entry, it is important to note the following:

1. If you intend to integrate ACCPAC Plus accounting modules, store the data for all of the programs in the same subdirectory of one disk, using the same data extension.

2. If you keep accounting records for more than one company or division, store each company's data in its own subdirectory. This increases processing speed when using the programs.

3. Do not store your data files in the program subdirectories on your hard disk.

4. Each Start Name must be unique; i.e., no duplicates are allowed.

ADDING TO THE START MENU

It is important that the start line be added accurately; otherwise, you may manipulate a company's records with data from another company.

You will make an entry telling ACCPAC Plus that you wish to use the General Ledger module with the data for E. & J. Enterprises that will be stored in a subdirectory on a disk in drive A. Use this same procedure to add start line information for other companies. To modify the start line information, you would highlight the line, press **Tab** and then complete the same sequence of data entry screens.

❏ Insert your working data disk in drive A.

❏ Press: [INSERT] to add to the Start Menu.

A data entry area will appear as shown in Figure 2–7.

Figure 2–7

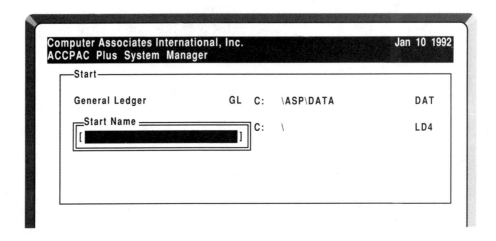

Note the instruction `Type name of item` and the highlighted data entry area with the flashing cursor. All data entry areas in ACCPAC Plus modules work the same way. You type the new data and then press **Enter** to indicate that the entry is complete.

❏ Type: `G/L E. & J. Enterprises`

❏ Press: Enter

A pop-up menu, listing the available ACCPAC Plus programs or modules, will appear on the screen, as shown in Figure 2–8.

Figure 2–8

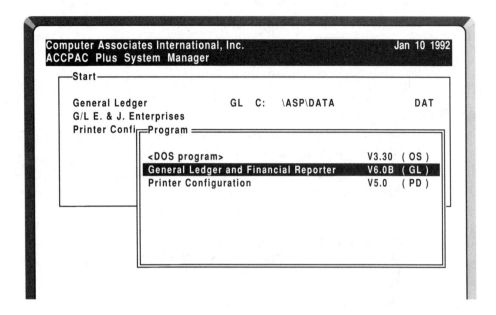

☐ Move the selector bar to `General Ledger and Financial Reporter`.

☐ Press: ⌈Enter⌋

A pop-up menu listing the disk drives installed on your system will appear, as shown in Figure 2–9.

Figure 2–9

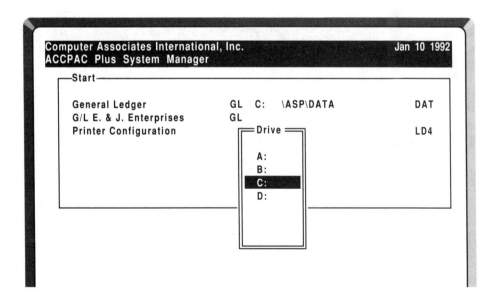

Your working data disk for E. & J. Enterprises is in drive A.

❏ Move the selector bar to `A:`

❏ Press: `Enter`

The next pop-up menu will ask you to `Choose or type in directory.`

Figure 2-10

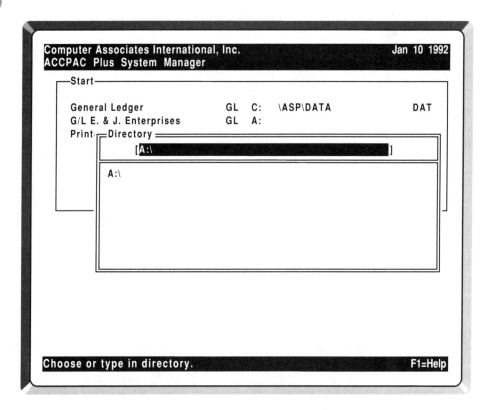

This menu is divided into two sections. You enter data in the top section, while the program lists available subdirectories on the selected disk drive in the bottom section. As the floppy disk in drive A does not have any subdirectories, the selector bar will be on `A:\` in the top section. If there were subdirectories on the disk, they would be shown in the lower portion of the screen.

You should store the data for each company in a separate directory. Use the letters "EJE" for E. & J. Enterprises.

❏ Type: `EJE`

The Directory data entry line should now read `A:\EJE`

❏ Press: [Enter] to accept the subdirectory EJE in the root directory of the disk in drive A.

If the subdirectory you specify does not currently exist, you will be asked if you want to create it.

```
┌─────────────────────────────────────────────┐
│                                             │
│           Create the subdirectory            │
│                  "EJE"                       │
│                                             │
│             Yes         No                   │
│                                             │
└─────────────────────────────────────────────┘
```

❏ Select: `Yes`

The final menu in this sequence will ask you to `Choose or type in data extension.` The data extension consists of the three characters following the period in a DOS filename. Each company's data files should be assigned a unique data extension when data files are created so that data for one company is not accidentally added to another company's records.

The data extension for the E. & J. Enterprises files is EJE. The pop-up menu displays the ACCPAC Plus default extension, DAT, in the highlighted data entry area. If your disk contains other files, the data extension for those files would be displayed in the lower section. To use a data selector displayed in the lower section, highlight it or type the three letters in the upper section, and then press **Enter**.

❏ Type: `EJE`
❏ Press: [Enter]

The Start Menu will appear on the screen with the selector bar on your new entry for E. & J. Enterprises. You use the same steps as described in this section to add any new company to the Start List. You can create the data files later.

You can change your Start Menu entries by highlighting the start line to be changed and pressing **Tab**. The sequence of menus is the same as for adding to the Start Menu. You make changes by entering new information in the data entry areas.

❏ Add a Start Line for Fred's Company General Ledger, using subdirectory FRED and data extension ZZZ on drive A, to the Start Menu. When you have finished, the Start Menu displayed on the screen should show a line for Fred's Company General Ledger.

USING HELP

ACCPAC Plus includes a large number of Help screens that provide information about the program menus and operations. The program displays help information in a window on the right side of the screen. To get help about the Start List, display the Start Menu on the screen.

❑ Press: [F1]

A Help screen for the Start List will appear as shown in Figure 2–11.

Figure 2–11

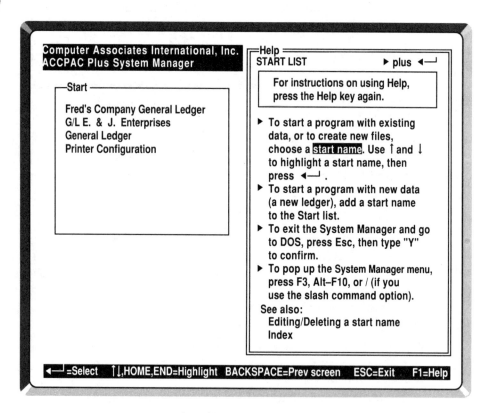

You may select highlighted "keywords" to obtain more information on the topics displayed on the Help screen.

❑ Move the selector bar to `add a start name`.

❑ Press: [Enter]

The program displays information on adding a start name to the Start Menu.

❑ Press the backspace key to display the previous Help screen in the help window.

Take a few minutes to look at the Help Index, choose a few topics, and look at the kind of help the program offers. Once you are accustomed to using the help function, you will find it a handy feature to turn to when you are confused about how to proceed.

❑ Press: [Esc] to exit from the help function.

EXITING FROM ACCPAC PLUS

To quit ACCPAC Plus from the Start Menu,

❑ Press: [Esc]

The program will request confirmation by showing the message,

```
┌─────────────────────────────────────────────────┐
│                                                   │
│   Do you really want to exit the system?          │
│                                                   │
│                 Yes       No                      │
│                                                   │
└─────────────────────────────────────────────────┘
```

❑ Select: Yes

REVIEW QUESTIONS

1. Name the command that you enter at the DOS C > prompt to load the ACCPAC Plus System Manager and display its Start Menu.
2. Which key do you press to display the System Manager Menu?
3. How do you select options from an ACCPAC Plus menu?
4. Which key do you use to add an entry to the Start Menu?
5. Describe the difference between program files and data files.
6. Why should data extensions be different for each company for which you maintain records?
7. Which key do you press to get help?
8. How do you exit ACCPAC Plus from the Start Menu?

EXERCISE

In this exercise, you will add a new selection to the Start List for the new company that bears your name.

If you are using double sided double density disks, you will require a new working disk and a new back-up disk for these exercises. If you are using high density disks you can store the exercise data files on the same disk that you are using for E. & J. Enterprises.

1. Enter the commands to access ACCPAC Plus.
2. Add a new line to the Start Menu using "G/L" and your name. The Start Menu line should use the ACCPAC Plus General Ledger and Financial Reporter module. The data files will be stored in the subdirectory "EXERCISE" in the root directory of drive A. Use your initials as the data extension. If your initials are EJE, enter EE.

II General Ledger & Financial Reporter

CHAPTER

3 General Ledger Creation

The ACCPAC Plus System Manager and the General Ledger and Financial Reporter Module should be installed on your computer. If necessary refer to Chapter 2 - The System Manager and complete the installation. In this chapter you will create the ledger files and company profile for E. & J. Enterprises.

STARTING THE SYSTEM MANAGER

If your computer system is part of a network or has a menu, ask a resource person how to access ACCPAC Plus.

To begin working with the ACCPAC Plus accounting system, insert your Working Data Disk in drive A and close the gate. At the DOS C > prompt,

❑ Type: Plus

❑ Press: [Enter]

A few seconds later, the Start Menu (Figure 3–1) will appear on the screen. If you have installed other ACCPAC Plus modules on your computer, the listing will be different from that shown.

If the start lines for G/L E. & J. Enterprises and Fred's Company General Ledger are not displayed on your screen, refer to Chapter 2 - The System Manager and add these two start lines.

Figure 3–1

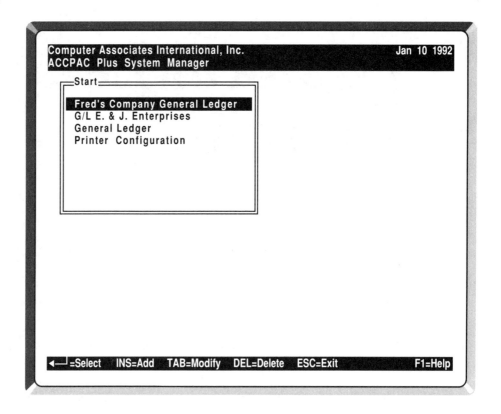

CREATING THE GENERAL LEDGER

The start line G/L E. & J. Enterprises that you added in Chapter 2 is now part of the System Manager. When you added this start line you also created a subdirectory "EJE" in the root directory of your working data disk. You will now create the basic General Ledger data files and store them on your working data disk.

❑ Move the selector bar to G/L E. & J. Enterprises.

❑ Press: Enter

The program will start and then search your data disk for the data files for the new company. Not finding any data files, ACCPAC Plus will display the title screen (Figure 3–2) with the current date as the "Last access date" and an option for creating the General Ledger data files.

❑ Press: C to create the General Ledger data files.

The first of a series of General Ledger Creation screens will appear, as shown in Figure 3–2.

Figure 3-2

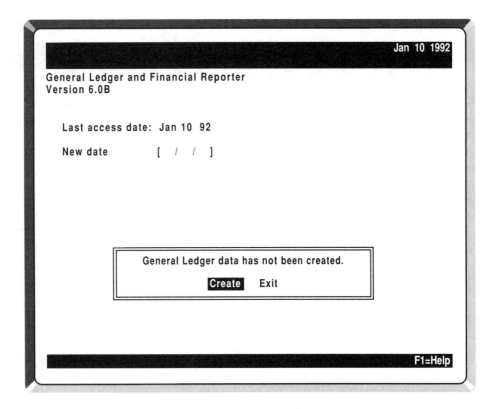

Fiscal Period

You may choose either a twelve- or thirteen-period fiscal year. Some companies use a thirteen-period fiscal year because that allows 28 days per period for comparison of the activity of identical periods. If you choose a thirteen-period fiscal year, you must specify which quarter will contain four periods when you are entering information on the next screen.

❏ Press: Enter to accept the default of 12 fiscal periods.

The "Month in which your current fiscal year began" refers to the month in the calendar year. For example, January would be month 1. E. & J. Enterprises was founded in November 1997.

❏ Type: 11

❏ Press: Enter

For the "Year in which your current fiscal year began" you will be using 1997.

❏ Type: 97

❏ Press: Enter

This information is used by the program to fill out fiscal period starting, ending, and report dates on the Fiscal Period Calendar screen.

Figure 3–3

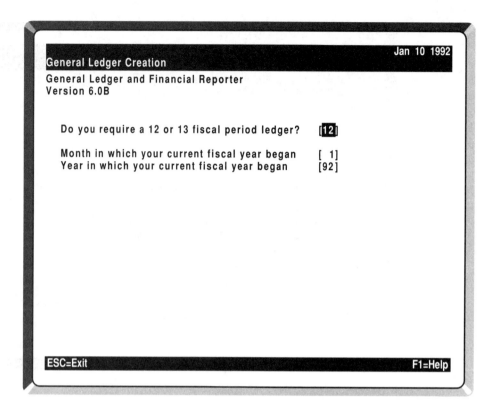

A menu will appear in the lower section of the screen.

If you have entered an incorrect date you could select Edit and make the necessary changes. If there are no errors,

❑ Press: N to display the next screen.

Company Data and Options

The General Ledger Creation - Company Data and Options screen (Figure 3–4), allows you to enter general information about the company. If you are using Version 6.0 A, the Allow provisional posting field will not be displayed on your screen.

❑ Press: E to edit the company data.

The menu box in the lower portion of the screen will disappear and the flashing cursor will appear in the Company name data entry area.

Figure 3–4

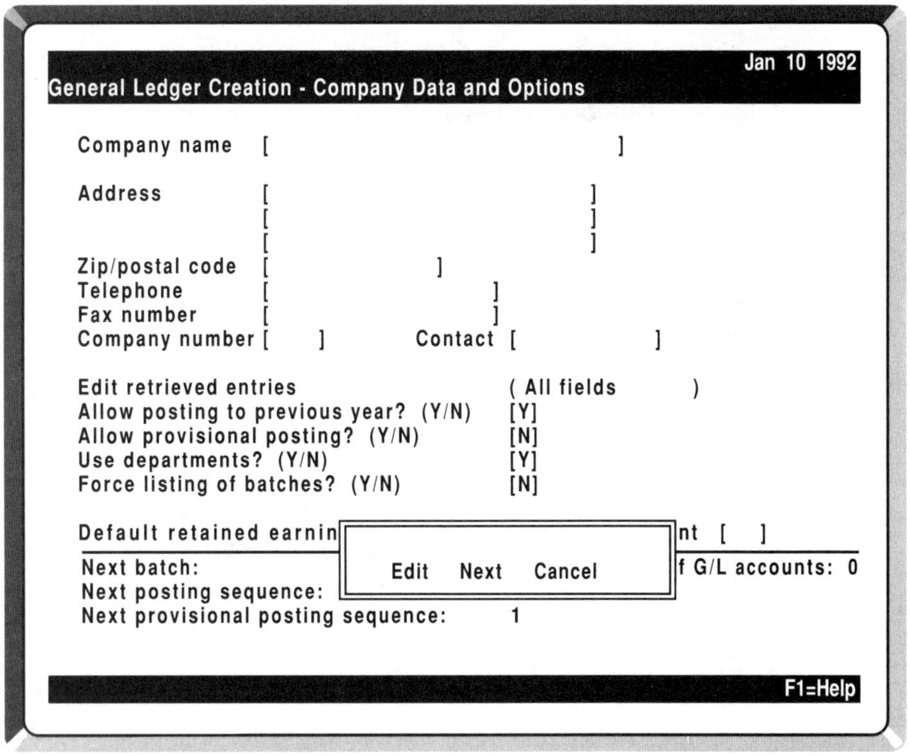

```
                                                    Jan 10 1992
 General Ledger Creation - Company Data and Options

        Company name   [                              ]

        Address        [                         ]
                       [                         ]
                       [                         ]
        Zip/postal code [                 ]
        Telephone      [                    ]
        Fax number     [                    ]
        Company number [     ]        Contact [          ]

        Edit retrieved entries           ( All fields    )
        Allow posting to previous year?  (Y/N)   [Y]
        Allow provisional posting?  (Y/N)        [N]
        Use departments?  (Y/N)                  [Y]
        Force listing of batches?  (Y/N)         [N]

        Default retained earnin┌──────────────────────┐nt  [   ]
        ──────────────────────│                      │──────────────
        Next batch:           │  Edit   Next   Cancel │f G/L accounts:  0
        Next posting sequence: └──────────────────────┘
        Next provisional posting sequence:     1


                                                      F1=Help
```

Company name

You may use a maximum of 36 characters for the company name. This name will appear on all subsequent reports produced, so be very careful when typing it. Use upper or lower case as you wish it to appear on the reports.

❏ Type: E. & J. Enterprises

❏ Press: [Enter]

Address

This field will hold a maximum of three 30-character lines.

❏ Type: 27 Nichole Circle in the first address field.

❏ Press: [Enter]

❏ Type: Georgetown in the second address field.

❏ Press: [Enter] twice.

Zip/postal code

This field will hold a maximum of 15 characters, allowing sufficient space for international codes.

❏ Type: 765JJ in the Zip/postal code field.

❏ Press: [Enter]

Telephone and fax

Both the Telephone and Fax number fields are large enough to accept international direct dial numbers.

❏ Type: `555-555-1212` in the Telephone field.

❏ Press: [Enter]

❏ Type: `555-555-1313` in the Fax number field.

❏ Press: [Enter]

Company number

You may use up to six alphanumeric characters to identify the company. The Company number field can be used to record a company's legal registration number or its client number for public accounting practice or some other form of identification.

❏ Type: `001` in the Company number field.

❏ Press: [Enter]

Contact

The Contact field is used to identify the person at the company to contact for information.

❏ Type: `Erin or Joan` in the Contact field.

❏ Press: [Enter]

Edit retrieved entries

When you press [Enter] in the Contact data entry field a menu will be displayed listing the options for Edit retrieved entries.

```
Edit Level

All Fields
Fiscal period only
No editing permitted
```

These options allow you to specify the types of changes or corrections you can make in batches transferred to the General Ledger from other ACCPAC Plus programs. The choices are to allow editing of all fields, to limit the editing to changing the fiscal periods associated with the entries, or to prevent any editing of the batches.

❑ Press: [Enter] to accept the default to permit editing of all fields.

Allow posting to previous year?

You can set up the General Ledger to allow or prevent posting of batches to periods in the prior year. You can make this choice during General Ledger creation or on the Edit Company Profile screen. The most common reasons to post to the prior year are to enter the last year's closing account balances to set up opening balances and historical data, or to enter auditor's adjustments for the prior year after the year is closed.

❑ Type: Y

❑ Press: [Enter] to allow posting to the previous fiscal year.

Allow provisional posting?

This feature allows you to post batches on a provisional basis to test the effects of transactions on the General Ledger and the financial statements, before you permanently post the data. Provisional posting is particularly useful for estimating period end or year end adjustments. When the final adjustments are known the provisional batch can be modified and permanently posted to the General Ledger.

❑ Select: Y

Departments

The Use departments option allows you to create cost centers in the ledger by defining departments and then entering department codes with the account codes. This would provide separate accounting for each department. Since E. & J. Enterprises is a small company, Erin has decided not to use departments.

❑ Type: N

❑ Press: [Enter]

Force listing of batches?

The Force Listing of Batches option requires you to print a listing for each batch and to correct any errors reported on the listing before you can post the batch. If this option is chosen, you must also reprint the batch listing each time you make changes to a batch. You can print batch listings to a printer, a file, or the screen. Using this option helps you to maintain a clear audit trail by ensuring that you will post only error-free batches, so that all transactions entered in a batch are posted together.

❑ Type: Y

❑ Press: [Enter]

Default retained earnings account

At year end, all corporations transfer the revenue and expense account balances to a "Retained Earnings" account. The procedure is much the same for a sole proprietorship. You should enter the account code for the Retained Earnings account to which you want to close these temporary accounts. The Retained Earnings account for E. & J. Enterprises will be account 690.

❑ Type: 690
❑ Press: Enter

Batch and posting report

The lower section of the screen is a report. As we have not entered transactions or posted transaction batches, the Next batch number and the Next posting sequence number should both be 1. The 690 for the Current number of G/L accounts represents the Default retained earnings account recorded earlier.

Review the screen. If all information has been entered correctly,

❑ Select: Next

Fiscal Period Calendar

The Fiscal Period Calendar lists the status, starting date, ending date, and report date for each period. This screen is the final creation screen, and becomes the second screen of the Edit Company Profile function. The starting month and year you specified earlier provide the default dates that now appear for each period on the Fiscal Period Calendar screen as shown in Figure 3-5.

The report date for each period appears on financial statements exactly as it is entered on the Fiscal Period Calendar screen. When entering report dates, be sure to use the format you require for your statements. The report dates are not updated by the program at the year end. You must modify them yourself as you begin each fiscal year.

As a protection against accidental posting to incorrect fiscal periods, you can define fiscal periods as either "open" or "closed". Transaction batches can only be posted to "open" fiscal periods. You may change the status of fiscal periods at any time, using the Edit Company profile function.

The menu in the lower portion of the screen has four options.

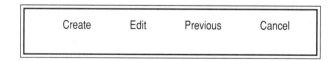

If the data on your screen does not agree with that shown in Figure 3–5, you would select "Edit" and enter the necessary changes.

Figure 3–5

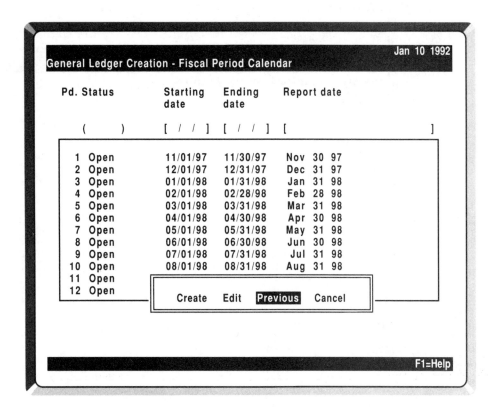

Both Create and Cancel start with the letter "C". To select either of these you must move the selector bar to the option you want and then press **Enter**.

❑ Move the selector bar to `Create`.

❑ Press: [Enter]

The computer will work for several moments creating the files and will then display the title screen.

INITIALIZATION

The company name, E. & J. Enterprises, and the system date should be displayed at the top of the screen. This confirms that ACCPAC was able to find the data files where you told it to look when you added the start line.

During initialization you enter the date that you wish to be recorded as the processing date. The `Last access date` is the last day that you worked with General Ledger files. The system date stored by your computer will be displayed in the `New date` field as shown in Figure 3–6. Both of these fields should display the current date.

Figure 3–6

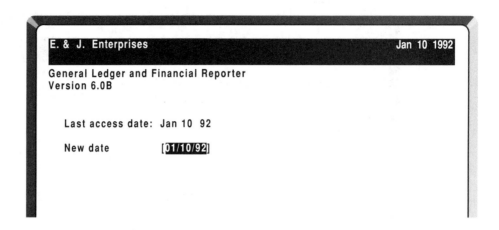

```
E. & J. Enterprises                                    Jan 10 1992

General Ledger and Financial Reporter
Version 6.0B


    Last access date:  Jan 10  92

    New date           [01/10/92]
```

On September 30, 1998 Erin and Joan decided to switch from a manual account-ing system to ACCPAC Plus.

❑ Type: 093098 in the New date field.

❑ Press: Enter

A warning will appear on the screen.

```
┌─────────────────────────────────────────────────┐
│                                                   │
│    New date is more than one week later than old date.│
│                                                   │
│          Accept          Edit                     │
│                                                   │
└─────────────────────────────────────────────────┘
```

If you had entered a date earlier than the last access date, a similar warning would be displayed.

```
┌─────────────────────────────────────────────────┐
│                                                   │
│         New date is earlier than old date.        │
│                                                   │
│          Accept          Edit                     │
│                                                   │
└─────────────────────────────────────────────────┘
```

These warnings help prevent errors in the recording or processing dates printed on ACCPAC Plus reports that become part of the audit trail. Verify that 09/30/98 is displayed in the New date field.

❑ Type: A to accept 09/30/98 as the new date.

GENERAL LEDGER MASTER MENU

The computer should now display the ACCPAC General Ledger Master Menu, as shown in Figure 3–7. The date you entered in the New date field should be dis-played on the top line of the screen.

Figure 3–7

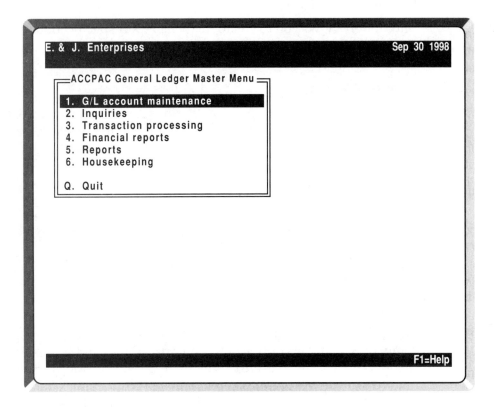

The menu choices are described below.

1. G/L account maintenance

This option allows you to add, delete, or modify General Ledger accounts; to edit historical data (month-end balances from the previous year); and to enter budget data, and export or import accounts for use in conjunction with other ACCPAC Plus modules or other programs.

2. Inquiries

This choice allows you to display transactions posted to specific General Ledger accounts or to display unposted transaction batches.

3. Transaction processing

The Transaction processing option allows you to add, modify, or delete batches. This option also allows you to create special purpose batches and to retrieve or import batches. You can also print batches, post batches, and print a posting journal of the batches that have been posted.

4. Financial reports

This option allows you to create financial report specifications and then to print the financial reports.

5. Reports

This option allows you to print out various reports, such as the Chart of Accounts, Trial Balance, General Ledger, Source Journals, Batch Status Report, and Company Profile.

6. Housekeeping

This option allows you to edit or change the Company Profile, financial report specifications, source codes, source journals, and account groups used in creating the financial report specifications. It is also used for periodic processing functions such as consolidating posted transactions and closing at year end.

Q. Quit

The Quit option should be used each time when you wish to stop working with a company's data. This option closes all opened files and writes data to disk. You cannot press **Escape** to leave this menu and return to the Start Menu. If you do not use the Quit option but simply remove your data disk and turn the computer off, you will probably lose data or damage your data files.

PRINTING THE COMPANY PROFILE

From the ACCPAC General Ledger Master Menu

❑ Select: `5. Reports` to display the Reports Menu.

The Reports Menu allows you to print six different reports (see Figure 3-8). As you work through this book, you will print each of these reports at the appropriate time. At this time you will print the company profile.

❑ Select: `6. Company profile`

After a few seconds a `Print` prompt will be displayed near the bottom of the screen.

❑ Turn your printer **off**.

❑ Press: [Enter] to start printing.

Figure 3–8

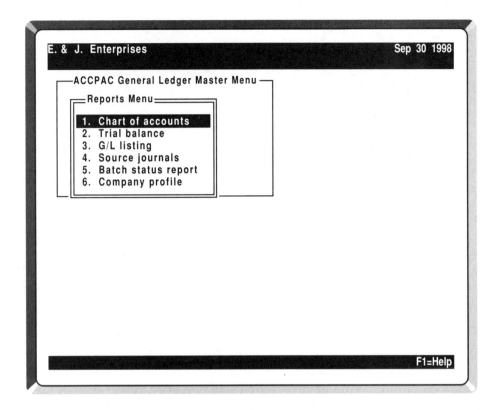

ACCPAC Plus is not able to send the report to your printer and displays the following printer-problem message.

❑ Set the printhead to the top of a page and turn your printer **on**.

❑ Press: c to Continue.

❑ Remove the printout from the printer and compare it to Table 3–1.

Table 3–1

```
Date: Sep 30 98    11:17am          E. & J. Enterprises          Page:   1
Company Profile

Company name:                       E. & J. Enterprises
Address:                            27 Nichole Circle
                                    Georgetown

Zip/postal code:                    765JJ
Telephone:                          555-555-1212
Fax number:                         555-555-1313
Company number:                     001
Contact:                            Erin or Joan

Edit retrieved entries:             All fields
Allow posting to previous year?     Yes
Allow provisional posting?          Yes
Use departments?                    No
Force listing of batches?           Yes

                          Account
Default retained earnings    690

Next batch number:                          1
Next posting sequence number:               1
Next provisional posting sequence:          1
Current number of G/L accounts:             1

Fiscal Period Calendar


Pd.   Status      Starting Date  Ending Date    Report Date

  1   Open        Nov 01 97      Nov 30 97      Nov 30 97
  2   Open        Dec 01 97      Dec 31 97      Dec 31 97
  3   Open        Jan 01 98      Jan 31 98      Jan 31 98
  4   Open        Feb 01 98      Feb 28 98      Feb 28 98
  5   Open        Mar 01 98      Mar 31 98      Mar 31 98
  6   Open        Apr 01 98      Apr 30 98      Apr 30 98
  7   Open        May 01 98      May 31 98      May 31 98
  8   Open        Jun 01 98      Jun 30 98      Jun 30 98
  9   Open        Jul 01 98      Jul 31 98      Jul 31 98
 10   Open        Aug 01 98      Aug 31 98      Aug 31 98
 11   Open        Sep 01 98      Sep 30 98      Sep 30 98
 12   Open        Oct 01 98      Oct 31 98      Oct 31 98
```

❏ Press: [Esc] to return to the ACCPAC General Ledger Master Menu.

EDITING THE COMPANY PROFILE

When the company profile was reviewed, it was decided that changes should be made. First, your name should be put in as the contact person. Second, the status of the first ten periods should be changed to closed. Finally, the report dates should use the full spelling for each month.

❑ Select: 6. Housekeeping from the ACCPAC General Ledger Master Menu.

Figure 3–9

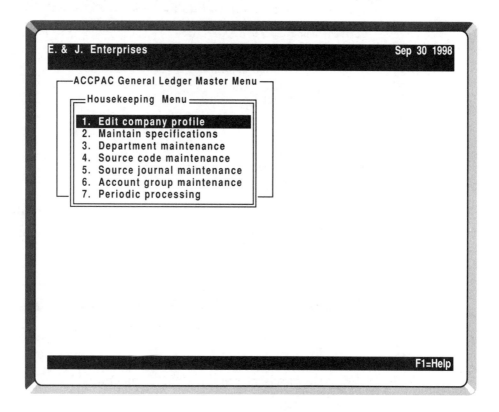

You will work through each of the housekeeping options at the appropriate time. Now you will change the name of the contact person, change the status of the first ten periods, and change the form of the report dates. You can then use these same procedures to correct any errors there may be in the company profile.

❑ Select: 1. Edit company profile from the Housekeeping Menu.

Company Data and Options

The screen displayed in Figure 3-10 is identical to that displayed during creation of the General Ledger files.

To Edit the information displayed on the Company Data and Options screen,

❑ Type: E

The menu at the bottom of the screen will disappear and the flashing cursor will be in the Company name field. Pressing either **Enter** or **Tab** will move the cursor to the next data entry field.

Figure 3–10

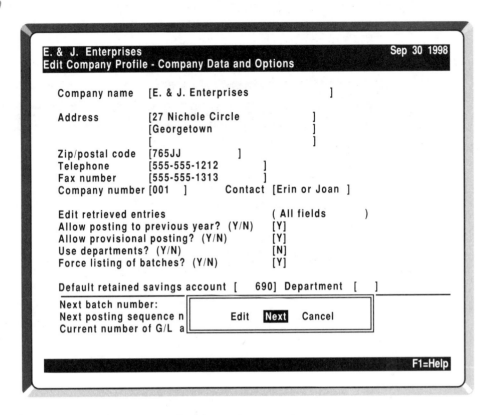

```
E. & J. Enterprises                                    Sep 30 1998
Edit Company Profile - Company Data and Options

   Company name    [E. & J. Enterprises              ]

   Address         [27 Nichole Circle        ]
                   [Georgetown               ]
                   [                         ]
   Zip/postal code [765JJ          ]
   Telephone       [555-555-1212      ]
   Fax number      [555-555-1313      ]
   Company number [001   ]        Contact [Erin or Joan ]

   Edit retrieved entries              ( All fields        )
   Allow posting to previous year?  (Y/N)    [Y]
   Allow provisional posting?  (Y/N)         [Y]
   Use departments?  (Y/N)                   [N]
   Force listing of batches?  (Y/N)          [Y]

   Default retained savings account  [    690] Department  [  ]
   ─────────────────────────────────────────────────────────
   Next batch number:
   Next posting sequence n |      Edit   Next   Cancel   |
   Current number of G/L  a |_____|


                                                        F1=Help
```

❏ Press: [Enter] to move the cursor to the Contact field.

❏ Type: YOUR NAME

❏ Delete any excess characters using the space bar or the delete key.

❏ Press: [Enter] to indicate that the data entry is complete for the Contact field.

❏ Press: [Esc] to tell ACCPAC Plus that no more changes are to be made to the data displayed on this screen.

The following menu box will appear at the bottom of the screen.

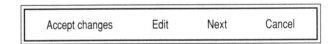

```
┌──────────────────────────────────────────────────────┐
│                                                        │
│   Accept changes      Edit      Next      Cancel       │
│                                                        │
└──────────────────────────────────────────────────────┘
```

If you only wanted to change information on this screen, you would press A to accept the changes that you had entered.

❏ Press: N to advance to the next edit screen.

Fiscal Period Calendar

❏ Press: E to edit.

The menu at the bottom of the screen will disappear and a selector bar will highlight the first fiscal period.

❏ Press: [Enter]

The data for the first fiscal period will be transferred to the data entry fields in the top portion of the screen and the following menu will appear.

```
Options

         Open
         Closed
```

❏ Select: Closed

The closed status prevents the posting of transactions to this period.

❏ Press: [Enter] twice to advance the cursor to the Report date field.

❏ Type: November 30, 1997

❏ Press: [Enter]

The data from the data entry area will now be displayed on the Fiscal Period Calendar and the selector bar will be on the second period.

❏ Complete the changes for the remaining periods. The status should be Closed for periods one through ten and Open for periods eleven and twelve.

❏ Press: [Esc] when the changes have been completed.

❏ Press: A to accept the changes.

❏ Press: [Esc] to return to the ACCPAC General Ledger Master Menu.

❏ Press: Q to return to the Start Menu.

YOUR TURN

❏ Create the General Ledger data files for Fred's Company.

Enter any data that you wish, but ensure that the default retained earnings account is account number 690 and that the fiscal year begins November 1997.

❏ Display the Start Menu on the screen.

EXITING ACCPAC PLUS

To quit ACCPAC Plus from the Start Menu,

❏ Press: [Esc]

The program will request confirmation by showing the message,

```
┌──────────────────────────────────────────────┐
│                                                │
│        Do you really want to exit the system?  │
│                                                │
│                  Yes      No                   │
│                                                │
└──────────────────────────────────────────────┘
```

❏ Select: Yes

The screen will again display the DOS C > prompt.

Every time you are finished working with ACCPAC Plus, you must quit using this method. If you do not quit properly, the data files may be damaged.

BACKING UP YOUR DATA FILES

It is very important to back up your data files systematically. Both floppy and hard disks are subject to damage and deterioration. You can lose all the information you have entered and hours of work. No matter how much expertise you have with computers, you will get into an occasional mess. You can reduce the work necessary to recover from these disasters by systematically backing up your data files.

The **live/father/grandfather** backup system uses three disks. The **live**, or current data disk, records current data as it occurs. Back up this disk several times each day onto the **father** disk.

Back up data weekly from the father disk onto a **grandfather** disk, which should be kept in another location. Many companies make arrangements for commercial storage of their grandfather disks. Try to avoid having more than two generations of the disks together at any one time. The grandfather disk protects against losing your files in a unpredicted event, such as explosion, fire, theft, or vandalism.

Since you have valuable data on your data disks and you will be shortly making journal entries to record transactions, you should back up the data on the live disk to the father disk before continuing. The live disk, in this case, is the working data disk you created earlier.

❏ Copy all the files in the "EJE" subdirectory of your working data disk to the "EJE" subdirectory of your backup data disk.

If you are not sure how to copy files on your computer system, refer to the Back-up Procedures Appendix. If necessary, ask your computer support person to show you how to copy files using your computer system.

❑   Copy the files for Fred's Company to the "FRED" subdirectory on your back-up disk.

REVIEW QUESTIONS

1. Why would a company choose to use a thirteen-period fiscal year?
2. What does the "Edit retrieved entries" option allow you to do?
3. Why would you want to allow posting to the previous fiscal year?
4. What are departments used for?
5. Why would you want to force the listing of transaction batches?
6. Why would you want to edit the Fiscal Period Calendar?
7. Describe the steps required to print the Company Profile.
8. Describe the steps necessary to change the address in the Company Profile.
9. Why should you back up your data files?

EXERCISE

In this exercise, you will create the General Ledger files for the new company that bears your name.

If you are using double sided double density disks, you will require a new working disk and a new back up disk for these exercises. If you are using high density disks you can store the exercise data files on the same disk that you are using for E. & J. Enterprises.

1. Enter the commands to access ACCPAC Plus.
2. If necessary add a new line to the Start Menu using "G/L" and your name. The Start Menu line should use the ACCPAC Plus General Ledger and Financial Reporter module. The data files will be stored in the "EXERCISE" subdirectory of the root directory of drive A. Use your initials as the data extension. If your initials are EJE, enter EE.
3. Create the General Ledger files for your company. Enter your full name as the company name. Use the data shown in Table 3–2 to complete the company profile.
4. Enter 093098 as the New date on the Title screen.
5. Print the Company profile and compare it to Table 3–2. Make any corrections necessary.
6. Exit from ACCPAC Plus and back up the data files for your company.

Table 3–2

```
Date: Sep 30 98     3:07pm          Your Name Co. Ltd.        Page:   1
Company Profile

Company name:                       Your Name Co. Ltd.
Address:                            123 Accounting St.
                                    Anytown

Zip/postal code:                    456MAIL
Telephone:                          777-555-1212
Fax number:                         777-555-1313
Company number:                     002
Contact:                            YOUR NAME

Edit retrieved entries:             All fields
Allow posting to previous year?     Yes
Allow provisional posting?          Yes
Use departments?                    No
Force listing of batches?           Yes
                              Account
Default retained earnings       690

Next batch number:                              1
Next posting sequence number:                   1
Next provisional posting sequence:              1
Current number of G/L accounts:                 1

Fiscal Period Calendar

Pd.    Status        Starting Date  Ending Date   Report Date

  1    Closed        Nov 01 97      Nov 30 97     November 30, 1997
  2    Closed        Dec 01 97      Dec 31 97     December 31, 1997
  3    Closed        Jan 01 98      Jan 31 98     January 31, 1998
  4    Closed        Feb 01 98      Feb 28 98     February 28, 1998
  5    Closed        Mar 01 98      Mar 31 98     March 31, 1998
  6    Closed        Apr 01 98      Apr 30 98     April 30, 1998
  7    Closed        May 01 98      May 31 98     May 31, 1998
  8    Closed        Jun 01 98      Jun 30 98     June 30, 1998
  9    Closed        Jul 01 98      Jul 31 98     July 31, 1998
 10    Closed        Aug 01 98      Aug 31 98     August 31, 1998
 11    Open          Sep 01 98      Sep 30 98     September 30, 1998
 12    Open          Oct 01 98      Oct 31 98     October 31, 1998
```

CHAPTER

4 Chart of Accounts

In this chapter you will add E. & J. Enterprises' Chart of Accounts to the General Ledger files that you created in Chapter 3. The Chart of Accounts will then be copied to Fred's Company.

GETTING READY

When you have the DOS C> prompt on the screen, enter the command to load ACCPAC Plus.

- ❑ Type: `Plus`
- ❑ Press: [Enter]

ACCPAC Plus should now be loaded into your system, ready for you to use with the Start Menu displayed on your screen. If `G/L E. & J. Enterprises` is not listed on your Start Menu, you must add it using the procedure for adding a company to a Start List, as described in Chapter 2.

- ❑ Move the selector bar to `G/L E. & J. Enterprises`.
- ❑ Press: [Enter]

The title screen will appear as shown in Figure 4–1.

Figure 4–1

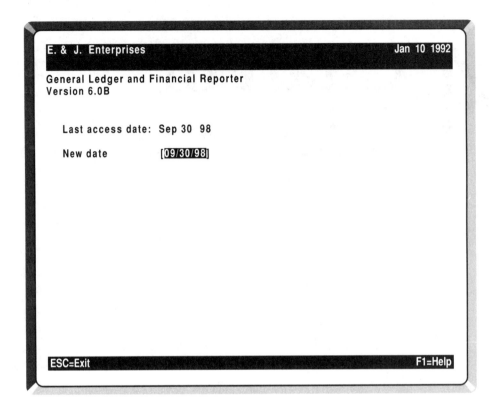

If `E. & J. Enterprises` is not displayed in the top line on the screen, or if
the message `General Ledger data has not been created` appears,
press **Esc** to return to the Start Menu. Then modify the entry for G/L E. & J.
Enterprises, following the outline in Chapter 2.

`Sep 30 98` should be displayed in the Last access date field and should be
shown as `09/30/98` in the New date field. If the correct date is displayed,

❑ Press: Enter to accept the information as displayed.

If a correction is required, type `093098` in the New date field and press **Enter**.
You do not enter the solidus (/) symbol.

After checking the data files for E. & J. Enterprises the computer will display the
ACCPAC General Ledger Master Menu, as shown in Figure 4–2.

Figure 4–2

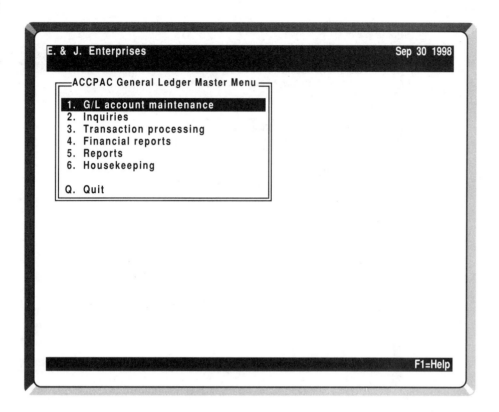

G/L ACCOUNT MAINTENANCE MENU

☐ Select: 1. G/L account maintenance

The G/L Account Maintenance Menu will appear as shown in Figure 4–3. The menu choices are explained below.

1. Add/modify/delete accounts

The add function of this option allows you to add General Ledger accounts to an existing Chart of Accounts or to create a Chart of Accounts for a new company. Modify allows you to change the name or type of an existing account. Finally, the delete option will allow you to delete inactive accounts only if the account balance is zero for both the current year and the previous year. This restriction ensures that comparative figures remain intact for use in financial statements.

2. Edit historical data

This option allows you to edit the historical data from the previous year. This data is used for comparative purposes in the financial statements.

Figure 4–3

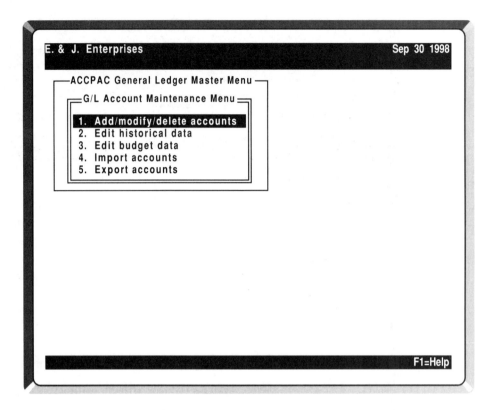

3. Edit budget data

This choice allows you to enter budget data for the current year. Several of the financial statements available use this information for comparing actual performance to budgeted performance.

4. Import accounts

This option allows you to copy data from other programs into the General Ledger to set up a Chart of Accounts, add new accounts, or update existing accounts.

5. Export accounts

This option allows you to copy account information from ACCPAC Plus to other file formats for use with different programs. The exported file can also be imported by ACCPAC Plus to create a duplicate Chart of Accounts for another company.

ADDING ACCOUNTS

❑ Select: `1. Add/modify/delete accounts` from the G/L Account Maintenance Menu.

Figure 4–4

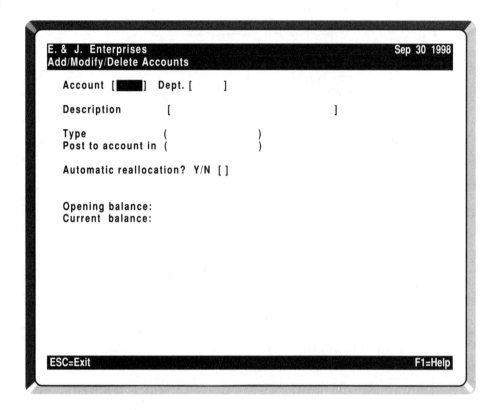

```
┌─────────────────────────────────────────────────────────────┐
│ E. & J. Enterprises                              Sep 30 1998  │
│ Add/Modify/Delete Accounts                                    │
│                                                               │
│     Account [▓▓▓▓]  Dept. [      ]                            │
│                                                               │
│     Description       [                           ]           │
│                                                               │
│     Type              (               )                       │
│     Post to account in (              )                       │
│                                                               │
│     Automatic reallocation?  Y/N  [ ]                         │
│                                                               │
│                                                               │
│     Opening balance:                                          │
│     Current  balance:                                         │
│                                                               │
│                                                               │
│                                                               │
│ ESC=Exit                                            F1=Help   │
└─────────────────────────────────────────────────────────────┘
```

All of the data entry fields will be blank as in Figure 4–4. The cursor should be in the Account field. If you are adding to or creating a Chart of Accounts, ensure that you leave sufficient numerical space between account codes so that other accounts can be added later. For example, "Advertising Expense" might be 810, with the next account numbered 835.

❑ Type: `100` in the Account field.

❑ Press: [Enter]

After a few seconds the cursor will move to the Description field and defaults will be displayed in the other data entry fields. For a better appearance of the printed output, type all account descriptions in a consistent style.

❑ Type: `Cash` in the Description field.

❑ Press: [Enter]

The following menu will appear for the Type field.

```
Type

Balance Sheet
Income Statement
Retained Earnings
```

❏ Move the selector bar to `Balance sheet.`

❏ Press: [Enter] to identify Cash as a Balance sheet item.

The next option is the "Post in" field.

```
Post in

Detail form
Consolidated form
```

When an account is posted in detail form, all the debits and credits posted to it are retained and can be listed individually on source journals and the G/L Listing. If the account is posted in consolidation form, the separate details are combined during posting into single amounts for each fiscal period and source code. The date assigned to each consolidated amount is the last date of the fiscal period to which the combined details were posted. Details for the account appear only in consolidated form on the G/L Listing and source journals.

Regardless of the posting form specified for an account, all the details posted to it are listed on the posting journal. Each detail posted to an account that uses the consolidated posting form will be marked with a letter "c". A summary is included at the end of the journal to list the consolidated amounts for each account, separated into totals for each fiscal period and source code.

❏ Move the selector bar to `Detail form.`

❏ Press: [Enter]

The Automatic reallocation (of account balances) option allows you to identify accounts whose balances will be periodically allocated to other accounts. The option is useful for reallocating revenue or expense account balances from head office accounts to department accounts. If you use this option, you must specify the accounts to receive the allocations, and the percentages to reallocate to each. You can reallocate amounts to any number of accounts, but the percentages must total exactly 100%.

You also can enter a reference and description for each account to which amounts are allocated. You cannot add comment lines to the reallocation information in the account record but, after you have created a reallocation batch, you can add comments and change other information for the reallocation entries, using the Add/Modify/Delete Batches function.

❑ Type: N in the Automatic reallocation field.

❑ Press: [Enter]

The menu box that now appears at the bottom of the screen allows you the option to either Add the account to the chart of accounts, Edit the information on the account, or Cancel the input you have created for this account. Review the fields on the screen. Once you are satisfied that they are correct,

❑ Move the selector bar to Add.

❑ Press: [Enter]

You have now added one General Ledger Account to your data files. Continue to add the following accounts. In all cases the posting to the account will be in Detail form, and there will be no reallocation of accounts. Use the **Spacebar** or **Delete** key to delete unwanted letters in the Description field.

❑ Add the accounts in Table 4–1.

Table 4–1

Account	Description	Type
105	Bank Account - Payroll	Balance sheet
200	Accounts Receivable	Balance sheet
210	Allowance for Doubtful Accts	Balance sheet
250	Inventory	Balance sheet
300	Prepaid Expenses	Balance sheet
406	Fixtures and Furniture	Balance sheet
408	Machinery and Equipment	Balance sheet
426	Accum. Dep. Fixtures & Furn.	Balance sheet
428	Accum. Dep. Machinery & Equip.	Balance sheet
500	Accounts Payable	Balance sheet
520	Sales Tax Payable	Balance sheet
540	Value Added Tax Payable	Balance sheet
542	Value Added Tax Recoverable	Balance sheet
680	Common Stock	Balance sheet
692	Dividends	Balance sheet
700	Sales	Income statement
710	Sales Discounts	Income statement
720	Sales, Accounting Services	Income statement
730	Interest Income	Income statement
750	Opening Inventory	Income statement
752	Purchases	Income statement
754	Purchase Discounts	Income statement
756	Freight-In	Income statement
780	Closing Inventory	Income statement
810	Bad Debt Expense	Income statement
835	Depreciation Expense	Income statement
880	Insurance Expense	Income statement
920	Rent, Office Space	Income statement
925	Rent, Equipment	Income statement
935	Salary Expense	Income statement
945	Supplies Expense	Income statement

The default Retained Earnings account (690) was added when you created the General Ledger data files in Chapter 3. If you used departments in your ledger, you could assign a separate retained earnings account for each department. If you do not use departments, you can close the revenue and expense accounts to only one retained earnings account.

❏ Press: [Esc] to indicate that no further accounts will be added at this time.

❏ Press: [Esc] again to return to the ACCPAC General Ledger Master Menu.

PRINTING THE CHART OF ACCOUNTS

❏ Select: 5. Reports

The Reports Menu will display the options shown in Figure 4–5.

Figure 4–5

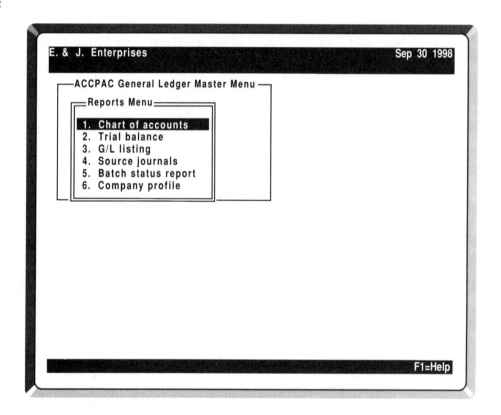

```
┌──────────────────────────────────────────────────────────┐
│ E. & J. Enterprises                           Sep 30 1998  │
│   ┌─ACCPAC General Ledger Master Menu─────────────┐        │
│   │ ┌─Reports Menu────────────────┐               │        │
│   │ │ 1.  Chart of accounts        │               │        │
│   │ │ 2.  Trial balance            │               │        │
│   │ │ 3.  G/L listing              │               │        │
│   │ │ 4.  Source journals          │               │        │
│   │ │ 5.  Batch status report      │               │        │
│   │ │ 6.  Company profile          │               │        │
│   │ └──────────────────────────────┘               │        │
│   └─────────────────────────────────────────────┘        │
│                                              F1=Help       │
└──────────────────────────────────────────────────────────┘
```

❏ Type: 1 to select the Chart of Accounts option.

The Chart of Accounts screen, Figure 4–6, displays the default settings for printing the Chart of Accounts. You can print the Chart of Accounts using these default settings or you can edit the settings. ACCPAC Plus assumes that you want to print all of the accounts in numerical order. Leaving the Print chart from account field blank causes the printing to start with the very first account. The zzzzzz in the to field specifies the last account in the chart of accounts.

E. & J. Enterprises does not use departments. If you use departments with another company, you could specify which departments you wish to print.

Figure 4–6

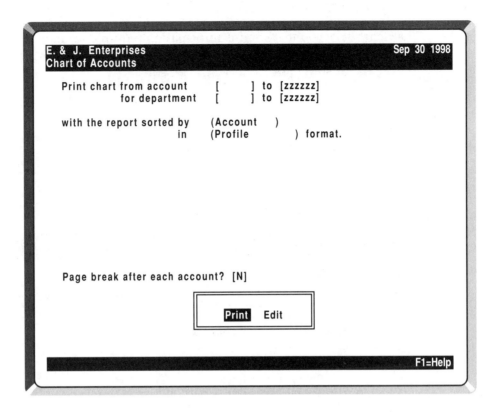

```
E. & J. Enterprises                                      Sep 30 1998
Chart of Accounts

    Print chart from account      [      ] to [zzzzzz]
                 for department    [      ] to [zzzzzz]

    with the report sorted by     (Account   )
                          in       (Profile          ) format.




    Page break after each account?  [N]

                          ┌─────────────────────────┐
                          │       Print   Edit       │
                          └─────────────────────────┘

                                                          F1=Help
```

The report is sorted by Account, and will print in numerical sequence. If you use departments with another company, you could specify that the report be sorted by department.

The Profile format means that the printed report will include the account code, description, type, and choices of consolidation and reallocation options. The Reallocations format adds details of reallocations to the printed report. Budget/History format adds the budget and history figures for each fiscal period, reported as net changes.

You would not normally have a page break after each account since that would print only one account per page.

❑ Select: Print

After the Chart of Accounts has been printed,

❑ Press: [Esc] to return to the ACCPAC General Ledger Master Menu.

CHART OF ACCOUNTS

The Chart of Accounts contains information required to maintain a complete set of General Ledger accounts. Review the Chart of Accounts printout for E. & J. Enterprises as shown in Table 4–2.

Table 4–2

```
Date: Sep 30 98   12:08pm              E. & J. Enterprises        Page:   1
Chart of Accounts

Print chart from account [     ] to [zzzzzz],
for department           [     ] to [zzzzzz],
sorted by                (Account   ),
in                       (Profile     ) format.

                                            Pstg.  Acct.
      Acct.  Dept.  Description         Type Form   Realloc.

      100           Cash                 B   Detail    No
      105           Bank Account - Payroll   B  Detail  No
      200           Accounts Receivable  B   Detail    No
      210           Allowance for Doubtful Accts  B  Detail  No
      250           Inventory            B   Detail    No
      300           Prepaid Expenses     B   Detail    No
      406           Fixtures and Furniture   B  Detail  No
      408           Machinery and Equipment  B  Detail  No
      426           Accum. Dep. Fixtures & Furn.  B  Detail  No
      428           Accum. Dep. Machinery & Equip. B  Detail  No
      500           Accounts Payable     B   Detail    No
      520           Sales Tax Payable    B   Detail    No
      540           Value Added Tax Payable   B  Detail  No
      542           Value Added Tax Recoverable  B  Detail  No
      680           Common Stock         B   Detail    No
      690           Retained Earnings    R   Detail    No
      692           Dividends            B   Detail    No
      700           Sales                I   Detail    No
      710           Sales Discounts      I   Detail    No
      720           Sales, Accounting Services  I  Detail  No
      730           Interest Income      I   Detail    No
      750           Opening Inventory    I   Detail    No
      752           Purchases            I   Detail    No
      754           Purchase Discounts   I   Detail    No
      756           Freight-In           I   Detail    No
      780           Closing Inventory    I   Detail    No
      810           Bad Debt Expense     I   Detail    No
      835           Depreciation Expense I   Detail    No
      880           Insurance Expense    I   Detail    No
      920           Rent, Office Space   I   Detail    No
      925           Rent, Equipment      I   Detail    No
      935           Salary Expense       I   Detail    No
      945           Supplies Expense     I   Detail    No

33 accounts printed.
```

The account codes used by E. & J. Enterprises consist of three digits. However, the system will allow the use of up to six digits. ACCPAC Plus does not require the creation of headings, subheadings, or totals in the General Ledger as do many other accounting software packages. It has embedded these specifications in the Financial Reporter portion of the program.

For E. & J. Enterprises, no department codes have been created; however, department codes are available as an option for companies that wish to use cost center accounting.

Account names up to 31 characters are printed in the Description column.

The fourth column, Type, refers to whether an account is a Balance Sheet item (B), Income Statement account (I), or a Retained Earnings account (R). Balance Sheet (B) accounts do not close from one period to the next. Income Statement (I) accounts will be closed at the end of the year to Retained Earnings, so be careful to flag all temporary proprietorship accounts with "I". The default Retained Earnings account, defined when creating the company profile, indicates to ACCPAC Plus where the Close Year function should place the retained net income from operations. In the case of a partnership, the balance in the default Retained Earnings account may be allocated to partnership equities through the automatic reallocation option.

The Posting Form column indicates if the account is posted in consolidated or detail form. The Account Reallocation column indicates if the account balance is to be reallocated to other accounts.

The Chart of Accounts for E. & J. Enterprises has account groups as follows:

100-399	Current Assets
400-420	Fixed Assets
421-499	Accumulated Dep'n, Fixed Assets
500-599	Current Liabilities
600-649	Long-Term Liabilities
650-699	Shareholders' Equity
700-749	Sales
750-799	Cost of Goods Sold
800-999	Operating Expenses

Each General Ledger account must be assigned a number within the specified range for its account type. These account groups will be used later for creating financial report specifications.

DELETING ACCOUNTS

Reviewing the Chart of Accounts, Erin noticed account 105, Bank Account - Payroll. As E. & J. Enterprises is a small company with only one bank account, Erin decided to delete account 105.

- ❏ Select: `1. G/L account maintenance` from the ACCPAC General Ledger Master Menu.
- ❏ Select: `1. Add/modify/delete accounts`

If you enter an Account code that presently exists, the program will assume that you either wish to modify or delete that account. The option to modify or delete the account appears at the bottom of the page when a current number is entered.

- ❏ Type: `105` in the Account field.
- ❏ Press: [Enter]

The option box allowing you to either Modify or Delete the account now appears at the bottom of the screen. The Delete option will allow you to delete inactive accounts only if the account balance is zero for both the current year and the previous year. This restriction ensures that comparative figures remain intact for use in financial statements.

- ❏ Move the selector bar to `Delete`.
- ❏ Press: [Enter]

The program will present a message, seeking confirmation that you definitely wish to delete the account.

```
+-------------------------------------------------------+
|                                                       |
|      Are you sure you want to delete this account?    |
|                                                       |
|                    Yes       No                       |
|                                                       |
+-------------------------------------------------------+
```

- ❏ Move the selector bar to `Yes`.
- ❏ Press: [Enter] to delete account 105.

MODIFYING EXISTING ACCOUNTS

Erin also noticed that account 408 was called Machinery and Equipment rather than Office Equipment.

- ❏ Type: `408` in the Account field.
- ❏ Press: [Enter] to display information about this account.
- ❏ Select: `Modify`
- ❏ Type: `Office Equipment` in the description field.
- ❏ Use the [SPACEBAR] or Delete key to delete any extra characters left in the field.
- ❏ Press: [Enter] to change the name of the account.

Since there are no other changes required for this account,

- ❏ Press: [Esc]

- ❑ Move the selector bar to `Accept changes`.
- ❑ Press: [Enter]

Now you must modify account 428 to reflect the change you made to the name of account 408. The new account name for account 428 will be "Accum. Dep. Office Equipment".

- ❑ Change the name of account 428.

Once you have finished, the cursor will return to the Account field, and wait for the next account number.

- ❑ Press: [Esc] to return to the G/L Account Maintenance Menu.
- ❑ Press: [Esc] again to return to the General Ledger Master Menu.
- ❑ Print the Chart of Accounts again and verify that account 105 has been deleted and the changes have been made to accounts 408 and 428.
- ❑ Enter the commands to return to the ACCPAC General Ledger Master Menu.

EXPORTING ACCOUNTS

When you created the General Ledger for Fred's Company, you did not create a Chart of Accounts. You could use the "Add/modify/delete accounts" option from the G/L Account Maintenance Menu to add each account individually. You may have to use this approach if the new Chart of Accounts is very different from any others you are already using. If you must create a Chart of Accounts using this technique, write out the information first, leaving five to ten numbers between accounts. Then, enter the accounts from your list of accounts.

If the Chart of Accounts for Fred's Company is the same as or very similar to that of E. & J. Enterprises, you can **export** the Chart of Account information from E. & J. Enterprises data files and then **import** that information to the data files for Fred's Company. You could modify the exported file using spreadsheet (Super-Calc or Lotus 1-2-3), data base management (dBASE III+ or dBASE IV), or wordprocessing software before it is imported. You can then add, delete, or modify accounts to customize the imported Chart of Accounts.

Assuming that Fred's Company will use the same Chart of Accounts as E. & J. Enterprises, you will export the Chart of Accounts from E. & J. Enterprises and then import that Chart of Accounts to Fred's Company.

- ❑ Select: `1. G/L account maintenance` from the General Ledger Master Menu.
- ❑ Select: `5. Export accounts` from the G/L Account Maintenance Menu (see Figure 4–7).

ACCPAC Plus has set the default options so that every bit of information in an account is exported. It is unlikely that you would export such a complete set of information. In this case you want to export only the Account code, Description, and Type.

Figure 4–7

❏ Move the selector bar to `Edit`.

❏ Press: [Enter]

The highlighted bar moves to the "Export to" field. This field describes the path that will be used for exporting the Chart of Accounts information. `A:\EJE` specifies that the file will be stored in the \EJE subdirectory of the root directory of the disk in drive A. `\GLMASTEX` is the head of a filename representing General Ledger Master Export. The `EJE` is the extension for E. & J. Enterprises. When you export information you must remember the path to the information.

❏ Press: [Enter] to accept the default path.

❏ Press: [Enter] twice more to accept the default settings for the first and last account numbers.

The selector bar will move into the `Export for Each Account` selection box. The spacebar is used as a toggle switch to turn on and off the various options for export. The selector bar is on the word `ALL` and each of the other options is marked with a triangular pointer.

❏ Press: [SPACEBAR] once to turn off the `ALL` option.

❏ Move the selector bar down to `Account code`.

This choice is turned on as indicated by the pointer. This is an unchangeable default to always export the Account code. Pressing the space bar will not turn the pointer off.

❑ Move the selector bar to `Description`.

❑ Press: [SPACEBAR] to turn the pointer on.

❑ Move the selector bar to `Type`.

❑ Press: [SPACEBAR] to turn the pointer on.

At this point there should be a triangular pointer beside `Account Code`, `Description`, and `Type`.

❑ Press: Esc to indicate that option selection is completed.

❑ Move the selector bar to `Export`.

❑ Press: Enter to display the Export Formats option box, Figure 4–8.

Figure 4–8

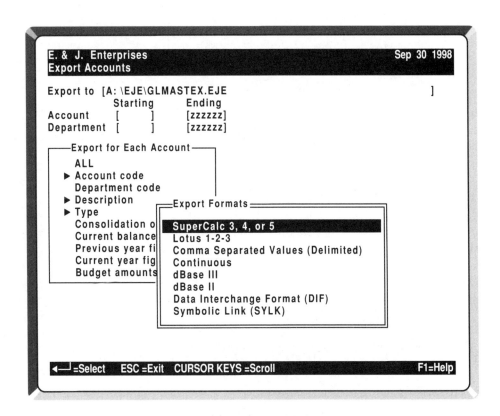

This option box allows you to select the way data is stored in your export file. If you were using a program other than ACCPAC Plus, you would select the format that can be used by that program. As you will import the file with ACCPAC Plus, it does not matter which format you select as long as the same format is selected when you import the file.

❑ Select: `SuperCalc 3, 4, or 5` as the format for the exported file.

The following prompt will be displayed.

```
The previous contents of the export file
must be emptied.

Empty          Cancel
```

❑ Select: Empty

After the program has completed exporting the accounts, the following message appears on the screen.

```
Export complete. Number of accounts exported: 32.

Continue
```

❑ Press: [Enter] to continue.
❑ Press: [Esc] to return to the General Ledger Master Menu.
❑ Type: Q to return to the Start Menu.

IMPORTING ACCOUNTS

❑ Select: Fred's Company General Ledger from the Start Menu.
❑ Type: 093098 in the New Date field.
❑ Press: [Enter] to accept the New date.
❑ Select: 1. G/L account maintenance from the ACCPAC General Ledger Master Menu.
❑ Select: 4. Import accounts

A warning will be displayed on the Import Accounts screen as shown in Figure 4–9.

If the General Ledger to which you were importing accounts contained data, you should back up that data. Then, if there were an accident during importing, you could use your back-up files.

Since no General Ledger data have been created for Fred's Company, you do not have to back up your files.

❑ Select: Yes to continue.

The Import Accounts screen will appear (Figure 4–10).

Figure 4–9

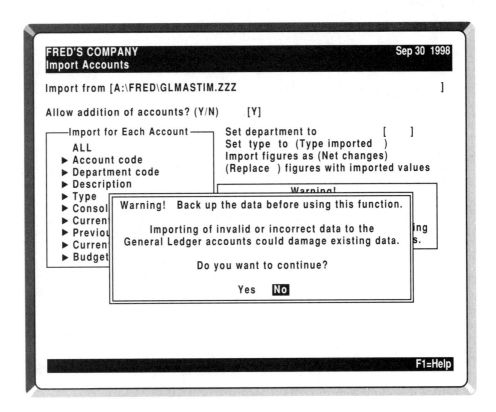

❑ Select: Edit

The Import from field shows the default import path

A:\FRED\GLMASTIM.ZZZ.

When you exported the account data, the path was

A:\EJE\GLMASTEX.EJE.

You will have to rename the Import from path so that ACCPAC Plus can find your exported file.

❑ Type: A:\EJE\GLMASTEX.EJE in the Import from field.

❑ Press: Enter

The next field will ask if you want to allow the addition of accounts.

❑ Type: Y

❑ Press Enter to allow the addition of accounts.

The selector bar will move to the Import for Each Account option box. You must now turn on only those options that you chose to export from EJE's files. As you recall, the exported format contained the Account Code, Description, and Type.

❑ Using the space bar turn off the All option, then turn on the Account code, Description, and Type options.

Figure 4–10

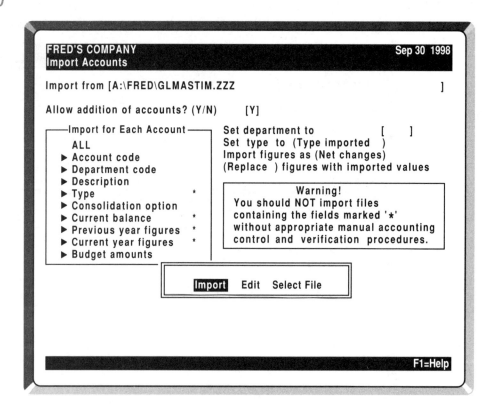

```
┌─────────────────────────────────────────────────────────────┐
│ FRED'S COMPANY                                    Sep 30 1998 │
│ Import Accounts                                               │
├─────────────────────────────────────────────────────────────┤
│ Import from [A:\FRED\GLMASTIM.ZZZ                          ]  │
│                                                               │
│ Allow addition of accounts? (Y/N)     [Y]                     │
│  ┌──Import for Each Account──┐  Set department to        [  ] │
│    ALL                          Set type to (Type imported  ) │
│  ▶ Account code                 Import figures as (Net changes)│
│  ▶ Department code              (Replace ) figures with imported values│
│  ▶ Description                                                │
│  ▶ Type                    *   ┌────────────────────────────┐ │
│  ▶ Consolidation option        │          Warning!          │ │
│  ▶ Current balance         *   │ You should NOT import files│ │
│  ▶ Previous year figures   *   │ containing the fields marked '*'│ │
│  ▶ Current year figures    *   │ without appropriate manual accounting│ │
│  ▶ Budget amounts              │ control and verification procedures.│ │
│  └────────────────────────┘    └────────────────────────────┘ │
│               ┌─────────────────────────────────────┐        │
│               │ Import   Edit   Select File          │        │
│               └─────────────────────────────────────┘        │
│                                                               │
│                                                      F1=Help  │
└─────────────────────────────────────────────────────────────┘
```

❏ Press: [Esc] to signify that editing is complete.

❏ Select: Import

❏ Select the Supercalc format for importing the accounts as you used this format when exporting.

ACCPAC Plus will make two passes through the data in the file to be imported. During the first pass ACCPAC Plus will verify each account, checking that the information selected for import is actually present.

If the file that you are trying to import does not contain the information above or has been exported with a different format, an error message will be displayed. If this happens, you must repeat the steps above to export the Chart of Account information and then import it to Fred's Company again.

During the second pass, the data will actually be imported into Fred's Company's General Ledger files. After the accounts have been imported, the following message will appear on the screen.

```
┌─────────────────────────────────────────────────────────┐
│                                                           │
│   Import complete. Number of accounts imported: 32.       │
│                                                           │
│                       Continue                            │
│                                                           │
└─────────────────────────────────────────────────────────┘
```

❏ Press: [Enter] to continue.

❏ Print the Chart of Accounts to verify that the accounts have the proper descriptions, types, and zero current balances.

❏ Quit ACCPAC Plus.

❏ Back up your data files!

REVIEW QUESTIONS

1. How do you select an item from the Start Menu?
2. Describe the functions available from the G/L Account Maintenance Menu.
3. What is the purpose of a Chart of Accounts?
4. How many digits can be incorporated into the account code of a Chart of Accounts?
5. You must identify the account type for each account. Name and describe the three types of General Ledger accounts.
6. What are the differences between detail and consolidated posting?
7. The number of accounts that can be identified as "default retained earnings" is restricted. Why?
8. Why will the "Delete Accounts" option work only if the account that you wish to delete has a zero balance for both the current year and the previous year?
9. Describe the steps you would take to print the Chart of Accounts.
10. You should leave unallocated account codes between the ledger accounts you create. Why?
11. Why would you export a Chart of Accounts?

EXERCISE

The purpose of this exercise is to continue setting up the company that was named after you.
1. Select your company from the Start Menu.
2. Enter 093098 as the New date on the Title screen.
3. Create a Chart of Accounts, as you did for E. & J. Enterprises. Use either "Export / import accounts" or "Add accounts" to add accounts. If you are using different disks for E. & J. Enterprises and your company, copy the file (GLMASTEX.EJE) from the disk for E. & J. Enterprises to your company's disk.
4. Once you have created all the accounts, print the Chart of Accounts and confirm that there are no errors.
5. Exit from ACCPAC Plus and back up your files again. Remember to use the proper subdirectory and extension.
6. Delete the files for Fred's Company and remove the subdirectory FRED from both your working and back-up data disks. If necessary refer to Appendix A for assistance with the necessary DOS commands.

5 Batch Processing

Working through this chapter, you will add the Source codes and then enter transaction information into one transaction batch. The information that you will enter represents the balances in E. & J. Enterprises' manual accounting system at the end of September 1998.

GETTING READY

❑ Enter the commands necessary to display the ACCPAC Plus Start Menu.

❑ Select: G/L E. & J. Enterprises from the Start Menu.

❑ Type: 093098 in the New date field to represent September 30, 1998.

❑ Press: [Enter]

ENTERING SOURCE CODES

You must define at least one source code before you can enter transactions. A source code consists of two letters to identify the ACCPAC Plus module in which the transaction originates, followed by a dash and two letters to represent the type of transaction. Erin and Joan have decided to use General Journal, Cash Receipts, Cash Disbursements, Purchases, Payroll, and Sales as source codes.

❏ Select: `6. Housekeeping` from the General Ledger Master Menu.

Figure 5–1

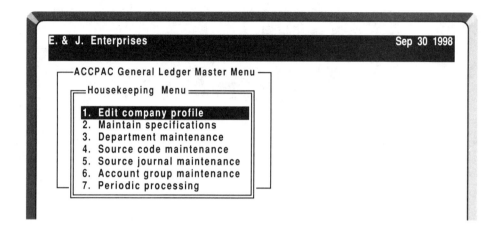

❏ Select: `4. Source code maintenance` from the Housekeeping Menu.

Figure 5–2

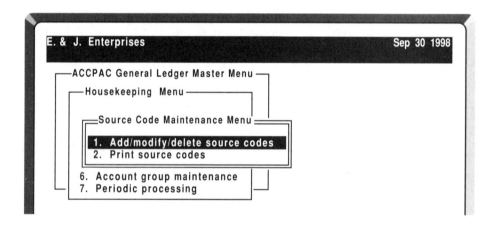

❏ Select: `1. Add/modify/delete source codes` from the Source Code Maintenance Menu.

Figure 5–3

❏ Type: `GLGJ` in the Source code field.

You do not have to type the dash or hyphen. GL indicates that this is a General Ledger Source code. GJ indicates that the source is the General Journal.

❑ Press: [Enter]

❑ Type: General Journal in the description field.

❑ Press: [Enter]

Review the entry. If necessary, select Edit and make corrections.

❑ Move the selector bar to Add.

❑ Press: [Enter]

❑ Add the Source codes GL–CR for Cash Receipts, GL–CD for Cash Disbursements, GL–PU for Purchases, GL–PA for Payroll, and GL–SA for Sales.

❑ Press: [Esc] to return to the Source Code Maintenance Menu.

PRINTING THE SOURCE CODES

As you will need the source codes when you enter transactions, you should print a list of the source codes that you have entered.

❑ Select: 2. Print Source codes from the Source Code Maintenance Menu.

Figure 5–4

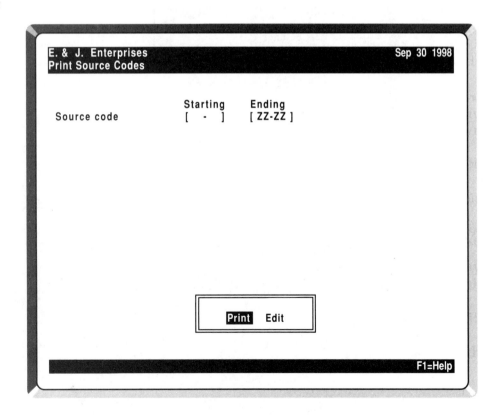

The default settings, as shown in Figure 5–4, of a blank Starting field and ZZ-
ZZ in the Ending field indicate that all source codes are to be printed.

❑ Press: [Enter] to print the source code list.

Review the printout to ensure that the six source codes have been entered properly. If necessary, edit the information to correct errors and reprint the source codes.

❑ Press: [Esc] twice to display the General Ledger Master Menu.

TRANSACTION PROCESSING

To access the Transaction Processing Menu, ensure that the ACCPAC General
Ledger Master Menu is displayed.

❑ Select: 3. Transaction processing

The Transaction Processing Menu, shown in Figure 5–5, will appear.
The menu options are described below.

Figure 5–5

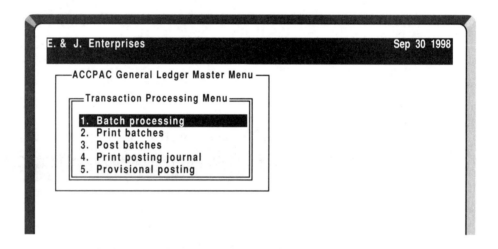

1. Batch processing

This option allows you to enter transactions into new or existing batches and to
edit unposted transactions. You will also use this option to retrieve batches from
other ACCPAC Plus modules or from other programs.

2. Print batches

You can use this option to print a specified unposted transaction batch or all unposted batches. These printouts can be used to identify errors and to verify the
batches before posting.

3. Post batches

This option allows you to post transaction batches to either the current or the previous fiscal year.

4. Print posting journal

This option is used to print an audit trail report of the transaction details posted by either the "Post batches" option on this menu or the Close Year function which will be used later.

5. Provisional posting

Selecting this option allows you to post a batch of transactions on a provisional, or temporary, basis before you permanently post the data. This option is useful when you are estimating year end adjustments before you receive the finalized adjustments from the company auditors.

BATCH PROCESSING

❏ Select: 1. Batch processing to display the Batch Processing Menu shown in Figure 5–6.

Figure 5–6

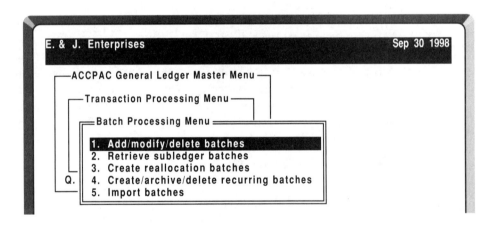

❏ Select: 1. Add/modify/delete batches to display the screen shown in Figure 5–7.

Figure 5–7

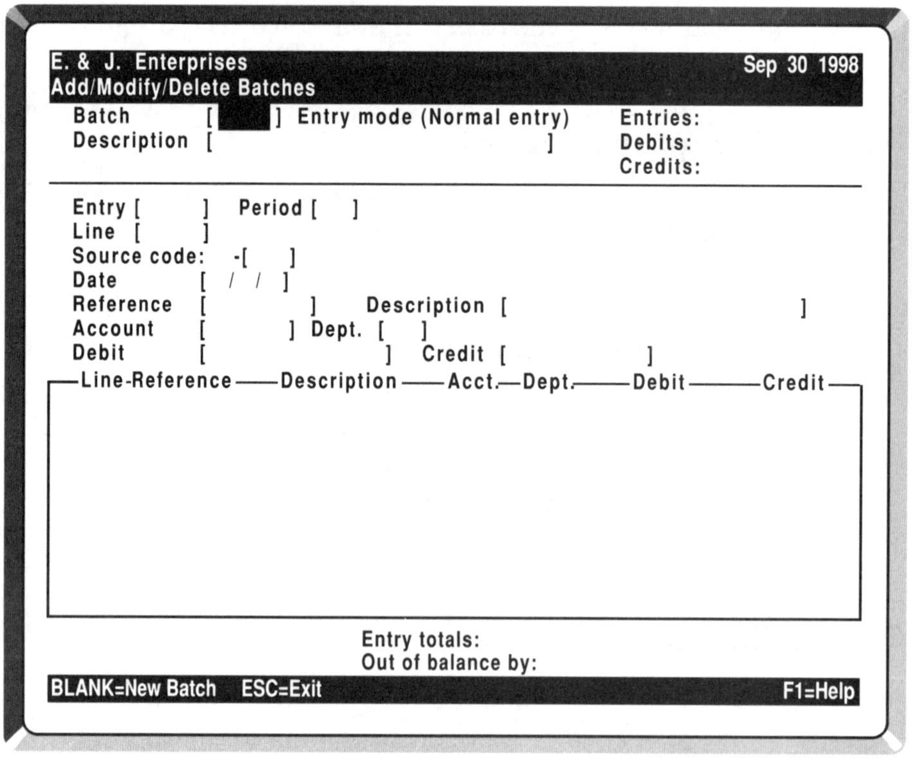

```
┌─────────────────────────────────────────────────────────────────────┐
│ E. & J. Enterprises                                    Sep 30 1998    │
│ Add/Modify/Delete Batches                                             │
│    Batch      [      ]  Entry mode (Normal entry)     Entries:        │
│    Description [                                  ]    Debits:         │
│                                                       Credits:        │
│   ─────────────────────────────────────────────────────────────────  │
│    Entry [    ]   Period [    ]                                        │
│    Line  [    ]                                                        │
│    Source code:   -[    ]                                             │
│    Date      [  /  /  ]                                               │
│    Reference   [          ]    Description [                      ]    │
│    Account     [        ] Dept. [    ]                                 │
│    Debit       [            ]  Credit [          ]                     │
│   ┌─Line-Reference──Description──Acct.─Dept.───Debit────Credit─┐       │
│   │                                                            │       │
│   │                                                            │       │
│   │                                                            │       │
│   │                                                            │       │
│   │                                                            │       │
│   │                                                            │       │
│   └────────────────────────────────────────────────────────────┘     │
│                         Entry totals:                                 │
│                         Out of balance by:                            │
│ BLANK=New Batch   ESC=Exit                              F1=Help       │
└─────────────────────────────────────────────────────────────────────┘
```

Batch

To maintain a clear audit trail, ACCPAC Plus assigns a new number to each new batch. The batch number is used to recall an existing batch for editing, deleting, or posting. Once a batch has been deleted, you cannot reuse its number. The Batch Status Report will keep track of open, posted, and deleted batches. Batch numbers are listed on the posting journals, the G/L Listing, and the source journal printouts. The batch number is reset to 1 by the Change Fiscal Year function at the end of the fiscal year.

❑ Type: 1 in the Batch field.

❑ Press: Enter

```
┌──────────────────────────────────────────────────────┐
│                                                        │
│     Error                                              │
│     Invalid Entry. Batch number does not exist.        │
│                                                        │
│     Press F2                                           │
│                                                        │
└──────────────────────────────────────────────────────┘
```

No batches exist, so you must create one.

❑ Press: F2 to clear the error message from the screen.

❑ Press: Enter with the Batch field blank to display the following prompt.

```
┌─────────────────────────────────────────────────────────┐
│                                                           │
│        Are you sure you want to create a new batch?       │
│                                                           │
│                    Yes        No                          │
│                                                           │
└─────────────────────────────────────────────────────────┘
```

❑ Select: `Yes`

ACCPAC Plus will now create a new batch and assign the batch number as indicated by the `1` in the Batch field.

Entry mode

When the batch has been created, the Entry mode selections box will appear on the screen.

```
┌─────────────────────────────────────────────────────────┐
│                                                           │
│     Entry Mode                                            │
│                                                           │
│     Normal entry                                          │
│     Quick entry                                           │
│                                                           │
└─────────────────────────────────────────────────────────┘
```

The Entry mode controls the fields at which the cursor stops as you enter transactions. You enter data in the Entry and Period fields only once for each entry. The cursor will move to each of the remaining fields for the first detail line.

When you use Normal Entry, the cursor continues to visit each field for every detail line. Use this mode if you want to assign different source codes, dates, references, or descriptions to individual detail lines.

In Quick Entry mode, the same source code, date, reference and description are used for each detail line. You can enter only the account code, the department code, and the debit or credit amount for each of the remaining detail lines. If you use the Quick Entry mode, you can enter only one set of comment lines for the entire entry, and you must enter that information before you begin entering the detail lines.

The selection you make just applies for the time you are working with the batch. If you recall an existing batch for editing, you select the entry mode again, and you can use Normal Entry mode to add comments or change information you entered earlier in the Quick Entry mode.

The transactions that you are going to enter will transfer the account balances from E. & J. Enterprises manual accounting system to ACCPAC Plus. The source code, date, reference, and description will be the same for each detail line.

❑ Select: `Quick entry`

Description

You may enter a short description for each transaction batch. This description will be printed on the batch listing produced by the Print Batches function and on the Batch Status Report.

❑ Type: `Transfer balances to ACCPAC`

❑ Press: [Enter]

Entry

Each entry is a complete transaction and is assigned a sequential number by AC-CPAC Plus. You use the number to recall an entry for editing or deleting, and to track the entry after posting. Entry numbers are listed on batch listings and posting journals. If the details are not consolidated, the entry numbers also appear on the G/L Listing and source journals.

When you delete an entry, you can reuse that number for your next entry. If you do not add a new entry to replace the deleted entry, when you post the batch the posting journal will include an error report which lists the entry number as deleted. The error report becomes your audit trail of the deleted entry number.

❑ Press: [Enter] to accept entry number 1.

Period

You must enter a fiscal period number with each entry. The period that corresponds with the New date you entered when starting the program is displayed, but you can change it. If the date you entered when you started the program is outside of the current fiscal year, the program enters a default number in the fiscal period field. If you start with a date which precedes the current year, `1` is displayed as the fiscal period number. If the date is after the current year, the number assigned is `12`, if you have a 12 period ledger; or `13`, if you use 13 periods. You must then edit the field if the number is incorrect.

You can enter only one fiscal period for each entry. However, a single batch can contain entries with different fiscal periods.

❑ Press: [Enter] to accept period 11.

Line

ACCPAC Plus automatically assigns a number to each detail line within a batch entry. This line provides a convenient means of selecting a detail for editing. The line number appears in the display area on the Add/Modify/Delete Batches screen immediately after you enter the period number or a detail line. Line numbers also appear on batch listings and can be used in tracing transactions back to their sources.

Comment lines

If you cannot fit all the descriptive text for an entry in the Reference and Description fields associated with the detail lines, you can use comment lines to add the remaining information. You tell ACCPAC Plus that you want to enter a comment line by pressing **Enter** when the cursor is in a blank Source code field. In some cases it may be necessary to use the spacebar to erase the contents of the Source code field before you press **Enter**.

If you are working in Normal entry mode, you can add as many comment lines as you need to clearly identify or explain an entry. You can insert comment lines at the beginning or ending of an entry, or before or after each detail.

When you are using Quick entry mode, you can enter only one set of comment lines for each entry, and you must enter comments before you begin entering the details. Later you can use the Normal entry mode to edit the entry adding additional comment lines if necessary.

The comment lines are printed on the batch listings and the posting journals. They do not appear on any other reports.

❑ Press: [Enter] in the blank Source code field.

❑ Type: `Transfer of account balances as of Sept. 30, 1998 from the`

❑ Press: [Enter] to move to the second comment field.

❑ Type: `manual accounting system to ACCPAC Plus.`

❑ Press: [Enter] to indicate that the second comment line is complete.

❑ Press: [Enter] in the blank comment field to indicate that the comment is complete and to add entry details.

Note the display of the comment lines in the box on the lower portion of the screen.

Source code

A source code must be included with each detail line in a batch entry to identify the type of transaction, such as a cash payment or receipt. If you do not use source journals, you need to define only one source code, then assign that code to all the details you enter.

Whether you are entering transactions directly into General Ledger, or you have retrieved or imported them, the first two characters of the code are fixed in the Add/Modify/Delete Batches function, and you cannot change them. You can enter or change the remaining one or two characters using the codes you defined earlier.

❑ Type: `GJ` the code for General Journal in the Source code field.

❑ Press: [Enter]

ACCPAC Plus will then verify that GJ has been entered as a Source code and display the journal name beside the Source code field.

Date

You must enter a date for each detail line. ACCPAC Plus will display the date entered as the "New date" when you started the program. You can enter any date for the detail line. The date entered with a detail line appears on the batch listing and posting journal. It is also included on the G/L Listing and source journals for unconsolidated accounts. The date assigned to details consolidated during posting is the last date of the fiscal period to which they were posted. The Consolidate Posting Transactions function assigns the current date to the details it consolidates.

Regardless of the dates you include in the detail lines of a single entry, all details in the entry are posted to only one fiscal period, and all entries in the batch are posted to the same year.

❑ Type: 093098 in the Date field if necessary.

❑ Press: [Enter]

Reference and description

When you are using Quick entry mode, you can enter only one reference and one description for all the detail lines in each entry. If the account is not consolidated, the reference and description are printed with the detail lines on the batch listing and posting journal for the batch and on the G/L Listing. For consolidated accounts, the G/L Listing lists a description of "Consolidated posting" for accounts which were consolidated by the Consolidate Posted Transactions function.

Because you can print source journals by reference, it is important to enter the same reference for associated details, such as multiple expense allocations for one check.

❑ Type: Balances Fwd in the Reference field.

❑ Press: [Enter]

❑ Type: Transfer Sept. 30 Balances in the Description field.

❑ Press: [Enter]

Account

For each detail line, you must enter the account code to which the debit or credit will be posted. If you enter an account code that has not been entered in the Chart of Accounts, the computer will "beep" and display the Finder in the lower portion of the screen. You could then select the proper Account code.

❑ Type: 111 in the Account field.

❑ Press: [Enter]

As ACCPAC Plus could not find Account 111 in the Chart of Accounts for E. & J. Enterprises, the Finder will be displayed. Compare the Account codes and descriptions in the Finder to your printout of E. & J. Enterprises' Chart of Accounts.

❑ Move the selector bar to account 100.

❑ Press: Enter

The name of the account will be displayed on the Account line and the cursor will move to the Debit field. Remember that E. & J. Enterprises does not use departments in its Chart of Accounts.

Debit or credit amount

You enter the amount for a detail in either the Debit or Credit field. If you press **Enter** in the Debit field without typing an amount, the ACCPAC Plus assumes the detail is to be a credit.

Do not type currency signs or commas, but you can insert the decimal point. If you do not type a decimal point, the program will insert one, allowing for the number of decimal places you use. Do not enter minus signs with credit details. If you enter a minus sign with either a debit or credit detail, the program will record the amount as the opposite entry.

Each debit or credit amount you enter is added to the total for the entry displayed at the bottom of the screen along with the amount by which the entry is out of balance. You can add an entry that does not balance, but you cannot post it until it does balance.

Each detail line you enter updates the displayed totals for the entry. The debit and credit totals for the batch, displayed in the upper right corner of the screen, are updated when you save the entry.

❑ Type: 7349.93 in the Debit field.

❑ Press: Enter

The cursor will return to the Account field and wait for the next transaction. All of the fields you filled in for the first line remain unchanged since the description, in the Quick Entry mode, will remain the same for all of them. The transaction that you have entered appears in the box in the lower portion of the screen below the comment lines. The portion of the screen above the box contains information currently being entered.

❑ Enter the balances in Table 5–1.

The credit of 5,500.00 for account 935 is a recording error that you will correct later.

Table 5–1

Account Number	Debit	Credit
200	5320.00	
250	2487.00	
300	700.00	
406	12735.00	
408	12845.00	
426		500.00
428		1250.00
500		1700.00
542	248.70	
680		31500.00
720		18160.63
752	2487.00	
780		2487.00
835	1925.00	
880	500.00	
920	2500.00	
925	500.00	
935		5500.00
945	500.00	

Once you have entered these balances, the debit Entry total should equal $50,097.63 and the credit Entry total should equal $61,097.63. The amount shown in the Out of Balance field should be $11,000.00. ACCPAC Plus will allow you to save a batch that is incomplete or out of balance but will not allow that batch to be posted.

❑ Press: [Esc] to indicate that you have finished working with this batch for now.

The options displayed at the bottom of the screen allow you to save the entry, edit the entry, select a line, or cancel everything you have done.

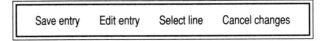

Save entry   Edit entry   Select line   Cancel changes

❑ Select: Save entry.

As the debits do not equal the credits in this batch a warning message will be displayed.

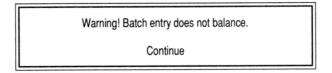

Warning! Batch entry does not balance.

Continue

You will save the out of balance batch and print a listing of the batch entries. In the next chapter you will modify the batch to correct the error in the entry for account 935.

❑ Press: [Enter] to Continue.

The computer will take a few moments to save the transaction. Once it has completed this process, the cursor will appear in the Entry number field, and wait for the next transaction.

❑ Press: [Esc] to exit from the Entry field.

❑ Press: [Esc] to exit from the Batch field and return to the Batch Processing Menu.

❑ Press: [Esc] to return to the Transaction Processing Menu.

PRINTING THE TRANSACTION BATCH LIST

The Transaction Batch List shows all the transactions in the batch. You should print this list so you will have a permanent printed copy of the transactions since ACCPAC Plus denies access to a batch once you have posted it to the General Ledger.

❑ Select: 2. Print batches from the Transaction Processing Menu.

Figure 5–8

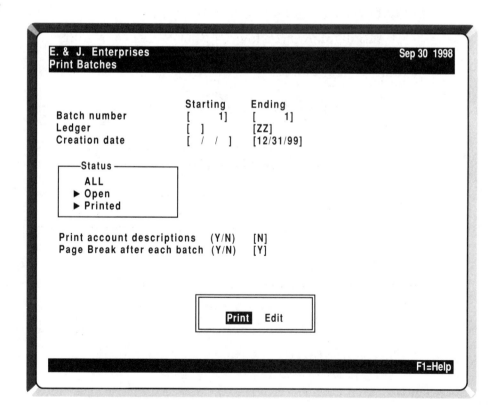

Edit

The selection box in the lower part of the screen (Figure 5–8) allows you to edit the specifications for printing the batch or to print the batch using the default specifications.

- ❏ Select: `Edit` to clear the selection box from the screen and to allow you to change the specifications shown on the screen.

Batch number

ACCPAC Plus allows you to specify which batches are to be printed. If you had entered 15 batches (batches 1 through 15) and only wanted to print the first five, you would enter 1 in the Starting Batch number field and 5 in the Ending Batch number field. For E. & J. Enterprises only one batch has been entered so AC-CPAC Plus displays Batch number 1 in both the Starting and Ending Batch number fields.

- ❏ Press: [Enter] to accept Starting Batch number 1.
- ❏ Press: [Enter] again to accept Ending Batch number 1.

Ledger

ACCPAC Plus allows you to print batches created by different ACCPAC Plus modules. At this time E. & J. Enterprises is only using the General Ledger module.

- ❏ Press: [Enter] to leave the Starting Ledger field blank.
- ❏ Press: [Enter] again to accept ZZ in the Ending Ledger field.

Accepting the blank in the Starting Ledger field and ZZ in the Ending Ledger field tells ACCPAC Plus to print batches created by all ACCPAC Plus modules.

Creation date

You could specify that you also want to print the batches created in a certain time period by entering the starting and ending dates of that time period. ACCPAC Plus displays a blank Starting Creation date which represents the creation date of the first batch created.

- ❏ Press: [Enter] to leave the Starting Creation date field blank.

The default 12/31/99 is displayed in the Ending creation date field.

- ❏ Press: [Enter] to accept the default Ending Creation date.

Status

The Status option box should now be highlighted. Selecting ALL allows you to print all of the batches that meet the specifications that you have entered. Selecting Open allows you to print only those batches which have not yet been printed and any batches that have been changed since printing. Selecting `Printed` prints only those batches that have already been printed and that have not been changed.

❑ Move the selector bar to `ALL`.

❑ Press: [Enter]

Print account descriptions

This option allows you to print the account descriptions with the account codes. An extra line is printed for each description.

❑ Type: `N` to specify that account descriptions are not to be included.

❑ Press: [Enter]

Page break after each batch

This option is used when you are printing more than one batch. If you insert a page break after each batch, ACCPAC Plus will print each batch starting at the top of a new page.

❑ Press: [Enter] to accept the default `Y`.

Print

Review the selections displayed on the screen. If necessary select `Edit` and make corrections.

❑ Select: `Print`

Once the batch has printed, the program will return to the Transaction Processing Menu.

ANALYSIS OF THE TRANSACTION BATCH LIST

Table 5–2

```
Date: Sep 30 98   10:48am            E. & J. Enterprises                        Page:   1
Batch Listing

Batch number        from [    1]    to [    1]
Source ledger       from [   ]      to [ZZ]
Creation date       from [          ] to [Dec 31 99]
Status(es) selected: Open, Printed

Batch number:    1  Transfer balances to ACCPAC     Creation date: Sep 30 98  Status: Printed

Entry  Line
Number No.  Pd. Srce. Date    Reference   Description          Acct. Dept.  Debits      Credits     Errors

   1     1  11 Transfer of account balances as of Sept. 30, 1998 from the
         2  11 manual accounting system to ACCPAC Plus
         3  11 GL-GJ Sep 30 98 Balances Fwd Transfer Sept. 30 Balances   100    7,349.93
         4  11 GL-GJ Sep 30 98 Balances Fwd Transfer Sept. 30 Balances   200    5,320.00
         5  11 GL-GJ Sep 30 98 Balances Fwd Transfer Sept. 30 Balances   250    2,487.00
         6  11 GL-GJ Sep 30 98 Balances Fwd Transfer Sept. 30 Balances   300      700.00
         7  11 GL-GJ Sep 30 98 Balances Fwd Transfer Sept. 30 Balances   406   12,735.00
         8  11 GL-GJ Sep 30 98 Balances Fwd Transfer Sept. 30 Balances   408   12,845.00
         9  11 GL-GJ Sep 30 98 Balances Fwd Transfer Sept. 30 Balances   426                500.00
        10  11 GL-GJ Sep 30 98 Balances Fwd Transfer Sept. 30 Balances   428              1,250.00
        11  11 GL-GJ Sep 30 98 Balances Fwd Transfer Sept. 30 Balances   500              1,700.00
        12  11 GL-GJ Sep 30 98 Balances Fwd Transfer Sept. 30 Balances   542      248.70
        13  11 GL-GJ Sep 30 98 Balances Fwd Transfer Sept. 30 Balances   680             31,500.00
        14  11 GL-GJ Sep 30 98 Balances Fwd Transfer Sept. 30 Balances   720             18,160.63
        15  11 GL-GJ Sep 30 98 Balances Fwd Transfer Sept. 30 Balances   752    2,487.00
        16  11 GL-GJ Sep 30 98 Balances Fwd Transfer Sept. 30 Balances   780              2,487.00
        17  11 GL-GJ Sep 30 98 Balances Fwd Transfer Sept. 30 Balances   835    1,925.00
        18  11 GL-GJ Sep 30 98 Balances Fwd Transfer Sept. 30 Balances   880      500.00
        19  11 GL-GJ Sep 30 98 Balances Fwd Transfer Sept. 30 Balances   920    2,500.00
        20  11 GL-GJ Sep 30 98 Balances Fwd Transfer Sept. 30 Balances   925      500.00
        21  11 GL-GJ Sep 30 98 Balances Fwd Transfer Sept. 30 Balances   935              5,500.00
        22  11 GL-GJ Sep 30 98 Balances Fwd Transfer Sept. 30 Balances   945      500.00
                                                                                ----------  ----------
                                                                                50,097.63   61,097.63   * 4
                                                                                ----------  ----------
                                                                                50,097.63   61,097.63
                                                                                ==========  =========

1 entry printed.    1 error found.

1 batch printed.

Error Description

   1   Account/department does not exist.
   2   Fiscal period closed or invalid.
   3   Source code does not exist.
   4   Batch entry does not balance.
```

Table 5–2 shows you the printed Transaction Batch List. The date and time that the batch was printed appears in the upper-left corner of the printout. The name of the company appears at the top of each page, centered between the date and the page number. The name of the printout, "Batch Listing", appears below the date and time. The next four lines show the specifications you choose. The next line lists the batch number and description, the date the batch was created, and the batch status.

The main part of the list has the following columns:

Entry Number   Entries are sequentially numbered to identify each transaction within the batch.

Line No.   Comment and detail lines are numbered sequentially within each entry.

Pd.   fiscal period

Srce.   source

Date

Reference

Description

Acct.   account code

Dept.   department code

Debits

Credits

Errors   are indicated by a code number beside the detail line or total containing the error. A description of the error codes is printed at the bottom of the batch listing.

At the end of each entry the debit and credit columns are totalled. Note the error code 4 on your printout. This error code draws your attention to the fact that the batch entry does not balance.

At the end of the list, the batch totals for the debit and credit columns are shown. The Transaction Batch List also shows the number of entries and errors in the batch.

❑   Quit ACCPAC Plus.

❑   Back up your data files.

REVIEW QUESTIONS

1. Why is it good practice to prepare a list of the transactions to be entered in the ACCPAC Plus system?
2. What are the functions of each option on the Transaction Processing Menu?
3. What is a transaction batch?
4. What are source codes?
5. What is the purpose of the Reference field? Why is this information important?
6. What will happen if you type an account number not included in the Chart of Accounts?
7. How do you know if an entry that you just made is not in balance?

8. Why should you print a Transaction Batch List before posting that batch to the General Ledger?
9. Describe the differences between the "Quick entry" and the "Normal entry" modes. Under what conditions would you use each of these options?
10. How can you make corrections to a batch already posted to the General Ledger?
11. What steps must you complete to print a Batch Listing?
12. Describe the error codes printed on a Batch Listing.

EXERCISE

In this part of the ongoing exercise you will enter the source codes and record the opening balances for the company that was named after you. Use September 30, 1998 as the New date.

1. Enter General Ledger source codes for General Journal, Cash Disbursements, Cash Receipts, Purchases, and Sales.
2. Print two copies of the Source Code List.
3. Enter the following opening balances for the new company that you created earlier. Assume that all accounts should have a natural balance. You should prepare a data-entry sheet, writing out each account and balance before entering it into the batch.

Table 5–3

100	Cash	900.00	
300	Prepaid Expenses	1,200.00	
406	Fixtures and Furniture	2,000.00	
408	Office Equipment	1,500.00	
500	Accounts Payable		4,800.00
542	Value Added Tax Recoverable	300.00	
680	Common Stock		4,100.00
752	Purchases	3,000.00	

4. Save the batch and print two copies of the Batch Listing for your records.
5. Quit ACCPAC Plus and back up the data files for your company.

CHAPTER

6 More Batch Processing

Working through this chapter you will edit the transaction batch that you created in the last chapter. Then you will enter transaction information into two more batches.

GETTING READY

❏ Enter the commands necessary to display the ACCPAC Plus Start Menu.

❏ Select: `G/L E. & J. Enterprises` from the Start Menu.

❏ Type: `103198` for October 31, 1998 as the New date.

❏ Press: [Enter]

As a protection against errors in the entry of a New date, ACCPAC Plus compares the New date to the Last access date. If the New date is more than seven days before or after the Last access date, a warning message is displayed.

```
┌─────────────────────────────────────────────────────┐
│  New date is more than one week later than old date.  │
│                                                       │
│            Accept          Edit                       │
└─────────────────────────────────────────────────────┘
```

❏ Select: `Accept`

EDITING A BATCH

In the last chapter you entered a batch to transfer the account balances from E. & J. Enterprises' manual accounting system to ACCPAC Plus. That Batch was out of balance because of an error in the balance for account 935. The amount was entered as a credit but it should have been entered as a debit.

❑ Select: `3. Transaction processing` from the ACCPAC General Ledger Master Menu.

❑ Select: `1. Batch processing` from the Transaction Processing Menu.

❑ Select: `1. Add/modify/delete batches` from the Batch Processing Menu.

If you have created additional batches, you should refer to your batch listings to find the correct batch number to use in this chapter.

❑ Type: `1` in the Batch field.

❑ Press: [Enter]

ACCPAC Plus will access the batch and display the batch description in the top portion of the screen. The top right corner of the screen will display the following information reflecting the error made in the entry for account 935.

Entries:	1
Debits:	50,097.63
Credits:	61,097.63

If your debit and credit totals are different from those shown above, you have made additional incorrect entries. Do not worry! When you have corrected the error in account 935, you can use the same technique to change any other line in the batch. A selection box is displayed in the lower portion of the screen.

Modify batch	Delete batch

If you select `Delete batch`, ACCPAC Plus would delete the whole batch and you would have to create a new batch and enter each line again. If you have additional batches, enter the batch number in the Batch field and use the "Delete batch" option to delete those additional batches. If necessary, return to Chapter 5 to enter the first batch again and then re-start this chapter.

❑ Select: `Modify batch`

❑ Select: `Quick entry` as the entry mode.

The cursor should move to the Description field in the top portion of the field.

❑ Press: Enter to accept `Transfer balances to ACCPAC` as the batch description.

The cursor will move to the Entry field which displays the number 2 . If you wished to add a second entry to the batch, you would press **Enter** and then add to the batch using the same techniques as in the last chapter. The error that Erin and Joan caused you to make should be in entry number 1.

❑ Type: `1` in the Entry field.

❑ Press: Enter

ACCPAC Plus will access the batch and display the screen shown in Figure 6–1.

Figure 6–1

```
E. & J. Enterprises                                    Oct 31 1998
Add/Modify/Delete Batches - Modify Batch
   Batch        [    1] Entry mode (Quick entry)   Entries:        1
   Description [Transfer balances to ACCPAC   ]   Debits:   50,097.63
                                                   Credits:  61,097.63

   Entry [    1]   Period [ 11 ]
   Line  [     ]
   Source code:  -[    ]
   Date       [  /  /  ]
   Reference  [         ]      Description  [                    ]
   Account    [         ] Dept. [    ]
   Debit      [              ]  Credit  [              ]
  ─Line-Reference────Description────Acct.─Dept.────Debit────Credit─┐
      1  Transfer of account balances as of Sept. 30, 1998 from the
      2  manual accounting system to ACCPAC Plus
      3  Balances Fwd Transfer Sept.   100          7,349.93
      4  Balances Fwd Transfer Sept.   200          5,320.00
      5  Balances Fwd ┌───────────────────────┐     7.00
      6  Balances Fwd │ Modify entry  Delete entry │ 0.00          ↓
                      └───────────────────────┘
                                                    7.63      61,097.63
                          Out of balance by:                  11,000.00

                                                             F1=Help
```

❑ Select: `Modify entry`

The cursor will move to the Period field which displays `11` , the correct fiscal period number.

❑ Press: Enter

The information box in the lower half of the screen will become active as indicated by increased brightness of the double line around the box.

❑ Move the selector bar to the line containing the details for account 935.

❑ Press: Enter

The details from this line should now be displayed in the data input fields in the middle portion of the screen. Any information that is correct can be accepted by pressing **Enter** when the cursor is in that data input field.

❑ Press: ⌈Enter⌉ five times to move the cursor to the Credit field.

❑ Press: [SPACEBAR] to erase the contents of the Credit field.

❑ Press: ⌈Enter⌉ to indicate that you have finished changing the information in this field.

The cursor will move back to the Debit field.

❑ Type: 5500.00 in the Debit field.

❑ Press: ⌈Enter⌉

The information box will be made active again and the debit and credit totals will be updated. If there are no other errors in the batch the totals should both be 55,597.63 , indicating a balanced entry.

❑ Press: ⌈Esc⌉ to exit.

❑ Select: Accept changes

ACCPAC Plus will then update the totals displayed at the top right of the screen and save the batch.

❑ Press: ⌈Esc⌉ to exit from the Entry field.

❑ Press: ⌈Esc⌉ again to exit from the Batch field.

❑ Print a batch listing.

Confirm that the error in account 935 has been corrected. The totals in both the debits and credits columns should be 55,597.63. If necessary use these steps to correct any other errors in batch 1 and print the batch again. Then display the ACCPAC General Ledger Master Menu on the screen.

OCTOBER 1998 TRANSACTIONS

You will now record a set of transactions for October 1998, representing a complete month's work. Have your printout of the Chart of Accounts readily available so that you can confirm the account codes. You should write down the entry details before you enter them.

❑ Select: 3. Transaction processing from the ACCPAC General Ledger Master Menu.

❑ Select: 1. Batch processing from the Transaction Processing Menu.

❑ Select: 1. Add/modify/delete batches from the Batch Processing Menu.

Batch

❏ Press: [Enter] in the blank Batch field.

❏ Select: `Yes` to create a new batch.

ACCPAC Plus will display the next available batch number in the Batch field. Since one transaction batch has been entered, this batch number should be 2.

Entry mode

❏ Select: `Quick entry` for the Entry mode.

In most cases it is best to use the Quick entry mode when first entering transaction information or editing that information. The Normal entry mode is best used when modifying or editing a batch that requires additional comment lines, or when different references or descriptions are required for each detail line.

Description

The description entered in this field describes the batch in general, not the individual entries in the batch.

❏ Type: `October 1998 Transactions` in the Description field.

❏ Press: [Enter]

The First Transaction

In working through this first entry, you will be entering the data to record the issuing of check #010, on October 1, 1998, to Home Realty in payment of October's office rent (account 920) for $400.

Entry

The Entry field will display the number 1 for the first entry in this batch. Remember that each entry should completely record one and only one transaction.

❏ Press: [Enter] to accept entry number 1.

Period

The cursor will move to the Period field which displays the number "12". Refer to the printout of the company profile and confirm that October 31, 1998 is in fiscal period 12.

❏ Press: [Enter] to accept the displayed fiscal period number.

Line

The sequential line number within each entry is automatically assigned by ACCPAC Plus. Each line consists of either a comment or a detail, and a debit or credit amount for a specific account.

Source code

The Source code field refers to the type of transaction. The source codes will be used to sort transactions into source journals after batches are posted. The six source codes used by E. & J. Enterprises are as follows:

1. CR Cash Receipts
2. CD Cash Disbursements
3. PU Purchases
4. PA Payroll
5. SA Sales
6. GJ General Journal

The source code for this transaction is "CD" for Cash Disbursements.

❑   Type: CD   in the Source code field.
❑   Press: [Enter]

Date

The Date field should display the date entered as the new date. You should enter the actual date of the transaction in this field.

❑   Type: 100198   in the Date field to indicate that the actual date of the transaction was October 1, 1998.
❑   Press: [Enter]

Reference

You use the Reference field to create an audit trail by entering information that enables you to trace the transactions. The reference could be a purchase order number for purchases, an invoice number for sales, a check number for cash disbursements, or the date of a cash receipt. You will use this information to organize the presentation of transaction data when you print the source journals. In this example the check number will be used as the reference.

❑   Type: CK 010
❑   Press: [Enter]

Description

The Description field allows you to record a short description of the entry. If a longer description is required, comment lines can be added at the beginning of the entry when you are using the Quick entry mode.

❑   Type: October 1998 Office Rent   in the description field.
❑   Press: [Enter]

Account

In the Account field, you enter the appropriate General Ledger account number from the Chart of Accounts. ACCPAC Plus will then confirm your entry by displaying the name of the account in highlighted characters to the right. If the account number that you enter is not found in the Chart of Accounts, the Finder will display account numbers and descriptions. You can then select the appropriate account. To see how the Finder works, work through the following steps.

❑ Type: `921`

❑ Press: [Enter]

Since ACCPAC Plus cannot find the account number you entered, the computer will beep and display adjacent account numbers. If the window displays the account you want, select the correct account number and press **Enter**. If the window does not display the account you want, scroll to the correct account number and select it.

❑ Move the selector bar to `920     Rent, Office Space.`

❑ Press: [Enter]

The name of the account, "Rent, Office Space", will appear to the right to allow you to verify the account entered.

The amount fields: debit and credit

Since we did not set up the Chart of Accounts to include departments, the cursor will move directly to the Debit field.

If you are entering a credit, press **Enter** or **Tab** to move the cursor to the Credit field. If the amount is a debit, stay in the Debit field.

If you accidentally move the cursor past the field you want, press **Esc** to return to the Source code field. Then, press **Enter** to advance to the correct field.

ACCPAC Plus assumes that the last two numbers you enter are cents unless you enter a decimal point. You may either enter the decimal or allow ACCPAC Plus to enter it for you. For example, to enter $100, you could type `10000` or `100.00`.

Now, enter October's office rent of $400.

❑ Type: `400.00` in the Debit field.

❑ Press: [Enter]

The cursor returns to the Account field to accept the next account number. Details of the first line of the entry are displayed in the information box and the entry totals are updated.

To record the credit portion of this transaction,

❑ Type: `100` in the Account field.

❑ Press: [Enter]

Make sure the confirmation "Cash" appears to the right.

❑ Move the cursor to the Credit field.

❑ Type: 400.00

❑ Press: [Enter]

The entry totals should now display 400.00 for both the debit and credit columns.

Save entry

You can now indicate that the entry recording one transaction is complete.

❑ Press: [Esc] with the cursor in the blank Account field.

Save entry	Edit entry	Select line	Cancel changes

This is one of the few ACCPAC Plus selection boxes that has more than one option starting with the same letter. If you wish to either `Save entry` or `Select line`, you must move the selector bar to the desired option and then press **Enter**.

❑ Move the selector bar to `Save Entry`.

❑ Press: [Enter] to save your first entry.

The cursor will return to the Entry field and ACCPAC Plus will be ready to accept the next entry into the transaction batch.

SALES TAXES

Governments are turning more and more to taxes on the sales of goods and services to generate revenue. Sales taxes are levied by most states in the United States and most provinces in Canada. Value added taxes are levied by the government of Canada and the governments of most European countries. As a result, you may have to record sales and value added tax data for several different governments. Each government has its own set of rules and regulations about these types of taxes. In this simulation you will work with a simplified sales and value added tax model.

No sales taxes are collected on the sale of services. As a provider of services, E. & J. Enterprises must pay sales tax (5%) and value added tax (10%) on equipment and supplies used in providing these services. These taxes are considered to be part of the cost of the equipment and supplies.

No sales taxes are collected on the purchase of goods for resale. Sales tax (5%) must be collected and rebated to the government on all sales to non-resellers of the goods. E. & J. Enterprises must collect sales tax on all merchandise sales unless the purchaser has the documents to prove that they are exempt from sales tax.

Value added tax (10%) must be paid on all purchases of goods but not services. Any purchase made by E. & J. Enterprises is subject to the 10% value added tax. If the purchase is for equipment, supplies, or services that will be used by E. & J. Enterprises the value added tax is considered part of the cost of the equipment, supplies or services. If the purchase is for items that will be resold, the value added tax paid on the purchase is deductible from the value added tax payable to the government when the items are resold.

CORRECTING ENTRY ERRORS

The next transaction that you will enter is for the October 4, 1998 purchase of software for resale (total price $2250) plus a 10% Value Added Tax ($225.00) on credit from Pear Computers Inc. E. & J. Enterprises' purchase order was number P0005. The instructions will cause an out-of-balance entry that you will be shown how to correct after saving the batch entry.

❑ Press: [Enter] to accept 2 in the Entry field.

❑ Press: [Enter] to accept fiscal period 12.

The description field is too short to enter a full description of this transaction. In this entry it will be used to identify the supplier and a more complete description will be entered as comments.

❑ Use the [SPACEBAR] or [DELETE] key to erase the contents of the Source code field.

❑ Press: [Enter] in the blank Source code field to enter comments.

❑ Type: Purchase of software packages for resale at a cost of $2250 in the first comment line.

❑ Press: [Enter]

❑ Type: plus value added tax of $225 from Pear Computers Inc. in the second comment line.

❑ Press: [Enter]

❑ Press: [Enter] in the blank comment line.

This transaction is a purchase, so the Source code should be "PU".

❑ Type: PU in the Source code field.

❑ Press: [Enter]

❑ Type: 100498 in the Date field.

❑ Press: [Enter]

You will use the purchase order number as a reference. If you always use the purchase order number as the reference for purchases, you can arrange the printout of the Purchases Journal in sequential order of purchase order numbers.

❑ Type: P0005 in the Reference field.

❑ Press: Enter

A more complete description of the transaction has been entered in the comment lines, so the description that you enter in the detail line may refer only to the supplier.

❑ Type: Pear Computers Inc. in the Description field.

❑ Press: Enter

Record the purchase of software for resale.

❑ Type: 752 in the Account field.

❑ Press: Enter

❑ Type: 2250.00 in the Debit field.

❑ Press Enter

❑ Type: 542 in the Account field.

❑ Press: Enter

❑ Type: 225.00 in the Debit field.

❑ Press Enter

❑ Type: 500 in the Account field.

❑ Press: Enter

❑ Move the cursor to the Credit field.

❑ Type: 2525.00 to record an **incorrect** amount.

❑ Press: Enter

The Entry totals will show 2,475.00 for debits and 2,525.00 for credits. The Out of balance by line will show 50.00 in the credit column, indicating that credits exceed debits by $50.00.

❑ Press: Esc to indicate that the entry is complete, even though it is incorrect.

ACCPAC Plus will now display a selection box.

```
┌─────────────────────────────────────────────────────────┐
│  Save entry    Edit entry    Select line    Cancel changes │
└─────────────────────────────────────────────────────────┘
```

❑ Move the selector bar to Select line.

❑ Press: Enter

The information box displays the details for entry 2. The only credit should be on line five.

❑ Type: 5 in the Line field.

❑ Press: Enter

The information box will be made active as indicated by the highlighted display and the double line outline. The selector bar should be on line 5, the credit to account 500 detail.

❑ Press: Enter to transfer the information to the input fields on the screen.

❑ Press: Enter to move the cursor until it reaches the Credit field.

❑ Type: 2475.00 to record the proper credit amount.

❑ Press: Enter

The Out of balance by should now show 0.00 , indicating that debits equal credits.

❑ Press: Esc to indicate that you have completed the changes to this entry.

❑ Select: Save entry to save the changes that you have entered.

MORE ENTRIES

Add the following transactions of E. & J. Enterprises to Transaction Batch 2 using the Quick entry mode and period number 12. Remember that each transaction should be a separate entry. Choose the source code from those used by E. & J. Enterprises. Enter the actual transaction dates, and meaningful references and descriptions. When necessary use a comment line to more fully describe the transaction. The account number and amount is shown for each debit or credit. Remember that the rate for sales tax is 5% and the rate for value added tax (VAT) is 10%

1. On October 4, 1998, E. & J. Enterprises sold a Micmac model B336 computer ($1,700.00) and a Ginzu model 300XZ printer ($300) on credit to Evans Ltd. The invoice number was 1015 and the amount was $2,300 including sales tax and VAT. Terms of all credit sales are n/30. Hint! Use the invoice number as a reference, the customer name in the description, and the details in a comment line.

200		2300.00	
	700		2000.00
	520		100.00
	540		200.00

2. On October 8, 1998 E. & J. Enterprises purchased an executive chair for Erin's office on purchase order number P0006 for $745, including sales and value added taxes, from O.K. Furniture Company. O.K. Furniture delivered the chair and invoice number OK0069 on October 10, 1998. The invoice, dated October 10, 1998 was for $745 and the terms were 2/10, n/30.

406		745.00	
	500		745.00

3. Received ACCPAC Plus accounting modules ordered on P0007 and invoice from Computer Associates. The invoice (CA54043, dated October 12, 1998) was for $3,000 plus VAT of $300 and the terms are n/30.

```
752              3000.00
542               300.00
       500                  3300.00
```

4. On October 17, 1998 E. & J. Enterprises received $2,300 payment from Evans Ltd. for the sale (invoice 1015) in first transaction.

```
100              2300.00
       200                  2300.00
```

5. On October 21, 1998 sold a Serene model DG3 ($2,000) computer and a Ginzu model 300XZ printer ($300) to Hibou Co. The invoice, dated that day, was number 1016.

```
200              2645.00
       700                  2300.00
       520                   115.00
       540                   230.00
```

6. Received word processing and graphics software ordered on P0008 from Dubai Software Co., invoice number 87795. The invoice for $1,650 including VAT, was dated October 25, 1998. Terms are n/30.

```
752              1500.00
542               150.00
       500                  1650.00
```

7. On October 29, 1998 issued check #011 to Computer Associates in payment of invoice CA54043 for $3,300.

```
500              3300.00
       100                  3300.00
```

8. On October 29, 1998 issued check #012 to Erin for $950 to pay October salary.

```
935               950.00
       100                   950.00
```

9. On October 29, 1998 issued check #013 to Joan for $1,000 to pay October salary.

```
935              1000.00
      100                    1000.00
```

10. On October 31, 1998 record $4,600 in cash sales (including sales tax and VAT) for October.

```
100              4600.00
      700                    4000.00
      520                     200.00
      540                     400.00
```

11. On October 31, 1998 issued invoice 1017 to PerCorp Inc. for monthly billing of $3,520 for accounting services.

```
200              3520.00
      720                    3520.00
```

12. On October 31, 1998 recorded $4,800 received from PerCorp Inc. in payment of invoice number 1014 for September accounting services.

```
100              4800.00
      200                    4800.00
```

Once you have entered these transactions, print the Transaction Batch Listing. The batch total should be $33,985. If necessary, make corrections using the Normal entry mode and reprint the Batch Listing.

PERIOD END ADJUSTMENTS

❑ Create a new batch for the October period end adjustments.

❑ Enter the following adjusting entries.

1. Expired insurance was $115.

```
880              115.00
      300                    115.00
```

2. Estimated depreciation was $135 on office equipment and $105 on furniture and fixtures.

```
835              240.00
      426                    105.00
      428                    135.00
```

After counting the inventory at the end of the month, E. & J. Enterprises found it had merchandise that cost $3,397 still on hand. To present the effect of the difference between the opening and closing inventory in the Income Statement and to update the inventory account in the Balance Sheet, you must enter the following transactions.

3. Transfer the beginning inventory from the balance sheet inventory account to the Income Statement opening inventory account.

```
750              2487.00
     250              2487.00
```

4. Debit the closing inventory for the month to the balance sheet inventory account and credit that amount to the Income Statement closing inventory account.

```
250              3397.00
     780              3397.00
```

❑ Print the Batch Listing.

The batch total should be $6,239.00. Review your printout and, if necessary, make corrections and reprint the Batch Listing.

DISPLAYING A BATCH

In addition to reviewing the printed Batch Listing, you can also display batches on the screen to make sure there are no errors.

❑ Select: 2. Inquiries from the ACCPAC General Ledger Master Menu.

Figure 6–2

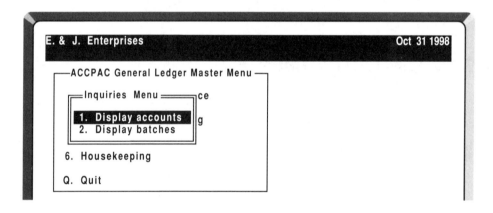

❑ Select: 2. Display batches from the Inquiries Menu.

The Transaction Batch Number field will show the number of the first unposted batch. To select a batch for viewing you enter the number of the batch. For E. & J. Enterprises, the October adjustments should be in batch 3. If you have used a different batch number, look it up on the Batch Listing. If you enter the number of a deleted or unused batch, ACCPAC Plus will display a listing of the unposted batches. You can then select the batch that you wish to display.

❑ Type: 15 in the Batch field.

❑ Press: [Enter]

Figure 6–3

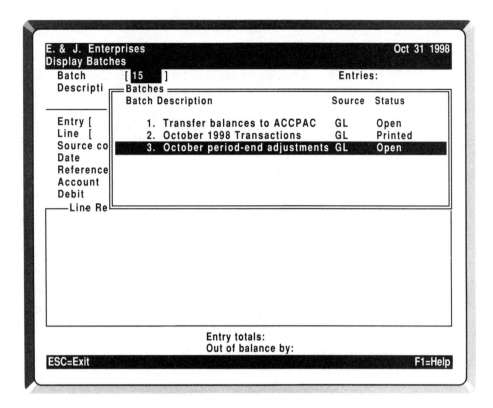

```
E. & J. Enterprises                                    Oct 31 1998
Display Batches
     Batch      [ 15  ]                          Entries:
     Descripti ┌─Batches ───────────────────────────────────────┐
               │ Batch Description              Source  Status   │
     ─────────  │                                                │
     Entry  [   │   1.  Transfer balances to ACCPAC  GL   Open   │
     Line   [   │   2.  October 1998 Transactions    GL   Printed│
     Source co  │   3.  October period-end adjustments GL  Open  │
     Date       │                                                │
     Reference  │                                                │
     Account    │                                                │
     Debit      │                                                │
     └Line Re───┘                                                │
               │                                                  │
               │                                                  │
               │                                                  │
               │                                                  │
               │                                                  │
               │                                                  │
               │          Entry totals:                           │
               │          Out of balance by:                      │
 ESC=Exit                                                 F1=Help
```

The Finder will display a list of the batches entered (see Figure 6–3).

❏ Move the selector bar to the batch that you created for the October period end adjusting entries.

❏ Press: Enter

ACCPAC Plus will display the batch description, number of entries in the batch and the debit and credit balances in the top portion of the screen. There should be 4 entries with debits and credits each totalling $6,239.00. Short form detail lines for the first entry will be displayed in the information box. To display the complete information on a detail line you use the "View" option.

❏ Press: V

The option box will disappear and the selector bar will be on the first line in the transaction.

❏ Move the selector bar to the credit detail line.

❏ Press: Enter

The complete information that you entered on this line will be displayed in the fields in the middle portion of the screen. Verify the information, noting any errors.

❏ Press: Esc to return to the option box.

❏ Select: Next entry to view entry 2.

❏ View each of the entries by selecting `Next entry` . Note any errors.

When there are no more entries to be displayed, ACCPAC Plus will display the following prompt.

```
No entry after this one

Continue
```

❏ Press: [Enter] to continue.

❏ Press: [Esc] to return the cursor to the Batch field.

❏ Press: [Esc] again to display the ACCPAC General Ledger Master Menu.

If necessary, correct any errors that you noted, and print the Batch Listing again.

❏ Exit from ACCPAC Plus.

❏ Back up your data files.

REVIEW QUESTIONS

1. What is a transaction batch?
2. Describe the steps that you would take to correct an error in a batch entry.
3. Why should you use the same source code for all transactions of a particular type?
4. Why would you use more than one transaction batch during a fiscal period?
5. How can you display the details of a transaction batch on the screen?
6. What is the difference between a batch and an entry?
7. When would you use comment lines in an entry?

EXERCISE

This part of the ongoing exercise has two sections: recording a series of transactions for October 1998 and recording month-end adjustments for October 1998. Create a separate batch for each section. Use October 31, 1998 as the New date.

Entering October 1998 Transactions

1. Prepare a data entry sheet for the following transaction. Terms for all merchandise sales are 2/10, n/30 and net 30 for services. Sales tax (5%) and value added tax (10%) are applied on merchandise sales to end users. Only value added tax is applied to purchases for resale. No sales taxes are charged on services.

Oct. 1	Sold software for $2,300 (the amount included $100 sales tax and $200 VAT) on credit to Barilak & Associates, invoice A001.
Oct. 1	Paid $600 to Masters Realty for October office rent, check C003.
Oct. 2	Invoiced Dillingham & Co. $1,920 for services rendered during September, invoice A002.
Oct. 7	Issued 3,000 shares, common stock, to you for $3,000 cash.
Oct. 10	Sold a Serene computer security device for $1725 (the amount included $75 sales tax and $150 VAT) on credit to H. Bazelton, Accountant, invoice A003.
Oct. 12	Cash sale of software for $759 (the amount included $33 sales tax and $66 VAT) to Jenna & Reyk recorded on invoice A004.
Oct. 15	Purchased software for resale on purchase order B005 from Serene Systems Inc. for $6,050, (which includes the original invoice amount of $5,500, plus VAT). The invoice amount of $5,500 did not include VAT. The invoice number SS4550 was dated October 15, with net 30 terms.
Oct. 15	Sold software for $960, plus $48 sales tax and $96 VAT, on credit to Graves & Dawn Co., invoice A005.
Oct. 23	Received a $1725 check (#1353) from H. Bazelton in payment of invoice A003.
Oct. 27	Received a check (#4890) from Graves & Dawn Co. for the amount of $1104 due on invoice A005.
Oct. 27	Sold printer for $560, plus $28 sales tax and $56 VAT, on credit to Hapick Ltd., invoice A006.
Oct. 27	Received a check (#2459) from Dillingham & Co. for $1920 in payment of invoice A002.
Oct. 29	Received check #187 from Hapick Ltd. for $632.80 in payment of invoice A006. Hint! 2% discount does not apply to sales or value added taxes.
Oct. 30	Invoice A007 to Dillingham & Co. in the amount of $2,150 for services rendered in October.
Oct. 30	Issued check C004 to you for $2,300 salary for the month of October.

2. Enter the transaction described above using a new batch.
3. After entering these transactions, print two copies of the Transaction Batch List for your records.

Month End Adjustments

4. Create a new batch, dated October 31, 1998, and make the following month end adjustments:
   a) Monthly depreciation on the office equipment was $35.
   b) Monthly depreciation on fixtures and furniture was $18.50.
   c) At the end of the month, the closing inventory was $3,990.
5. Print two copies of the Transaction Batch List for your records.
6. Exit from ACCPAC Plus. Remember to back up your files!

CHAPTER

7 Period End

In this chapter, you will post the transaction batches created in Chapters 5 and 6 to the General Ledger. You will then print a series of reports.

GETTING READY

- ❑ Enter the commands necessary to display the ACCPAC Plus Start Menu.
- ❑ Select: `G/L E. & J. Enterprises` from the Start Menu.
- ❑ Type: `103198` in the New date field.
- ❑ Press: Enter

BATCH STATUS REPORT

Before you post batches to the General Ledger, you should verify the status of each batch. The Batch Status report tells you about the activity that has taken place in all the unposted batches and in batches that have been posted or deleted since the last time the data for the report was cleared. This report includes the number of errors in the unposted batches. It can be used as an audit trail of batch numbers and dates of activity in the batches.

You may print the Batch Status Report any time. The only time you must print and clear this report is before running the Change Fiscal Year function as will be described in Chapter 9.

❑ Select: `5. Reports` from the ACCPAC General Ledger Master Menu.

❑ Select: `5. Batch status report`

Figure 7–1

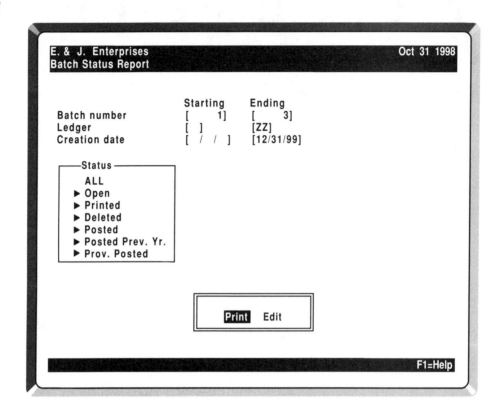

The area at the top of the Batch Status Report screen (Figure 7–1) contains a number of options that allow you to specify which batches will be included in the report. You can select batches by batch number, ledger, and batch creation date.

The "Status" box on the left side of the screen allows you to select batches for the report based on their status.

ALL	This default setting selects all batches without considering the status of each batch.
Open	This option selects only unposted batches that have not been printed since the last change was made to the batch.
Printed	This option is used to select only those batches for which listings have been printed.
Deleted	Only batches that have been deleted using the Add/Modify/Delete Batches function are selected when this option is chosen.
Posted	This option selects only batches that have already been posted to the General Ledger for the current fiscal year.
Posted Prev. Yr.	Only those batches that have been posted to the previous fiscal year are selected by this option.

Prov. Posted   This option selects only those batches that have been provisionally posted to the General Ledger. This feature is only available if you are using Version 6.0B or higher.

If you wanted to change the report options, you would select Edit from the option box in the lower portion of the screen. You could then enter new information in the Batch number, Ledger, or Creation date fields. When the selector bar appears in the Status box, you use the space bar to turn the options on and off. When an option has been chosen, a triangular pointer appears to its left. To exit the Status box, you would press **Enter**.

ACCPAC Plus sets the defaults on the Batch Status Report Screen to include all batches that have not been cleared from the data files.

❑ Move the selector bar to Print.

❑ Press: Enter

If you have deleted or posted any batches, the following prompt would appear at the bottom of the screen once the Batch Status Report has printed.

```
Do you want to clear all posted and deleted batches
              within the specified range?
                   Yes          No
```

The curser will be resting on No . If you have deleted any batches you could select Yes to clear the deleted batches from the data files.

As shown in Table 7–1, the first area on the Batch Status Report identifies the date and time that the report was printed. It also indicates the selections entered on the Batch Status Report screen.

The second area lists each batch by batch number and describes the batch in a series of columns.

An Open status indicates that the batch has not been printed since the last time that you called it up. Any batch with an Open status must be printed before posting is allowed.

Each of the printed batches should have a 0 in the Errors/Posting Sequence column. If your report shows a number in the error column you must modify the batch to correct the error and print the batch again before continuing.

The third area on the report summarizes information by batch status.

Press: Esc to return to the ACCPAC General Ledger Master Menu.

Table 7–1

```
Date: Oct 31 98    2:37pm           E. & J. Enterprises        Page:   1
Batch Status Report

Batch number           from [    1]    to [    3]
Ledger                 from [    ]     to [ZZ]
Creation date          from [         ] to [Dec 31 99]
Status(es) selected: Open, Printed, Deleted, Posted, Posted Prev. Yr, Prov. Posted


                                                            Errors/
Batch                            Creation           Status  Posting No. of
Number Description        Srce. Date    Status       Date   Sequence Entries  Debits       Credits

    1 Transfer balances to ACCPAC  GL   Sep 30 98 Printed  Oct  1 98    0      1     55,597.63     55,597.63
    2 October 1998 Transactions    GL   Oct 31 98 Printed  Oct 31 98    0     14     33,985.00     33,985.00
    3 October period-end adjustments GL Oct 31 98 Printed  Oct 31 98    0      4      6,239.00      6,239.00
                                                                       19     95,821.63     95,821.63
                                                            ===========================================

3 batches printed.
0 errors found.

                      No. of        Total        Total
Status        Batches Entries       Debits       Credits

Open            0        0           0.00          0.00
Printed         3       19        95,821.63     95,821.63
Deleted         0        0           0.00          0.00
Posted          0        0           0.00          0.00
Posted Prev. Yr. 0       0           0.00          0.00
```

POSTING TO THE GENERAL LEDGER

❑ Select: 3. Transaction processing from the ACCPAC General Ledger Master Menu.

❑ Select: 3. Post batches from the Transaction Processing Menu.

The G/L Account Posting Menu, which should appear on the screen, offers two options.

Figure 7–2

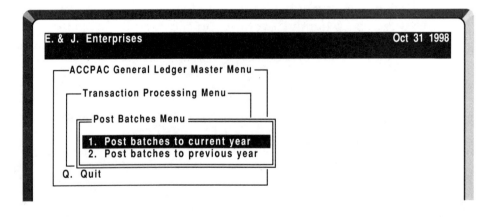

The `Post batches to previous year` function is normally used to post adjustments to the previous fiscal year. When amounts are posted to revenue or expense accounts, this function creates transactions to close these accounts, again transferring the amounts to retained earnings.

❏ Select: 1. `Post batches to current year`

After a few seconds, a message appears on the screen warning you to make a back-up copy of the data disk before proceeding.

Figure 7–3

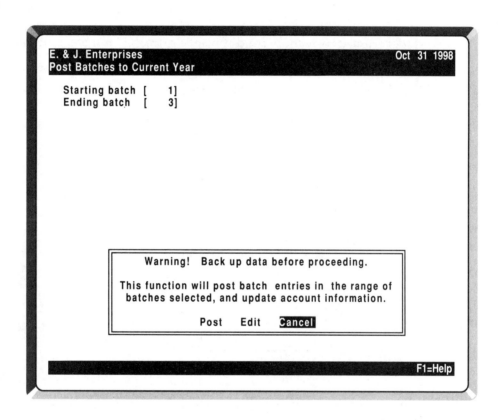

```
E. & J. Enterprises                                    Oct  31  1998
Post Batches to Current Year

        Starting batch  [    1]
        Ending batch    [    3]




                ┌──────────────────────────────────────────────┐
                │  Warning!  Back up data before proceeding.     │
                │                                                │
                │  This function will post batch entries in the  │
                │  range of batches selected, and update account │
                │  information.                                  │
                │                                                │
                │         Post     Edit     Cancel               │
                └──────────────────────────────────────────────┘

                                                          F1=Help
```

If you did not make a back-up copy of the E. & J. Enterprises files at the end of Chapter 6 or if you have made any changes in the batches, press C to exit from the posting procedure. Return to the Start Menu and go to DOS through the System Manager. Back up the E. & J. Enterprises data files. Then start the posting procedure again and display the "Post Batches to Current Year" screen again.

❏ Move the selector bar to `Post` .

❏ Press: [Enter]

If there are errors in the batches, the program will display an error message at the bottom of the screen:

```
┌─────────────────────────────────────────────────────┐
│                                                       │
│        Errors in batches - No Posting allowed.        │
│                                                       │
│                     Press F2                          │
│                                                       │
└─────────────────────────────────────────────────────┘
```

If you receive this error message, go back to the Reports Menu. Print the Batch Status Report to identify the faulty batch. Then return to the Transaction Processing Menu and print the batch that contains the error. Review it for errors, make the necessary corrections, and reprint the transaction batch. Repeat the posting routine again.

Once posting is complete, a new message will appear on the screen:

```
┌─────────────────────────────────────────────────────┐
│                                                       │
│                  Posting complete.                    │
│                                                       │
│                     Continue                          │
│                                                       │
└─────────────────────────────────────────────────────┘
```

❑ Press: [Enter]

The Post Batches Menu will reappear. If you are not certain that you posted the General Ledger, try to make a duplicate posting while the Post Batches Menu is still displayed.

❑ Select: 1. Post batches to current year again.

ACCPAC Plus will display an error message:

```
┌─────────────────────────────────────────────────────┐
│                                                       │
│                There are no batches to post.          │
│                                                       │
│                     Continue                          │
│                                                       │
└─────────────────────────────────────────────────────┘
```

❑ Press: [Enter]

The program will again return to the Post Batches Menu.

As you can see, ACCPAC Plus will not allow you to post a batch twice. People who have posted manual General Ledgers know what it is like to be interrupted and then to spend the next ten minutes trying to remember where they were, only to miss an account or post one twice. ACCPAC Plus will prevent this from happening. The only danger of error is that you might record an entry in more than one batch or in one batch twice, so be very careful when entering data. It is best to write each batch on a data entry form before sitting down at the keyboard.

❑ Press: [Esc] to display the Transaction Processing Menu.

PRINTING THE POSTING JOURNAL

The Posting Journal provides an audit trail of all details posted in the last posting run.

☐ Select: 4. Print posting journal from the Transaction Processing Menu.

The Print Posting Journal screen is shown in Figure 7–4. ACCPAC Plus will automatically insert numbers in the Starting and Ending Posting sequence number fields to print a posting journal for all posting sequences that have not been cleared. If you had posted each batch separately the Starting number would be 1 and the Ending number would be 3.

The default, Print report in Posting sequence order, prints the journal sorted in order of posting sequence, batch number, and entry number. You can also print the report sorted in order of account codes.

☐ Select: Print

Figure 7–4

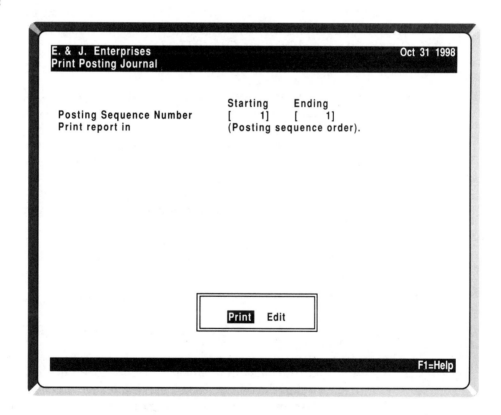

E. & J. Enterprises   Oct 31 1998
Print Posting Journal

                                    Starting   Ending
Posting Sequence Number   [1]   [1]
Print report in   (Posting sequence order).

                              ┌──────────────────────┐
                              │ Print   Edit   │
                              └──────────────────────┘

                                                        F1=Help

After the Posting Journal is printed, ACCPAC Plus will display the following prompt.

```
┌─────────────────────────────────────────────┐
│                                               │
│      Do you want to clear all posting journals│
│          within the specified range?          │
│                                               │
│              Yes        No                    │
│                                               │
└─────────────────────────────────────────────┘
```

If your printout is not readable or complete, or if you wished to print the journal in account order, you could select "No" and then print the posting journal again.

☐ Select: No

☐ Select: 4. Print posting journal again.

☐ Select: Edit

☐ Select: Account order in the Print report in field.

☐ Print the posting journal.

You must clear the posting journals before you can run the Change Fiscal Year function (Chapter 9). When you clear the posting journals, the detail information in the source journals and the General Ledger is unaffected.

☐ Select: Yes

The first part of the posting journal is a detailed listing of each entry from your transaction batches. Compare your batch listings with the posting journal. If you had chosen consolidated posting for an account, c would be printed beside the credit column for each account that is to be consolidated during posting.

The second part of the posting journal is a Consolidated Transaction Report. Had you chosen consolidated posting for an account, the details that are to be consolidated during posting would be printed sequentially by account number.

Compare the two versions of the posting journal that you have printed. Management may select to have one or both of these printed as part of the audit trail documentation.

☐ Press: [Esc] to display the ACCPAC General Ledger Master Menu.

SOURCE JOURNALS

Printing the source journals after transactions have been posted provides the opportunity to check that the entries have been made and provides a more complete audit trail. A source journal is a listing of transactions of a specific type recorded by an ACCPAC Plus accounting module. You may have as many journals as needed, but you must define the contents of each journal.

CREATING SOURCE JOURNALS

❑ Select: 6. Housekeeping from the ACCPAC General Ledger Master Menu.

Figure 7–5

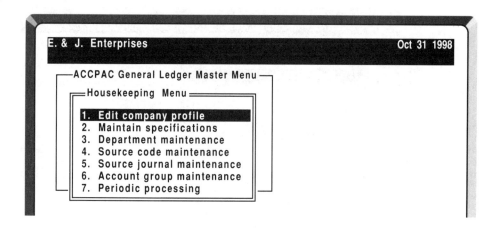

❑ Select: 5. Source journal maintenance from the Housekeeping Menu.

The Source Journal Maintenance Menu will appear on the screen.

Figure 7–6

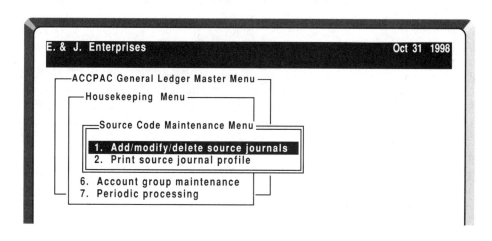

❑ Select: 1. Add/modify/delete source journals

The first step in defining a source journal is to enter the journal name.

❑ Type: General Journal in the Source journal field.

❑ Press: Enter

As soon as you press Enter, two boxes appear on the screen as shown in Figure 7–7.

Figure 7–7

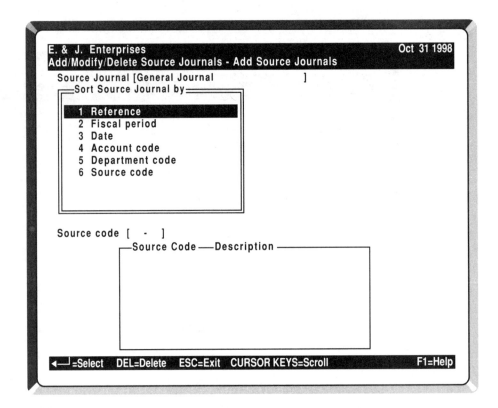

The upper box, Sort Source Journal by , will be highlighted. The order of the selections in this box determines the order in which information is sorted and then presented in columns on the printed report. Erin and Joan have decided that for the General Journal the information should be sorted in the following sequence.

Fiscal period
Date
Account code
Posting sequence
Batch number
Reference

This order specifies that the transactions will first be sorted by fiscal period. If there is more than one transaction for a fiscal period, then these transactions will be sorted by date. Any transactions in the same fiscal period and with the same date will then be sorted by account code. If there were any transactions with the same fiscal period, date, and account code, they would then be sorted by posting sequence, batch, and reference.

To change the sequence you would first select the order number and then select the information that you want displayed in that column.

❏ Move the selector bar to row 1 in the Sort Source Journal by box.

❏ Press: Enter

A "Choices" box will appear, listing the information that can be included in the report, as shown in Figure 7–8.

Figure 7–8

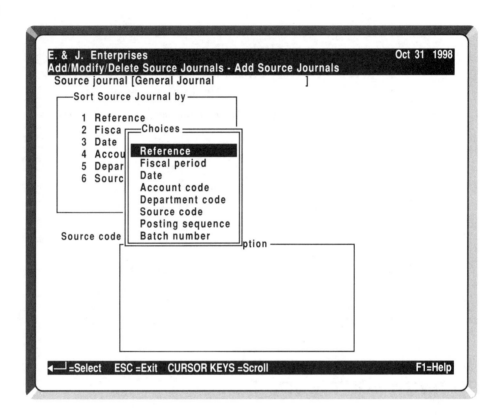

❏ Move the selector bar to Fiscal period in the Choices box.

❏ Press: Enter

Fiscal period should now be displayed in row 1 of the Sort Source Journal by box and Reference will have moved to the second row.

❏ Move the selector bar to row 2 in the Sort Source Journal by box.

❏ Press: Enter

❏ Move the selector bar to Date in the Choices box.

❏ Press: Enter

❏ Repeat this process for rows 3 through 6 to specify the order of information described above.

As E. & J. Enterprises does not use departments, the departments column should be deleted.

- ❑ Move the selector bar to row ` 7. Department code `.
- ❑ Press: [DELETE]

This journal will only list entries with the GL-GJ source code.

- ❑ Delete the Source code row.

Verify that the information is in the desired sequence in the rows and make any corrections necessary.

- ❑ Press: [Esc] to exit from the ` Sort Source Journal by ` box.

The cursor should move to the Source code field. If you remember the Source codes you could type the proper code and then press **Enter**. If you do not remember the Source code, you can use the Finder.

- ❑ Press: [F5] to display a listing of the Source codes and descriptions.
- ❑ Select: ` GL-GJ General Journal `
- ❑ Select: ` Accept ` to accept the GL–GJ source code.

If you wished to include more than one source code in a journal, you would repeat the last step, selecting the desired source codes.

- ❑ Press: [Esc] to indicate that you do not wish to include any more source codes for this journal.
- ❑ Select: ` Add ` to add the specifications for the General Journal.
- ❑ Press: [Esc] to exit from the Source journal field.
- ❑ Press: [Esc] twice to return to the ACCPAC General Ledger Master Menu.

PRINTING A SOURCE JOURNAL

- ❑ Select: ` 5. Reports ` from the ACCPAC General Ledger Master Menu.
- ❑ Select: ` 4. Source journals ` from the Reports Menu.
- ❑ Type: ` General journal ` in the Print source journal field.
- ❑ Press: [Enter]

If you make a typing error, ACCPAC Plus will not find the source journal specifications and will display the Finder. You could then select the source journal from the Finder box.

The following screen, Figure 7–9, will appear.

Figure 7–9

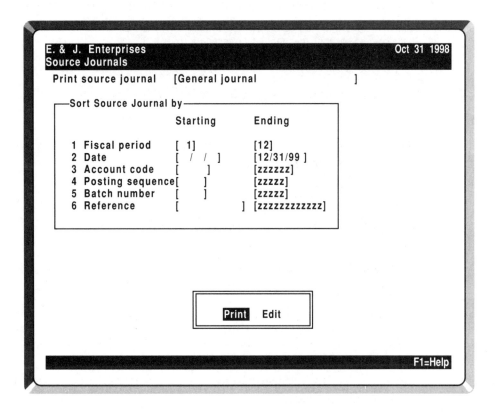

```
E. & J. Enterprises                                    Oct 31 1998
Source Journals
Print source journal    [General journal                    ]

 ┌─Sort Source Journal by──────────────────────────────────────┐
 │                      Starting        Ending                  │
 │                                                              │
 │  1 Fiscal period      [ 1]           [12]                    │
 │  2 Date               [  /  /  ]     [12/31/99 ]             │
 │  3 Account code       [      ]       [zzzzzz]                │
 │  4 Posting sequence   [     ]        [zzzzz]                  │
 │  5 Batch number       [     ]        [zzzzz]                  │
 │  6 Reference          [              ] [zzzzzzzzzzzz]        │
 │                                                              │
 └──────────────────────────────────────────────────────────────┘



                      ┌──────────────────────┐
                      │     Print   Edit      │
                      └──────────────────────┘



                                                         F1=Help
```

The options identify the column sequence and the default ranges of information for printing the General Journal. If you wished to change the ranges you would select Edit and enter the changes. The default ranges displayed on the screen will print all the transactions that you have entered with GL-GJ as the source code.

❏ Select: Print

Once the journal is printed, ACCPAC Plus will display the Reports Menu.

❏ Press: [Esc] to return to the ACCPAC General Ledger Master Menu.

YOUR TURN

❏ Add a Source Journal for each Source code, using the information in Table 7–2. Select the first row as indicated and choose a logical order for the remaining rows. As each Source Journal will use only one source code, you should delete the source code column.

Table 7-2

Journal Name	Sort by	Source Code
Cash Receipts Journal	Date	GL CR
Cash Disbursements Journal	Reference	GL CD
Purchases Journal	Reference	GL PU
Payroll Journal	Reference	GL PA
Sales Journal	Reference	GL SA

❑ Print the Source Journal profiles.

PRINTING THE GENERAL LEDGER

The next step is to print the General Ledger Listing. You should have the ACCPAC General Ledger Master Menu on your screen.

❑ Select: `5. Reports`

The Reports Menu will appear.

❑ Select: `3. G/L listing`

The top two lines of the G/L Listing screen (Figure 7–10) allow you to set the range of accounts and departments that are to be printed. The default is to print all accounts for all departments. You could change the range to specify a group of accounts by selecting **Edit** and then entering the first and last account codes in the range. As E. & J. Enterprises does not use departments, the cursor would skip the department fields.

The third line allows you to select the fiscal periods to be included in the printout and to sort the data by either account or department. The default is to print data for all fiscal periods and to sort the data by account number as E. & J. Enterprises does not use departments.

You may choose to print the G/L Listing in either Standard or Extended format. The Extended format adds the posting entry and batch entry for each line in the report and presents the period net change and balance in a different format. The default is to print the G/L Listing in Standard Format.

The last line allows you to insert a page break after each account. You would normally not use this option since it would print only one account per page, resulting in a longer printout.

Figure 7–10

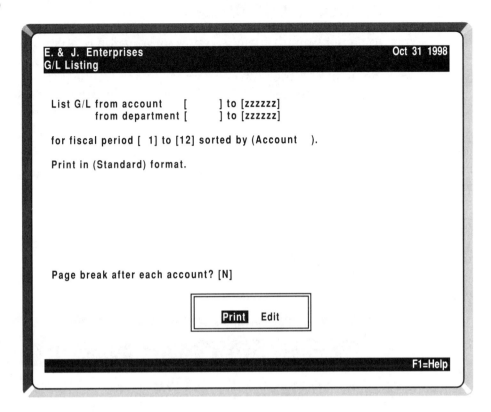

E. & J. Enterprises   Oct 31 1998
G/L Listing

List G/L from account   [   ] to [zzzzzz]
         from department [   ] to [zzzzzz]

for fiscal period [1] to [12] sorted by (Account   ).

Print in (Standard) format.

Page break after each account? [N]

            Print   Edit

                                                      F1=Help

❑   Move the selector bar to   Print .

❑   Press: [Enter] to proceed with printing.

After the printer has stopped, remove the General Ledger printout and review it carefully. Each account shows the details posted. The Debit and Credit columns show the amounts for each detail. The Net Change and Balance columns show the initial account balance, the net change for each fiscal period and the balance at the end of each fiscal period.

❑   Print the G/L Listing for account 100 to 200 in the Extended format.

Compare the presentation of the posted transaction data in each format. Which do you prefer?

❑   Press: [Esc] to display the ACCPAC General Ledger Master Menu.

CONSOLIDATE POSTED TRANSACTIONS

You would not want the detailed entry information to accumulate in the General Ledger accounts indefinitely since this wastes storage space on your disk and slows down processing. You can combine many transaction details into a single line using the Consolidate Posted Transactions function. You should consolidate the posted transactions after printing the Source Journals, as the last step in your period end procedures.

❑ Back up your data files before consolidating the posted entries.

❑ Select: 6. Housekeeping from the ACCPAC General Ledger Master Menu.

❑ Select: 7. Periodic processing

❑ Select: 1. Consolidate posted transactions to display the Consolidate Posted Transactions screen shown in Figure 7–11.

Figure 7–11

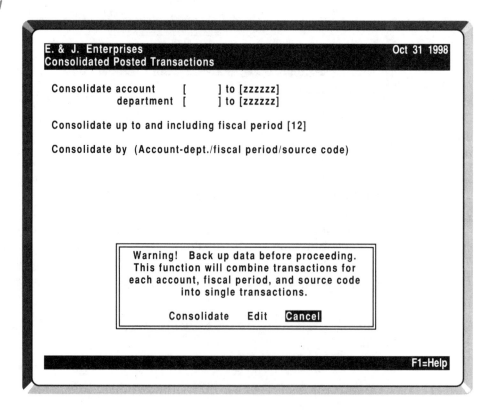

```
E. & J. Enterprises                                    Oct 31 1998
Consolidated Posted Transactions


Consolidate account    [       ] to [zzzzzz]
           department  [       ] to [zzzzzz]

Consolidate up to and including fiscal period [12]

Consolidate by  (Account-dept./fiscal period/source code)




                  ┌──────────────────────────────────────┐
                  │ Warning!  Back up data before proceeding. │
                  │ This function will combine transactions for │
                  │ each account, fiscal period, and source code │
                  │       into single transactions.       │
                  │                                      │
                  │   Consolidate    Edit    Cancel      │
                  └──────────────────────────────────────┘



                                                       F1=Help
```

If you did not back up your data files you should do so now.

The defaults shown on the Consolidate Posted Transaction screen will combine transactions for all accounts up to and including the current fiscal period. For each account the transactions will be combined by source code for each fiscal period.

❏ Select: `Consolidate`

❏ Print the General Ledger Listing.

Compare the new General Ledger Listing with that printed earlier. Note the consolidated postings and the reduced number of transactions printed.

❏ Exit from ACCPAC Plus.

❏ Back up your data files.

REVIEW QUESTIONS

1. Describe the steps that you would take to post a batch to the General Ledger.
2. What is the purpose of the Batch Status Report?
3. Is it possible to post a transaction batch twice? What will happen if you try?
4. What type of error is an accounting package unable to prevent? Give several examples.
5. Describe a good control system that would allow you to review transactions before posting them to the General Ledger.
6. Describe the sequence of menus you must pass through to arrive at the "G/L listing" option.
7. When printing the General Ledger, is it necessary to print all of the accounts? Describe how you would limit the range of accounts to be printed.
8. What is a Source Journal?
9. Why would you want to change the order of the columns in a Source Journal?
10. What is the purpose of the Consolidate Posted Transactions function?

EXERCISE

1. In the previous chapter, you printed the Batch Lists for the new company identified by your initials. Print a Batch Status Report to verify that there are no errors in the batches. If there are errors, correct them, print the Transaction Batch List again, and back up your data files.
2. Post all transaction batches to the General Ledger.
3. Print and clear the Posting Journal.
4. Add the Source Journals and then print the Source Journal profiles.
5. Consolidate the posted transaction details.
6. Print the General Ledger Listing.
7. Exit from ACCPAC Plus.
8. Back up your data files.

CHAPTER

8 Financial Reports

In this chapter, you will use the data that you posted to the General Ledger in Chapter 7 to produce financial statements for the year ending October 31, 1998.

GETTING STARTED

☐ Enter the commands necessary to access the ACCPAC Plus Start Menu.

☐ Select: `G/L E. & J. Enterprises` from the Start Menu.

☐ Enter the date 10/31/98 in the New date field.

ACCPAC Plus allows you to create financial statements for your company through a computer-driven set of commands. ACCPAC Plus uses fifteen account groups in this process. The financial report specifications you generate may be only a starting position on which to build the statements for your company. These statement formats have two limitations:

1. They create a line for every account group in the ledger rather than grouping similar accounts, such as cash accounts.

2. The order of presentation of account information within a statement may not be that desired by management.

EDITING ACCOUNT GROUPS

You must first edit the account groups. All related accounts should be numerically grouped with related accounts; for example, all fixed assets should be together, with no current assets or expenses included within their numerical range.

❑ Select: 6. Housekeeping from the ACCPAC General Ledger Master Menu.

❑ Select: 6. Account group maintenance

The Account Group Maintenance Menu shown in Figure 8–1 will appear.

Figure 8–1

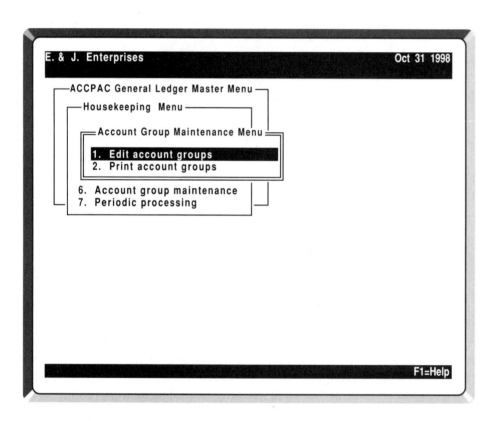

The first option allows you to edit the account groups so that they correspond to the chart of accounts you created earlier. The second option prints a listing of the groupings by number, description, and account ranges. If you have to review the account groupings before updating them, this will give you the information to work on.

❑ Select: 1. Edit account groups

Figure 8–2

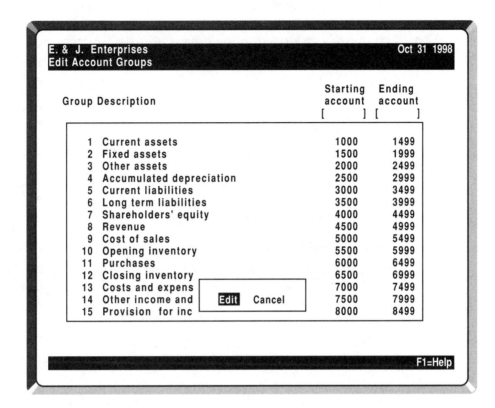

The account codes, as shown in Figure 8–2, were installed by Computer Associates when they created the software. You must edit the account ranges to correspond to E. & J. Enterprises' chart of accounts. Look at the Chart of Accounts printed in Chapter 4. The Quick Report Writer uses 15 account groups. Identify the account numbers that conform to the groups shown in Table 8.1.

Table 8–1

1	Current assets	100-399
2	Fixed assets	400-419
3	Other assets	none
4	Accumulated depreciation	420-449
5	Current liabilities	500-599
6	Longterm liabilities	none
7	Shareholder's equity	600-699
8	Revenue	700-749
9	Cost of sales	none
10	Opening inventory	750-750
11	Purchases	751-779
12	Closing inventory	780-780
13	Costs and expenses	800-999
14	Other income and expenses	none
15	Provision for income taxes	none

When you change the account code range for any group, you must type the correct opening and closing account numbers in the appropriate fields. If there are no accounts in a group, you should use the spacebar or the delete key to leave both fields blank.

❏ Select: `Edit`

The selector bar will move to Group 1   `Current assets`.

❏ Press: [Enter] to edit this account group.

The information for Group 1 should now be displayed in the upper portion of the screen with the cursor in the Starting account field.

❏ Type: `100`

❏ Use [SPACEBAR] or [DEL] to erase any excess numbers.

❏ Press: [Enter] to move the cursor to the Ending account field.

❏ Type: `399`

❏ Use [SPACEBAR] or [DEL] to erase any excess numbers.

❏ Press: [Enter] to indicate that you are finished editing the account ranges for Group 1.

❏ Edit the remaining account groups using the information in Figure 8–1.

You must place every ledger account into one of the groups. After you complete the last group, verify that all the changes have been entered correctly and make any corrections necessary.

❏ Press: [Esc] to indicate that you have finished editing the account group ranges.

The following message will appear:

```
┌──────────────────────────────────────────────────────┐
│                                                        │
│        Accept changes        Edit        Cancel        │
│                                                        │
└──────────────────────────────────────────────────────┘
```

You now have the opportunity to cancel the changes or to accept them and update this information for E. & J. Enterprises.

❏ Select: `Accept changes`

ACCPAC Plus will then check the account ranges for each group. If there are no accounts within the range defined for group, an error message will be displayed. If an account number has not been included in any account group, no error message will be displayed.

PRINTING THE ACCOUNT GROUPS

❏ Select: `2. Print account groups` from the Account Group Maintenance Menu.

❏ Press: ⌜Enter⌟ to print.

Compare this printout to your printed chart of accounts. If any accounts have not
been included in the group account ranges, or if any accounts have been included in two account groups, re-edit the account groups making the necessary
corrections.

❏ Press: ⌜Esc⌟ twice to return to the ACCPAC General Ledger Master Menu.

CREATING REPORT SPECIFICATIONS

❏ Select: 4. Financial reports to display the Financial reports screen
    shown in Figure 8–3.

Figure 8–3

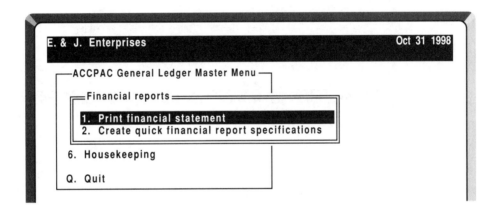

The first option, Print financial statement , prints statements using
specifications that have been created and stored with the data files for the company. The second option allows you to create statement specifications. Statements have not yet been created for E. & J. Enterprises. You can now use the
Create quick financial report specifications option to create
specifications that can be used to print financial statements.

ACCPAC Plus, unlike many other accounting packages, gives you the option of
using different preconfigured income statements and balance sheets. You may
also customize these statements for your specific needs, as you will see later.

❏ Select: 2. Create quick financial report specifications
    from the Financial reports screen.

The screen, Figure 8–4, will show the names of three different Balance Sheets and
three Income Statements. The word "ALL" should be in bold with the statements
names below in subdued letters. You may choose to create all the specifications
or you may select any of them. For E. & J. Enterprises, you will select Balance
Sheet and Income Statement .

❏ Select: Edit

Figure 8–4

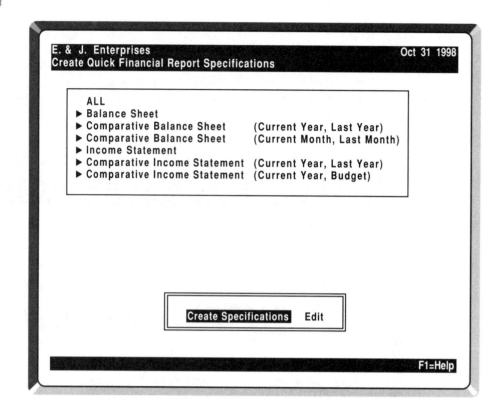

The triangular pointers indicate which statement specifications will be created.

❑ Press: [SPACEBAR] to turn off the ALL option.

❑ Move the selector bar down to Balance Sheet .

❑ Press: [SPACEBAR].

The triangular pointer should appear to the left of the statement.

❑ Move the selector bar to Income Statement .

❑ Press: [SPACEBAR]

❑ Press: Esc to exit from the selection box.

❑ Select: Create Specifications from the box displayed in the lower portion of the screen.

ACCPAC Plus will take a few moments to check the account groupings and write the specifications for the new statements to the data disk. ACCPAC Plus will then return to the Financial reports screen.

PRINTING THE FINANCIAL STATEMENTS

❑ Select: 1. Print financial statement

After a few seconds, your monitor will display the Print Financial Statement screen shown in Figure 8–5. Preselected report options are highlighted. You could change these options by selecting Edit and entering the changes.

Figure 8–5

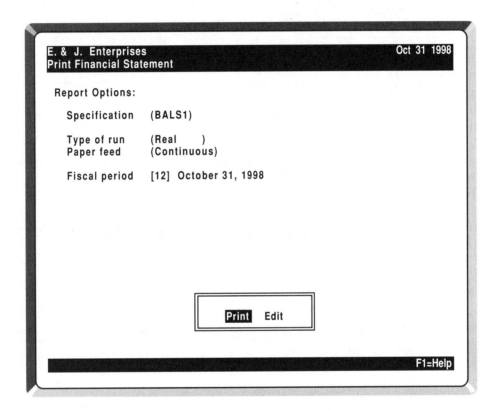

```
E. & J. Enterprises                              Oct 31 1998
Print Financial Statement

   Report Options:

      Specification    (BALS1)

      Type of run      (Real    )
      Paper feed       (Continuous)

      Fiscal period    [12]  October 31, 1998




                          ┌─────────────────┐
                          │  Print   Edit   │
                          └─────────────────┘


                                              F1=Help
```

Specification

The screen should indicate BALS1 as the specification to be used with the three highlighted report options. The specification BALS1 refers to the first Balance Sheet on the Create Quick Financial Report Specifications screen.

Type of run

The Type of run option has two possible settings:

Real   prints the report using actual data.

Practice   prints a prototype report showing 9's in the number column. You can use this setting to test new or modified report specifications.

Paper feed

Within the `Paper feed` option, you have two choices.

Continuous   indicates that your printer is either using continuous-form paper or is equipped with an automatic sheet feeder.

Sheet   indicates that your printer uses a manual sheet feeder. The printer s after each page to allow you to insert another sheet of paper. Then you would press **Enter** to print each succeeding page of the report.

Fiscal period

ACCPAC Plus allows you to print statements as at the end of any fiscal period.

Before printing the Balance Sheet, check that the printer is ready.

❑ Select: `Print`

ACCPAC Plus will take a few moments to check the specifications, perform the necessary calculations, and print the desired document. You may suspend printing by pressing the spacebar or stop it by pressing **Esc** once. When printing is complete, the `Print` and `Edit` options will reappear on the screen. Compare your printed Balance Sheet to that shown in Table 8–2.

Printing Other Statements

❑ Select: `Edit`

A pop-up specifications menu will appear. The specification `INCS1` refers to the second Income Statement on the Create Quick Financial Report Specifications screen.

❑ Move the selector bar to `INCS1` .

❑ Press: [Enter]

❑ Select: `Real` from the pop-up `Run Options` menu.

❑ Select: `Continuous` from the Pop-up `Feed Options` menu.

❑ Press: [Enter] to accept Fiscal period 12.

❑ Select: `Print`

Compare your printout with the Statement of Earnings shown in Table 8–3.

Table 8–2

```
                    E. & J. Enterprises
                       Balance Sheet
                      October 31, 1998

                         Unaudited

                          ASSETS
                         ——-—


Current assets:
  Cash                                            13,399.93
  Accounts Receivable                              6,685.00
  Allowance for Doubtful Accts                         0.00
  Inventory                                        3,397.00
  Prepaid Expenses                                   585.00
                                                 ———————-
  Total current assets                            24,066.93

Fixed assets:
  Fixtures and Furniture                          13,480.00
  Office Equipment                                12,845.00
  Less accumulated depreciation                    1,990.00
                                                 —————————
                                                  24,335.00
                                                 —————————
                                                  48,401.93
                                                 ============


           LIABILITIES AND SHAREHOLDERS' EQUITY
           ——————————————————————————————


Current liabilities:
  Accounts Payable                                 6,570.00
  Sales Tax Payable                                  415.00
  Value Added Tax Payable                            830.00
  Value Added Tax Recoverable                       (923.70)
                                                 —————————
  Total current liabilities                        6,891.30

Shareholders' equity:
  Common Stock                                     31,500.00
  Retained Earnings                                     0.00
  Dividends                                             0.00
  Profit (loss) for period                         10,010.63
                                                 —————————
  Total shareholders' equity                       41,510.63
                                                 —————————
                                                   48,401.93
                                                 ============
```

Table 8–3

```
                         E. & J. Enterprises
                       Statement of Earnings
                   12 Periods Ended October 31, 1998

                            Unaudited

                                                         Current
                                                             YTD
                                                         _____


Revenue:
   Sales                                                8,300.00
   Sales Discounts                                          0.00
   Sales, Accounting Services                          21,680.63
   Interest Income                                          0.00
                                                        _____
                                                       29,980.63


Cost of sales:
   Opening Inventory                                        0.00
   Purchases                                            9,237.00
   Purchase Discounts                                       0.00
   Freight-In                                               0.00
   Closing Inventory                                   (3,397.00
                                                        _____
                                                        5,840.00
                                                        _____

Gross profit                                           24,140.63

Costs and expenses:
   Bad Debt Expense                                         0.00
   Depreciation Expense                                 2,165.00
   Insurance Expense                                      615.00
   Rent, Office Space                                    2,900.00
   Rent, Equipment                                        500.00
   Salary Expense                                        7,450.00
   Supplies Expense                                       500.00
                                                        _____
                                                       14,130.00
                                                        _____

Earnings (loss) from operations                        10,010.63
                                                        _____

Earnings (loss) before income taxes                    10,010.63
                                                        _____

Net earnings (loss) for period                         10,010.63
                                                       ===========
```

ANALYZING THE FINANCIAL STATEMENTS

The world of accounting is founded on the Balance Sheet equation: Assets = Liabilities + Owner's Equity. Revenues increase owner's equity, while expenses decrease it. Net income is the difference between the two. If a company has a residual net income, its owner's equity (or, more likely, retained earnings) increases. A net loss has the opposite effect. ACCPAC Plus financial statement specifications should automatically transfer this difference to the retained earnings line of the Balance Sheet. The only time the Income Statement and Balance Sheet might not balance is when you have added accounts to the General Ledger but not to the account groups or the report specifications. This, however, is a human error, not a system error.

❑ Press: [Esc] twice to return to the ACCPAC General Ledger Master Menu.

PRINTING STATEMENT SPECIFICATIONS

Now you can print the specifications you have created.

❑ Select: 6. Housekeeping from the ACCPAC General Ledger Master Menu.

❑ Select: 2. Maintain specifications

The Maintain Specifications Menu will appear on the screen as shown in Figure 8–6.

Figure 8–6

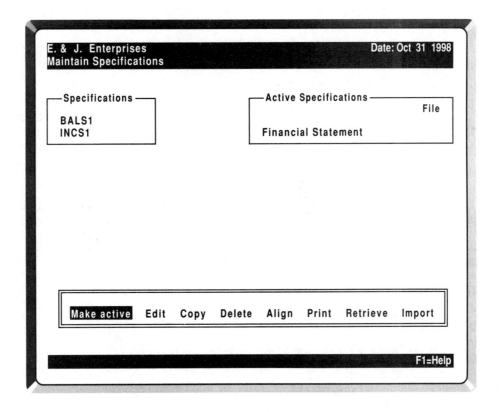

The menu choices are described below:

Make active   sets the default specification for the "Print financial statements".

Edit   allows you to change or create specifications to print a particular financial statement.

Copy   duplicates an existing specification file and allows you to choose a different name for the new file.

Delete   allows you to eliminate a report specification file. Treat this activity with great respect, since you may find it difficult to recover a deleted file.

Align   tests column alignment and layout. In the test, printout characters will be replaced with X's and numbers with 9's.

Print   prints the contents of the specification file for the chosen statement.

Retrieve   allows you to create statement specifications with the EasyWriter II wordprocessing program and bring them into the General Ledger.

Import   enables you to import a standard DOS text file (ASCII text file) to the financial statement of your choice; you could create a title page using wordprocessing software, export it to a DOS file, and then import the DOS file into the General Ledger.

From the options bar at the bottom of the Maintain Specifications Menu,

❑ Select: `Print`

❑ Select: `BALS1` , the specifications for the Balance Sheet that you created earlier.

❑ Type: `10` in the `With an indent of:` field.

❑ Press: ⌸Enter⌸ to set the indent, or left margin, to ten spaces.

❑ Press: ⌸Enter⌸ to continue.

Repeat the process to print the specifications for INCS1.

The specification printouts are really printouts of programs created by ACCPAC Plus in its own programming language. Making major changes in these programs is beyond the scope of this book. As you complete the following sections you will be shown basic procedures and how to make minor changes to specifications for the Balance Sheet, BALS1. You will then create the specifications to print a title page.

COPYING STATEMENT SPECIFICATIONS

Never make changes to the original specifications for a financial statement, since you may create a statement that does not work. Instead, you should copy the original specifications to another file, which you can then modify. Make sure that your screen shows the Maintain Specifications screen.

❑ Move the selector bar to `Copy` .

❑ Press: `Enter`

ACCPAC Plus will ask you which file you want to copy from. Move the selector bar down in the `Copy from` section until it rests on `BALS1` .

❑ Press: `Enter`

ACCPAC Plus will then ask you the name of the `Copy to` file. To create a new file named "BS1",

❑ Type: `BS1` in the `Copy to` field.

❑ Press `Enter` to create a set of Balance Sheet specifications identical to `BALS1` .

You may now alter the working copy until you are satisfied with the results, without risking damage to the original set of specifications.

EDITING SPECIFICATIONS

Before editing statement specifications, you should print them and compare the printout with the printed financial statement. You can write any changes on the printout and then enter them.

Editing balance sheet specifications

❑ Select: `Edit` from the menu at the bottom of the Maintain Specifications screen.

❑ Select: `BS1` to indicate the specification file you wish to edit.

The contents of the specification file will be displayed on the screen. It shows "BALS1" as the Specification name since it is the identical copy that you have just made.

Reviewing the Balance Sheet printout, Erin and Joan have decided that they would like to have the Cash, Inventory, and Prepaid Expenses reported as separate items but to report Net Accounts Receivable (Accounts Receivable less the Allowance for Doubtful Accounts).

Before you make any changes, you should be aware of a couple of keystrokes used to edit the statement specifications:

1. Pressing **Enter** will insert a new line where the cursor is resting. You must avoid pressing **Enter** unless you want to insert a new line.
2. When you wish to scroll up or down, use the directional keys, not **Enter**.
3. Pressing **F6** will delete the line where the cursor is.
4. If you press the page-down or page-up keys on the right side of the keyboard, you will move to the top or bottom of the screen without moving through each line.
5. Holding down **Home** and pressing a directional key will move the cursor as far as it can go in a particular direction.
6. **Del** or **Delete** will delete a single character in the space occupied by the cursor.
7. Pressing **F5** twice will display the Chart of Accounts. Once you have selected the account number, press **Enter** to insert the number in the current specification.
8. Pressing **Esc** will allow you to exit from the file. You may save or cancel your changes when exiting.

The first group of lines, starting with two periods (..), are comment lines that are used to describe the program and are not used in printing the statement. You should change the Specification name from "BALS1" to "BS1"

If you are not using an extended keyboard, with separate directional and numeric key pads, you should turn the **Num Lock** off.

❑   Move the cursor to the A of BALS1 on the first line.

❑   Press [DELETE] twice to erase AL .

❑   Move the cursor until it rests on the detail line that reads,

The five lines for Current Assets on the Balance Sheet (BALS1) printout are printed by this one line in the specification. This is a Detail Line specification. It tells the Financial Reporter to retrieve the current balance and account description for all accounts in the range 100 to 399. The descriptions are then printed 3 spaces from the left margin and the balances are printed in a column at the right margin. The information is printed sequentially by account numbers on separate lines. The account balances are summed and stored in an accumulator called T1.

❑   Use [DELETE] to erase ^ and ~399.

The changed line should now look like this.

This detail line causes the information about account 100 to be printed on one line in the report.

❑   Move the cursor to the end of the line.

❑   Press: [Enter] to create a new blank line.

❑   Type: 200+210   :T1   @>3   Accounts Receivable, Net

The plus sign between the account numbers causes the account balances to be added and then reported as one number. Because more than one account number was included in the detail line, it is necessary to type in the description for the line otherwise ACCPAC Plus would insert the name of the first account in the printed report.

❑ Press: [Enter] to create a new blank line.

❑ Type: ^250~399   :T1   @>3   \DESC

The ^ causes each account in the range to be printed on a separate line.

❑ Enter the changes necessary to print "Value Added Tax Liability, Net" on one line. Remember that you must also modify the specification to print Accounts Payable and Sales Tax Payable on individual lines. When you finish, the detail lines should look like the following.

```
          ^500~520    :T4    @>3    \DESC
   540 + 542  :T4    @>3    Value Added Tax Liability, Net
```

❑ Press: [Esc] to indicate that you have finished editing the specification.

❑ Select: Save changes

❑ Print the revised Balance Sheet specifications, BS1.

Your editing may have changed the alignment of the accumulators, the indents or other parts of the specification. Do not worry!

❑ Print the revised Balance Sheet.

If there are errors within the specifications you have just created, you will receive the following message when you attempt to print the revised Balance Sheet.

```
          There are errors in the specification.
          Do you wish to print the error report?

                    Yes        No
```

If you receive this message select Yes to print the error report. Read the error messages, then go back to the Maintain Specifications Menu and make corrections. Once the corrections have been entered, save the revised specifications, and then try to print the statement again.

CREATING A SPECIFICATION

☐ Enter the commands necessary to display the Maintain Specifications screen.

☐ Select: `Edit`

☐ Type: `TITLE` as the specification file you want to edit.

☐ Press: `Enter`

The Maintain Specifications screen will clear and a flashing cursor followed by 19 lines of crosses will appear. The following symbols will be used in TITLE specifications as shown in Figure 8–7.

Figure 8–7

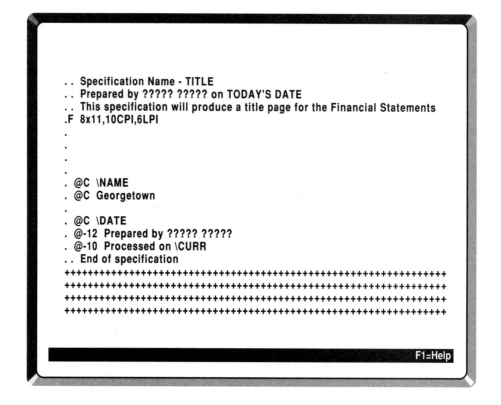

```
.. Specification Name - TITLE
.. Prepared by ????? ????? on TODAY'S DATE
.. This specification will produce a title page for the Financial Statements
.F  8x11,10CPI,6LPI
.
.
.
.
.
.  @C  \NAME
.  @C  Georgetown
.
.  @C  \DATE
.  @-12  Prepared by ????? ?????
.  @-10  Processed on \CURR
.. End of specification
+++++++++++++++++++++++++++++++++++++++++++++++++++++++++++++++++++++
+++++++++++++++++++++++++++++++++++++++++++++++++++++++++++++++++++++
+++++++++++++++++++++++++++++++++++++++++++++++++++++++++++++++++++++
+++++++++++++++++++++++++++++++++++++++++++++++++++++++++++++++++++++
```

F1=Help

..	indicates that a line is for programming comments and that the line is not used in printing the statement.
.	indicates that the line contains either text or specifications.
.F	indicates a form specification that controls the printing of the report.
8x11	indicates that the paper the report will be printed on is 8.5 inches wide and 11 inches high. Because 8.5 inches is a standard paper width, ACCPAC Plus interprets a width of 8 as 8.5 inches. This is the only place that a number is interpreted in this illogical way.
10CPI	causes 10 characters per inch to be printed across each line.
6LPI	causes 6 lines to be printed per inch of height.
. @C	centers the text.
. @R	right justifies the text.
. @-n	prints the text "n" lines from the bottom of the page.

In the specification `@-10 Processed on \CURR` the instruction `. @-10` indicates that this line will print ten lines from the right bottom of the page. The words `Processed on` print as text on the title page. However, `\CURR` is a text variable that allows you to print information from the data files. Two other text variables used in the title page specification are

\NAME	prints the company name in the General Ledger's Company Profile.
\DATE	prints the report date.

❑ Enter each line as shown in Figure 8–7.

Type in your first and last names in place of the question marks after `Prepared by` . When you have finished,

❑ Press: [Esc] to tell ACCPAC Plus you have completed editing the specifications.

The next prompt will ask if you wish to save, cancel changes, or edit. If you made errors in your changes, you could select `Edit` and correct those errors.

❑ Select: `Save changes`

❑ Print the new title page using the `TITLE` specification.

If there are errors within the specifications you have just created, you will receive the following message when you attempt to print the TITLE page.

```
+-----------------------------------------------+
|      There are errors in the specification.   |
|      Do you wish to print the error report?   |
|                                               |
|              Yes        No                    |
+-----------------------------------------------+
```

If you receive this message, print the error report. Read the error messages, then go back to the Maintain Specifications Menu and make corrections. Once the corrections have been entered, save the revised specifications, and then try to print the statement again.

❑ Quit ACCPAC Plus.

❑ Back up your data files.

REVIEW QUESTIONS

1. What are the weaknesses of statements produced by the Create Quick Financial Report Specifications function?
2. List the names of the account groupings available from the Edit Account Groups screen.
3. What are your major considerations when identifying account ranges on the Edit Account Groups screen?
4. List and describe the types of Income Statements and Balance Sheets available from the "Create quick financial report specifications" option.
5. Before you edit a set of statement specifications, you should copy the current set. Why?
6. List the steps necessary to create a copy of a statement specification.
7. Some keys have special functions for editing specifications. What are they and what are their functions?
8. How do you move the cursor when editing specifications?

EXERCISE

1. Edit the Account Groups using the same account ranges as you used with E. & J. Enterprises.
2. Create one Balance Sheet and one Income Statement specification for your company.
3. Print each statement and its specifications.
4. Edit the statements to appear as you want them. Reprint the statements and their specification files.
5. Using the new title page printout for E. & J. Enterprises as a model, create a title page for your statements.
6. Exit from ACCPAC Plus and back up your data files.

CHAPTER

9 Year End

In this chapter, you will be working on the year end closing of the General Ledger. If you allowed provisional posting in the company profile, you could provisionally post the estimated year end adjustments and print provisional financial statements for the year.

You should make permanent copies of your data files before closing the accounts at year end. In addition to using these files to print provisional financial statements, you would post the auditor's finalized adjustments to these files and then print the financial statements. A business would normally keep several identical copies of these files in different locations as a safety precaution.

After closing the accounts, you will prepare a post-closing trial balance, an opening Income Statement, and a Balance Sheet showing the starting position for the new year. In the new fiscal year you will post an identical set of the auditor's finalized adjustments to the previous fiscal year.

GETTING STARTED

❑ Enter the commands necessary to access the ACCPAC Plus Start Menu.

❑ Select: `G/L E. & J. Enterprises` from the Start Menu.

❑ Enter the date 10/31/98 in the New date field.

BATCH STATUS REPORT

You must print a Batch Status Report and clear all posted and deleted batches before completing the year end closing procedures. The Batch Status Report will also allow you to verify that all batches have been posted to the General Ledger.

❑ Select: `5. Reports` from the ACCPAC General Ledger Master Menu.

❑ Select: `5. Batch status report`

If necessary `Edit` the options displayed on the screen to ensure that `ALL` batches will be included in the report.

❑ Select: `Print`

Verify that all batches have either been "Posted" or "Deleted". The Total Debits and Total Credits columns should balance at 95,821.63. If there are "Open" or "Printed" batches you must either post or delete these batches. If necessary, print and clear the new posting journals, and then print the Batch Status Report again.

When the report has been printed, the following message will be displayed on the screen.

```
┌─────────────────────────────────────────────┐
│                                               │
│  Do you want to clear all posted and deleted batches │
│           within the specified range?         │
│                                               │
│             Yes          No                   │
│                                               │
└─────────────────────────────────────────────┘
```

All posted and deleted batches must be cleared before you can complete the year-end procedures.

❑ Select: `Yes`

When ACCPAC Plus has completed this function, the screen will display the Reports Menu.

TRIAL BALANCE WORKSHEET

You should print the General Ledger Trial Balance worksheet before you close the books, since you will transfer the balances from the temporary proprietorship accounts to retained earnings upon closing. ACCPAC Plus allows you to print the closing General Ledger trial balance in a worksheet format with columns for the auditor's adjusting entries, or in a report format. Normally, an auditor's adjustments would be returned a few months after the year end, so you would enter these adjustments through the "Post batches to previous year" option on the Post Batches Menu. An identical batch containing the auditor's adjustment must also be posted to your permanent copies of the previous year's data files.

The procedure for printing the Trial Balance worksheet is described below.

❑ Select: `2. Trial balance` from the Reports Menu.

The Trial Balance screen (Figure 9–1) will appear.

Figure 9–1

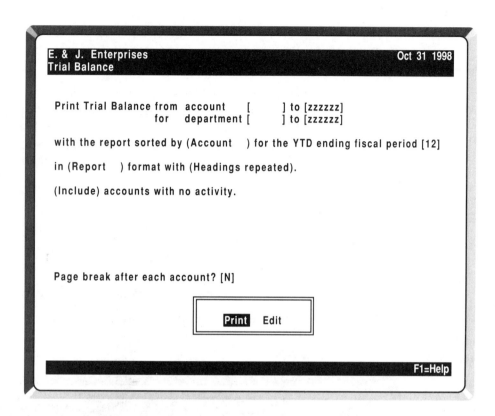

The default options are to print all of the accounts sequentially and to include the information up to and including the twelfth period. In the Report format, the balances of the accounts will print out in a traditional Trial Balance format with all the numbers listed as either a debit or a credit and column headings repeated at the top of each page.

❏ Select: `Print`

Once the Trial Balance has finished printing the screen will return to the Reports Menu.

❏ Select: `2. Trial balance` again.

In the Worksheet format the report will be printed with debits and credits columns for Trial Balance, Adjustments, Income Statement, and Balance Sheet.

❏ Select: `Edit`

❏ Press: [Enter] three times to accept the account range and fiscal period defaults.

❏ Select: `Worksheet` from the Format Options.

❏ Select: `Headings repeated` from the Print Options.

❏ Press: [Esc] to indicate that editing is completed.

❏ Select: `Print`

When printing is complete, return to the ACCPAC General Ledger Master Menu.

CLOSING THE GENERAL LEDGER

The closing function will create and post a batch of entries to close the General Ledger. Before using this function you should make two back-up disks. The first will be an archive data disk that will be put away in case you later find that you should not have closed the year at this time. The second back-up is your protection in case the power fails or your computer malfunctions during the closing process.

❏ Back up your data files.

❏ Enter the commands to return to the ACCPAC General Ledger Master Menu.

❏ Select: `6. Housekeeping` from the ACCPAC General Ledger Master Menu

❏ Select: `7. Periodic processing` from the Housekeeping menu.

The Periodic Processing Menu will appear as shown in Figure 9–2.

Figure 9–2

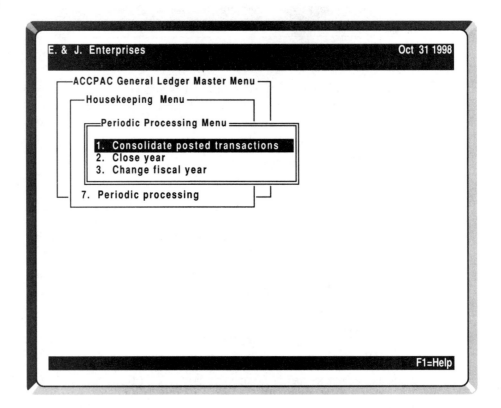

❑ Select: 2. Close year

ACCPAC Plus will display the Close Year screen with a warning message to back up your data files.

Figure 9–3

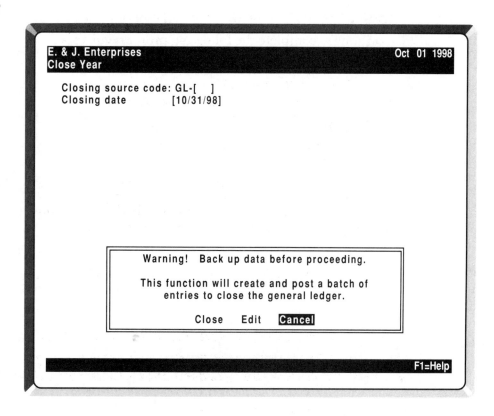

```
E. & J. Enterprises                                    Oct  01  1998
Close Year

      Closing source code: GL-[   ]
      Closing date         [10/31/98]




                ┌──────────────────────────────────────────┐
                │  Warning!   Back up data before proceeding. │
                │                                            │
                │  This function will create and post a batch of │
                │     entries to close the general ledger.   │
                │                                            │
                │          Close     Edit     Cancel         │
                └──────────────────────────────────────────┘


                                                           F1=Help
```

Two of the options in the warning start with the letter C . To select either you must move the selector bar to the option and then press **Enter**.

❑ Select: Close

The computer will beep and display the following error message.

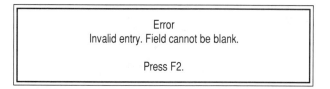

```
┌────────────────────────────────────────────┐
│                    Error                     │
│        Invalid entry. Field cannot be blank. │
│                                              │
│                  Press F2.                   │
└────────────────────────────────────────────┘
```

❑ Press: F2

The cursor will move to the Closing source code field. You must specify a Source code for the closing entries. This source code would normally be General Journal.

❑ Type: GJ

❑ Press: Enter

The warning message will again appear.

❏ Select: Close

The computer will require a few moments to complete the closing of the accounts and will then display the Print Posting Journal screen.

❏ Press: Enter to print the G/L Posting Journal.

When printing is complete the following prompt will appear.

```
┌─────────────────────────────────────────────┐
│                                             │
│      Do you want to clear all posting journals │
│            within the specified range?        │
│                                             │
│              Yes          No                 │
│                                             │
└─────────────────────────────────────────────┘
```

If you select the "Yes" option, the information in the posting journal files will be cleared and the posting sequence number will reset to "1". You select the "No" option if the printed G/L Posting Journal is unclear or incomplete. Print the posting journal again and clear it before completing the closing process.

❏ Select: Yes

Table 9–1

```
Date: Oct 31 98    9:52pm          E. & J. Enterprises        Page:   1
G/L Posting Journal

Posting sequence number from        [    2] to       [    2]

Posting sequence number:     2

Posting Batch Entry
Entry  No.   No.    Pd.
       Date  Srce.  Description                Reference   Acct.  Dept.      Debits        Credits

  1      4     1  12
       Oct 31 98 GL-GJ Close yr. to retained earnings   690     700          8,300.00
       Oct 31 98 GL-GJ Close yr. to retained earnings   690     720         21,680.63
       Oct 31 98 GL-GJ Close yr. to retained earnings   690     750                          2,487.00
       Oct 31 98 GL-GJ Close yr. to retained earnings   690     752                          9,237.00
       Oct 31 98 GL-GJ Close yr. to retained earnings   690     780          5,884.00
       Oct 31 98 GL-GJ Close yr. to retained earnings   690     835                          2,165.00
       Oct 31 98 GL-GJ Close yr. to retained earnings   690     880                            615.00
       Oct 31 98 GL-GJ Close yr. to retained earnings   690     920                          2,900.00
       Oct 31 98 GL-GJ Close yr. to retained earnings   690     925                            500.00
       Oct 31 98 GL-GJ Close yr. to retained earnings   690     935                          7,450.00
       Oct 31 98 GL-GJ Close yr. to retained earnings   690     945                            500.00
       Oct 31 98 GL-GJ Close yr. from income accounts           690                         10,010.63

                                                                    ─────────────   ─────────────
                                                                       35,864.63        35,864.63   *

                                                    Posted Total     35,864.63        35,864.63
                                                                    =============   =============

1 posting entry printed.
```

The batch created by the closing process is documented in the G/L Posting Journal as shown in Table 9–1. The description, "Close yr. to retained earnings", and the reference to account "690" identifies that each of the revenue and expense accounts have been closed to the retained earnings account.

❑ Print the Trial Balance again.

Review the printout of the Trial Balance carefully to ensure that the program has reduced all the income and expense accounts to zero. If you have set up the account codes incorrectly when you created the General Ledger accounts, an Income Statement account may show a Balance Sheet code or vice versa. This would cause an incorrect closing of accounts. The program updates retained earnings by the net income.

CHANGE FISCAL YEAR

The Change Fiscal Year function will prepare the General Ledger for processing in the next fiscal year. Before using this function you should back up your data files again in case there is a power or computer failure during the change process.

❑ Back up your data files.

❑ Enter the commands to return to the ACCPAC General Ledger Master Menu.

❑ Select: 6. Housekeeping

❑ Select: 7. Periodic processing

❑ Select: 3. Change fiscal year

The screen will display the message shown in Figure 9–4.

❑ Select: Yes

ACCPAC Plus will display the following error message.

```
                            Error
    Incorrect Procedure. Print and clear batch status report
                   before changing fiscal year.

                          Press F2.
```

Figure 9–4

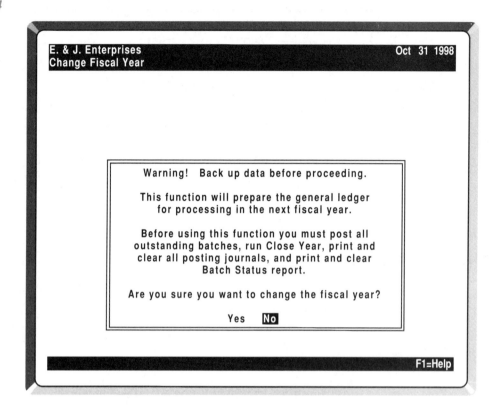

The closing procedure created a batch that was posted to close the fiscal year. The batch status report must be printed and cleared before you can proceed.

❑ Press: [F2]

❑ Press: [Esc] twice to return to the ACCPAC General Ledger Master Menu.

❑ Print and clear the Batch Status Report.

❑ Select: 6. Housekeeping from the ACCPAC General Ledger Master Menu.

❑ Select: 7. Periodic processing

❑ Select: 3. Change fiscal year

❑ Select: Yes

Watch the line at the bottom of the screen while the program is updating the accounts. When the process has been completed, the following message will be displayed.

```
┌─────────────────────────────────────────────────┐
│ ╔═══════════════════════════════════════════════╗ │
│ ║                                               ║ │
│ ║        Change Fiscal Year complete.           ║ │
│ ║                                               ║ │
│ ║   You should now edit the Fiscal Period Calendar screen ║ │
│ ║     to update fiscal period statuses and enter the report ║ │
│ ║              dates for the new year.          ║ │
│ ║                                               ║ │
│ ║                  Continue                     ║ │
│ ║                                               ║ │
│ ╚═══════════════════════════════════════════════╝ │
└─────────────────────────────────────────────────┘
```

❏   Press: Enter to continue.

❏   Press: Esc twice to return to the ACCPAC General Ledger Master Menu.

❏   Press: Q   to return to the Start Menu.

FISCAL PERIOD CALENDAR

Your first task in the new fiscal year will be to update the Fiscal Period Calendar.

❏   Select: G/L E. & J. Enterprises

❏   Type: 110198   in the New date field.

❏   Press: Enter

❏   Select: 6. Housekeeping

❏   Select: 1. Edit company profile

❏   Select: Next   to display the Fiscal Period Calendar.

The Status for all periods should be changed to "Open". Note that the Starting and Ending dates have been adjusted. The Report dates, which you entered as text, must be changed to dates in the new fiscal year.

❏   Select: Edit

❏   Press: Enter   to select period 1.

❏   Select: Open

❏   Press: Enter   twice to accept the Starting and Ending dates.

❏   Change: November 30, 1997 to November 30, 1998.

❏   Press: Enter

Repeat this process, editing each fiscal period to change the Status to "Open" and to correct the Report date. When you have changed the information for all twelve periods,

❏   Press: Esc

❏   Select: Accept changes

❏   Press: Esc to return to the ACCPAC General Ledger Master Menu.

PREPARING OPENING FINANCIAL STATEMENTS

After you have closed the General Ledger for the year, confirm that the opening Income Statement figures are all zeros and that the new opening Balance Sheet exactly reflects the General Ledger.

❑ Select: `5. Reports`

❑ Print the General Ledger Listing.

❑ Press: `Esc` to return to the ACCPAC General Ledger Master Menu.

Note that each account has now been reduced to one line showing the ending balance from the previous year. The income statement account balances should be zero. When batches are posted to the General Ledger in the new fiscal year, this ending balance will become the opening balance for each account.

❑ Select: `4. Financial reports` from the ACCPAC General Ledger Master Menu.

❑ Print the Balance Sheet and the Income Statement.

In the Income Statement, the last year column should display zeros as there were no transactions at the beginning of the first fiscal year for E. & J. Enterprises. The dates of these statements are incorrect. You must write over the "Nov 30" date with "Nov 1" and then note on the cover that this statement is to prove the clearing of the accounts for the beginning of the year.

❑ Press: `Esc` twice to display the ACCPAC General Ledger Master Menu.

❑ Press: `Q` to return to the Start Menu.

PREVIOUS YEAR ADJUSTMENTS

In most cases you are not able to process all your year end adjustments until some time after you have closed the ledger and changed the fiscal year. Your auditor may take weeks or months to finalize the year end adjustments. ACCPAC Plus will allow you to make a special posting to the previous year for such adjustments.

❑ Select: `G/L E. & J. Enterprises`

❑ Type: `111598` in the New date field.

❑ Press: `Enter`

❑ Select: `Accept` in response to the prompt.

When you record entries that are to be posted to a previous year you must enter the period in which you want the entries to be posted, not the current fiscal period number. The year end adjusting should be posted to the last period of the previous fiscal year.

❑ Record the batch entries as shown in Table 9–2.

Table 9–2

```
te: Nov 15 98    11:34am            E. & J. Enterprises              Page:   1
tch Listing

tch number         from [    1]   to [    1]
urce ledger        from [   ]     to [ZZ]
eation date        from [        ] to [Dec 31 99]
atus(es) selected: Open, Printed

tch number:     1  Prior year adjustments        Creation date: Nov 15 98  Status: Printed

try  Line
mber  No.   Pd. Srce. Date      Reference    Description         Acct. Dept.      Debits      Credits     Errors

   1    1   12 uncollectable invoice #1004 to Mini-Pictures which has gone
        2   12 out of business
        3   12 GL-GJ Nov 15 98 prior yr adj bad debt              810     320.00
        4   12 GL-GJ Nov 15 98 prior yr adj bad debt              200                320.00
                                                                  _____    _____
                                                                   320.00      320.00       *

   2    1   12 Adjustment for depreciation of office equipment.
        2   12 GL-GJ Nov 15 98 prior yr adj office equipment depreciation  835   927.00
        3   12 GL-GJ Nov 15 98 prior yr adj office equipment depreciation  428             927.00
                                                                  _____    _____
                                                                   927.00      927.00       *
                                                                 1,247.00    1,247.00
                                                               =============== ===============

entries printed.  0 errors found.

batch printed.
```

❑ Print the Batch Listing.

❑ Select: 3. Post batches from the Transaction Processing Menu.

❑ Select: 2. Post batches to previous year

Figure 9–5

```
E. & J. Enterprises                                    Nov  15 1998
Post Batches to Previous Year

    Starting batch [1    ]
    Ending batch   [    1]

    Closing source code: GL-[   ]
```

❑ Press: [Enter] twice to accept 1 in both the Starting and Ending batch fields as shown in Figure 9–5.

❑ Type: GJ in the Closing source code field.

❑ Press: [Enter]

❑ Select: Post

After posting is complete,

❑ Press: [Enter] again to continue.

❑ Press: [Esc] to return to the Transaction Processing Menu.

❑ Print and clear the Posting Journal.

As this batch includes amounts to be posted to expense accounts, ACCPAC Plus creates the closing entries and posts them. The closing entries are also created and posted if the batch includes amounts to be posted to revenue accounts. These entries are shown in the Posting Journal with the description "Close to Retained Earnings".

❑ Use the Reports function to print the General Ledger Listing.

Each detail posted to the General Ledger is marked "Special Posting(s) - Previous Year". No beginning balance is indicated for the accounts affected.

You should also post an identical batch to the back up data files that you created before closing. You could then use that back up disk to produce accurate financial statements for the previous fiscal year.

❑ Quit ACCPAC Plus and back up your data files.

REVIEW QUESTIONS

1. What is the purpose of closing a General Ledger at year-end?
2. Why is it important to make a permanent file copy of the General Ledger before closing the year's accounts?
3. What steps must you complete before you can close the General Ledger?
4. What would happen if you failed to post a transaction batch before closing?
5. What is the purpose of the G/L Posting Journal that you print after closing has been completed?
6. What does the Change Fiscal Year function do?
7. What changes should you make to the Fiscal Period Calendar at the beginning of a new fiscal year?
8. Why would you post a batch to the previous fiscal year?

EXERCISE

In this exercise, you will apply the procedures you just learned to your company.
1. Print and clear the Batch Status Report.
2. Print the General Ledger Trial Balance worksheet.
3. Close the General Ledger using the General Journal as the source code.
4. Change the fiscal year editing the batch status and report dates.
5. Print opening financial statements for the new year.
6. Back up the data files.
7. Exit from ACCPAC Plus.

10 Inquiry, History & Budgets

In this chapter you will use Inquiries Menu to display account information on the screen and G/L Account Maintenance Menu to edit historical and budget data.

GETTING READY

❑ Enter the commands to display the ACCPAC Plus Start Menu.

❑ Select: `G/L E. & J. Enterprises`

❑ Type: `111598` in the New date field.

❑ Press: [Enter]

INQUIRIES

❑ Select: `2. Inquiries` from the ACCPAC General Ledger Master Menu.

The Inquiries Menu will appear on your screen.

```
Inquiries Menu

1. Display accounts
2. Display batches
```

❑ Select: `1. Display accounts`

There are three options for displaying information on the screen.

```
Screens

Chart Display
Transactions
Budget/History
```

☐ Select: Chart display

☐ Type: 100 in the from Account field.

☐ Press: [Enter]

You can display the accounts with their balances at the end of any fiscal period in the current year. As this is the first period of the fiscal year and no transactions have been posted to the current year, ACCPAC Plus will display the beginning balances.

Figure 10–1

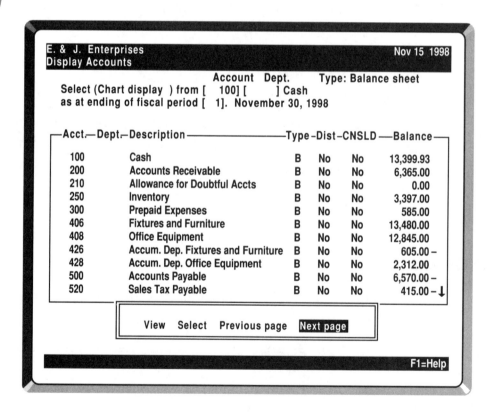

☐ Press: [Enter] to accept the default of fiscal period 1.

ACCPAC Plus will display a list of the accounts in numerical order, beginning with the account number you chose as shown in Figure 10–1. This screen shows the account and department codes, account description, account type, automatic distribution, posting mode, and current balance for each account. The option box at the bottom of the screen can be used to display additional accounts.

❑ Select: Next page to display the next eleven accounts.

❑ Select: Previous page to display the first eleven accounts.

❑ Select: Select to return to the "Screens" option box.

❑ Press: T for Transactions.

Your screen would now display transactions that have been posted to the selected account, but there are no transactions in the accounts for E. & J. Enterprises for the current year. To display additional accounts you could select either "Next account" or "Previous account". To display a specific account you would press **Escape**, and then enter the account number and the fiscal period.

❑ Press: S to return to the "Screens" option box.

The "Budget/History" option will allow you to compare current year figures to both historical and budgeted figures.

❑ Select: Budget/History

Figure 10–2

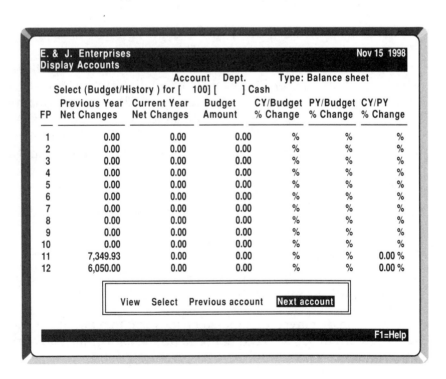

The display, Figure 10–2, consists of six pieces of information for account 100 for each fiscal period.

The first column for each period lists the net changes in the account for each period of the previous year. The figure in period 11 was entered in the first transaction batch, which transferred the account balances from E. & J. Enterprises' manual accounting system to ACCPAC Plus. The figure in period 12 represents the change in the account balance between the end of period 11 and the end of period 12. This change resulted from the entries posted through batch 3.

The column "Current Year Net Changes" should show 0.00 for each period as you have not posted any transactions to the current year. The "Budget Amount" column should also show 0.00 for each period. You will add budget data to some accounts later in this chapter. The three percentage comparison columns are blank as there is no data to make these calculations.

❏ Press: [Esc] to return the cursor to the Account field.

If you wished to display information about another account, you would type the account number and press **Enter**.

❏ Press: [Esc] to display the Screens option box.

❏ Press: [Esc] twice to return to the ACCPAC General Ledger Master Menu.

EDITING HISTORICAL DATA

Now you will use the "Edit historical data" option to enter monthly data for fiscal periods of the previous year. This option is normally used only when converting from another accounting system to ACCPAC Plus. The first batch that you entered in Chapter 5 transferred E. & J. Enterprises' account balances as of the end of the eleventh period (September 1998) from their manual system to ACCPAC Plus. You also entered batches for the October 1998 transactions and adjustments. When you completed the Change Fiscal Year procedure, the program automatically transferred the account information for the year that you were closing to account history. This historical data provides comparative information for financial statements.

❏ Select: 1. G/L account maintenance from the ACCPAC General Ledger Master Menu.

❏ Select: 2. Edit historical data

ACCPAC Plus will display the Edit Historical Data screen with the warning message as shown in Figure 10–3.

The warning displayed on this screen tells you that you must back up the data before continuing. If you did not back up the data at the end of the last chapter, do so now.

Figure 10–3

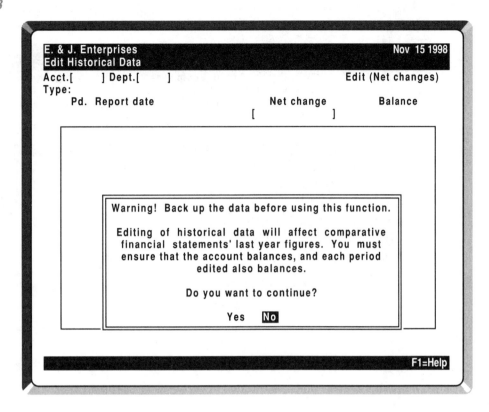

Editing the historical data will change the last year figures in comparative financial statements. As each edited account and fiscal period must balance, you will not be able to produce accurate comparative financial statements after saving the example changes you are about to enter.

❏ Select: Yes   to clear the warning message.

Now, you must enter the account code to add historical data to an account.

❏ Type: 925

❏ Press: [Enter] to select the account Rent, Equipment.

The "Edit as" option box will appear in the upper right corner of the screen.

"Net changes" allows you to input the amount of the net change in the account balance during a period. The net change entered for one period is then added to the balance for the previous period to calculate the new balance for the period being edited.

❏ Select: Net changes

Figure 10–4

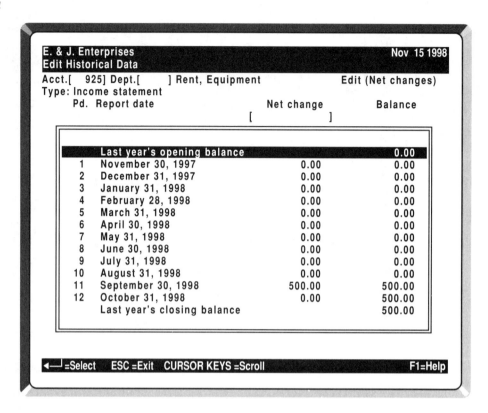

```
E. & J. Enterprises                                        Nov 15 1998
Edit Historical Data
Acct.[   925] Dept.[   ] Rent, Equipment          Edit (Net changes)
Type: Income statement
        Pd.  Report date              Net change        Balance
                                    [            ]

        Last year's opening balance                       0.00
         1   November 30, 1997          0.00              0.00
         2   December 31, 1997          0.00              0.00
         3   January 31, 1998           0.00              0.00
         4   February 28, 1998          0.00              0.00
         5   March 31, 1998             0.00              0.00
         6   April 30, 1998             0.00              0.00
         7   May 31, 1998               0.00              0.00
         8   June 30, 1998              0.00              0.00
         9   July 31, 1998              0.00              0.00
        10   August 31, 1998            0.00              0.00
        11   September 30, 1998       500.00            500.00
        12   October 31, 1998           0.00            500.00
             Last year's closing balance               500.00


◄──┘=Select   ESC =Exit   CURSOR KEYS =Scroll              F1=Help
```

For revenue and expense accounts, the figures displayed in the Balance column are the amounts that were in the account immediately before the ledger was closed at the end of the fiscal year. In the example shown in Figure 10–4, the only net change occurs in period 11, reflecting the transfer of the $500.00 balance to the Rent, Equipment expense account. This balance resulted from an equipment rental expense of $125.00 in June, July, August and September.

❑ Move the selector bar to period 8   June 30, 1998 .

❑ Press: [Enter] to transfer this information to the edit line above the displayed information.

❑ Type: 125.00 in the Net change field.

❑ Press: [Enter]

The information box will be highlighted again and the selector bar will be on the next period, period 9 July 31, 1998. The 125.00 net change will be displayed in period 8 and the balances will be changed for periods 8 through 12.

❑ Press: [Enter] to select period 9.

❑ Type: 125.00 in the Net change field.

❑ Press: [Enter] again.

Note how the net changes have accumulated in the Balance column.

❑ Press: [Esc]

❏ Select: `Accept changes`

ACCPAC Plus will save the changes even though the "Last year's closing balance" of 750.00 did not agree with the information as originally displayed.

❏ Type: `925` in the Acct. field.

❏ Press: [Enter]

"Balances" allows you to change the balance in the account at the end of each period. The new balance and the previous period balance are then used to calculate the net change.

❏ Select: `Balances` from the option box.

The information displayed will change as the Net changes column is erased from the display. The equipment rental for each of the periods was $125.00, so the balance for Rent, Equipment should increase by $125.00 each period.

❏ Move the selector bar to `10 August 31, 1998`

❏ Press: [Enter]

❏ Type: `375.00` in the Balance field.

❏ Press: [Enter]

The selector bar again moves down to the next period.

❏ Change the balances for periods 11 and 12 to $500.00

❏ Press: [Esc]

❏ Select: `Accept changes`

This sample editing of historical data has made changes for one debit balance account over four periods. The "Last year's closing balance" was restored to its proper value but the periods are now out of balance. If you were maintaining the accounts for a real company, you would now have to balance each period by editing a corresponding credit balance account. However, editing historical data for one account should be enough for you to understand the process.

❏ Press: [Esc]

ACCPAC Plus will return to the G/L Account Maintenance Menu.

EDITING BUDGET DATA

You can enter, edit, and review budget data with the "Edit budget data" option. This data can then be used for comparisons in several financial statements.

❏ Select: `3. Edit budget data`

Figure 10–5

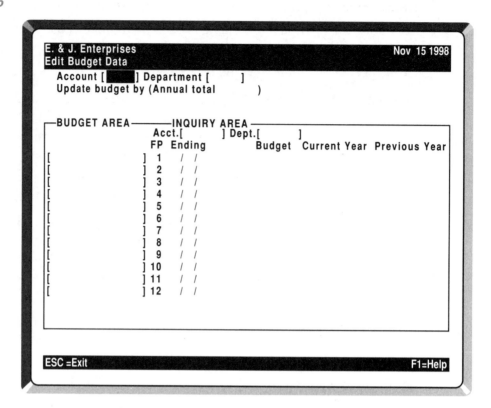

```
 E. & J. Enterprises                                    Nov 15 1998
 Edit Budget Data
    Account [     ] Department [        ]
    Update budget by (Annual total        )


 ┌─BUDGET AREA───────INQUIRY AREA──────────────────────────────────┐
 │                 Acct.[       ] Dept.[        ]                   │
 │                 FP  Ending           Budget  Current Year Previous Year
 │ [             ]  1   /  /                                        │
 │ [             ]  2   /  /                                        │
 │ [             ]  3   /  /                                        │
 │ [             ]  4   /  /                                        │
 │ [             ]  5   /  /                                        │
 │ [             ]  6   /  /                                        │
 │ [             ]  7   /  /                                        │
 │ [             ]  8   /  /                                        │
 │ [             ]  9   /  /                                        │
 │ [             ] 10   /  /                                        │
 │ [             ] 11   /  /                                        │
 │ [             ] 12   /  /                                        │
 │                                                                 │
 │                                                                 │
 └─────────────────────────────────────────────────────────────────┘


 ESC =Exit                                                  F1=Help
```

The Edit Budget Data screen will appear in three sections, as shown in Figure 10–5. The data entry area at the top of the screen is used to enter account numbers, to select a method of entering budget amounts, and to enter the budget amounts and calculation factors. The INQUIRY AREA is used to display budget, current year and previous year information. The BUDGET AREA displays the new budget amounts for each period. The cursor will be in the Account field at the top of the screen.

❑ Type: 880

❑ Press: [Enter]

This is the account code for Insurance Expense. The program will display current budget data in both the BUDGET AREA and INQUIRY AREA. As you have not yet entered budget data, the program will display zeros in both budget columns. Current year and previous year account balances will be displayed in the Inquiry Area.

You may enter budget figures in different ways, using the options shown in the "Select Options" box overlaying the Inquiry area. The following options are available:

Annual total	allows you to enter a annual total for the year, which the program will allocate in equal amounts to each period.
Constant amount	lets you enter a constant amount to be budgeted for each month.
Entering values	allows you to enter individual amounts for each fiscal period and is most useful when budgeting for business subject to seasonal fluctuations.
Incremental amount	calculates a series of arithmetically increasing or decreasing amounts for each period, starting from a base value.
Moving values	allows you to move the budget, current year, or previous year amounts from the INQUIRY AREA to the BUDGET AREA. You can move the amounts as they are, or change them by either a percentage or a fixed amount, or as an annual total.
Percentage increment	allows you to enter a base budget amount in the first period and to increase each following period by a fixed percent.

Entering Annual Total

❑ Select: `Annual total` from Select Options.

The "Update budget by" field will display `Annual total` and the cursor will be in the data entry field. The amount that you enter in this field will be divided by the number of periods in the fiscal year and allocated equally to each period in the year. If necessary the amount displayed in the last period will be adjusted to force the sum of the period amounts to equal the annual total.

Insurance Expense is a debit balance account. If the budget amount that you were to enter is a credit, you would enter a minus sign before or after the amount.

❑ Type: `1950.10`

❑ Press: Enter

The budget amounts for each period will be calculated and displayed in the BUDGET AREA. If necessary the amount displayed in the last period will be rounded to force the sum of the period amounts to equal the annual total. Verify the amounts in the BUDGET AREA. In this example the first 11 periods should display 162.51 and period 12 will show 162.49 to balance the annual entry.

❑ Press any key to continue.

The options displayed at the bottom of the screen offer you several alternatives:

Accept changes	Edit	Select	Inquiry	Cancel

Accept changes	transfers the information from the BUDGET AREA to the recorded information, clears the screen, and returns the cursor to the Account field in the top portion of the screen.
Edit	clears the option box in the lower portion of the screen and places the cursor in the first period of the BUDGET AREA. You could then edit the amounts for each period. Then you would press **Esc** to return to the option box.
Select	returns you to "Select Options". You may then select a method for updating the budget for the account that you entered in the top portion of the screen.
Inquiry	allows you to display the information for another account in the INQUIRY AREA. If you are using the Moving Values option, you could then transfer these amounts to the BUDGET AREA.
Cancel	erases any budget data calculations that you have made and have not saved by using "Accept changes".

❏ Select: `Accept Changes` to accept the annual budget total of $1950.10 for Insurance expense.

Entering Constant Amounts

❏ Type: `880` as the account code again.

❏ Press: ⌈Enter⌉

Note that budget data you just entered is displayed in both the BUDGET AREA and INQUIRY AREA.

❏ Select: `Constant amount`

The `Update budget by` field will change to Constant amount.

❏ Type: `155.00`

❏ Press: ⌈Enter⌉

The display in the BUDGET AREA will change to show 155.00 in each period for a total of 1,860.00, but the display in the INQUIRY AREA will not be changed.

❏ Press any key to continue.

If you were not satisfied with the entries, you could choose "Select", then choose "Constant amount" again and enter a new amount.

❏ Select: `Cancel` to cancel the changes and return the cursor to the Account field in the top portion of the screen.

Entering Values

The "Entering values" option allows you to enter budget amounts for each period. This option is especially useful for businesses that experience cyclical revenues and/or expenses. For example, a motel in Florida might experience peak room rentals in the January through April period while a restaurant in Cape Cod or Muskoka may only be open in the May to September season. E. & J. Enterprises prepares personal income tax returns, a service that is concentrated in February, March, and April of each year. December and January are slow months due to Christmas and New Year, as are July and August, the summer vacation period.

❏ Type: `720` in the Account field.

❏ Press: [Enter]

❏ Select: `Entering values` from the Select Options box.

The cursor will move into the data entry area for the first period in the Budget area. Typing a minus sign before or after an amount indicates a credit.

E. & J. Enterprises does not expect an increase in billings for accounting services for November 1998 from October 1998. Verify that the period 12 Previous Year sales for accounting services was $3,520.00. Erin and Joan have established the following forecast for the sale of the types of accounting services offered by E. & J. Enterprises.

Period	Ending	Amount
1	11/30/98	$3,520
2	12/31/98	$2,200
3	01/31/99	$2,200
4	02/28/99	$5,600
5	03/31/99	$7,200
6	04/30/99	$6,900
7	05/31/99	$4,000
8	06/30/99	$3,750
9	07/31/99	$2,500
10	08/31/99	$2,500
11	09/30/99	$3,600
12	10/31/99	$3,900

❏ Type: `-3520.00` in the data entry field for period 1.

❏ Press: [Enter]

Remember that revenue accounts are normally credit balance accounts and you must type a minus sign before or after the amount to indicate credit values.

❏ Enter the budget amounts for the next eleven periods. When you press **Enter** after typing the value in the field for period 12, the total should be 47,870.00-.

❏ Press any key to continue.

❏ Select: `Accept changes`

Using the Finder

If ACCPAC Plus cannot find the account code you enter, it will open a window in the center of the screen and display the seven closest accounts to the one entered. To explore this function,

❑ Type: `715` as the account code.

❑ Press: [Enter]

The computer may beep and the disk drive will work for a few seconds. Then the Finder window will appear.

❑ Select: `700 Sales`

Entering Values Changed by a Standard Increment

❑ Select: `Incremental amount`

A minus sign after a value indicates a credit.

❑ Type: `1000.00-`

This is the amount by which the budget figure will increase each period.

❑ Press: [Enter]

The cursor will move to the base amount field.

❑ Type: `9000.00-`

❑ Press: [Enter]

The BUDGET AREA displays the base amount in the first period. Each succeeding field equals the amount in the previous period incremented by $1,000.

❑ Press any key to continue.

❑ Select: `Accept changes`

Moving Values

This option allows you to move amounts that are displayed in the INQUIRY AREA to the BUDGET AREA.

❑ Type: `700` in the account field in the upper portion of the screen.

❑ Press: [Enter]

❑ Select: `Moving values`

The Column Options box will appear in the upper right part of the screen.

```
┌─────────────────────────────────────────────────┐
│  Column Options                                   │
│                                                   │
│  Budget                                           │
│  Current year                                     │
│  Previous year                                    │
└─────────────────────────────────────────────────┘
```

You may select one of the three columns of data displayed in the INQUIRY AREA to copy to the BUDGET AREA.

❑ Select: `Budget` from the Column Options box.

The Move Options are described below:

Move as is   copies the amounts unchanged into the BUDGET AREA. You could use this option to copy information from the Previous year figures to the current year budget.

Percentage increment   moves the amounts and at the same time increments them by a percentage that you specify.

Increment amount   moves the amounts and increases or decreases them by a dollar amount that you specify.

Annual total   allocates the total amount equally across the periods in the BUDGET AREA.

❑ Select: `Annual total`

ACCPAC Plus will copy the annual total for the budget column in the INQUIRY AREA to the BUDGET AREA and distribute that total equally to the twelve periods.

❑ Press any key to continue.

❑ Select: `Cancel`

❑ Enter the commands to select account 700, Moving values, and the Budget column data from the Inquiry Area.

Joan and Erin feel that the budget amounts displayed in the Inquiry Area are at least 15% too high.

❑ Select: `Percentage increment` from the Move Options box.

❑ Type: `-15.00` in the percent field to reduce each budget amount by 15 percent.

❑ Press: [Enter]

The amounts displayed in the BUDGET AREA should now be 15% less than the amounts displayed in the Budget column of the INQUIRY AREA.

❑ Press any key to continue.

❑ Select: `Accept changes`

The Increment amount option works in the same manner as the Percentage increment.

Entering Values Incremented by a Percentage

This option allows you to select a base amount for the first fiscal period, and then to increase or decrease the base amount on a month by month basis.

❑ Type: `700` in the Account field to select Sales.

❑ Press: [Enter]

❑ Select: `Percentage increment`

❑ Type: `3.25` in the percent field.

This will cause the base amount to increase by 3.25% each period. If you wished to decrease the base amount each period you would enter a minus sign either before or after the numbers for the percentage change.

❑ Press: [Enter]

❑ Type: `-9000.00` in base amount field.

❑ Press: [Enter]

The BUDGET AREA will then display the base amount in the first field. The value shown for each succeeding field equals the amount in the previous period plus 3.25 percent.

❑ Press any key to continue.

❑ Select: `Cancel` to cancel the changes that you have just entered.

❑ Press: [Esc] twice to return to the ACCPAC General Ledger Master Menu.

❑ Exit from ACCPAC Plus.

❑ Back up your data files.

REVIEW QUESTIONS

1. What is the purpose of the "Inquiries" option?
2. Briefly describe the purpose of each of the options available through the "Display batches" option.
3. Describe the purpose of the "Edit historical data" option.
4. Why do you not have to use the "Edit historical data" option at each year end?
5. Describe the two methods used to edit historical data.
6. Describe the purpose of the "Edit budget data" option.
7. List and describe the choices available through the "Edit budget data" option.
8. How do you identify a number as a credit when adding it to the Edit Budget Data screen?
9. List and describe the functions available through the "Moving values" option.

EXERCISES

1. Using November 1, 1999 as the new date, access your company's General Ledger.
2. Create budgets for the following accounts:
   a) For Account 880, Insurance Expense, enter a budget amount of $200 per month.
   b) For account 835, Depreciation Expense, enter an annual budget of $700.
   c) For account 200, Accounts Receivable, enter a budget with the first period having a balance of $4,500 and each subsequent period increasing by $100.
   d) For account 925, Rent, Equipment, enter a budget with a monthly increment of 5% on a base of $75.
3. Exit from ACCPAC Plus and back up your data files.

11 Macavity & Co. Case

The names of the characters in the Macavity cases are from *Old Possum's Book of Practical Cats*, a book of poems by T.S. Eliot.

Macavity & Co. was created on July 1, 1997 by two cool but active cats known as Mongojerrie and Rumpelteazer. The company supplies the latest fad, fish bone toothpicks. Rum Tum Tugger, the manager, has hired you to set up and maintain the company books. Macavity & Co.'s fiscal year begins on July 1, 1997 and ends June 30, 1998. In the world of cats there is a 5% retail sales tax and a 10% value added tax.

After completing this case, organize and submit Macavity & Co.'s printouts. Each printout *must* contain your initials following the company name. Save the data files for your instructor to evaluate.

1. ADDING TO THE START MENU

Create a new line on the Start Menu using the following information:

Start Name	Macavity G/L
Program	General Ledger and Financial Reporter
Drive	A:
Data Directory	CAT
Data Extension	CAT

2. CREATING THE GENERAL LEDGER

Create the General Ledger files using the following data:

Number of periods	12
Month in which the fiscal year began	7
Year in which the current fiscal year began	97
Company Name	Macavity & Co. (followed by your init▶
Address	1313 Fishbone Alley
	Alleycat Junction
	Meowville
	KIT-KAT
Telephone	111-555-9999
Fax	111-555-9998
Company number	9
Contact	Rum Tum Tugger
Edit retrieved fields	All fields
Allow posting to previous year	Yes
Allow provisional posting	No
Departments	No
Force Listing of batches	Yes
Default retained earnings account	3105

Reset the Fiscal Period Calendar to report the date into a fully written-out format (for example "August 31, 1997"; not "Aug 31 97"). All periods will have an "Open" status.

Using July 1, 1997 as the new date, print the company profile.

3. ADDING THE SOURCE CODES

Add the following source codes:

1. **GL-GJ** General Journal
2. **GL-SA** Sales
3. **GL-PU** Purchases
4. **GL-CD** Cash Disbursements
5. **GL-PA** Payroll
6. **GL-CR** Cash Receipts

Print the source codes.

4. ADDING THE SOURCE JOURNALS

Add source journals to correspond to the source codes created above. Accept the sort options as shown in the "Sort Source Journal by" option box.

1. **General Journal**	GL-GJ
2. **Sales Journal**	GL-SA
3. **Purchases Journal**	GL-PU
4. **Cash Disbursements Journal**	GL-CD
5. **Payroll Journal**	GL-PA
6. **Cash Receipts Journal**	GL-CR

Print the source journal profile.

5.   CREATING THE CHART OF ACCOUNTS

Create a new Chart of Accounts by adding the accounts listed in Table 11–1 to the General Ledger. Be careful to identify each account by the proper type (Income Statement, Balance Sheet). All accounts are to be posted in "Detail form". There will be no automatic reallocations.

Table 11–1

Account	Name of Account
1101	Cash Working Funds
1105	Cash Payroll Funds
1201	Accounts Receivable
1205	Allowance for Doubtful Accounts
1250	Inventory
1301	Office Supplies Inventory
1401	Prepaid Expenses
1501	Office Equipment
1601	Accum. Dep'n, Office Equip.
2101	Accounts Payable
2105	Sales Tax Payable
2110	Value Added Tax Payable
2111	Value Added Tax Recoverable
2120	Bank Loan Payable
3101	Common Stock
4101	Sales, Toothpicks
4110	Sales, Other
4115	Sales Allowances and Discounts
4500	Opening Inventory
4510	Purchases
4520	Purchase Discounts
4530	Freight-In
4550	Closing Inventory
5210	Bank Interest and S/C Expense
5220	Depreciation Expense
5230	Entertainment Expense
5240	Insurance Expense
5250	Office Supplies Expense
5260	Payroll Expense
5270	Property Rent Expense
5300	Interest Income

Print the chart of accounts.

6. EDITING ACCOUNT GROUPS

Edit the account groups as shown in Table 11–2 in preparation for creating the financial statements.

Table 11–2

Group	Account Name	From	To
1	Current Assets	1101	1499
2	Fixed Assets	1501	1550
3	Other Assets		
4	Accumulated Depreciation	1601	1699
5	Current Liabilities	2101	2150
6	Long Term Liabilities		
7	Shareholders Equity	3000	3199
8	Revenue	4101	4199
9	Cost of Sales		
10	Opening Inventory	4500	4500
11	Purchases	4510	4549
12	Closing Inventory	4550	4550
13	Costs and Expenses	5200	5299
14	Other Income and Expenses	5300	5300
15	Provision for Income Taxes		

Print the account groups to ensure that all the information has been recorded properly.

7. CREATING QUICK FINANCIAL REPORT SPECIFICATIONS

Rum Tum Tugger wants the simple Balance Sheet and the simple Income Statement. Create these two statements for Macavity & Co. Print both of the statement specifications. Print the financial statements. Since no data has been entered the statements will have zero balances.

8. TITLE PAGE

Create a Title page specification for Macavity & Co.'s financial reports. Include your name on the title page and then print the specification and the statement.

9. EDITING THE FINANCIAL STATEMENTS

Rum Tum Tugger wants you to combine accounts for the Balance Sheet. It is not necessary to do so for the Income Statement. Combine the following accounts:

```
Accounts 1101 and 1105    Cash
Accounts 1201 and 1205    Accounts Receivable, Net
Accounts 2110 and 2111    Value Added Tax Payable, Net
```

Print the revised Balance Sheet.

10. ENTERING THE INITIAL BALANCES

Create a transaction batch as shown in Table 11–3 to record the initial account balances in the General Ledger as of July 1, 1997.

Table 11–3

Account Name	Debit	Credit
Cash, Working Funds	910.00	
Cash, Payroll Funds	100.00	
Purchases	1900.00	
Office Supplies	40.00	
Office Equipment	2650.00	
Value Added Tax Payable		190.00
Accounts Payable		410.00
Common Stock		5000.00

Print the Transaction batch listing.

11. ENTERING THE JULY TRANSACTIONS

On July 31, create another transaction batch to record the following transactions for July. Assume that all sales are subject to 5% retail sales tax and 10% value added tax.

a) The cash sales of toothpicks amounted to $750.
b) Sale of toothpicks on credit to Mistoffelees for $100 plus sales tax and value added tax dated July 13. Invoice number 001.
c) Sale of toothpicks on credit to Skimbleshanks dated July 27, invoice number 002, for $150.00 plus sales tax and value added tax.
d) Purchases of $350 from Cat Morgen Trading Company were made on credit. Macavity's purchase order number was M201. Cat Morgen's invoice number was MORG 001, dated July 31, 1999.

e) Macavity & Co. purchased a one-year insurance policy from Feline Casualty Insurance for $120 on July 1, using check number 101.

f) On July 31, payment of $70 was made to Kitty, the office employee, from the Cash, Payroll Funds account. The check number was PR001.

g) Rent on the property for July was $50, paid by check number 102 issued on July 29 to Old Possum Realty.

h) Entertainment expenses for a howling good time amounted to $5 plus sales tax and value added tax for fish dip. This was paid with check number 103 on July 29. The check was payable to Crabcakes Inc.

Print the transaction batch listing.

12. MAKING ADJUSTING ENTRIES

Prepare a third Transaction Batch to record the necessary adjustments based on the following information:

a) At the end of July, you found that the office supplies inventory (account 1301) was reduced by $10.

b) Toothpick inventory (account 1250) at the end of the month was $1,650.

c) Estimated monthly depreciation on the office equipment was $80.

d) By July 31, the first month's insurance had expired ($10).

Print the transaction batch listing.

13. PERIOD END

Post the transaction batches to the General Ledger, then print and clear the posting journal. Print the General Ledger Listing. Print a Title page, Income Statement, and Balance Sheet for Macavity & Co. at the end of the first month of operation.

III ACCOUNTS RECEIVABLE

12 Accounts Receivable Data Creation

In Unit III, you will add the ACCPAC Plus Accounts Receivable module for E. & J. Enterprises. This company is already using the General Ledger and Financial Reporter module. You would follow similar procedures to use the Accounts Receivable module with a manual or non-ACCPAC General Ledger. Each chapter will guide you through one step in setting up and operating the ACCPAC Plus Accounts Receivable module.

 If you have not completed Unit I, Introduction, and Unit II, General Ledger, you should read Chapter 1, Using ACCPAC Plus, and work through Chapter 2, The System Manager. If you have not completed the General Ledger Unit, you will not be able to import Accounts Receivable transactions into the General Ledger, nor will you be able to use the Finder to identify General Ledger account codes.

Erin and Joan have decided to add the Accounts Receivable module to their AC-CPAC Plus accounting system for the next fiscal year. They will use the following policies:

1. All cash receipts will be deposited intact daily in the company's current account.

2. Monthly bank reconciliations will be prepared.

3. Terms for credit sales will normally be 2/10, n/30, but may be adjusted for individual customers.

4. The company's year end is October 31.

5. Monthly unaudited financial statements, including an Accounts Receivable trial balance, will be prepared for management.

GETTING READY

If the ACCPAC Plus has not been installed on your computer system, you must install both the System Manager and the Account Receivable module. If your Accounts Receivable module was supplied with a later version of the System Manager than is installed on your computer system, you must install the new System Manager and the Accounts Receivable module.

❏ Install the System Manager and the Accounts Receivable module.

If necessary turn to Chapter 2, The System Manager, for step-by-step instructions for installing the System Manager and your Accounts Receivable module.

Before you can work with Accounts Receivable you must also add a line to the Start Menu. This line should read A/R E. & J. Enterprises . You should select Accounts Receivable from the Program Menu, Drive A:, Directory A:\EJE and Extension EJE so that the Accounts Receivable can integrate with the General Ledger data files created in Unit II.

❏ Add this line to the Start Menu.

If necessary turn to Chapter 2, The System Manager, for step-by-step instructions for adding to the Start Menu.

CREATING ACCOUNTS RECEIVABLE DATA

❏ Select: A/R E. & J. Enterprises from the Start Menu.

The title screen will appear and display the following prompt:

```
Accounts Receivable data has not been created

        Create    Edit
```

❏ Select: Create

ACCPAC Plus will present a series of data entry screens that allow you to create Accounts Receivable data files for a company.

Figure 12–1

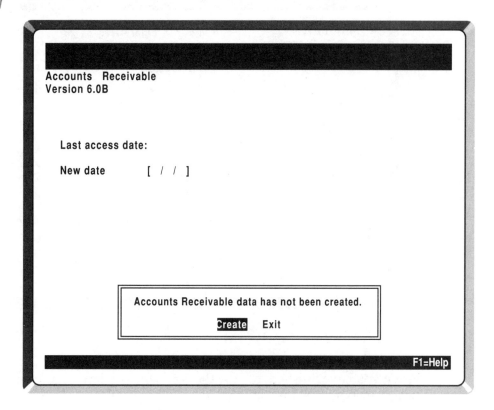

Company Data

The first screen records basic information about the company.

❑ Enter the information about E. & J. Enterprises, as shown in Figure 12–2.

Figure 12–2

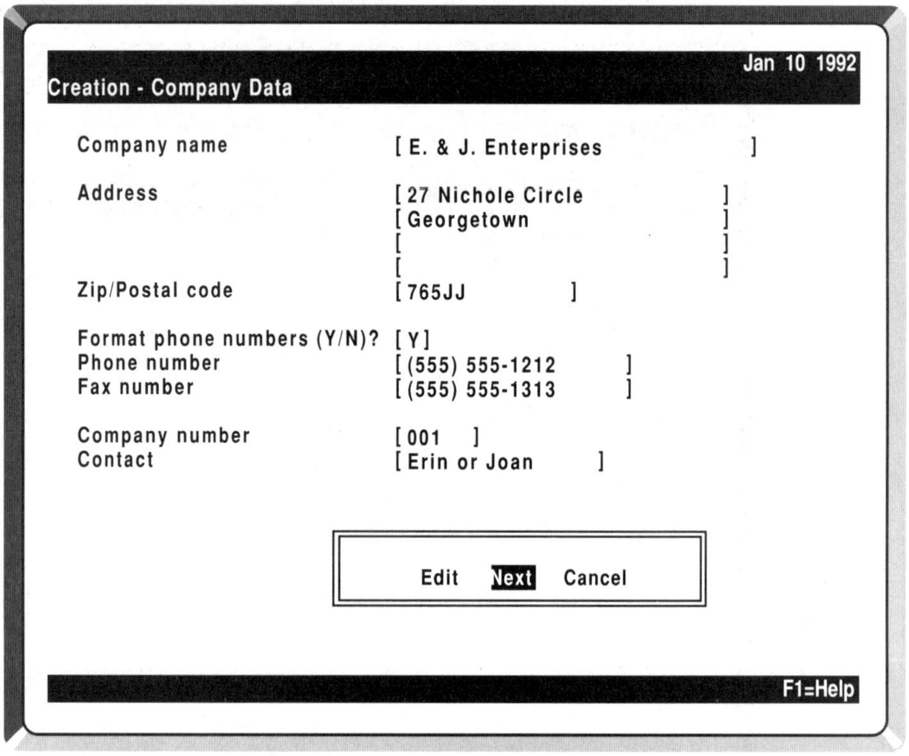

```
                                                      Jan 10 1992
 Creation - Company Data

     Company name          [ E. & J. Enterprises         ]

     Address               [ 27 Nichole Circle       ]
                           [ Georgetown               ]
                           [                          ]
                           [                          ]
     Zip/Postal code       [ 765JJ          ]

     Format phone numbers (Y/N)?  [ Y ]
     Phone number          [ (555) 555-1212      ]
     Fax number            [ (555) 555-1313      ]

     Company number        [ 001  ]
     Contact               [ Erin or Joan     ]


                    ┌─────────────────────────────┐
                    │   Edit   Next   Cancel      │
                    └─────────────────────────────┘


                                                      F1=Help
```

When you have finished, review the screen. If you have made an error, select
Edit   to loop back through the fields and make necessary corrections. Once you
have made corrections and are ready to proceed,

❑ Select: Next

System Options and Interest Charges

The System Options and Interest Charges screen (Figure 12–2) lets you specify
how ACCPAC Plus will handle customer accounts. To simplify the adding of
new customer accounts, you should select the options that will apply to most of
your customers. You can change these defaults if you add new customers who
require other arrangements.

System options

The   Process recurring charges   option allows preset recurring charges
to be applied to a customer's account (see Chapter 18). This option reduces the
amount of data entry required. E. & J. Enterprises will be offering accounting services to some customers for a monthly fee. Erin and Joan want to use the
Process recurring charges   option to record these monthly fees in customer accounts.

❑ Type: Y

Figure 12–3

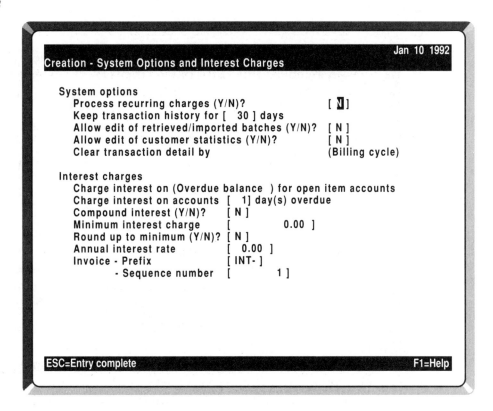

```
                                                          Jan 10 1992
Creation - System Options and Interest Charges

     System options
        Process recurring charges (Y/N)?            [ N ]
        Keep transaction history for [   30 ] days
        Allow edit of retrieved/imported batches (Y/N)?  [ N ]
        Allow edit of customer statistics (Y/N)?   [ N ]
        Clear transaction detail by                (Billing cycle)

     Interest charges
        Charge interest on (Overdue balance  ) for open item accounts
        Charge interest on accounts  [   1] day(s) overdue
        Compound interest (Y/N)?    [ N ]
        Minimum interest charge     [             0.00 ]
        Round up to minimum (Y/N)?  [ N ]
        Annual interest rate        [   0.00 ]
        Invoice - Prefix            [ INT- ]
               - Sequence number    [            1 ]




 ESC=Entry complete                                        F1=Help
```

❑ Press: [Enter]

The `Keep transaction history for [   ] days` option allows you to control the number of days that fully paid transactions will be retained in a history file. This information can then be displayed on the screen using the Display Customer Transactions option on the Inquiries Menu or printed in the Customer Transactions report.

❑ Press: [Enter] to accept the default of `30` days.

`Allow edit of retrieved/imported batches` controls whether you can edit batches retrieved from other ACCPAC Plus modules or imported from another program. If you select this option and then edit retrieved or imported batches, the audit trail reports printed by the source program will not be accurate.

❑ Type: N

❑ Press: [Enter]

The `Allow edit of customer statistics` option enables you to view and edit statistics for each customer. You can revise year-to-date and last year invoice sales, payments, discounts taken, interest charges, and credit notes, as well as total days to pay and total paid invoices. This option is useful when you are converting to ACCPAC Plus from another accounting system. If you do not choose this option, you can view the statistics using the Display Customer Transactions option on the Inquiries Menu, but you cannot edit them.

❏ Type: Y

❏ Press: Enter

The `Clear transaction detail by` option determines when fully paid transactions are removed from customer accounts and transferred to the history file. If you select "Billing cycle", ACCPAC Plus clears the fully paid transactions for all customers assigned to the billing cycle selected when you print statements. Even if you print statements for only certain types of customer balances, the paid transactions for all customers would be cleared. If you select "Period End", the paid transactions are cleared when you run the Period End function.

❏ Select: `Period End`

Interest charges

E. & J. Enterprises' policy is to charge interest on overdue balances to encourage their customers to keep their accounts current. After much discussion, Erin and Joan decided to charge 12.5% interest per year and to apply a minimum interest charge of $3.00 to customers owing a minimum of $3.00 in interest.

Balance forward customers are always charged interest on the net balance overdue on their accounts. The `Charge interest on (        ) for open item accounts` option allows interest to be calculated in two ways for open item accounts. You would select the "Overdue invoices" method if you wanted to calculate interest on each overdue invoice, without considering unapplied debit notes, credit notes, cash, and adjustments. Erin and Joan have decided to use the "Overdue balance" method to calculate interest on the customer's net balance (the total of overdue invoices and unapplied cash, credit notes, debit notes, and adjustments).

❏ Select: `Overdue balance`

The `Charge interest on accounts [  ] day(s) overdue` option allows you to control when interest charges begin. You enter the number of days from the invoice due date that the invoice amount can be overdue before interest is charged. If you did not wish to charge interest, you would enter a zero in this field. Erin and Joan have decided to allow E. & J. Enterprises' customers three days before charging interest.

❏ Type: 4

❏ Press: Enter

The `Compound interest` option allows you to calculate interest on overdue amounts or on the overdue amount plus accrued interest. E. & J. Enterprises will calculate interest on the overdue amounts and not on the accrued interest.

❏ Type: N

❏ Press: Enter

The `Minimum interest charge` field allows you to charge a minimum amount of interest on overdue accounts. To enter the amount, you type the amount including the decimal but no currency sign and then press **Enter**. E. & J. Enterprises' minimum interest charge will be $3.00.

❏ Type: `3.00`

❏ Press: [Enter]

The `Round up to minimum` option allows you to tell ACCPAC Plus to round up to the minimum interest charge any interest charge that is less than the minimum. If you do not select this option, any interest less than the minimum interest charge will not be charged to the customer.

❏ Type: `N`

❏ Press: [Enter]

The `Annual interest rate` field enables you to specify the rate of interest that ACCPAC Plus will use to calculate interest charges. E. & J. Enterprises has decided to charge a 12.5% annual interest rate on overdue accounts. To enter the percentage rate, you type the numbers including the decimal but no percentage sign and then press **Enter**.

❏ Type: `12.5`

❏ Press: [Enter]

ACCPAC Plus treats an interest transaction the same way it does any other invoice transaction, except that it automatically generates invoice numbers for interest charges. Each of these invoice numbers has a four character prefix to identify the transaction as an interest charge. The default invoice prefix is "INT-".

❏ Press: [Enter] to accept the prefix `INT-` .

ACCPAC Plus will then sequentially assign a number to identify the specific interest transaction. ACCPAC Plus displays the default sequence number "1", as the Accounts Receivable module has not yet been used to generate interest invoices.

❏ Press: [Enter] to accept the number 1 as the next interest invoice number.

Your computer should now display the completed System Options and Interest Charges screen as shown in Figure 12–4. Compare the entries to those displayed on your screen. If there are errors, select `Edit` and make the necessary corrections.

❏ Select: `Next` to display the next data entry screen.

Customer Defaults and Statement Options

This screen is used to record the default entries for customer account type, credit limit, printing statements, charging interest on overdue accounts, aging periods, and dunning messages. To simplify the adding of new customer accounts, you should select the options that will apply to most of your customers. You can change these defaults if you add new customers who require other arrangements.

Figure 12–4

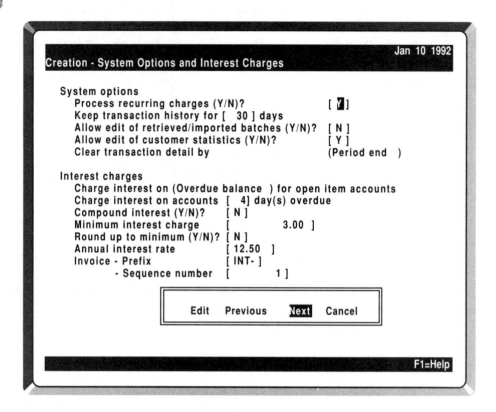

```
                                                        Jan 10 1992
Creation - System Options and Interest Charges

    System options
       Process recurring charges (Y/N)?              [ Y ]
       Keep transaction history for [  30 ] days
       Allow edit of retrieved/imported batches (Y/N)?  [ N ]
       Allow edit of customer statistics (Y/N)?      [ Y ]
       Clear transaction detail by                   (Period end  )

    Interest charges
       Charge interest on (Overdue balance  ) for open item accounts
       Charge interest on accounts  [  4] day(s) overdue
       Compound interest (Y/N)?     [ N ]
       Minimum interest charge      [          3.00 ]
       Round up to minimum (Y/N)?   [ N ]
       Annual interest rate         [ 12.50  ]
       Invoice - Prefix             [ INT- ]
             - Sequence number      [        1 ]

                    ┌─────────────────────────────────────┐
                    │   Edit    Previous    Next   Cancel  │
                    └─────────────────────────────────────┘


                                                        F1=Help
```

Customer defaults

The `Account type` default allows you to choose either the "Open item" or "Balance forward" method for maintaining customer accounts. You can change the default for a specific customer as required. The "Balance forward" option may be chosen if it is not necessary to keep itemized transactions from previous periods. Most of E. & J. Enterprises' customers will have "Open item" accounts. This option provides detailed information on unpaid invoices and, thus, better control of Accounts Receivable.

❑ Select: `Open item`

The `Credit limit` default field allows you to enter the standard credit limit offered to customers. If you do not have any credit limit, enter a number that your customers' outstanding balances will never exceed. When you add a new customer, you can change the default if necessary. ACCPAC Plus will produce a warning message if an invoice is posted for a customer whose balance exceeds the credit limit. E. & J. Enterprises has decided to use a credit limit of $2,000.00 for most customers.

❑ Type: `2000.00`

❑ Press: [Enter]

The `Statements` option sets the default for printing customer statements. You would type Y and press **Enter**, if you want the program to print statements for most customers. Erin and Joan have decided that E. & J. Enterprises will send statements to customers on a regular basis.

❏ Type: Y
❏ Press: [Enter]

The `Interest` default allows interest charges to be calculated for all overdue customer accounts. When you add a new customer, you can change the default. E. & J. Enterprises will charge interest on overdue accounts.

❏ Type: Y
❏ Press: [Enter]

Statement options

The "Statement options" allow you to specify aging periods for the Accounts Receivable, a dunning or reminder message to be printed on customer statements based on the status of the account and the printing of statements for zero balance accounts.

❏ Press: [Enter] three times to accept the default settings of 30, 60, 90, and over 90 days for the Accounts Receivable aging periods.

The cursor will move to the `Dunning messages` field for current aging. Dunning messages are usually short messages asking customers to keep their accounts up to date. In this case E. & J. Enterprises have decided to include dunning messages on their statements.

❏ Type: `Thanks for keeping your account current.` in the Current Dunning messages field.
❏ Press: [Enter]
❏ Type: `Payment overdue-please pay amount shown.` in the 1 to 30 days field for Dunning messages.
❏ Press: [Enter]
❏ Type: `Please settle your account immediately!` in the 31 to 60 days field for Dunning messages.
❏ Press: [Enter]
❏ Type: `ACCOUNT IN ARREARS - COLLECTION PENDING` in the 61 to 90 days field for Dunning messages.
❏ Press: [Enter]
❏ Type: `PAY IMMEDIATELY - LEGAL ACTION PENDING` in the over 90 days field for Dunning messages.
❏ Press: [Enter]

The `Print zero balance statements` allows you to choose to print statements for customers with no outstanding balances in addition to printing statements for customers with outstanding balances. As this option would print statements for fully paid accounts that have not been active, Erin and Joan have decided not to print statements for zero balance accounts.

❑ Type: N

❑ Press: Enter

The `Analysis report options` will not be displayed on your screen if you are using Version 6.0A of the Accounts Receivable software. This option allows you to leave blank spaces on analysis reports rather than printing zeros. E. & J. Enterprises will include zeros in printed analysis reports.

❑ Type: N

❑ Press: Enter

Figure 12–5

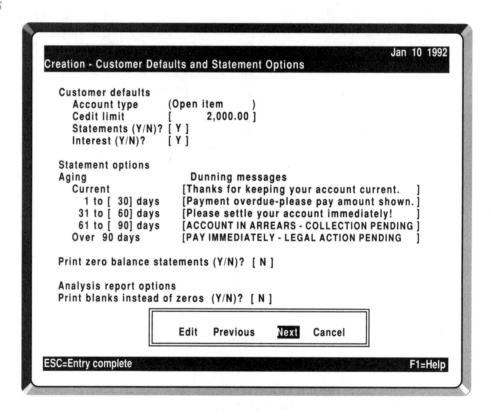

Compare the information displayed on your computer screen to that shown in Figure 12–5. If you have made any data entry errors, select `Edit` and correct the entries.

❑ Select: Next

ACCPAC Plus Integration

The choices entered on this screen enable you to integrate your Accounts Receivable data with the ACCPAC Plus General Ledger and Job Costing modules and to use retainage accounting. E. & J. Enterprises will integrate the Accounts Receivable module with the General Ledger module, but will not use the Job Costing module or retainage accounting.

General Ledger

Version 6 of the ACCPAC Plus software assumes that you will integrate the Accounts Receivable module with the General Ledger Module. Accounts Receivable transaction batches are prepared in a format that can be retrieved by the General Ledger module. If you were not using the ACCPAC Plus General Ledger module you could print these batches and manually transfer them to your General Ledger.

E. & J. Enterprises wants to integrate the Accounts Receivable module with the General Ledger module. E. & J. Enterprises did not use departments in the Chart of Accounts in General Ledger module.

❑ Type: `N` in the `G/L departments` field.

❑ Press: Enter

When Accounts Receivable transactions are retrieved by the General Ledger module, cash payment, interest invoice and recurring charge invoice information is transferred to the Reference field as determined by ACCPAC Plus. The `Send to G/L reference field` allows you to select the information that you want to appear in the reference field for other transactions when they are retrieved by the General Ledger.

❑ Select: `Document reference`

The first part of the description field for transactions retrieved by the General Ledger module consists of a posting sequence number, a batch number, and an entry number which are assigned by ACCPAC Plus. The `Send to G/L description field` allows you to control the information that appears as the last 13 characters of the description field for transactions when they are retrieved by the General Ledger.

❑ Select: `Document description`

Job Cost

Erin and Joan have decided not to use the Job Costing module. If the Job Cost module is required in the future, you can activate the Job Cost option then.

❑ Type: `N`

❑ Press: Enter

Retainage Accounting

You would use the `Retainage accounting` option if your customers with-hold part of the payment for goods or services for an agreed period of time. This is a common practice in the construction industry or in the sale of complex computer installations. E. & J. Enterprises will not use this option. If you require it in the future, you can activate it as long as Accounts Receivable doesn't have any unposted transactions.

❑ Type: N

❑ Press: Enter

Figure 12–6

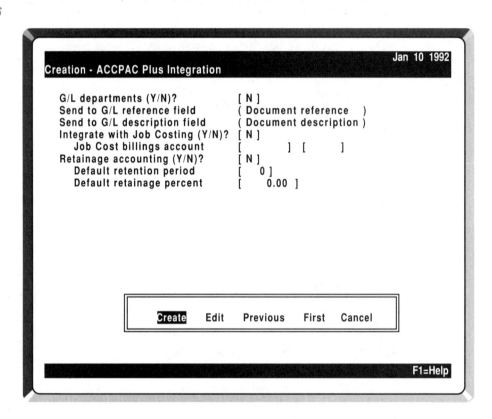

```
                                                              Jan 10 1992
Creation - ACCPAC Plus Integration

    G/L departments (Y/N)?                 [ N ]
    Send to G/L reference field            ( Document reference   )
    Send to G/L description field          ( Document description )
    Integrate with Job Costing (Y/N)?      [ N ]
        Job Cost billings account          [          ] [        ]
    Retainage accounting (Y/N)?            [ N ]
        Default retention period           [    0 ]
        Default retainage percent          [     0.00 ]




                    Create   Edit   Previous   First   Cancel



                                                              F1=Help
```

At this point, the options screen will appear at the bottom of the screen as shown in Figure 12–6. If you have made any errors, select `Edit` and make the necessary corrections.

❑ Select: `Create`

The computer will work for several moments creating the files and will then display the title screen.

INITIALIZATION

The company name, E. & J. Enterprises, and the system date should be displayed at the top of the title screen. During initialization you enter the date that you wish to be recorded as the processing date. The system date stored by your computer will be displayed in the "New date" field as shown in Figure 12–7.

Figure 12–7

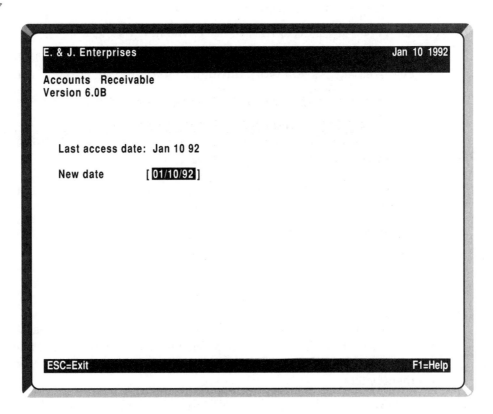

On November 1, 1998, Erin and Joan decided to add the Accounts Receivable module to their ACCPAC Plus accounting system.

❑ Type: 110198 in the New date field.

❑ Press: Enter

A warning will appear on the screen.

> New date is more than one week later than old date.
>
> Accept   Edit

If you had entered a date earlier than the last access date a similar warning would be displayed.

```
┌─────────────────────────────────────────────────────────────┐
│ ┌─────────────────────────────────────────────────────────┐ │
│ │                                                           │ │
│ │              New date is earlier than old date.           │ │
│ │                                                           │ │
│ │                  Accept          Edit                     │ │
│ │                                                           │ │
│ └─────────────────────────────────────────────────────────┘ │
└─────────────────────────────────────────────────────────────┘
```

These warnings help prevent errors in the recording or processing dates printed on ACCPAC Plus reports that become part of the audit trail. Verify that `11/01/98` is displayed in the New date field.

❑ Type: `A` to accept 11/01/98 as the new date.

After several moments the ACCPAC Accounts Receivable Master Menu will then be displayed. As you work through this simulation you will use each of the options on this menu.

PRINTING THE COMPANY PROFILE

To verify the information you have just entered, you can print a Company Profile. It will specify all the options you have selected.

❑ Select: `4. Reports` from the ACCPAC Accounts Receivable Master Menu.

❑ Select: `4. General reports`

❑ Select: `2. Company profile`

❑ Press: [Enter] to print the Company Profile.

The first four sections of this report show the information that you entered as you created the Accounts Receivable Data. The final section, Batch Status, is generated by ACCPAC Plus to show the status of the invoice, cash, and adjustment batches.

❑ Press: [Esc] twice to display the ACCPAC Accounts Receivable Master Menu.

EDITING THE COMPANY PROFILE

When the company profile was reviewed, it was decided that your name should be put in as the contact person.

❑ Select: `6. Housekeeping` from the ACCPAC Accounts Receivable Master Menu.

You will work through each of the options shown on the Housekeeping Menu (Figure 12–8) at the appropriate time. Now you will change the name of the contact person in the company profile. You can then use these same procedures to correct any errors there may be in the company profile.

❑ Select: `1. Edit company profile`

Figure 12–8

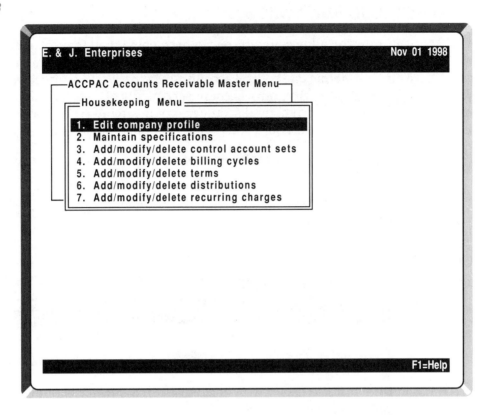

The screen displayed is identical to that displayed during the creation of the Accounts Receivable data.

- ❑ Select: `Edit`
- ❑ Press: [Enter] to move the cursor to the `Contact` field.
- ❑ Type: `YOUR NAME`
- ❑ Use [SPACEBAR] or [DELETE] to erase any excess characters.
- ❑ Press: [Enter] to indicate that data entry is complete for the contact field.

The following menu box will appear at the bottom of the screen.

If you wished to make additional changes you would select "Next" until the screen requiring the change was displayed and then "Edit" that screen. When all changes have been made

- ❑ Select: `Accept changes`

CONTROL ACCOUNT SETS

This function allows you to specify the General Ledger accounts to be used when Accounts Receivable transaction information is posted to the General Ledger. You must define one control account set before any customers are added to the customer list. Each control account set consists of a receivable control account, a bank account, a payment discounts account, an interest income account, and a retainage control account if the retainage function has been selected.

Erin and Joan have a simple set of books, and will need to create only one Control Account Set.

❑ Select: 3. Add/modify/delete control account sets from the Housekeeping Menu.

Figure 12–9

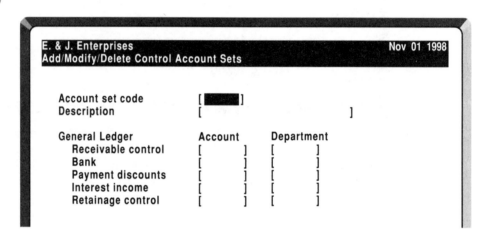

The cursor will be resting in the Account set code field as shown in Figure 12–9. You must enter a name or number for each Control Account Set.

❑ Type: 1

❑ Press: [Enter]

❑ Type: Accounts Receivable - General in the Description field.

❑ Press: [Enter]

The cursor will move to the Receivable control field in the General Ledger section of the screen. You must enter the Accounts Receivable Control account code from the General Ledger so that the information which is accumulated for posting will be charged to the proper account.

❑ Type: 200

❑ Press: [Enter]

If ACCPAC Plus cannot find the General Ledger account code that you entered, it will display the Finder window in the lower right portion of the screen. You would then move the selector bar to the proper account and press **Enter**.

- ❏ Type: `110` in the `Bank` field.
- ❏ Press: Enter
- ❏ Move the selector bar to `100` `Cash`.
- ❏ Press: Enter
- ❏ Repeat the above process, entering account 710 for Payment Discounts and account 730 for Interest Income.

The program will skip the Retainage control account field as this option was not chosen when the Accounts Receivable data was created.

- ❏ Select: `Add`
- ❏ Press: Esc to return to the Housekeeping Menu.

BILLING CYCLES

This function allows you to enter and maintain billing cycle information for charging interest, printing customer statements, and clearing paid transactions. You must add one billing cycle before you can add any customer accounts. If you chose to clear transaction detail by billing cycle in the company profile, all fully paid transactions for a billing cycle will be cleared after statements are satisfactorily printed for that cycle.

Erin and Joan have decided to use a single billing cycle: the end of each month. They will clear transaction detail by period end rather than by billing cycle. The date that transactions are cleared is updated for all billing cycles when you clear transaction detail after running the Period end function. If they were to choose to clear transaction detail by billing cycle, the date is updated when they printed statements for that billing cycle.

- ❏ Select: `4. Add/modify/delete billing cycles`
- ❏ Type: `1` in the `Billing cycle code` field.
- ❏ Press: Enter
- ❏ Type: `Monthly` in the `Description` field.
- ❏ Press: Enter

The cursor will move to the Frequency field. If you wanted to change the time interval between customer statements, you would type over the default number of days with the interval you have decided upon, and then press **Enter**.

- ❏ Press: Enter to accept 30 days.

Since you have not printed customer statements, the cursor will move to the bottom of the screen, skipping the "Statements last printed", "Interest last invoiced", and "Transactions last cleared" fields.

- ❏ Select: `Add`
- ❏ Press: Esc to display the Housekeeping Menu.

TERMS

This function allows you to set up payment terms to use in calculating invoice due dates, discount dates, and discount amounts. At least one set of terms must be defined before customer accounts can be added.

The invoice due dates and discount dates can be set up in a number of different ways. They can be due in a certain number of days, at the end of the next month, on a specific day of next month, or within a certain number of days from a specific day of the month. E. & J. Enterprises will offer terms of 2%/10 days, net 30 days on merchandise sales and net 30 days on accounting service fees. A third term will be used for cash sales as Erin and Joan want to use the Accounts Receivable to gather statistics on all customers.

❑ Select: `5. Add/modify/delete terms` from the Housekeeping Menu to display the data entry screen shown in Figure 12–10.

Each of the terms codes that you will enter are in lower case. The use of lower case will reduce the number of keystrokes required when entering transaction data.

❑ Type: `sales` in the `Terms code` field.

Figure 12–10

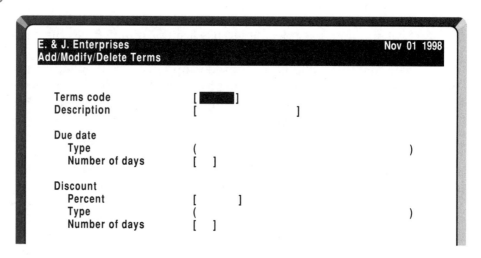

❑ Press: [Enter]

❑ Type: `2/10,n/30` in the `Description` field.

❑ Press: [Enter]

The Due Date Type option box will appear.

❑ Select: `Specific number of days`

❑ Type: `30` in the `Number of days` field.

❑ Press: [Enter]

The cursor will move to the Percent field in the Discount section of the screen. You would enter zero as the discount percent if you did not want to give early payment discounts.

❑ Type: `2.0`

❑ Press: Enter

❑ Select: `Specific number of days` again.

❑ Type: `10` in the `Number of days` field.

❑ Press: Enter

❑ Select: `Add`

❑ Add terms code `fees` for the net 30 days terms E. & J. Enterprises will apply to accounting service fees. Use `n/30` as the description.

❑ Add terms code `cash` for cash sales.

❑ Press: Esc to display the Housekeeping Menu.

DISTRIBUTIONS

This function allows you to enter and maintain General Ledger distribution codes to speed up the entry of invoices, payments, and adjustments. You can also store and print information on any distribution code using the tax tracking feature. When creating the distribution code you should use a name or short form that is easy to remember. This distribution code can be up to six characters long. You can also enter the General Ledger account code.

E. & J. Enterprises will use the following distribution codes:

fees	Accounting Fees	account 720
sales	Merchandise Sales	account 700
stax	Sales Tax Payable	account 520
vat	Value Added Tax Payable	account 540

The Tax tracking option will apply to the Sales Tax Payable (5.0%) and Value Added Tax Payable (10.0%) distributions.

❑ Select: `6. Add/modify/delete distributions` from the Housekeeping Menu to display the screen shown in Figure 12–11.

Figure 12–11

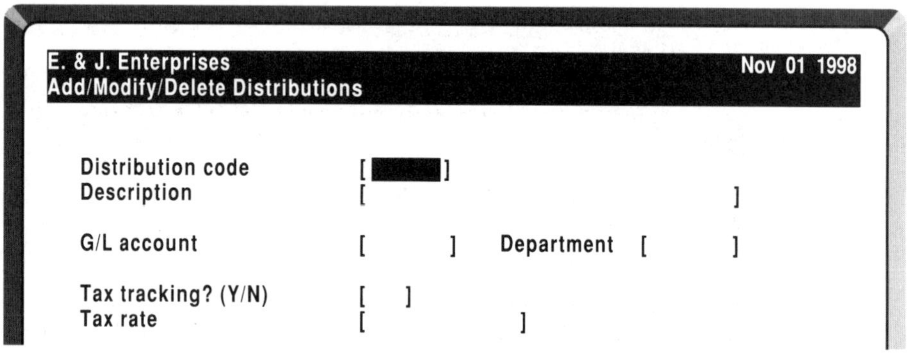

```
┌─────────────────────────────────────────────────────────────────┐
│ E. & J. Enterprises                                  Nov 01 1998  │
│ Add/Modify/Delete Distributions                                   │
│                                                                   │
│      Distribution code        [▮▮▮▮▮▮]                           │
│      Description              [                              ]    │
│                                                                   │
│      G/L account              [       ]   Department  [     ]    │
│                                                                   │
│      Tax tracking? (Y/N)      [   ]                              │
│      Tax rate                 [              ]                    │
│                                                                   │
└─────────────────────────────────────────────────────────────────┘
```

❑ Type: fees in the Distribution code field.

❑ Press: Enter

❑ Type: Accounting Fees in the Description field.

❑ Press: Enter

❑ Type: 720 in the G/L account field.

❑ Press: Enter

If ACCPAC Plus cannot find the General Ledger account code that you entered, it will display the Finder window in the lower right portion of the screen. You would then move the selector bar to the proper account and press **Enter**.

❑ Type: N in the Tax tracking field.

❑ Press: Enter

Review the data entry screen. If there are errors you would select "Edit", and then make the necessary corrections.

❑ Select: Add

❑ Add the distributions for **sales**, **stax**, and **vat**.

Remember to specify tax tracking for **stax** and **vat**. The tax rates are 5% for **stax** and 10% for **vat**.

❑ Press: Esc to return to the Housekeeping Menu.

RECURRING CHARGES

This function allows you to add, modify, or delete recurring charges that you regularly apply to customer accounts. Such charges could be for the rental of space or equipment, or monthly fees for routine services. Using this option reduces the amount of data entry required for customers invoiced a standard fee each month. Erin and Joan have a number of clients who are charged a standard fee each month for accounting or bookkeeping services.

❑ Select: 7. Add/modify/delete recurⲧing charges

Figure 12–12

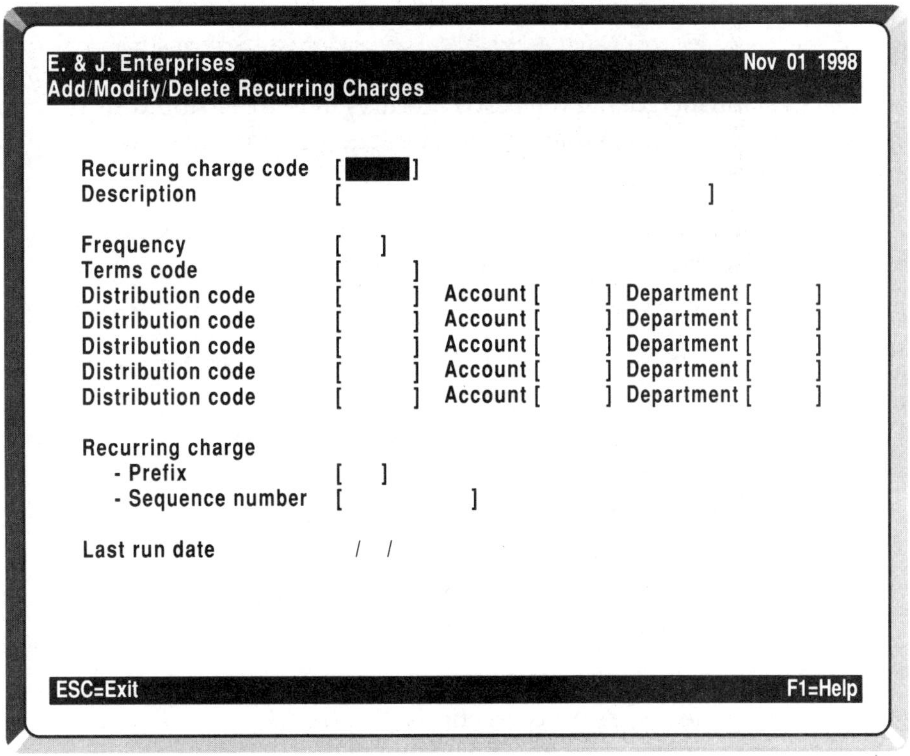

```
E. & J. Enterprises                                    Nov 01 1998
Add/Modify/Delete Recurring Charges


        Recurring charge code   [       ]
        Description             [                                    ]

        Frequency               [    ]
        Terms code              [        ]
        Distribution code       [       ] Account [    ] Department [    ]
        Distribution code       [       ] Account [    ] Department [    ]
        Distribution code       [       ] Account [    ] Department [    ]
        Distribution code       [       ] Account [    ] Department [    ]
        Distribution code       [       ] Account [    ] Department [    ]

        Recurring charge
          - Prefix              [    ]
          - Sequence number     [              ]

        Last run date               /  /




   ESC=Exit                                             F1=Help
```

- ❑ Type: `fees` in the `Recurring charges code` field.
- ❑ Press: [Enter]
- ❑ Type: `Monthly Accounting Fees` in the `Description` field.
- ❑ Press: [Enter]
- ❑ Press: [Enter] to accept the "30" in the `Frequency` field to indicate that the recurring charges will be processed monthly.

The cursor will move to the Terms field. You have already set up the terms code "fees" for net 30 days terms for accounting fees.

- ❑ Type: `fees`
- ❑ Press: [Enter]

ACCPAC Plus will search the terms that you have entered and display the confirmation "n/30" beside the Terms code field. If ACCPAC Plus could not find the terms code entered the Finder would display the terms code recorded in the Finder window. You could then select the appropriate terms code by moving the selector bar to the appropriate code and pressing **Enter**.

The next step identifies the distribution codes to be used when you post transaction information to the General Ledger. The distribution code for the sale of Accounting services is "fees".

❑ Type: fees

❑ Press: [Enter]

ACCPAC Plus will automatically insert the General Ledger account number you established using the Add/modify/delete distributions function in the Account field to confirm that General Ledger account 720 matches the distribution code "fees".

In this simulation no sales or value added taxes are charged on services, so no additional distribution codes are necessary.

❑ Press: [Enter] twice to move the cursor to the Prefix field.

You must enter a prefix of up to four characters for all invoices created through the recurring charge option.

❑ Type: MAF- for monthly Accounting fees.

❑ Press: [Enter]

❑ Press: [Enter] to accept "1" as the Sequence number.

ACCPAC Plus updates the recurring charge sequence number each time a recurring charge invoice is created.

Review the entries. If there are any errors you would select Edit and then make the necessary corrections.

❑ Select: Add

❑ Press: [Esc] twice to return to the ACCPAC Accounts Receivable Master Menu.

PRINTING GENERAL REPORTS

Can you remember all the codes and information that you have entered for account set, billing cycles, terms, distributions, and recurring charges? ACCPAC Plus can supply this information in two ways.

1. You can use the Finder by pressing **F5** when the square cursor is displayed in a data entry field and then you can select the appropriate information.

2. You can print the information using the "Reports" option on the ACCPAC Accounts Receivable Master Menu.

To document and verify the codes and information you will now print a series of reports.

❑ Select: 4. Reports from the ACCPAC Accounts Receivable Master Menu.

❑ Select: 4. General reports

❑ Select: 3. Control account sets

The default settings displayed on the screen will print the information for all control account sets.

❑ Select: `Print`

❑ Print the reports for billing cycles, terms, distributions, and recurring charges.

❑ Press: `Esc` twice to display the ACCPAC Accounts Receivable Master Menu.

Table 12–1a

```
ate: Nov 01 98    3:06pm              E. & J. Enterprises                              Page:   1
ontrol Account Sets
ontrol account set [      ] to [zzzzzz]
ccount      Receivable Ctl      Bank       Payment   Discounts  Interest Income   Retainage Ctl
t Code   Description      Account   Dept  Account  Dept   Account  Dept    Account  Dept   Account   Dept
     1   Accounts Receivable - General    200             100            710            730
     1 control account set(s) printed.
```

Table 12–1b

```
ate: Nov 01 98    3:06pm              E. & J. Enterprises                              Page:   1
illing Cycles
illing cycle [      ] to [zzzzzz]
   Billing                                          Statements    Interest      Transactions
ycle Code   Description                  Frequency  Last Printed  Last Invoiced  Last Cleared
       1    Monthly                          30
 1 billing cycle(s) printed.
```

Table 12–1c

```
Date: Nov 01 98    3:07pm              E. & J. Enterprises                              Page:   1
Terms
Terms [     ] to [zzzzzz]
Terms code   Description         Discount %  Due  Date Type             Discount Type
     cash    Cash Sales             0.00     Specific    number of days  Specific number of days
                                             Number of Days :   0        Number of Days :   0
     fees    n/30                   0.00     Specific number of days     Specific number of days
                                             Number of Days :  30        Number of Days :   0

    sales    2/10, n/30             2.00     Specific number of days     Specific number of days

                                             Number of Days :  30        Number of Days :  10


 3 terms code(s) printed.
```

Table 12-1d

```
Date: Nov 01 98    3:07pm              E. & J. Enterprises           Page:   1
Distributions
Distribution [      ] to [zzzzzz]
Distribution                            G/L                  Tax           Tax
       Code    Description            Account   Department  Tracking      Rate
        vat    Value Added Tax Payable    540                  Yes     10.00000
       fees    Accounting Fees            720                  No       0.00000
       stax    Sales Tax Payable          520                  Yes      5.00000
      sales    Merchandise Sales          700                  No       0.00000
   4 distribution(s) printed.
```

Table 12-1e

```
Date: Nov 01 98    3:07pm              E. & J. Enterprises           Page:   1
Recurring Charges
Recurring charge [      ] to [zzzzzz]
   Recurring                                Terms
Charges Code   Description                   Code   Last Run    Frequency
        Dist1 _Acct1_ Dept1 _Dist2_ Acct2   Dept2  Dist3 _Acct3_ Dept3 _Dist4_ _Acct4_ Dept4 _Dist5_ _Acct5_ Dept5
       fees    Monthly Accounting Fees       fees                   30
               fees    720
   1 recurring charge(s) printed.
```

Compare your printouts with those shown in Tables 12–1, a – e. If necessary use the Housekeeping option of the ACCPAC Accounts Receivable Master Menu to correct any errors and print the reports again.

EXITING FROM ACCPAC PLUS

❏ Select: Q. Quit from the ACCPAC Accounts Receivable Master Menu.

❏ Press: [Esc] at the Start Menu.

ACCPAC Plus will ask,

```
┌─────────────────────────────────────────────┐
│                                             │
│     Do you really want to exit the system?  │
│                                             │
│              Yes        No                  │
│                                             │
└─────────────────────────────────────────────┘
```

❏ Select: Yes

The screen will display the DOS C> prompt.

❏ Back up your data files. Refer to the Back-up Procedures Appendix if necessary.

REVIEW QUESTIONS

1. What is the function of the Start Menu line "A/R E. & J. Enterprises"?
2. Why should you save the Accounts Receivable files for a company in the same subdirectory used for that company's General Ledger files?
3. Describe the choices displayed on the System Options and Interest Charges screen.
4. What is the function of the "Process recurring charges" option?
5. Explain the differences between "Balance forward" and "Open item" accounts.
6. Why is it important to set a realistic credit limit for each account?
7. What is a "Dunning message"?
8. What information is printed on the Company Profile report?

EXERCISE

You should use the same disks for the Accounts Receivable exercises as you used for the General Ledger exercises. If you used double sided double density 5.25 inch disks for the General Ledger and saved both E. & J. Enterprises and the exercise data files on the same disk, you should copy the exercise files to a subdirectory called "EXERCISE" on a new disk.

If you have not completed the General Ledger exercises you will not be able to use **F5,** the Finder, or post the Accounts Receivable transactions to the General Ledger.

1. Add a new line called "A/R" and your name to the Start Menu. Use the Accounts Receivable module. The data files will be stored in the subdirectory "EXERCISE" in the root directory of drive A. Use your initials as the data extension.
2. Select your company's Accounts Receivable module from the Start Menu.
3. Create the Accounts Receivable ledger files using the information provided in Table 12–2.
4. Print a copy of the Company Profile dated November 1, 1998.
5. Define Account Sets, Billing Cycles, Terms, Distributions, and Recurring Charges the same as for E. & J. Enterprises.
6. Print reports showing the codes in use.
7. Exit from ACCPAC Plus.
8. Back up your data files.

Table 12–2

```
Company Data
    Name     Your Name Co. Ltd.
    Address  123 Accounting St.
             Anytown
             456MAIL
    Phone    777-555-1212
    Fax      777-555-1313
    Contact  Your Name
System Options
    Process recurring charges
    Keep transaction history for 60 days
    Do not allow edit of retrieved/imported batches
    Allow edit of customer statistics
    Clear transaction detail by period-end
Interest Charges
    Charge interest on overdue balance for open item accounts
    Charge interest on accounts 1 day overdue
    Compound interest
    $2.50 minimum interest charge
    Do not round up to minimum
    14.6% annual interest charge
    Next invoice number I-009
Customer Defaults
    Open item accounts
    $3,500 credit limit
    Send statements
    Charge interest
Statement Options
    30, 60 & 90 day aging
    Your choice of dunning messages
    Print zero balance statements
    Print blanks instead of zeros
ACCPAC Plus Integration
    General Ledger only, no departments
    Send document number to G/L reference field
    Send document reference to G/L description field
    Do not integrate with job costing
    Retainage accounting will not be used
```

CHAPTER

13 Customer Data

Now that you have created Accounts Receivable ledger files, you must add customer account information. As customer information changes, you will also modify existing customer account information.

❑ Enter the commands necessary to display the ACCPAC Plus Start Menu.

❑ Select: A/R E. & J. Enterprises from the Start Menu.

The title screen (Figure 13–1) will appear.

Figure 13–1

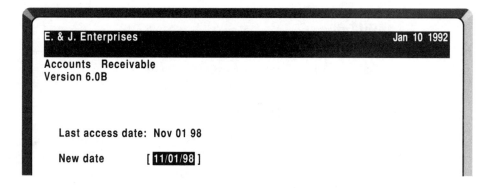

```
E. & J. Enterprises                                      Jan 10 1992

Accounts   Receivable
Version 6.0B



   Last access date:  Nov 01 98

   New date        [ 11/01/98 ]
```

If your computer does not display this title screen, press **Escape** to return to the Start Menu. Use the information in Chapter 2 to edit the Start Menu line and try the selection again.

ACCPAC Plus should display "Nov 01 98" as the Last access date and "11/01/98" in the New date field. If the New date is incorrect, type "110198" and press **Enter** to change the date.

If the New date is correct,

❏ Press: [Enter]

ACCPAC ACCOUNTS RECEIVABLE MASTER MENU

ACCPAC Plus will display the ACCPAC Accounts Receivable Master Menu (Figure 13–2).

Figure 13–2

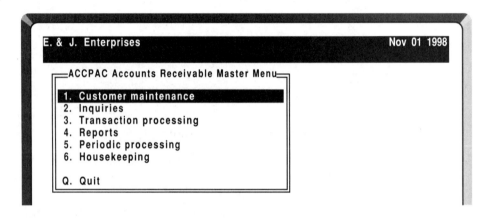

1. Customer maintenance

This option allows you to add, modify, and delete customer accounts. You can also import and export customer records between ACCPAC Plus and other programs.

2. Inquiries

This choice enables you to display customer information, current and historical transactions, and the status of Invoice, Cash, or Adjustment batches.

3. Transaction processing

This function allows you to add, modify, or delete invoice, cash, or adjustment batches. It also includes functions for retrieving or importing transaction batches. You can then print the batches, post them to the Accounts Receivable ledger, and print the posting journal.

4. Reports

This function allows you to print Customer statements, letters, and labels. It enables you to print and consolidate the G/L transactions for posting to the General Ledger. By using this option you can also print analysis reports based on the posted transactions and general reports such as you printed in Chapter 12.

5. Periodic processing

This option allows you to charge interest on overdue accounts or to process recurring (usually monthly) charges. It also allows you to process the period end and year end procedures.

6. Housekeeping

You have already worked with this menu. It allows you to edit the company profile, maintain the specifications that make the statements work, and Add/modify/delete control account sets, billing cycles, terms, distributions, and recurring charges.

THE CUSTOMER MAINTENANCE MENU

❑ Select: 1. Customer maintenance from the ACCPAC Accounts Receivable Master Menu.

The Customer Maintenance Menu (Figure 13–3) will appear. Using the options from this menu, you will be able to maintain the data on E. & J. Enterprises' customers.

Figure 13–3

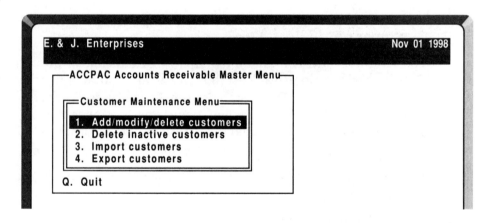

ADDING NEW CUSTOMERS

Now you will record data for several customers of E. & J. Enterprises.

❑ Select: 1. Add/modify/delete customers to display the data entry screen (Figure 13–4) used for adding new customers to the Accounts Receivable data files.

The first customer you will add to the system is Evans Ltd.

Figure 13–4

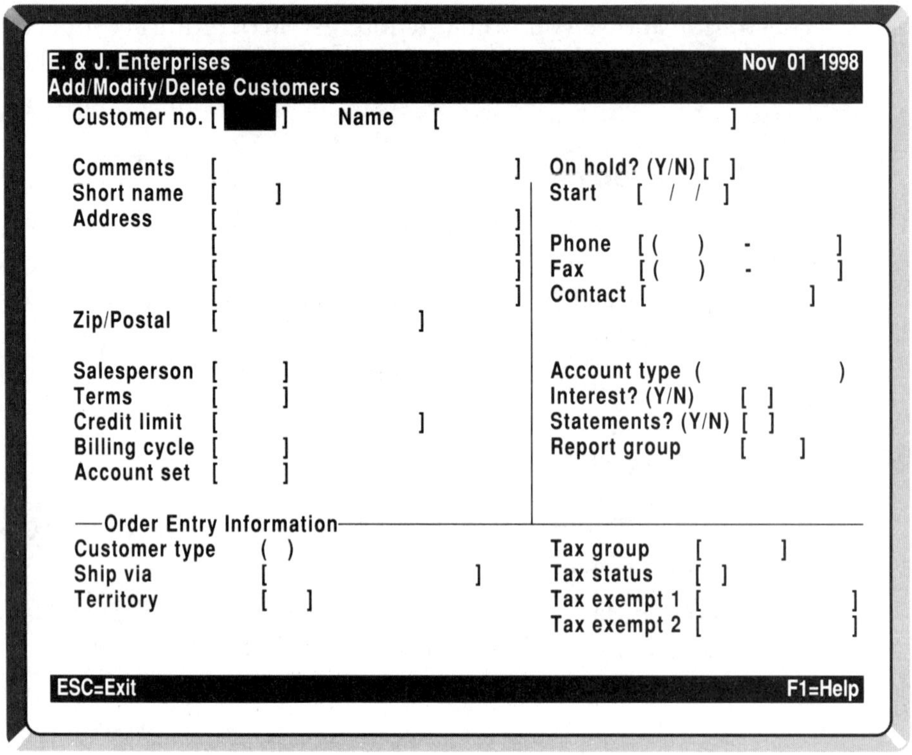

```
┌──────────────────────────────────────────────────────────────────┐
│ E. & J. Enterprises                                  Nov 01 1998   │
│ Add/Modify/Delete Customers                                        │
│    Customer no. [    ]     Name    [                            ]  │
│                                                                    │
│    Comments    [                    ]   On hold? (Y/N) [ ]         │
│    Short name  [      ]                  Start    [  /  / ]         │
│    Address     [                    ]                              │
│                [                    ]   Phone   [ (   )  -      ]   │
│                [                    ]   Fax     [ (   )  -      ]   │
│                [                    ]   Contact [              ]    │
│    Zip/Postal  [              ]                                     │
│                                                                    │
│    Salesperson [     ]                   Account type  (        )   │
│    Terms       [     ]                   Interest? (Y/N)   [ ]      │
│    Credit limit [          ]             Statements? (Y/N) [ ]      │
│    Billing cycle [    ]                  Report group    [    ]     │
│    Account set  [    ]                                              │
│                                                                    │
│   ─Order Entry Information────────────────                         │
│    Customer type   (  )                  Tax group     [      ]    │
│    Ship via        [            ]        Tax status    [ ]         │
│    Territory       [    ]                Tax exempt 1 [        ]    │
│                                          Tax exempt 2 [        ]    │
│                                                                    │
│ ESC=Exit                                              F1=Help      │
└──────────────────────────────────────────────────────────────────┘
```

Customer no.

You can choose any combination of up to six characters or digits as a customer number. You should use at least four characters to allow for an increase in the number of customers. The customer number can be used to determine the order in which records will be printed on many reports. You cannot change customer numbers after you have created the customer data record. E. & J. Enterprises will use a simple sequential numbering system.

❑ Type: 1000 in the Customer no. field.

❑ Press: [Enter]

Name

The customer name may have up to 30 letters and/or digits. You must enter it exactly as you want it to appear on statements and reports.

❑ Type: Evans Ltd. in the Name field.

❑ Press: [Enter]

Comments

The Comments field allows you to store short, important reminders or notes about a customer. Comments can be printed on customer statements and on the Customer List and Statistics report. At this time E. & J. Enterprises does not want to add any comments.

❑ Press: [Enter] in the blank `Comments` field.

On hold

If you place a customer on hold, a warning appears on the invoice entry screen when you enter transactions for that customer. The customer is also flagged as "on hold" on the Customer List and Statistics report. You can change this selection later if necessary.

❑ Type: `N`

❑ Press: [Enter]

Short name

ACCPAC Plus creates a nickname for the customer, composed of the first five letters of the name entered in the Name field. For several reports you can sort the customer accounts according to this short name. If you wished to change the default short name, you would type the new name over the default name and press **Enter**.

❑ Press: [Enter] to accept "Evans".

Address

ACCPAC Plus provides four fields for entering the customer's address.

❑ Type: `1234 Yellowbrick Rd.`

❑ Press: [Enter]

❑ Type: `Lionville`

❑ Press: [Enter]

❑ Press: [Enter] twice more to leave the last two lines of the address blank.

Zip/Postal

The Zip/Postal code field has room for up to fifteen characters.

❑ Type: `35201`

❑ Press: [Enter]

Salesperson

ACCPAC Plus allows the use of up to six letters and/or digits to identify the
E. & J. Enterprises salesperson responsible for a customer. Companies with large
sales forces and/or fixed sales territories could use this field to enter a sales territory code. E. & J. Enterprises will identify the salesperson by name.

❏ Type: `Jones`

❏ Press: [Enter]

Terms

You have already identified three terms codes using the Housekeeping function.
You can use the Finder to display these codes on the screen and then select the
appropriate code. Evans Ltd. purchases merchandise from E. & J. Enterprises
and is not expected to be a client for accounting services.

❏ Press: [F5]

❏ Move the selector bar to `sales`.

❏ Press: [Enter]

Credit limit

ACCPAC Plus will display the credit limit of $2,000.00 that you entered while
creating the Accounts Receivable data. You may change this limit at any time for
any individual customer. Erin and Joan have decided to leave the credit limit for
Evans Ltd. at $2,000.

❏ Press: [Enter]

You must record a credit limit for each customer, since ACCPAC Plus flags accounts exceeding their limit every time you print an Accounts Receivable Aged
Trial Balance. If you don't set a limit, the program will flag all accounts with a
debit balance.

Billing cycle

E. & J. Enterprises decided on a period end billing cycle for all clients and assigned this the billing cycle code "1".

❏ Type: `1`

❏ Press: [Enter]

The confirmation "Monthly" should then be displayed beside the Billing cycle
field.

Account set

Each customer must be assigned an Account set to allow posting to a General
Ledger control account. E. & J. Enterprises created only one control account set
and that was assigned the code "1".

- ☐ Type: 1
- ☐ Press: [Enter]

Start

This field allows you to enter the date on which this customer started doing business with the company. The default should display "11/01/98", the date you entered as the New date on the title screen. Evans Ltd.'s first purchase from E. & J. Enterprises was made on October 4, 1998.

- ☐ Type: 100498 in the Start field.
- ☐ Press: [Enter]

Phone

The Phone field holds up to sixteen digits as a telephone number. If you use telephone numbers from other countries that require international access codes, you should use a consistent format.

- ☐ Type: 9995551212
- ☐ Press: [Enter]

Fax

The fax data entry field is identical to the phone data entry field.

- ☐ Type: 9995551313
- ☐ Press: [Enter]

Contact

You may want to keep a record of the name of the person to be contacted about collecting outstanding accounts. The name of the contact person may have up to 18 characters.

- ☐ Type: Dorothy Leslie in the Contact field.
- ☐ Press: [Enter]

Account type

The Account type field allows you to choose either the "Open item" or "Balance forward" method for maintaining customer accounts. The "Balance forward" option may be chosen if it is not necessary to keep itemized transactions from previous periods. The "Open item" option provides detailed information on unpaid invoices and thus, better control of Accounts Receivable.

- ☐ Select: Open item

Interest

When you created the Accounts Receivable data in Chapter 12, you set the Interest defaults to charge customers interest on overdue accounts. You can change this default for an individual customer here when you add that customer to the records. E. & J Enterprises will charge interest when Evans Ltd. is overdue.

❑ Press: [Enter] to accept "Y".

Statements

In Chapter 12, you also determined what the statement default would be. You can change this default setting when you add a new customer. For E. & J. Enterprises, the default is to print statements for all customers with non-zero balances when you run the statement option.

❑ Press: [Enter] to accept "Y".

Report group

The report group field is a code that groups customers for reporting purposes. To add a group, you will type the new code into the customer record. All records that you assign to this code will be in the same group. For example, you could assign all customers in a certain geographical area to the same report group. When you sort data for analysis reports by report group, all customers with the specified code will be included. The report group can be printed on customer statements and on the Customer List and Statistics report. Erin and Joan have decided to assign customers to either report group "East" or "West" based on the customer's location. Lionville is in report group "West".

❑ Type: West
❑ Press: [Enter]

Customer type

The Customer type code is used with the ACCPAC Plus Order Entry module to determine the price level discounts allowed to a customer. As Erin and Joan have decided not to use the ACCPAC Plus Order Entry module, all customers should be assigned to the "Base" Customer type.

❑ Select: Base

Ship via

This field in the customer records describes the method by which goods are usually sent to the customer. This information can be printed on Customer statements and on the Customer List and Statistics report.

❑ Type: Local Delivery
❑ Press: [Enter]

Territory

The two-character Territory code you enter in the customer record is displayed for the customer when you use the Order Entry module. In addition, analysis reports can sort customer data using the Territory code. The Territory code can also be printed on customer statements and on the Customer List and Statistics report. Erin and Joan have decided not to use territory codes.

❏ Press: [Enter]

Tax group

If you use the ACCPAC Plus Order Entry module, you must enter in the customer record in Accounts Receivable one of the groups of tax jurisdictions and associated tax tables defined in the Order Entry module. The tax group can be printed on customer statements and on the Customer list and statistics report. As E. & J. Enterprises will not be using the Order Entry module, you can leave this field blank.

❏ Press: [Enter]

Tax status

The Tax status code indicates the type of sales on which the customer is charged sales tax. Zero is the default. If you use the ACCPAC Plus Order Entry module, you must enter one of the Tax status codes identified in that program. Since the Order Entry program is not being used,

❏ Press: [Enter] to accept the default of "0".

Tax exempt

The two tax exemption fields record the customer's tax exemption identification numbers. The numbers you enter in these fields are displayed for the customer in Order Entry, but they are for reference purposes only. The tax exemption numbers can be printed on customer statements and on the Customer List and Statistics report. All of E. & J. Enterprises' customers must pay the applicable sales and value added taxes.

❏ Press: [Enter] twice.

Compare the information you have input for this customer to the screen shown in Figure 13–5. If there are errors, you should select the "Edit" option and make the necessary corrections. If there are no errors,

❏ Select: Next

Figure 13–5

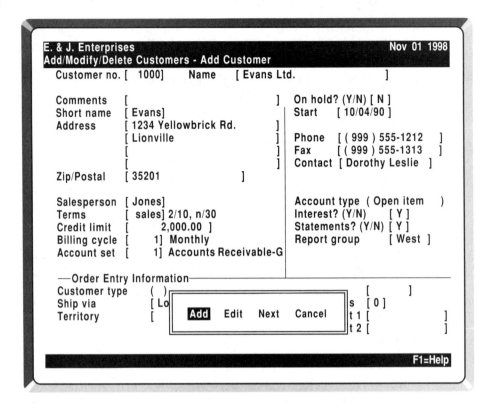

Historical Data

The second data entry screen, as shown in Figure 13–6, allows you to enter information about the customer's previous history with the company. Evans Ltd. made one purchase from E. & J. Enterprises for $2,300 on October 4, 1998 and paid the invoice thirteen days later.

Figure 13–6

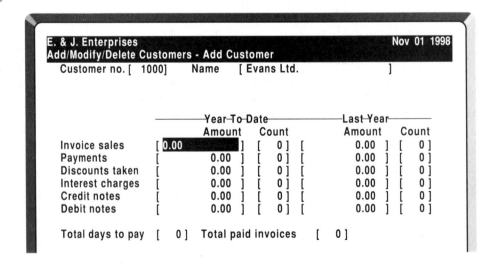

❏ Press: [Enter] or [⇆] to move the cursor to the `Last- Year` columns in the sales row.

❏ Type: `2300.00` in the `Amount` field.

❏ Press: [Enter]

❏ Type: `1` in the `Count` field.

❏ Press: [Enter] three times to move the cursor to the `Last-Year` columns in the `Payments` row.

❏ Type: `2300.00` in the `Amount` field.

❏ Press: [Enter]

❏ Type: `1` in the `Count` field.

❏ Press: [Enter]

If Evans Ltd. had taken any discounts, been charged interest, or been issued credit or debit notes, this information could be added in the appropriate fields.

❏ Press: [Enter] sixteen times to advance the cursor to the "Total days to pay" field.

❏ Type: `13`

❏ Press: [Enter]

❏ Type: `1` in the `Total paid invoices` field.

❏ Press: [Enter]

Add	Edit	Previous	Next	Cancel

❏ Select: `Next`

Recurring Charges

The final screen used in adding customers, as shown in Figure 13–7, controls the recurring charges that may be invoiced to the customer.

E. & J. Enterprises has also just agreed to provide payroll services to Evans Ltd., purchase order number EV-6943. The fee is $225 per month for the next 12 months for a total of $2,700.

Figure 13–7

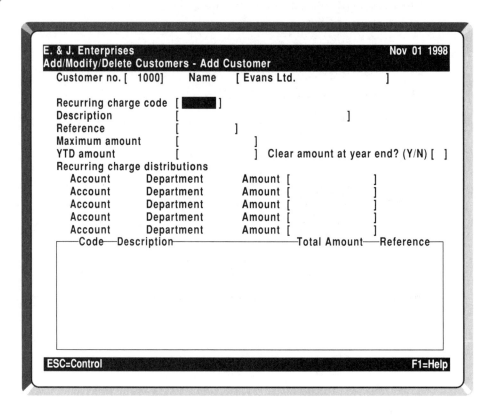

```
┌─────────────────────────────────────────────────────────────┐
│ E. & J. Enterprises                              Nov 01 1998  │
│ Add/Modify/Delete Customers - Add Customer                    │
│    Customer no. [  1000]     Name    [ Evans Ltd.          ]  │
│                                                               │
│    Recurring charge code  [▮▮▮▮▮▮ ]                           │
│    Description            [                              ]    │
│    Reference              [            ]                      │
│    Maximum amount         [                ]                  │
│    YTD amount             [                ] Clear amount at year end? (Y/N) [  ] │
│    Recurring charge distributions                             │
│      Account      Department      Amount [            ]        │
│      Account      Department      Amount [            ]        │
│      Account      Department      Amount [            ]        │
│      Account      Department      Amount [            ]        │
│      Account      Department      Amount [            ]        │
│     ┌─Code─Description───────────────────Total Amount──Reference─┐ │
│     │                                                          │ │
│     │                                                          │ │
│     │                                                          │ │
│     │                                                          │ │
│     │                                                          │ │
│     └──────────────────────────────────────────────────────────┘ │
│ ESC=Control                                          F1=Help  │
└─────────────────────────────────────────────────────────────┘
```

Recurring charge code

❑ Type: fees   in the Recurring charge code field.

❑ Press: [Enter]

Description

The Description field should display "Monthly Accounting Fees".

❑ Type: Monthly Payroll Processing

❑ Use [SPACEBAR] or [DELETE] to erase any extra characters.

❑ Press: [Enter]

Reference

You should enter a verifiable reference in this field. If possible, enter the purchase order number, contract number, or the date of the agreement.

❑ Type: EV-6943

❑ Press: [Enter]

Maximum amount

This field allows you to enter the maximum amount that can be charged to the customer. ACCPAC Plus will not generate recurring charges invoices that cause the accumulated billings to a customer to exceed this maximum amount.

- ❏ Type: `2700.00`
- ❏ Press: [Enter]

YTD amount

You would enter an amount in the YTD amount field when converting from another system to record the amounts that the customer has already been charged. New customers would not normally have been charged any recurring charges.

- ❏ Press: [Enter]

Clear amount at year end?

Many contracts run for one year, but not all start on the first day of the new fiscal year. If the contract extends into the next fiscal year you would select "N". Evans Ltd.'s purchase order does not extend into the next fiscal year.

- ❏ Type: `Y`
- ❏ Press: [Enter]

Recurring charge distributions

You could distribute the recurring charge to several General Ledger accounts. For example, a fitness club may distribute the monthly charge to accounts for basic membership fees, locker rentals, and special activity fees. E. & J. Enterprises will distribute all recurring charges to General Ledger account 720 as specified by the recurring charge code "fees".

- ❏ Type: `225.00` in the `Amount` field.
- ❏ Press: [Enter]

The cursor will return to the Recurring charge code, in case you have other recurring charges to enter. Since there are no others,

- ❏ Press: [Esc]
- ❏ Select: `Add`

YOUR TURN

Create records for the five customers shown in Table 13–1. Verify each customer's information before adding it to the files. Note that PerCorp Inc. has a balance forward account. Customer no. 9999 will be used to record miscellaneous cash sales.

Table 13–1a

Customer no.	1010	1040
Name	PerCorp Inc.	Hibou Co.
On hold	No	No
Short name	PerCo	Hibou
Address 1	Suite 1902	927 Warehouse Rd.
Address 2	17 Hopewell Cres.	Vancouver
Address 3	Oakton	
Postal code	GGG 7YU	L9H 777
Salesperson	Smith	Jones
Terms	fees	sales
Credit limit	$2,000	$2,000
Billing cycle	1	1
Account set	1	1
Start	Sept. 19, 1998	Sept. 5, 1998
Phone	416-555-1212	614-555-1212
Fax	416-555-1313	614-555-1313
Contact	John Murmark	Mr. Nightengale
Account type	Balance forward	Open item
Interest	Yes	Yes
Statements	Yes	Yes
Customer type	Base	Base
Ship via	Messanger	Air Freight
Tax status code	0	0
Last year sales	$8,320	$2,845
Last year count	2	2
Last year payments	$4,800	
Last year count	1	
Total days to pay	31	
Total paid invoices	1	
Recurring charge code		fees
Description		Monthly Payroll
Reference		H325
Maximum amount		$3,000
YTD amount		0
Clear amount at year end		Yes
Distribution code		fees
Distribution amount		$250

Table 13–1b

Customer no.	1020	1030	9999
Name	NorWest Export Co.	Mukrob Industries	Miscellaneous
On hold	No	No	No
Short name	NWest	Mukro	Misc.
Address 1	1515 Valley Rd.	342 Tobaka Rd.	
Address 2	Hillsboro	Atlantus	
Address 3			
Postal code	19287-900	99864	
Salesperson	Jones	Smith	Office
Terms	sales	sales	cash
Credit limit	$2,000	$2,000	
Billing cycle	1	1	1
Account set	1	1	1
Start	Nov. 1, 1998	Nov. 1, 1998	Nov. 1, 1998
Phone	415-333-1212	404-999-1212	
Fax	415-333-1313	404-999-1313	
Contact	Rudy Zergen	Mr. Marlboro	
Account type	Open Item	Open item	Open item
Interest	Yes	Yes	No
Statements	Yes	Yes	No
Customer type	Base	Base	Base
Ship via	Rail	Staff	Pick Up
Tax status code	0	0	0

❏ Press: [Esc] to return to the Customer Maintenance Menu.

MODIFYING A CUSTOMER RECORD

When information about a customer changes, you will have to modify the existing customer record. You have discovered that some information for customer number 1000 (Evans Ltd.) must be changed. Evans Ltd. has been awarded a large government contract and Erin wants to increase its credit limit to $5,000.

❏ Select: `1. Add/modify/delete customers` from the Customer Maintenance Menu.

❏ Type: `1000` in the `Customer no.` field.

❏ Press: [Enter]

After a few seconds, the information for customer number 1000 will appear in the appropriate fields and an option box will be displayed in the lower portion of the screen.

```
┌──────────────────────────────────────────────────┐
│                                                    │
│             Modify        Delete                   │
│                                                    │
└──────────────────────────────────────────────────┘
```

❏ Select: `Modify`

The option box will change.

```
                 Edit      Next      Cancel
```

❑ Select: Edit

❑ Press: [Enter] or [⇆] to move the cursor to the Credit limit field.

❑ Type: 5000.00 over the numbers displayed.

If necessary, you can use **Delete** or **Spacebar** to blank out any extra numbers left in the field.

❑ Press: [Enter]

❑ Press: [Esc] to indicate that the entry is complete. The following message will appear:

```
          Accept changes    Edit     Next     Cancel
```

If you wished to edit the historical data or the recurring charge information for this customer you would select "Next" to display the appropriate screen and the select "Edit" to enter the changes.

❑ Select: Accept changes

❑ Change PerCorp Inc.'s credit limit to $6,000.

DELETING A CUSTOMER RECORD

When E. & J. Enterprises loses a customer, you may choose to delete the relevant customer record.

❑ Type: 1020 in the Customer no. field.

❑ Press: [Enter]

ACCPAC Plus will display the information for NorWest Export Co. and the following option box.

```
                 Modify       Delete
```

❑ Select: Delete

ACCPAC Plus will display a second option box.

```
┌─────────────────────────────────────────────────────┐
│              Do you really want to delete this customer?          │
│                         Yes        No                 │
└─────────────────────────────────────────────────────┘
```

This prompt, with the highlight on the "No" option, is a precaution to prevent the accidental deletion of customer data. If you wanted to delete the customer you must select "Yes". If you just press **Enter**, the customer will not be deleted. This time, keep the customer record.

❑ Press: [Enter]

❑ Press: [Esc] twice to return to the ACCPAC Accounts Receivable Master Menu.

You cannot delete a customer unless the customer's balance is zero, there are no outstanding transactions, and there are no transactions in the customer's history file.

MAKING A CUSTOMER DATA INQUIRY

Sometimes, you may wish to display customer records on the screen to get information, such as customers' telephone numbers or credit limits.

❑ Select: 2. Inquiries from the ACCPAC Accounts Receivable Master Menu.

The Inquiries Menu, Figure 13–8, has three options.

Figure 13–8

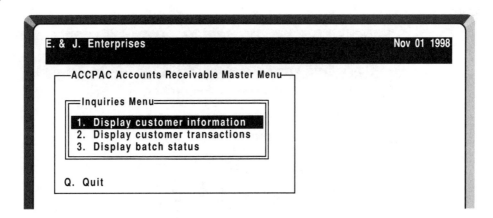

Customer Information

The Display customer information option displays the information entered on the first data entry screen used to add or modify customers.

❑ Select: 1. Display customer information

❑ Type: 1020 in the Customer no. field.

❑ Press: [Enter]

ACCPAC Plus will display the customer profile for NorWest Export Co. with an option box in the lower portion of the screen.

View	Select	Previous customer	Next customer

❑ Select: View to clear the option box from the screen so that you can see the full display.

❑ Press: [Esc] to display the option box again.

You can view customer profiles in sequential order by selecting either Previous customer or Next customer. If you chose Select you can type in a specific customer number and press **Enter**.

❑ Press: [Esc] twice to return to the Inquiries Menu.

❑ Press: [Esc] again to display the ACCPAC Accounts Receivable Master Menu.

PRINTING THE CUSTOMER LIST AND STATISTICS

❑ Select: 4. Reports from the ACCPAC Accounts Receivable Master Menu.

❑ Select: 3. Analysis reports

The Analysis Reports Menu (Figure 13–9) will appear.

Figure 13–9

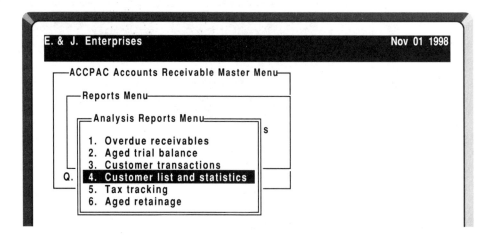

Note that 6. Aged retainage is not available as indicated by the lower intensity of the display. E. & J. Enterprises did not select retainage accounting when the Account Receivable data was created.

❑ Select: 4. Customer list and statistics

The Customer list and statistics screen (Figure 13–10) will appear.

Figure 13–10

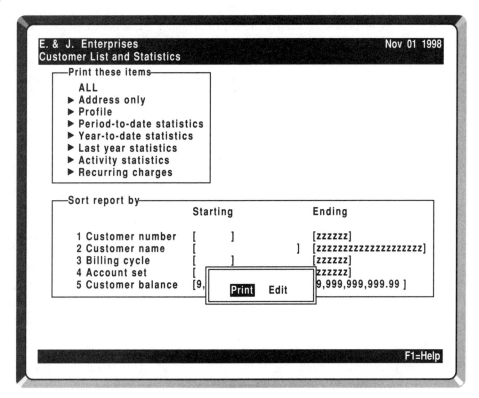

The options in the `Print these items` portion on the screen allows you to choose the information that will be included in the report. The pointers indicate which items will be printed. If you choose `ALL` a complete report would be printed including the customer profile, statistics on the customers' invoiced sales and payments, and a description of any recurring charges. If you are using Version 6.0A and you select `Statistics`, a complete statistical report will be printed for each customer. If you are using Version 6.0B you may select the statistical information that you want included in the report.

❑ Select: `Edit`

❑ Move the selector bar to `Profile`.

❑ Press: [SPACEBAR]

As E. & J. Enterprises has not processed any transactions in the new fiscal year, the only information in the statistics section of the report should be that you entered for the previous fiscal year when you added the customer's account.

❑ Move the selector bar to `Last year Statistics`.

❑ Press: [SPACEBAR]

❑ Move the selector bar to `Recurring charges`.

❑ Press: [SPACEBAR]

❑ Press: [Enter]

The selector bar will move into the Sort report by portion on the screen. You can choose to sort the report by any of twelve options. The order that customers will be printed in is indicated by the numbered lines or rows. The default is to print all customers in order of the customer number. As ACCPAC Plus does not allow you to enter duplicate customer numbers, no further sorting will take place.

❑ Press: [Esc] to indicate that you have finished editing this screen.

❑ Select: Print

Once the report has completed printing, the screen will return to the Analysis Reports Menu.

❑ Select: 4. Customer list and statistics again.

You can use the "Sort report by" options to organize reports in many useful ways. You could sort by salesperson and company number to create a customer list for each sales person. Erin wants a report of customer profiles sorted by customer name and then by customer number. If more than one customer had the same company name, as is common with franchises, the customers with duplicated customer names would then be sorted by customer number.

❑ Select: Edit

❑ Select: Address only and Profile from the Print these items options.

❑ Press: [Enter]

The Sort report by option box will now become active and the selector bar will be on row 1. The current setting is to first sort the customers by customer number. Erin wants the report to be sorted by customer name and then by customer number if there are duplicated customer names.

❑ Press: [Enter]

❑ Select: Customer name

You can select the customers to be included in the report by entering information in the Starting and Ending fields. The default of a blank Starting field and a row of zs in the Ending field will include all customers in the report.

❑ Press: [Enter] twice to accept the defaults.

The selector bar will move to row 2, which should now display Customer number. Erin wants any duplicated customer names to be sorted by customer number. If row 2 did not display Customer number you would press ENTER, select Customer number and accept the defaults to include all customer numbers.

❑ Press: [Enter] twice to accept both the blank Starting field and "z's" in the Ending field.

❑ Press: [Esc]

❑ Select: `Print`

After the report has been printed,

❑ Press: [Esc] twice to display the ACCPAC Accounts Receivable Master Menu.

Review both printed reports noting the different order of customers in each.

❑ Quit ACCPAC Plus.

❑ Back up your data files.

REVIEW QUESTIONS

1. Briefly describe each of the ACCPAC Accounts Receivable Master Menu options.
2. Explain why you would add the following information to a new customer account: contact, credit limit, and account set.
3. What is the purpose of the customer short name?
4. If ACCPAC Plus gave an unacceptable short name to a customer, how would you change it?
5. What is the Inquiries Menu used for?
6. Describe the information contained in the Customer List and Statistics Report.

EXERCISE

You have decided on the following Accounts Receivable policies for your company:
All customers will have a credit limit of $3,500 until they display a satisfactory payment history and show a need for greater credit. You will send statements to all customers, charge them interest on overdue accounts, and keep their invoices on an open-item rather than balance-forward basis.

1. Enter `11/01/99` as the new date.
2. Add the customers listed in Table 13–2 to the Accounts Receivable files that you created in the last exercise. They are the same customers as you used in the General Ledger and Financial Reporter module.
3. Once you have entered these customers, print a Customer List and Statistics Report and review it for errors. Make any corrections necessary.
4. Back up your data files and quit ACCPAC Plus.

Table 13–2a

Customer no.	6500	5320
Name	Barilak & Assoc.	Dillingham & Co.
On hold	No	No
Short name	Baril	Dilli
Address 1	1870 Duke St.	12 College St.
Address 2	Rexdale	Burlington
Address 3		
Postal code	98542	Z500A
Salesperson	Lisa	Brenda
Terms	fees	fees
Credit limit	$3,500	$3,000
Billing cycle	1	1
Account set	1	1
Start	Oct. 1, 1998	Sept. 1, 1998
Phone	562-555-1212	765-555-1212
Fax	562-555-1313	765-555-1313
Contact	Ihor	Bruce Dillingham
Account type	Open item	Open item
Interest	Yes	Yes
Statements	Yes	Yes
Report group		
Customer type	Base	Base
Ship via	Boat	Air
Tax status code	0	0
Last year sales	$2,300	$4,070
Last year count	1	2
Last year payments		$1,920
Last year count		1
Total days to pay		25
Total paid invoices		1
Recurring charge code	fees	fees
Description	Monthly Payroll	General Accounting
Reference	BA1122	DIL-A-867
Maximum amount	$3,000	$8,400
YTD amount	0	0
Clear amount at year end	Yes	Yes
Distribution amount	$250	$700

Table 13–2b

Customer no.	3467	7854	1111
Name	H. Bazelton	Graves & Dawn Co.	Miscellaneous
On hold	No.	No	No
Short name	Bazel	Grave	Misc.
Address 1	1184 Oak St.	1112 Woodlawn Ave.	
Address 2	Amherst	Chatham	
Address 3			
Postal code	3423ZIP	46812	
Salesperson	Lisa Lost	Brenda Black	Office
Terms	sales	sales	sales
Credit limit	$2,500	$1,500	
Billing cycle	1	1	
Account set	1	1	
Start	Oct. 10, 1998	Oct. 15, 1998	Nov. 1, 1998
Phone	876-555-1212	863-555-1212	
Fax			
Contact	H. Bazelton	Ruth Dawn	
Account type	Open item	Open item	Open item
Interest	Yes	Yes	No
Statements	Yes	Yes	No
Report group			
Customer type	Base	Base	Base
Ship via	Courrier	Staff	Pick Up
Tax status code	0	0	0
Last year sales	$1,725	$1,104	
Last year count	1	1	
Last year payments	$1,725	$1,104	
Last year count	1	1	
Total days to pay	13	11	
Total paid invoices	1	1	

14 Opening Invoices

You are adding the Accounts Receivable module to a system that includes the General Ledger module and existing data. The next step is to record outstanding invoices already posted to the Accounts Receivable control account in the General Ledger. When recording invoices are already posted to the Accounts Receivable account in the General Ledger, you must take special care to ensure that these transactions are not duplicated in the General Ledger.

❏ Enter the commands necessary to display the ACCPAC Plus Start Menu.

❏ Select: A/R E. & J. Enterprises.

ACCPAC Plus should display the title screen with "Nov 01 98" as the Last access date and "11/01/98" as the New date. If the New date is incorrect, type 110198.

❏ Press: [Enter]

INVOICE PROCESSING MENU

❏ Select: 3. Transaction processing from the ACCPAC Accounts Receivable Master Menu.

❏ Select: 1. Invoice processing from the Transaction Processing Menu.

The Invoice Processing Menu (Figure 14–1) will appear on the screen.

Figure 14–1

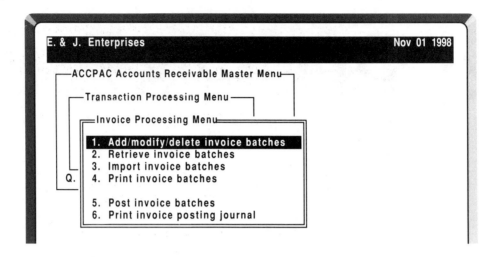

```
E. & J. Enterprises                                    Nov 01 1998

   ┌─ACCPAC Accounts Receivable Master Menu─┐
     ┌─Transaction Processing Menu─┐
       ┌─Invoice Processing Menu──────┐
       │ 1.  Add/modify/delete invoice batches │
       │ 2.  Retrieve invoice batches          │
       │ 3.  Import invoice batches            │
   Q.  │ 4.  Print invoice batches             │
       │                                       │
       │ 5.  Post invoice batches              │
       │ 6.  Print invoice posting journal     │
       └───────────────────────────────────────┘
```

The "Retrieve invoice batches" option allows you to bring invoice batches from other ACCPAC Plus or ACCESS programs into Accounts Receivable. The "Import invoice batches" option allows you to transfer invoice batches from non-ACCPAC Plus programs to the Accounts Receivable. You could then modify, print, and post the batch before printing the posting journal.

ENTERING AN INVOICE - SINGLE DISTRIBUTION

Now you are ready to enter the outstanding invoices into Accounts Receivable. The first invoice is number 1012 to Hibou Co., dated September 5, 1998, for accounting services in the amount of $200.00.

❑ Select: 1. Add/modify/delete invoice batches

The Add/Modify/Delete Invoice Batches screen (Figure 14–2) will appear.

If you make a typing error when entering the invoice information, you can correct it by pressing the backspace key and typing over your mistake. If you have already entered and accepted the information, you can correct it by selecting Edit at the final authorization inquiry and correcting the invoice.

Figure 14–2

```
E. & J. Enterprises                                  Nov 01 1998
Add/Modify/Delete Invoice Batches
    Batch number       [    ]                    Entries:
    Batch description [                    ]  Total:
    Entry number      [        ]

    Type         (              )
    Customer no. [    ]                      Terms    [   ]
    Document no.[         ]                   [                  ]
    Date        [ / / ]                      Discount [ / / ]
    Reference   [            ]               Percent  [     ]%
    Description [                         ]  Due date [ / / ]
    ─────────────────G/L INVOICE DISTRIBUTIONS────────────
    Code [    ] Account [    ] Department [    ]  Amount   [        ]
    Desc.                                         Tax base [        ]
    ┌─Code──Account─Department────Amount─┐       Tax rate       %
    │                                    │
    │                                    │       Document total
    │                                    │       Discount base [      ]
    │                                    │
    │                                    │
    │                                    │
    └────────────────────────────────────┘
BLANK=New batch    ESC=Exit                              F1=Help
```

❑ Press: [Enter] in the blank `Batch number` field.

The following message will appear:

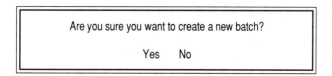

Are you sure you want to create a new batch?

Yes   No

❑ Select: `Yes`

ACCPAC Plus assigns the next available Batch number, number "1", to the new invoice batch file, displays "0" in the Entries field and "0.00" in the Total field at the top right of the screen. The cursor will then move to the Batch description field.

❑ Type: `Invoices posted to G/L`

❑ Press: [Enter]

Since this transaction is the first one to be entered, the Entry number field will display "1".

❑ Press: [Enter]

A box will appear on the screen, requiring you to identify the type of document that is being entered. Invoices are billings to clients for goods or services rendered and increase the accounts receivable. Credit notes are used to document decreases in accounts receivable that occur for a reason other than the customer making a payment. A debit note signifies an increase in the amount of the accounts receivable. This first item is an invoice.

❑ Select: `Invoice`

In the `Customer no.` field, you must enter the customer number as shown on the Customer List you printed earlier. If you do not have the list available and cannot remember Hibou Co.'s number, you can use the Finder. If you enter a customer number that has not been assigned, the Finder window will appear on the screen, listing customer numbers near the one you entered in error. You would then move the selector bar to the correct customer number and press **Enter**.

❑ Press: F5

❑ Move the selector bar to `1040 Hibou Co.`

❑ Press: Enter

ACCPAC Plus will display the customer name and move the cursor to the `Document no.` field. ACCPAC Plus will not accept an invoice entry without a document number.

❑ Press: Enter to try to enter a blank.

❑ Press: F2 to clear the error message from the screen.

❑ Type: `1012` in the `Document no.` field to record the invoice number.

❑ Press: Enter

The `Date` field automatically displays the date entered as the new date.

❑ Type: `090598` to record the date of the invoice, September 5, 1998.

❑ Press: Enter

You would normally use the `Reference` field for a customer's purchase order number or the name of the person ordering the goods or services.

❑ Type: `H2235` to represent Hibou Co.'s purchase order number.

❑ Press: Enter

The highlighted bar now moves to the `Description` field.

❑ Type: `Accounting Services`

❑ Press: Enter

The terms code displayed is the default that you entered when adding the customer. This code can be changed for a different type of transaction.

❑ Type: `fees`

❑ Use [DELETE] or [SPACEBAR] to delete any excess letters.

❑ Press: Enter

ACCPAC Plus will display the terms code description (n/30) and the discount percentage (0.00%). The due date will also be displayed and the cursor will move to the G/L INVOICE DISTRIBUTIONS portion of the screen.

❏ Type: `fees` in the `Code` field.

❏ Press: [Enter]

ACCPAC Plus will search the distributions codes that you created in Chapter 12. If the code is not found, the Finder will be displayed and you can select the code `fees`. If the code is found, the code description and the General Ledger account number will be displayed.

❏ Type: `200.00` in the `Amount` field.

❏ Press: [Enter]

The cursor will return to the Code field for further distributions on this invoice.

❏ Press: [Esc] to indicate that the distribution is complete.

The cursor will move to the `Discount base` field, which displays "0.00" indicating that no discount is available on this invoice.

❏ Press: [Enter]

An option box will now appear at the bottom of the screen as shown in Figure 14–3.

Figure 14–3

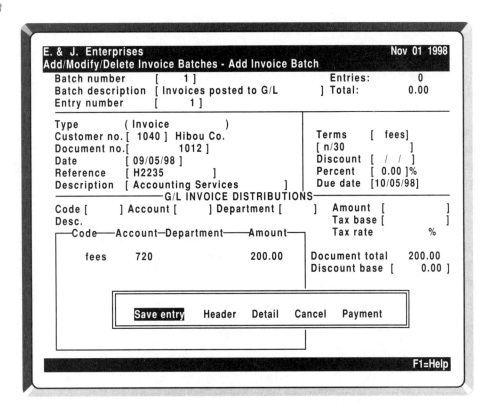

Review the data entered carefully. If there are errors in the upper portion of the screen, select "Header" and make the necessary corrections. If there are errors in the General Ledger distributions, select "Detail" to enter corrections. Once you are satisfied that there are no errors,

❑ Select: `Save entry`

The Entries field in the upper right corner will change to "1" and the Total field will change to 200.00. The Entry number field will display the next entry number in sequence and the Document Types option box will be displayed.

ENTERING AN INVOICE - MULTIPLE DISTRIBUTIONS

The next invoice to be entered is number 1016 to Hibou Co., dated October 21 1998 for the sale of a computer and printer ($2,300). The invoice totalled $2,645 including sales tax of $115 and value added tax of $230. Hibou Co.'s purchase order was H2334. This entry will require distribution to three General Ledger accounts.

❑ Select: `Invoice`

ACCPAC Plus will display the customer number, document number, and date of the last entry.

❑ Press: Enter to accept the customer number for Hibou Co.

❑ Type: `1016` in the `Document no.` field.

❑ Press: Enter

❑ Type: `102198` in the `Date` field.

❑ Press: Enter

❑ Type: `H2334` in the `Reference` field.

❑ Press: Enter

❑ Type: `Computer & Printer` in the `Description` field.

❑ Press: Enter

❑ Press: Enter to accept `sales` as the Terms code.

A common data entry error is recording an incorrect amount in one of the General Ledger invoice distributions. The distributions that you are now going to enter contain an error which you will correct later. The distributions to the General Ledger will be to the sales, sales tax payable, and value added tax payable accounts.

❑ Type: `sales` in the `Code` field.

❑ Press: Enter

❑ Type: `2645.00` in the `Amount` field.

❑ Press: Enter

❑ Type: `stax` in the `Code` field.

❑ Press: [Enter]

❑ Type: `115.00` in the `Amount` field.

❑ Press: [Enter]

Using the amount of the tax and the tax rate ACCPAC Plus will calculate the amount that the tax was based on and display the calculated amount in the Tax base field.

❑ Press: [Enter] to accept `2300.00` .

❑ Type: `vat` in the `Code` field.

❑ Press: [Enter]

❑ Type: `230.00` in the `Amount` field.

❑ Press: [Enter]

❑ Press: [Enter] to accept `2300.00` in the `Tax base` field.

❑ Press: [Esc] to indicate that the distribution is complete.

Discounts are not normally extended on sales tax or value added tax. The Discount base field will display the total of the distributions and you must change that to the amount before tax.

❑ Type: `2300.00` in the `Discount base` field.

❑ Press: [Enter]

❑ Select: `Save entry`

The following warning message will appear on the screen.

```
Warning! Customer is over the credit limit.

Continue
```

❑ Press: [Enter] to continue.

Your Turn

❑ Enter the information for the following invoice.

Invoice number 1017, dated Oct. 31, 1998, to PerCorp. Inc. for $4,800. PerCorp's purchase order number was PC9506. No sales or value added tax apply as this invoice is for accounting services.

When you have saved the above entry,

❑ Press: [Esc] three times to return to the Invoice Processing Menu.

PRINTING AN INVOICE BATCH

The Invoice Batch lists all the invoices you have entered in the batch.

❑ Select: `4. Print invoice batches` from the Invoice Processing Menu.

The Print Invoice Batches screen (Figure 14–4) will appear.

Figure 14–4

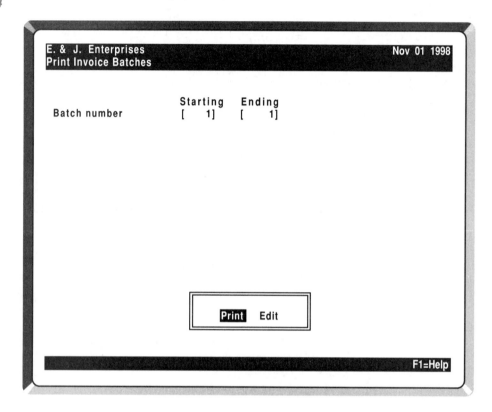

Ensure that the printer is ready and on line to your computer. If you had entered several Invoice batches you could select "Edit", and enter the number of the batch that you wanted to print in the "Starting" and "Ending Batch number" fields.

❑ Press: [Enter] to print the Invoice Batch.

After you have printed the Invoice Batch (shown in Table 14–1), review it for errors. Note the "e" beside entry number 1 and the explanation at the bottom of the printout that the "terms code has been changed".

Table 14–1

```
ate: Nov 01 98   11:52am                 E. & J. Enterprises                              Page:   1
/R Invoice Batches

atch number      :      1
atch description :   Invoices posted to G/L

ntry     Cust.      Document Document          Discount  Disc.   Due     Distr. GL Acct-Dept/
  No. Type No.          No. Date     Reference  Date   Percent Date      Code Description        Amount

   1 IN    1040         1012 Sep 05 98 H2235             0.00  Oct 05 98   fees Accounting Fe      200.00  e
      Customer Name : Hibou Co.                                                                 _____
      Description   : Accounting Services      Discount Base: 0.00           Total     :          200.00  *

   2 IN    1040         1016 Oct 21 98 H2334   Oct 31 98  2.00  Nov 20 98  sales Merchandise S   2,645.00
                                                                           stax Sales Tax Pay      115.00
                                                                           vat Value Added T       230.00
      Customer Name : Hibou Co.                                                                 _____
      Description   : Computer & Printer       Discount Base: 2,300.00       Total     :        2,990.00  *

   3 IN    1010         1017 Oct 31 98 PC9506            0.00  Nov 30 98   fees Accounting Fe    4,800.00
      Customer Name : PerCorp Inc.                                                              _____
      Description   : Accounting Services      Discount Base: 0.00           Total     :        4,800.00  *


                                                                           Total Invoices  :    7,990.00
                                                                                                _____
                                                                           Batch Total      :   7,990.00
                                                                                                ================
e : terms code has been changed.

  3 transaction(s) printed.
```

EDITING AN INVOICE BATCH

If an invoice batch contains any mistakes, you can edit it using the "Add/modify/delete invoice batches" option on the Invoice Processing Menu. You can edit a batch any time before it is posted to the Accounts Receivable ledger. After it has been posted, you are not permitted to make changes to that batch.

The batch total shown on the Invoice Batch you just printed is $7,990, but the balance in the General Ledger Accounts Receivable account was only $6365. Someone made an error in recording the amounts of invoice number 1016 to Hibou Co. and invoice 1017 to PerCorp Inc. The correct amount of the distribution to sales for invoice 1016 is $2,300.00, not $2,645.00 as entered.

❏ Select: 1. Add/modify/delete invoice batches from the Invoice Processing Menu.

❏ Type: 1 in the Batch number field.

❏ Press: [Enter]

An option box will appear at the bottom of the screen.

```
          Modify batch        Delete batch
```

❑ Select: `Modify batch`

❑ Press: Enter to accept the `Batch description`.

The cursor will move to the `Entry number` field. Look at the Invoice Batch you just printed to find the error. You can see that it occurs in batch entry number 2.

❑ Type: `2` in the `Entry number` field.

❑ Press: Enter

The invoice entry for Hibou Co. will be displayed, as shown in Figure 14–5.

Figure 14–5

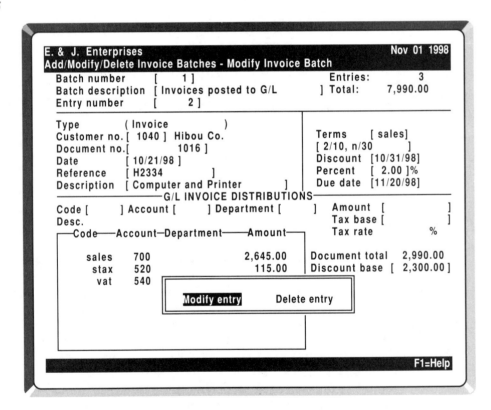

❑ Select: `Modify entry`

The invoice should have recorded the distribution to "sales" of $2,300, not $2,645.

❑ Select: `Detail`

The selector bar will move to the information box at the lower left of the screen.

- ❏ Move the selector bar to the `sales` distribution.
- ❏ Press: [Enter] to select this entry line for correction.
- ❏ Press: [Enter] to accept the distribution code `sales` .
- ❏ Type: `2300.00` in the `Amount` field.
- ❏ Press: [Enter]
- ❏ Press: [Esc] to indicate that you have finished editing details.

The cursor will move to the Discount base field, which displays the re-calculated amount of the Document total.

- ❏ Type: `2300.00`
- ❏ Press: [Enter]
- ❏ Select: `Save entry`

Hibou Co. is still over its credit limit.

- ❏ Press: [Enter] to continue.
- ❏ Press: [Esc] to return to the Entry number field.
- ❏ Modify entry number 3 and change the amount of the invoice to $3,520.

After you "Save entry" the total amount of the batch should be $6,365.00 as shown at the top right of the screen. If a different amount is displayed on your screen you should review the three entries to locate the error. You can then correct the error using the steps described in this section.

- ❏ Press: [Esc] three times to return to the Invoice Processing Menu.
- ❏ Print the Invoice batch again to document the changes made.

POSTING TO THE ACCOUNTS RECEIVABLE LEDGER

After you have printed and reviewed the revised Accounts Receivable Invoice Batch and corrected all the entry errors, you may post the batch to the Accounts Receivable ledger.

- ❏ Select: `5. Post invoice batches` from the Invoice Processing Menu.

The Post Invoice Batches screen will appear with the following warning.

```
Warning!  Back up data before proceeding.
This function will post entries in the selected range of batches.

          Post     Edit     Cancel
```

In case there is a power fluctuation or a computer problem, you should back up your data files before posting this batch.

- ❏ Select: `Cancel`

❑ Press: ⌐Esc⌐ twice to display the ACCPAC Plus Accounts Receivable Master Menu.

❑ Press: Q to return to the Start Menu.

❑ Press: ⌐F3⌐ to access the System Manager.

❑ Select: DOS

❑ Enter the DOS commands to back up your data files.

❑ Type: exit to return to the System Manager.

❑ Press: ⌐Esc⌐ to return to the Start Menu.

❑ Enter the commands necessary to return to the Post Invoice Batches screen.

❑ Select: Post to proceed with the posting.

Each time you post batches to the Accounts Receivable ledger a new posting sequence number will be assigned. ACCPAC Plus will not allow you to post a batch twice. If the batch that is being posted contains an error that ACCPAC Plus can detect, a warning message will be displayed on the screen. The entry that contains the error will be transferred to the next available batch. You should then correct the error, and then print and post the new batch.

Once posting is complete, ACCPAC Plus will display the following message.

```
Posting complete.

Continue
```

❑ Press: ⌐Enter⌐ to continue.

PRINTING THE INVOICE POSTING JOURNAL

❑ Select: 6. Print invoice posting journal

The Print Invoice Posting Journal screen allows you to select the posting journals to be printed by posting sequence number as shown in the "Starting" and "Ending" fields in Figure 14–6.

❑ Select: Edit

❑ Press: ⌐Enter⌐ twice to accept the default Starting and Ending posting sequence numbers.

The default setting prints the Invoice Posting Journal sorted by Customer number. You can also print the posting journals sorted by Document date for a chronological printout or by "Document number".

❑ Press: ⌐Enter⌐ to accept the default sorting by Customer number .

Figure 14–6

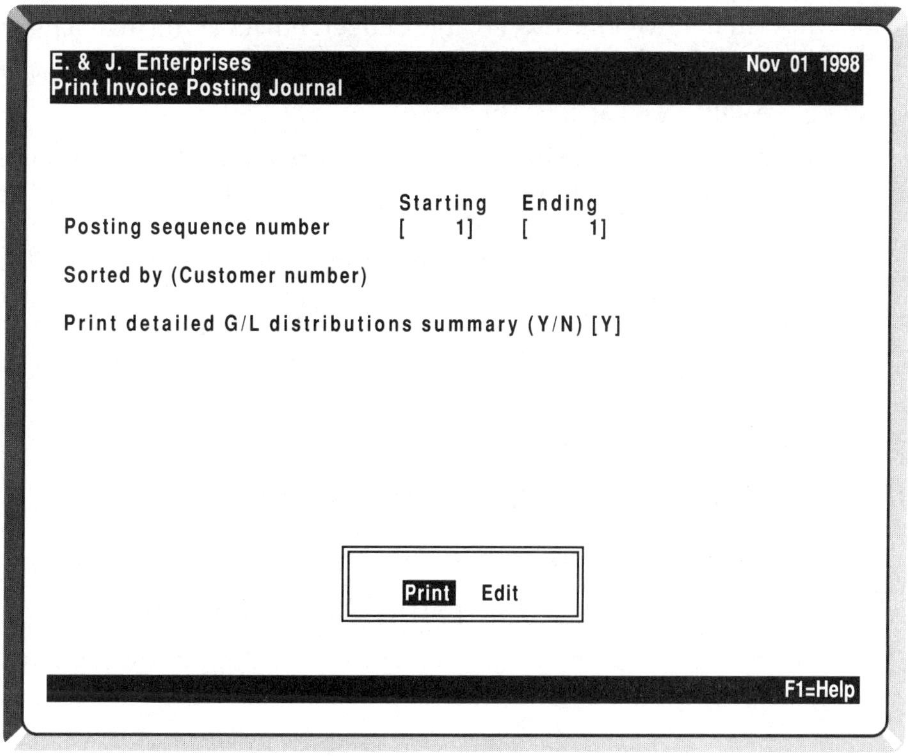

```
┌─────────────────────────────────────────────────────────────────────┐
│ E. & J. Enterprises                                    Nov 01 1998    │
│ Print Invoice Posting Journal                                         │
│                                                                       │
│                                                                       │
│                                 Starting   Ending                     │
│         Posting sequence number    [    1]   [      1]                │
│                                                                       │
│         Sorted by (Customer number)                                   │
│                                                                       │
│         Print detailed G/L distributions summary (Y/N) [Y]            │
│                                                                       │
│                                                                       │
│                                                                       │
│                              ┌──────────────────┐                     │
│                              │   Print  Edit     │                     │
│                              └──────────────────┘                     │
│                                                                       │
│                                                          F1=Help      │
└─────────────────────────────────────────────────────────────────────┘
```

The `Print detailed G/L distributions summary` field controls the information printed in the last portion of the journal. If you select "N", the General Ledger distributions will be summarized on one line. If you select "Y" the General Ledger distributions will be summarized by distribution code.

❑ Type: `Y`

❑ Press: `Enter`

❑ Select: `Print`

When the printing is finished, ACCPAC Plus will display the following message:

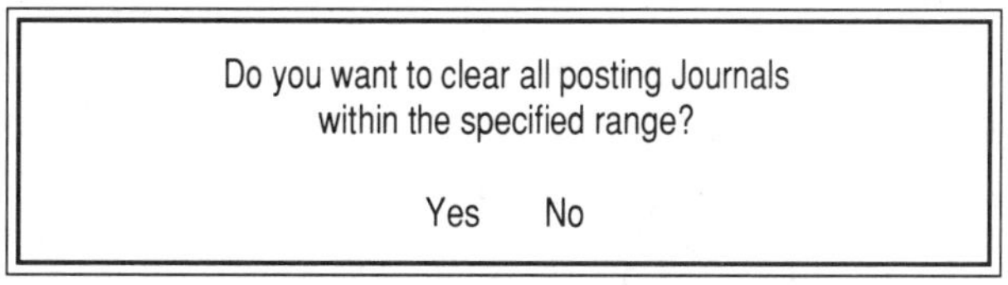

```
┌─────────────────────────────────────────────┐
│                                               │
│      Do you want to clear all posting Journals│
│             within the specified range?       │
│                                               │
│                    Yes    No                  │
│                                               │
└─────────────────────────────────────────────┘
```

If you wish to print the posting journal again, you would select "N" and the posting journal information would not be erased. You could then print the posting journal again and, if necessary, sort it by "Document date" or "Document number".

❑ Select: `Yes`

Once you have cleared the posting data, ACCPAC Plus will clear the invoice batch. Clearing does not remove all traces of the posted invoices, since they are now in the Accounts Receivable Ledger; however, the batch itself no longer exists.

❑ Press: [Esc] twice to return to the ACCPAC Accounts Receivable Master Menu.

Printed copies of the Invoice Posting Journal form the audit trail necessary to verify that posting is accurate. The first part of the report describes each entry that was posted. The second part of the report is the General Ledger Summary. The third part of the report is only printed if ACCPAC Plus detected an error in an entry. The report identifies the batch number and entry number containing the error and the number of the new batch created by ACCPAC Plus. You can use this information to correct the error before posting the new batch.

PRINT/CONSOLIDATE G/L TRANSACTIONS

The next step is to prepare the data for transfer to the General Ledger.

❑ Select: 4. Reports from the ACCPAC Accounts Receivable Master Menu.

❑ Select: 2.Print/consolidate G/L transactions from the Reports Menu.

The default setting, as shown in Figure 14–7, will sort and summarize the General Ledger transactions by General Ledger account numbers. If you wished to sort the transaction by "Journal entry" or "Transaction date", you would select "Edit" and then select the sort option.

❑ Select: Print

After the report has been printed, ACCPAC Plus will display the following message.

```
┌─────────────────────────────────────────────────────┐
│                                                       │
│     Do you want to consolidate the G/L transactions?  │
│                                                       │
│              Yes        No                            │
│                                                       │
└─────────────────────────────────────────────────────┘
```

❑ Select: No

❑ Press: [Esc] to return to the ACCPAC Accounts Receivable Master Menu.

❑ Press: Q to return to the Start Menu.

Figure 14–7

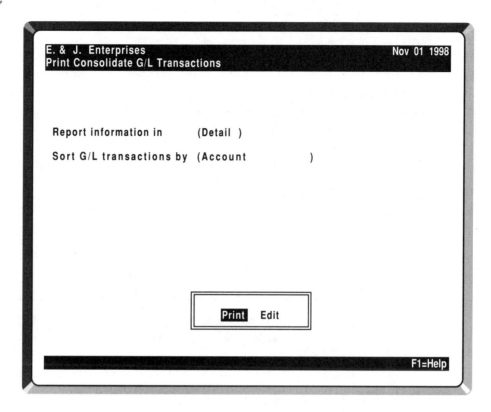

```
E. & J. Enterprises                                      Nov 01 1998
Print Consolidate G/L Transactions



     Report information in        (Detail  )

     Sort G/L transactions by  (Account            )







                            ┌─────────────────────┐
                            │    Print   Edit      │
                            └─────────────────────┘



                                                          F1=Help
```

DELETING THE INVOICE BATCH IN THE GENERAL LEDGER

You have already posted these transactions to the General Ledger when you were working through Unit II, General Ledger and Financial Reporter. If you were to post the transactions just completed, it would result in a duplicate posting of these transactions to the General Ledger.

If you were using a manual General Ledger, you could clear the information after running the "Print/consolidate G/L transactions" function. If your Accounts Receivable is integrated with the General Ledger module, you must bring the information into the General Ledger and then delete the General Ledger batch.

The following deletion process is used only when converting to the ACCPAC Plus Accounts Receivable when you are using the ACCPAC Plus General Ledger. It is not used in the processing of invoices that are part of normal on-going accounting procedures.

If `G/L E.& J. Enterprises` is not displayed on the Start Menu, refer to Chapter 2 for the necessary steps to create the proper Start Menu line.

❏ Select: `G/L E. & J. Enterprises`

❏ Type: `110198` in the `New date` field.

❏ Press: [Enter]

❏ Select: `Accept` to confirm the date.

ACCPAC Plus will start the General Ledger program and determine if there are any batches to be retrieved.

> There are outstanding subledger batches to be retrieved.
>
> Continue

❑ Press: [Enter] to continue.

❑ Select: 3. Transaction processing from the ACCPAC General Ledger Master Menu.

❑ Select: 1. Batch processing from the Transaction Processing Menu.

❑ Select: 2. Retrieve subledger batches

Figure 14–8

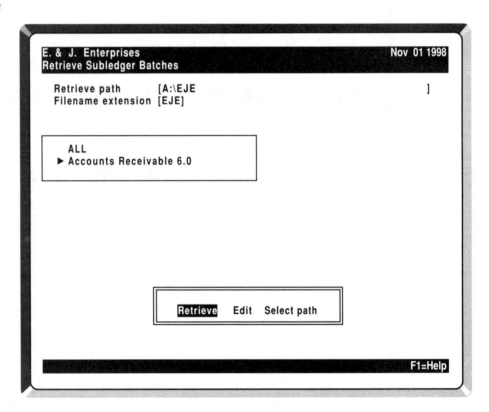

The Retrieve Subledger Batches screen (Figure 14–8) identifies that there are Accounts Receivable batches to be retrieved.

❑ Select: Retrieve

Figure 14–9

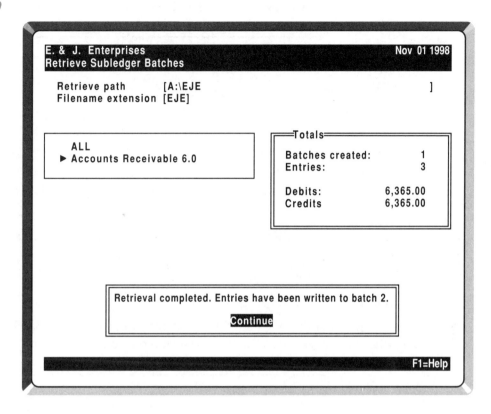

The next screen display, as shown in Figure 14–9, identifies that one batch with three entries has been created. The debits and credits totals equal $6,365.00.

❏ Press: Enter to continue.

In a few moments the screen will display the Batch Processing Menu.

❏ Select: 1. Add/modify/delete batches
❏ Press: F5 in the Batch field.
❏ Move the selector bar to the batch Retrieved from AR.
❏ Press: Enter

The general information on the batch (description, number of entries, and debit and credit amounts) will appear in the upper part of the screen. An option box at the bottom of the screen will display the following choices.

❏ Select: Delete batch

ACCPAC Plus will ask you to confirm that you wish to delete the Batch.

```
┌─────────────────────────────────────────────────────────┐
│ ┌───────────────────────────────────────────────────┐   │
│ │        Are you sure you want to delete this batch?  │   │
│ │                                                     │   │
│ │                    Yes    No                        │   │
│ └───────────────────────────────────────────────────┘   │
└─────────────────────────────────────────────────────────┘
```

❑ Select: Yes

You have now deleted the retrieved Accounts Receivable batch so the information it contained cannot be posted to the General Ledger again.

❑ Press: [Esc] three times to return to the ACCPAC General Ledger Master Menu.

You should confirm that the batch has been deleted in the General Ledger module.

❑ Select: 2. Inquiries

❑ Select: 2. Display batches

After a few seconds ACCPAC Plus will present the Display Batches screen with the following message in the lower portion of the screen.

```
┌─────────────────────────────────────────────────────────┐
│ ┌───────────────────────────────────────────────────┐   │
│ │          There are no batches to display.           │   │
│ │                                                     │   │
│ │                    Continue                         │   │
│ └───────────────────────────────────────────────────┘   │
└─────────────────────────────────────────────────────────┘
```

❑ Press: [Enter]

❑ Press: [Esc] to return to the ACCPAC General Ledger Master Menu.

❑ Quit the ACCPAC Plus General Ledger.

❑ Back up your data files.

REVIEW QUESTIONS

1. Describe the options available on the Invoice Processing Menu.
2. Describe how you would make changes to an invoice batch after you have entered it and printed the Invoice Batch Listing.
3. At what point is it impossible to correct an invoice batch?
4. Why is it very important that you back up your data files before you post invoice batches to the Accounts Receivable ledger?
5. Why would you want to have the Invoice Posting Journal sorted by document number or document date?
6. Why is it an advantage to print the G/L distributions summary in the Invoice Posting Journal?
7. Describe the procedure to transfer information from the Accounts Receivable to the General Ledger.

8. When adding previously Accounts Receivable to General Ledger, what steps must you take to record in the Accounts Receivable transactions that have been posted to the General Ledger without duplicating these transactions in the General Ledger?

EXERCISE

If you review the closing General Ledger for the company you used in the earlier exercises, you will see that the closing balance of Accounts Receivable is $4,450. This closing balance consists of the following invoices and amounts.

TABLE 14–2

```
Invoice A001
   Customer: Barilak & Associates
   Date: Oct. 1, 1998
   Purchase order: Bar 93
   Merchandise sales: $2,000.00
   Sales Tax: $100.00
   Value Added Tax: $200.00
Invoice A007
   Dillingham & Company
   Date: Oct. 30, 1998
   Purchase order: 13525
   Accounting Fees: $2,150
```

1. Create an invoice batch consisting of the October 31 unpaid items. Use Nov. 1, 1998 as the new date.
2. Print the Invoice Batch Listing.
3. Post the batch to Accounts Receivable.
4. Print the Invoice Posting Journal and clear the posting data.
5. Transfer the information to the General Ledger.
6. Print the General Ledger Batch.
7. Delete the General Ledger Batch.
8. Exit from ACCPAC Plus.
9. Back up your data disk.

15 Regular Invoices

In previous chapters, you created the Accounts Receivable data and entered the opening invoices. You are now ready to enter regular invoices that have arisen in the normal course of business since that time.

❑ Enter the commands necessary to display the ACCPAC Plus Start Menu.

❑ Select: `A/R E. & J. Enterprises` from the Start Menu.

❑ Type: `113098` in the `New date` field.

❑ Press: [Enter]

The screen will indicate that the new date is more than one week later than the last access date.

```
┌─────────────────────────────────────────────────────┐
│  New date is more than one week later than old date.  │
│                                                       │
│              Accept        Edit                       │
└─────────────────────────────────────────────────────┘
```

❑ Select: `Accept`

CASH SALES

E. & J. Enterprises has decided to record all cash sales in Accounts Receivable. Cash sales are made to customers who come to the office to make their purchases and pay for them at the time of purchase. Rather than adding each as a new customer, Erin has decided to use customer number 9999 for those customers not assigned a customer number.

The first cash sale in November, recorded on invoice 1021, was made on November 10, 1998 to Sam Sharidon, a student at the local college. Sam purchased a wordprocessing package for $150.00. He also paid $7.50 sales tax and $15.00 value added tax.

❑ Select: `3. Transaction processing` from the ACCPAC Accounts Receivable Master Menu.

❑ Select: `1. Invoice processing`

❑ Select: `1. Add/modify/delete invoice batches`

❑ Press: [Enter] in the blank `Batch number` field to create a new batch.

The following message will appear:

```
Are you sure you want to create a new batch?

            Yes        No
```

❑ Select: `Yes`

ACCPAC Plus will create Batch number 2.

❑ Type: `November 1998 Invoices` in the `Batch description` field.

❑ Press: [Enter]

❑ Press: [Enter] to accept "1" in the `Entry number` field.

❑ Select: `Invoice` as the document type.

❑ Type: `9999` in the `Customer no.` field.

❑ Press: [Enter]

ACCPAC Plus will display "Miscellaneous" beside the Customer no. field.

❑ Type: `1021` in the `Document no.` field.

❑ Press: [Enter]

❑ Type: `111098` in the `Date` field.

❑ Press: [Enter]

❑ Type: `S.Sharidon` in the `Reference` field.

❑ Press: [Enter]

❑ Type: `WP software` in the `Description` field.

❑ Press: [Enter]

The code "cash" should be displayed in the "Terms" field. If necessary, type in the proper code and delete any excess characters.

❑ Press: [Enter] to accept "cash" as the Terms code.

The cursor will move to the Code field in the lower section of the screen.

❑ Type: `sales`

❑ Press: [Enter]

❑ Type: 150.00 in the Amount field to record the sale of software for $150.

❑ Press: [Enter]

The Document total field in the lower section of the screen will change to reflect the $150. The cursor will then return to the Code field to allow you to enter another portion of the invoice with a different distribution code.

❑ Type: stax

❑ Press: [Enter]

❑ Type: 7.50 in the Amount field.

❑ Press: [Enter]

❑ Press: [Enter] to accept 150.00 in the Tax base field.

❑ Type: vat in the Code field.

❑ Press: [Enter]

❑ Type: 15.00 in the Amount field.

❑ Press: [Enter]

❑ Press: [Enter] again to accept the Tax base of 150.00.

❑ Press: [Esc] to indicate that the distribution is complete.

❑ Press: [Enter] to accept the Discount base of 0.00.

The following option box will be displayed at the bottom of the screen.

Save entry	Header	Detail	Cancel	Payment

❑ Select: Payment

The screen, as shown in Figure 15–1, will display an area in which the payment information is entered. ACCPAC Plus uses this information to generate and post a Cash batch when the Invoice batch is posted.

Figure 15–1

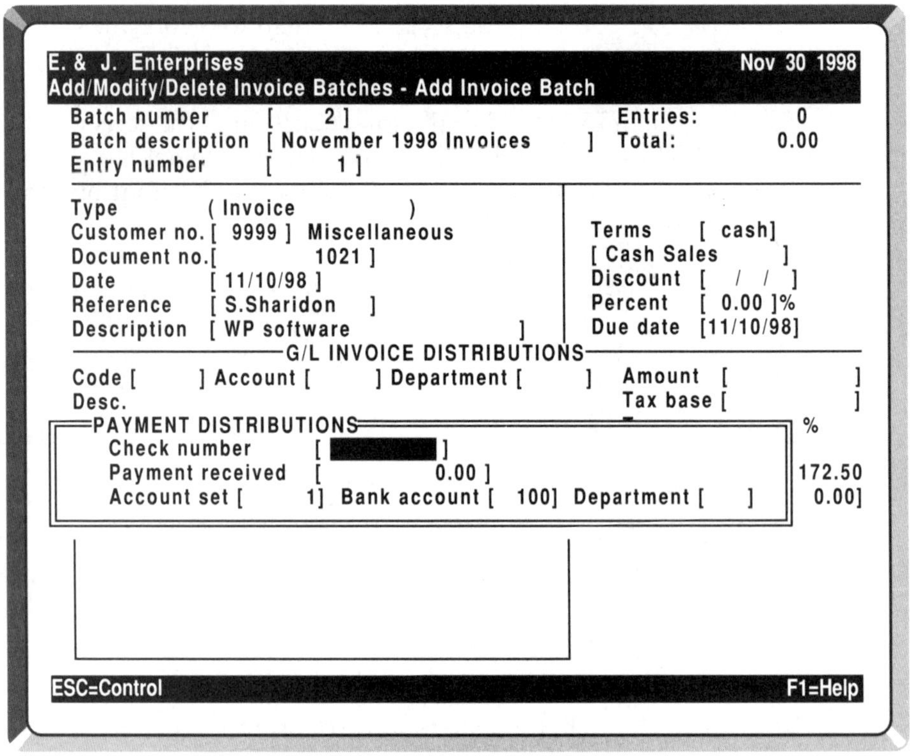

```
┌──────────────────────────────────────────────────────────────────┐
│ E. & J. Enterprises                                    Nov 30 1998 │
│ Add/Modify/Delete Invoice Batches - Add Invoice Batch              │
│   Batch number      [     2 ]                    Entries:       0  │
│   Batch description [ November 1998 Invoices  ]  Total:      0.00  │
│   Entry number      [     1 ]                                      │
│  ───────────────────────────────────                              │
│   Type       ( Invoice      )                                      │
│   Customer no. [ 9999 ]  Miscellaneous         Terms    [ cash]    │
│   Document no.[        1021 ]                   [ Cash Sales    ]   │
│   Date          [ 11/10/98 ]                   Discount  [  /  / ] │
│   Reference     [ S.Sharidon   ]               Percent   [ 0.00 ]% │
│   Description   [ WP software            ]     Due date  [11/10/98]│
│  ───────────────────G/L INVOICE DISTRIBUTIONS──────────           │
│   Code [    ] Account [    ] Department [   ]   Amount  [        ] │
│   Desc.                                        Tax base [        ] │
│  ┌═PAYMENT DISTRIBUTIONS═════════════════════════════┐      %      │
│  │  Check number       [████████████]                │             │
│  │  Payment received   [            0.00 ]            │     172.50  │
│  │  Account set [     1] Bank account [  100] Department [   ] 0.00]│
│  └────────────────────────────────────────────────────┘           │
│                                                                    │
│                                                                    │
│ ESC=Control                                              F1=Help   │
└──────────────────────────────────────────────────────────────────┘
```

You must enter a unique reference in the Check number field before you can record the amount of the payment. For cash sales you could enter the invoice number plus "cash" or the customer's check number. For a credit card purchase, you could enter the invoice number plus the name of the credit card. If the information in the Check number field is duplicated errors will be detected during posting and additional Cash "Errors" batches will be generated. Any letters typed in this field will automatically be displayed in upper case.

❑ Type: `1021CASH`

❑ Press: `Enter`

The cursor will move to the Payment received field which displays 172.50, the Document total. You would record a partial payment by typing in the amount and pressing **Enter**. ACCPAC Plus will not accept an amount greater than the amount displayed.

❑ Press: `Enter` to accept `172.50` as the `Payment received`.

❑ Press: `Enter` to accept `Account set 1`.

❑ Press: `Enter` to accept `Bank account 100`.

❑ Select: `Save entry`

YOUR TURN

❏ The following invoices are made up of cash and charge sales as indicated. Enter these invoices to the same batch, using the appropriate distribution codes. The discount base should not include sales tax or value added tax. You should write out your entries on a data entry form first.

1. Invoice 1018 to Evans Ltd., dated Nov. 2, 1998, for $300 for the purchase of a computer table plus $15 sales tax and $30 value added tax. Evans Ltd.'s purchase order number was 2112.

2. Invoice 1019 to PerCorp Inc., dated Nov. 7, 1998, referenced to their purchase order number 98-887 for a laser printer. The selling price of the printer was $1900 plus $95 sales tax and $190 value added tax.

3. Invoice 1020 to Hibou Co., dated Nov. 7, 1998, $275 for accounting services requested by Mr. Nightingale. Erin authorized these services after talking to Mr. Nightingale about payment of Hibou Co.'s account.

4. Invoice 1022 to Mukrob Industries Inc., dated Nov. 14, 1998, referenced to their purchase order AA321. The amounts invoiced were $4200 for hardware and software purchased plus $210 sales tax and $420 value added tax. This sale was authorized by Joan.

5. A cash sale to Helen Wilde for a box of computer paper was recorded on invoice 1023, dated Nov. 19, 1998. The selling price of the paper was $25.00 a box plus $1.25 sales tax and $2.50 value added tax. Remember to use a unique Check number when recording this entry.

6. Invoice 1020 to NorWest Export Co., dated Nov. 19, 1998, for the purchase of 5,000 computer disks for $0.50 each on purchase order NWE567. As these disks were for resale only value added tax (10%) is charged. This sale was authorized by Erin. (You will correct the duplication of invoice numbers in the next section.)

Print the Invoice Batch Listing for this batch (shown in Table 15–1).

Table 15–1

```
Date: Nov 30 98    2:04pm                E. & J. Enterprises                        Page:   1
A/R Invoice Batches

Batch number      :    2
Batch description : November 1998 Invoices
```

Entry No.	Type	Cust. No.	Document No.	Document Date	Reference	Discount Date	Disc. Percent	Due Date	Distr. Code	GL Acct-Dept/ Description	Amount
1	IN	9999	1021	Nov 10 98	S.Sharidon		0.00	Nov 10 98	sales	Merchandise S	150.00
									stax	Sales Tax Pay	7.50
									vat	Value Added T	15.00

```
           Customer Name : Miscellaneous
           Description   : WP Software        Discount Base: 0.00         Total       :      172.50 *
           Cash Payment: 172.50        Check:    1021CASH Bank Acct:100    Dept:    Set:1
```

2	IN	1000	1018	Nov 02 98	2112	Nov 12 98	2.00	Dec 02 98	sales	Merchandise S	300.00
									stax	Sales Tax Pay	15.00
									vat	Value Added T	30.00

```
           Customer Name : Evans Ltd.
           Description   : Computer Table     Discount Base: 300.00       Total       :      345.00 *
```

3	IN	1010	1019	Nov 07 98	98-887	Nov 17 98	2.00	Dec 07 98	sales	Merchandise S	1,900.00 e
									stax	Sales Tax Pay	95.00
									vat	Value Added T	190.00

```
           Customer Name : PerCorp Inc.
           Description   : Laser Printer      Discount Base: 1,900.00     Total       :    2,185.00 *
```

| 4 | IN | 1040 | 1020 | Nov 07 98 | Erin | | 0.00 | Dec 07 98 | fees | Accounting Fe | 275.00 e |

```
           Customer Name : Hibou Co.
           Description   : Accounting Services  Discount Base: 0.00       Total       :      275.00 *
```

5	IN	1030	1022	Nov 14 98	AA321	Nov 24 98	2.00	Dec 14 98	sales	Merchandise S	4,200.00
									stax	Sales Tax Pay	210.00
									vat	Value Added T	420.00

```
           Customer Name : Mukrob Industries
           Description   : Harhware and Software  Discount Base: 4,200.00  Total      :    4,830.00 *
```

6	IN	9999	1023	Nov 19 98	H. Wilde		0.00	Nov 19 98	sales	Merchandise S	25.00
									stax	Sales Tax Pay	1.25
									vat	Value Added T	2.50

```
           Customer Name : Miscellaneous
           Description   : Computer Paper     Discount Base: 0.00         Total       :       28.75 *
           Cash Payment: 28.75         Check:    1023CASH Bank Acct:100    Dept:    Set:1
```

| 7 | IN | 1020 | 1020 | Nov 19 98 | NWE567 | Nov 29 98 | 2.00 | Dec 19 98 | sales | Merchandise S | 2,500.00 |
| | | | | | | | | | vat | Value Added T | 250.00 |

```
           Customer Name : NorWest Export Co.
           Description   : Computer Disks     Discount Base: 2,500.00     Total       :    2,750.00 *



                                                          Total Invoices  :     10,586.25

                                                          Batch Total     :     10,586.25
                                                                                =================
e : terms code has been changed.
```

```
ch number       :      2
ch description  :   November 1998 Invoices

ry      Cust.    Document Document             Discount Disc.  Due      Distr. GL Acct-Dept/
No. Type No.          No. Date      Reference   Date   Percent Date      Code Description        Amount


                                                                    Total Cash Payments:        201.25

transaction(s) printed.
```

Check your printout for errors. If you find errors, write the corrections on your printout. You will be able to correct errors after the next section.

MODIFYING AN INVOICE BATCH

You can make changes to a batch at any time before the batch is posted to the Accounts Receivable ledger. Someone made an error in entry number 7, the invoice to NorWest Export Co. The invoice number is the same as that for entry number 4 for Hibou Co. Your investigation reveals that the invoice to NorWest Export Co. should be number 1024. If you did not correct the error now, ACCPAC Plus would generate an error invoice batch when posting. The entry with the duplicate document number would not be posted to the Accounts Receivable ledger; it would be transferred to the error batch. You would then have to modify that batch and post it.

❑ Select: 1. Add/modify/delete invoice batches from the Invoice Processing Menu.

❑ Type: 2 in the Batch number field.

❑ Press: Enter

The following option box will appear at the bottom of the screen:

```
┌──────────────────────────────────────────────────────┐
│                                                        │
│        Modify batch        Delete batch                │
│                                                        │
└──────────────────────────────────────────────────────┘
```

❑ Select: Modify batch

❑ Press: Enter to accept the batch description.

❑ Type: 7 in the Entry number field.

❑ Press: Enter

The following option box will appear:

```
┌──────────────────────────────────────────────────────┐
│                                                        │
│        Modify entry        Delete entry                │
│                                                        │
└──────────────────────────────────────────────────────┘
```

❑ Select: Modify entry

The option box will change to:

```
┌─────────────────────────────────────────────────────────────┐
│ ┌───────────────────────────────────────────────────────┐   │
│ │ Save entry    Header    Detail    Cancel    Payment   │   │
│ └───────────────────────────────────────────────────────┘   │
└─────────────────────────────────────────────────────────────┘
```

The "Header" option allows you to change information in the portion of the screen above the "G/L INVOICE DISTRIBUTIONS". The "Detail" option allows you to change information displayed in the "G/L INVOICE DISTRIBUTIONS" section of the screen.

❑ Select: Header

❑ Press: [Enter] to move the cursor to the Document no. field.

❑ Type: 1024 over "1020" in the Document no. field.

❑ Press: [Enter]

❑ Press: [Esc] to indicate that the entry is complete.

❑ Select: Save entry

❑ Press: [Enter] to continue.

❑ Press: [Esc] to return to the Entry number field.

If there are other errors in the batch, use the same steps to correct them before continuing.

❑ Press: [Esc] twice to exit from the batch and return to the Invoice Processing Menu.

Print the Invoice Batch Listing and verify that ACCPAC Plus has recorded all the corrections.

POSTING TO THE ACCOUNTS RECEIVABLE LEDGER

After you have printed and reviewed the revised Invoice Batch Listing, you can post the batch to the Accounts Receivable ledger.

❑ Back up your data files before continuing.

❑ Enter the commands to return to the Invoice Processing Menu.

❑ Select: 5. Post invoice batches

To proceed with the posting,

❑ Select: Post

During posting, ACCPAC Plus will generate and post a Cash batch if any of the invoice batch entries include a payment received. The cash receipt portion of the transaction will automatically be transferred to the Cash batch.

If ACCPAC Plus finds an error during posting it will display an error message on the screen. If the error is a duplication of document numbers, the entry with the duplication will not be posted and will be transferred to a new invoice batch generated by ACCPAC Plus. If the error is a duplication of check number information for an invoice entry involving a payment received, the cash receipt portion of the entry will be transferred to a new cash batch generated by ACCPAC Plus but the invoice portion will be posted to the Accounts Receivable ledger. In either case, you would have to modify the new batch to correct the error, print the batch, and post it.

Once posting is complete,

❏ Press: [Enter] to continue.

ACCPAC Plus will return to the Invoice Processing Menu.

PRINTING THE INVOICE POSTING JOURNALS

The Invoice Posting Journals will give you a listing of all the invoices you have posted but not cleared.

❏ Select: 6. Print invoice posting journal

Figure 15–2

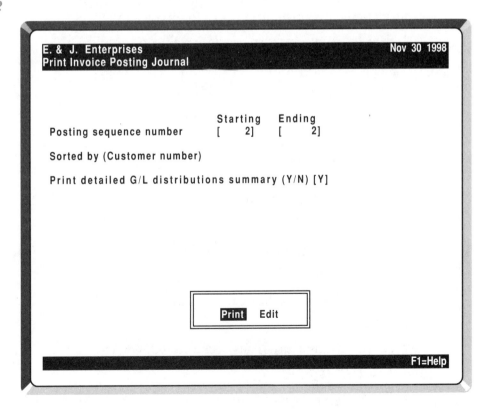

The defaults displayed, as shown in Figure 15–2, will print the posting journal for posting sequence 2, sorted by customer number, with a detailed General Ledger distributions summary.

❏ Select: `Print`

When printing is completed, ACCPAC Plus will display the following message:

```
Do you want to clear all posting journals
within the specified range?

      Yes          No
```

❏ Select: `No` to retain the posting journal data.

Review your printout carefully. The first section lists the entries by customer account number. If there are two or more entries for a customer, these are sorted by document type and then document number. The second section lists the General Ledger distributions by code and account number. The third section is a Posting Error Report that identifies any error that ACCPAC Plus was not able to transfer to another batch, such as a deleted entry. Errors transferred to a new batch are identified by their original batch and entry numbers. New batches generated by ACCPAC Plus are identified by type, Invoice or Cash, and batch number.

Erin and Joan also want to see the posting journals sorted by document number as part of their control procedures for invoice numbers.

❏ Select: `6. Print invoice posting journal`

❏ Select: `Edit`

❏ Press: [Enter] twice to accept the Posting sequence numbers.

ACCPAC Plus will display an option box.

```
Sort journal by
Customer number
Document date
Document number
```

❏ Move the selector bar to `Document number`

❏ Press: [Enter]

❏ Press: [Esc] to indicate that the entry is complete.

❏ Select: `Print`

When the posting journal has been printed, you can clear the posting data.

❏ Select: `Yes`

❏ Press: [Esc] twice to return to the ACCPAC Accounts Receivable Master Menu.

CUSTOMER TRANSACTION INQUIRY

You can display customer account details on the screen.

❑ Select: `2. Inquiries`

❑ Select: `2. Display customer transactions`

An option box will appear on the left side of the screen.

```
Screens

Current Transactions
Historical Transactions
Age Transactions by Due Date
Age Company Grand Total
```

The "Current Transactions" option will display details that are either outstanding or paid but not yet cleared. The "Historical Transactions" option will display fully paid details that have been cleared and transferred to the historical file. If you are using Version 6.0B, you can also display aged statistics on the screen for current transactions by selecting either "Age Transactions by Due Date" or "Age Company Grand Total". E. & J. Enterprises has not yet entered data to record the payment of any invoices.

❑ Select: `Current Transactions`

❑ Type: `1010` in the Customer no. field.

❑ Press: [Enter]

The screen (Figure 15–3) will display summarized information for the account of PerCorp Inc. It shows the last date of activity (invoice, payment, or adjustment), the last statement date, last invoice date, and the last payment date. It shows the sales to date for the year, and the last year sales. The final information displayed is the number of outstanding invoices and their balance. There are two outstanding invoices for a total of $5,705.00.

The cursor will be in the "Starting date" field. To display the details of the transactions starting from a certain date you type in the date and press **Enter**.

Figure 15–3

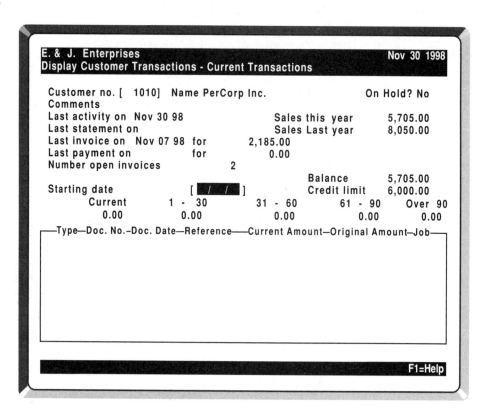

```
┌─────────────────────────────────────────────────────────────────────┐
│ E. & J. Enterprises                                    Nov 30 1998    │
│ Display Customer Transactions - Current Transactions                  │
│                                                                        │
│  Customer no. [  1010]  Name PerCorp Inc.              On Hold? No    │
│  Comments                                                              │
│  Last activity on  Nov 30 98           Sales this year     5,705.00   │
│  Last statement on                     Sales Last year     8,050.00   │
│  Last invoice on   Nov 07 98  for         2,185.00                    │
│  Last payment on            for              0.00                     │
│  Number open invoices              2                                  │
│                                        Balance            5,705.00    │
│  Starting date           [ ▓ / ▓ ]     Credit limit       6,000.00    │
│       Current       1 - 30      31 - 60      61 - 90     Over 90      │
│        0.00          0.00         0.00         0.00        0.00       │
│ ─Type─Doc. No.─Doc. Date─Reference──Current Amount─Original Amount─Job─│
│ ┌───────────────────────────────────────────────────────────────────┐ │
│ │                                                                   │ │
│ │                                                                   │ │
│ │                                                                   │ │
│ │                                                                   │ │
│ │                                                                   │ │
│ └───────────────────────────────────────────────────────────────────┘ │
│                                                          F1=Help       │
└─────────────────────────────────────────────────────────────────────┘
```

❑ Type: `100198` for October 1, 1998.

❑ Press: [Enter]

The lower portion of the screen will display a one-line summary for each detail posted to the Accounts Receivable for PerCorp Inc. between October 1, 1998 and November 30, 1998. Invoices 1017 and 1019 have been posted to PerCorp Inc.'s account.

```
┌──────────────────────────────────────────────────────────────────┐
│  View       Select      Previous customer      Next customer      │
└──────────────────────────────────────────────────────────────────┘
```

The option box allows you to "Select" another customer by customer number, or to display information for the "Previous customer" or the "Next customer". You can also display more complete details for each transaction.

❑ Select: `View`

The option box will disappear and the selector bar will highlight the first transaction, invoice 1017.

❑ Press: [Enter]

ACCPAC Plus will display all of the information concerning this invoice as shown in Figure 15–4. Since this invoice is unpaid, the "Last activity on" date is October 31, 1998, the date of the original invoice.

Figure 15–4

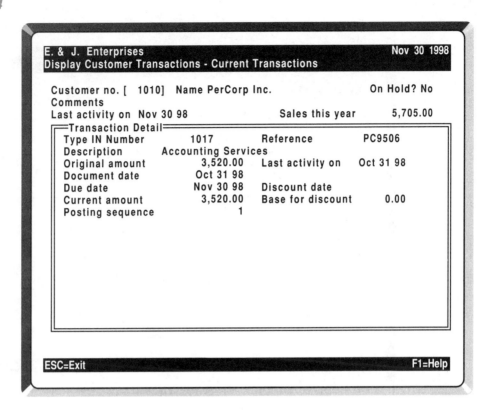

```
┌──────────────────────────────────────────────────────────────────┐
│ E. & J. Enterprises                                    Nov 30 1998 │
│ Display Customer Transactions - Current Transactions               │
├──────────────────────────────────────────────────────────────────┤
│                                                                    │
│   Customer no. [  1010]  Name PerCorp Inc.          On Hold? No    │
│   Comments                                                         │
│   Last activity on  Nov 30 98           Sales this year   5,705.00 │
│   ┌─Transaction Detail─────────────────────────────────────────┐  │
│   │ Type IN Number        1017      Reference        PC9506     │  │
│   │ Description        Accounting Services                      │  │
│   │ Original amount        3,520.00  Last activity on  Oct 31 98│  │
│   │ Document date         Oct 31 98                             │  │
│   │ Due date              Nov 30 98  Discount date              │  │
│   │ Current amount         3,520.00  Base for discount    0.00  │  │
│   │ Posting sequence             1                              │  │
│   │                                                             │  │
│   └─────────────────────────────────────────────────────────────┘ │
│                                                                    │
│ ESC=Exit                                                  F1=Help  │
└──────────────────────────────────────────────────────────────────┘
```

❏ Press: [Esc] to return to the selection box.

❏ Press: [Esc] to return to the option box.

❏ Select: Previous customer

❏ Type: 100198

❏ Press: [Enter]

The screen will display the information for Evans Ltd., customer number 1000.

❏ Press: [Esc] four times to return to the ACCPAC Accounts Receivable Master Menu.

CUSTOMER TRANSACTION REPORT

In addition to displaying the transactions for selected customers you can also print a transaction report.

❏ Select: 4. Reports

❏ Select: 3. Analysis reports

❏ Select: 3. Customer transactions to display the Customer Transactions screen, Figure 15–5.

Figure 15–5

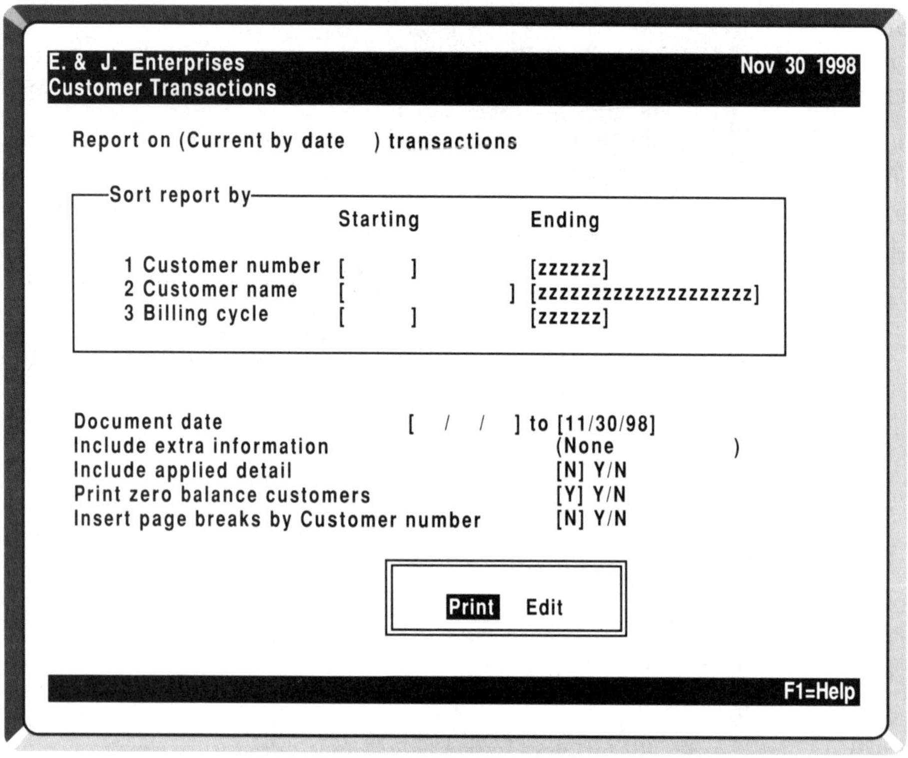

```
┌────────────────────────────────────────────────────────────┐
│ E. & J. Enterprises                              Nov 30 1998 │
│ Customer Transactions                                        │
│                                                              │
│   Report on (Current by date   ) transactions               │
│                                                              │
│    ┌─Sort report by──────────────────────────────────────┐  │
│    │              Starting        Ending                  │  │
│    │                                                       │  │
│    │  1 Customer number  [     ]    [zzzzzz]               │  │
│    │  2 Customer name    [       ]  [zzzzzzzzzzzzzzzzzzzz]  │  │
│    │  3 Billing cycle    [     ]    [zzzzzz]               │  │
│    └───────────────────────────────────────────────────────┘ │
│                                                              │
│   Document date                  [  /  /  ] to [11/30/98]    │
│   Include extra information               (None          )   │
│   Include applied detail                  [N] Y/N            │
│   Print zero balance customers            [Y] Y/N            │
│   Insert page breaks by Customer number   [N] Y/N            │
│                                                              │
│                        ┌──────────────────┐                 │
│                        │  Print   Edit     │                 │
│                        └──────────────────┘                 │
│                                                              │
│                                                    F1=Help   │
└────────────────────────────────────────────────────────────┘
```

❑ Select: Edit

You can print the report for current transactions either by date or by document number. You may also print a report that includes historical information.

❑ Select: Current by date

The report can be sorted by up to three variables. To change the sorting you move the selector bar to the variable you wish to change and press **Enter**. You then select a new variable from the "Choices" option box and enter the appropriate information in the starting and ending fields. Using these steps you could sort the report by territory and customer number, or report group and customer name. The defaults shown on the screen print all customers in order of customer number.

❑ Press: [Esc] to move the cursor to the Document date field.

If you are using Version 6.0A, the first date field will display the default date "01/01/80". This date is a DOS default date that is displayed by ACCPAC Plus to ensure that all transactions are included in the report.

❑ Type: 090198 for September 1, 1998.

❑ Press: [Enter]

The second date field displays "11/30/98", the date you entered in the New date field of the title screen.

❑ Press: Enter

You can include extra information in the report.

```
Extra Information

Contact/phone/credit
Space for comments
All of the above
None
```

Erin has decided to review all customers over their credit limit and may contact these companies.

❑ Select: Contact/phone/credit

❑ Press: Enter so that the report does not include applied detail.

❑ Type: N in the Print zero balance customer's field.

❑ Press: Enter

❑ Press: Esc to indicate that the entry is complete.

❑ Select: Print

Review your printed report. The "c" to the right of the Customer Balance indicates the customer has exceeded their credit limit. The "Days Del" column tells you the number of days that a customer is delinquent in making a payment on an invoice. Erin will contact Mr. Nightingale at Hibou Co. about invoice 1012 that is 56 days past due but will not worry about the other customers over their credit limits until the cash receipts have been posted.

PRINTING THE AGED TRIAL BALANCE

❑ Select: 2. Aged trial balance

If you are using Version 6.0A, you can only calculate balances as of the date entered in the next field.

If you are using Version 6.0B, you have two choices for the calculation type. You could select Age as of to age all outstanding transactions, including those dated after the date displayed. These future-dated transactions are shown as current on the printed report. You could select Calculate as of to include only those transactions dated before the date displayed.

❑ Select: Calculate as of

The date field should show 11/30/98, the date that you entered in the New date field on the title screen. You could change this date by typing the desired date and pressing **Enter**. If you change the date you would not be able to sort the report by customer balance.

❏ Press: [Enter] to accept 11/30/98 as the date.

Figure 15–6

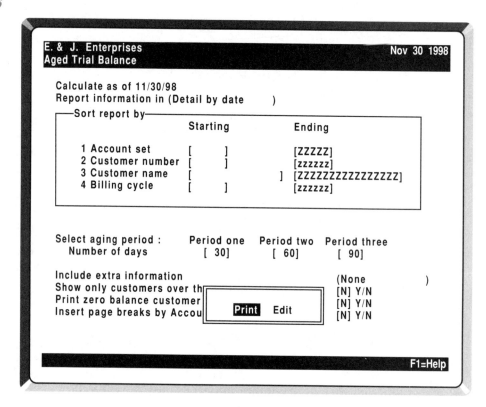

❏ Select: Edit

The Report Type option box allows you to the amount of information included in the report for each customer. If you select either Detail by date or Detail by document , the report will include one line for each transaction.

❏ Select: Summary for the report type.

The Sort report by option box allows you to control which customers are included in the report and the order in which they are printed. If you are using Version 6.0A, this option box will be slightly different in appearance but is used in the same way as described below for Version 6.0B.

ACCPAC Plus allows you to select and sort customers by up to four variables from a list of ten possible variables. For example, you could choose to have the report sorted by salesperson, territory, customer name and customer number, and to include all customers in the report. As E. & J. Enterprises has a short customer list, Joan wants to print a report for all customers sorted by customer number.

❏ Move the selector bar to 1.

❏ Press: [Enter]

The ten variables that you can use for selecting and sorting customers will be displayed in the "Choices" box. Erin wants the report to be sorted by customer number.

❑ Move the selector bar to `Customer number`

❑ Press: [Enter]

❑ Press: [Enter] in the Starting and Ending fields to instruct ACCPAC Plus to list all the Accounts Receivable accounts.

As each customer has a unique customer number, it is not necessary to enter further choices. All the customers will be included in the report.

❑ Press: [Esc] to move the cursor to `Select aging period` section.

❑ Press: [Enter] three times to accept the defaults of 30, 60, and 90 days.

❑ Select: `Contact/Phone/Credit` for extra information.

❑ Press: [Enter] to accept the default "N" in the `Show only customers over their credit limit` field.

Suppress the printing of accounts with zero balances.

❑ Type: `N`

❑ Press: [Enter]

❑ Press: [Enter] to accept no page breaks between customers.

❑ Select: `Print`

Note how the report flags customers who exceed their credit limits.

TAX TRACKING

The Tax Tracking report provides documentation for the sales tax and value added tax that you have charged customers. When you created the distribution codes, you indicated which codes would accumulate information for this report. The report shows all tax information recorded since the last time the report was printed and cleared.

❑ Select: `5. Tax tracking`

The default settings will print a report including each distribution for which tax tracking was specified. The report will provide detailed information for each transaction allocated to a tax tracking distribution. E. & J. Enterprises specified tax tracking for sales tax and value added tax.

If you wished to change the defaults, you would select "Edit", enter the changes and then press **Escape**.

❑ Select: `Print`

After the report is printed the following message will appear on the screen:

```
┌─────────────────────────────────────────────────────────┐
│                                                           │
│            Do you want to clear all tax tracking records  │
│                   within the specified range?            │
│                                                           │
│                      Yes       No                         │
│                                                           │
└─────────────────────────────────────────────────────────┘
```

Review the Tax Tracking Report. If it is clearly printed you would file it and then clear the records.

❑ Select: Yes

❑ Press: [Esc]   twice to return to the ACCPAC Accounts Receivable Master Menu.

BATCH STATUS INQUIRY

The third option on the Inquiries menu is "Display batch status". This option displays batch activity since the last time batch status data was cleared.

❑ Select: 2. Inquiries

❑ Select: 3. Display batch status

An option box appears allowing you to choose either Invoice, Cash, or Adjustment batches.

❑ Select: Invoice Batches

Information is displayed in two sections on the screen as shown in Figure 15–7. The lower portion of the screen summarizes batch information by the type of batch and the batch status. For E. & J. Enterprises two invoice batches have been "Entered" and "Posted" with 10 entries totalling $16,951.25.

The upper portion of the screen displays information on each batch. If you had five batches you would move the selector bar down to display the fifth batch.

❑ Press: [Esc]

❑ Select: Cash Batches

The display will show that one cash batch totalling $201.25 has been generated and posted by ACCPAC Plus. This is the batch generated when the transactions involving payments were posted.

❑ Press: [Esc]   three times to return to the ACCPAC Accounts Receivable Master Menu.

❑ Quit ACCPAC Plus.

❑ Back up your data files.

Figure 15–7

```
┌─────────────────────────────────────────────────────────────────────┐
│ E. & J. Enterprises                                    Nov 30  1998   │
│ Display Batch Status - Invoice Batches                                │
│ Batch status for (Invoice Batches  )                                  │
│                                                                       │
│  ┌Batch══No. of═══════════════Date═══════Date Last═══════════════     │
│   Number Entries    Batch Total  Created    Accessed  Status  Type    │
│  ┌──────────────────────────────────────────────────────────────┐    │
│  │    1      3       6,365.00    Nov 01 98  Nov 01 98  Posted  Entered │
│      Description: Invoices posted to G/L                              │
│       2      7      10,586.25    Nov 30 98  Nov 30 98  Posted  Entered │
│      Description: November 1998 Invoices                              │
│                                                                       │
│                                                                       │
│  ──────────────────────────────────────────────────────────────     │
│  Type     Total amount Entrs. Batches  Status Total amount Entrs. Batches │
│  Entered    16,951.25   10      2      Open       0.00     0      0   │
│  Retrieved       0.00    0      0      Printed    0.00     0      0   │
│  Imported        0.00    0      0      Deleted    0.00     0      0   │
│  Recurring       0.00    0      0      Posted  16,951.25  10      2   │
│  Interest        0.00    0      0                                     │
│  Generated       0.00    0      0                                     │
│ ESC=Exit   CURSOR KEYS=Scroll                              F1=Help    │
└─────────────────────────────────────────────────────────────────────┘
```

REVIEW QUESTIONS

1. What happens if you try to enter a customer number that has not been assigned to a customer?
2. What happens if you fail to type a document number when recording an invoice?
3. Why is it important to complete the Reference field when entering an invoice?
4. How do you correct a typing error before you have accepted the information?
5. If you have accepted incorrect information in recording an invoice, how do you correct the error?
6. Why should you print the Invoice Batch Listing before posting it?
7. Describe the procedure used to record a cash sale through the Accounts Receivable.
8. What would happen if you recorded a duplicate reference in the "Check number" field when recording a payment?
9. What is the purpose of the Aged Trial Balance?
10. What is the purpose of the Batch Status Inquiry?

EXERCISE

1. Create a new batch using November 30, 1998 as the New date, to record the following invoices for the company you have set up:

    a) November 2, Barilak & Associates, Production software, purchase order Bar101, Invoice A008, $1000 charge to sales plus $50 sales tax and $100 value added tax.
    b) November 7, Dillingham & Co., P.O. 13579, graphics software, Invoice A009 in the amount of $750 charged to sales plus $37.50 sales tax and $75 value added tax.
    c) November 13, H. Bazelton, P.O. HG 235 for computer and printer, Invoice A010, $2,500 charge to sales plus $125 sales tax and $250 value added tax.
    d) November 16, Graves & Dawn, P.O. ADV400 for accounting services, Invoice A011 for $350, charge to fees.
    e) November 20, Dillingham & Co., P.O. 13600 for graphics adaptor, Invoice A012, for $500 charge to sales plus $25 sales tax and $50 value added tax.
    f) The cash sale of 4 printer ribbons to Lisa Barb for $20, plus $1 sales tax and $2 value added tax, on November 25. Recorded on Invoice A013.

2. Print the new invoice and review it for errors. Correct any errors and then print a revised Invoice Batch Listing.
3. Once you are satisfied that the batch reflects the above information exactly, post it to the Accounts Receivable ledger. Print two different Invoice Posting Journals and clear the posting data after printing the second report.
4. Print the Aged Trial Balance.
5. Back up your data disk.

CHAPTER

16 Cash Receipts

You will now record cash payments received by E. & J. Enterprises. Assume that the amounts recorded are correct. These payments are representative and are not intended to illustrate a complete month's work.

❏ Enter the commands necessary to display the ACCPAC Plus Start Menu.

❏ Select: `A/R E. & J. Enterprises`

❏ Press: [Enter] to accept `11/30/98` as the New date.

RECORDING CASH PAYMENTS

❏ Select: `3. Transaction processing` from the ACCPAC Accounts Receivable Master Menu.

❏ Select: `2. Cash processing`

ACCPAC Plus will display the Cash Processing Menu, which is almost identical to the Invoice Processing Menu that you used in Chapter 15.

❏ Select: `1. Add/modify/delete cash batches`

The Add/Modify/Delete Cash Batches screen (Figure 16–1) will appear.

Figure 16–1

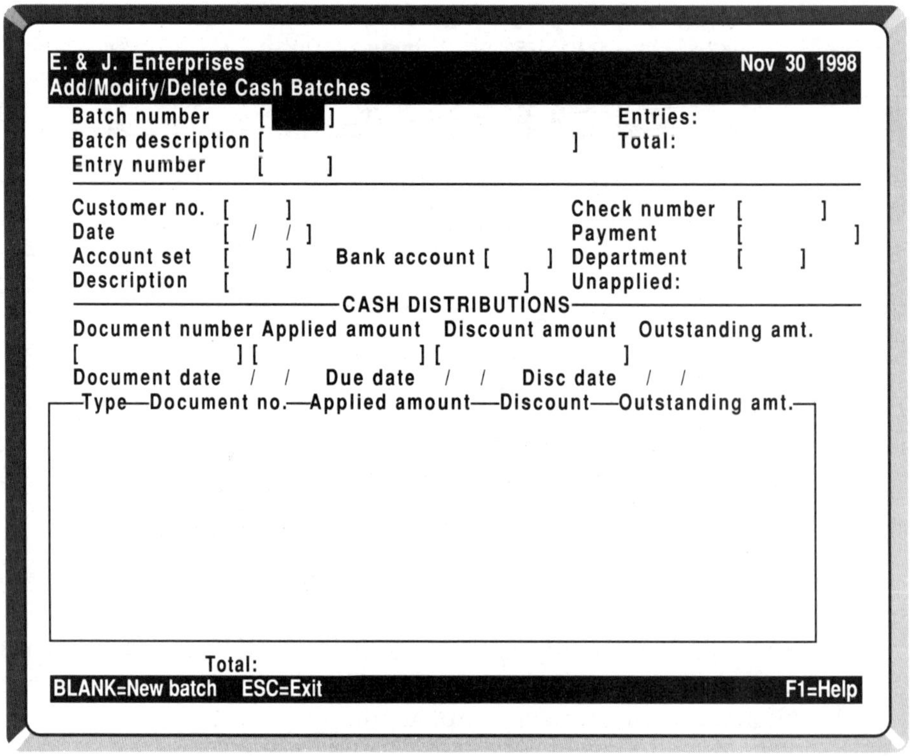

```
┌─────────────────────────────────────────────────────────────────────┐
│ E. & J. Enterprises                               Nov 30 1998         │
│ Add/Modify/Delete Cash Batches                                        │
│   Batch number      [      ]                      Entries:            │
│   Batch description [                    ]        Total:              │
│   Entry number      [      ]                                          │
│   ─────────────────────────────────────────────────────────────────  │
│   Customer no.  [     ]                    Check number  [       ]    │
│   Date          [  /  / ]                  Payment       [        ]   │
│   Account set   [    ]   Bank account [     ]  Department [     ]      │
│   Description   [                         ]  Unapplied:               │
│   ─────────────────────CASH DISTRIBUTIONS──────────────────────────   │
│   Document number Applied amount  Discount amount  Outstanding amt.   │
│   [           ] [            ] [                 ]                     │
│   Document date  /  /   Due date  /  /   Disc date  /  /              │
│   ┌─Type─Document no.─Applied amount─Discount─Outstanding amt.─┐       │
│   │                                                            │       │
│   │                                                            │       │
│   │                                                            │       │
│   │                                                            │       │
│   │                                                            │       │
│   │                                                            │       │
│   └────────────────────────────────────────────────────────────┘     │
│              Total:                                                   │
│ BLANK=New batch   ESC=Exit                              F1=Help       │
└─────────────────────────────────────────────────────────────────────┘
```

RECORDING A SINGLE INVOICE PAYMENT

The first payment you will record is a $339 payment from Evans Ltd. for invoice 1018. Their check, number ABC123, arrived Nov. 10, 1998.

❑ Press: [Enter] in the blank `Batch number` field to indicate that you want to create a new Cash Batch.

```
┌─────────────────────────────────────────────┐
│ ┌─────────────────────────────────────────┐ │
│ │   Are you sure you want to create a new batch? │ │
│ │                                         │ │
│ │             Yes        No               │ │
│ └─────────────────────────────────────────┘ │
└─────────────────────────────────────────────┘
```

❑ Select: `Yes`

ACCPAC Plus will select the next available batch number (2) and insert the number in the Batch number field. Remember that a Cash Batch was created and posted for the cash sales recorded in Chapter 15. The cursor then will move to the Batch description field.

❑ Type: `Nov. 1998 Cash Receipts`

❑ Press: [Enter]

❑ Press: [Enter] to accept `1` as the Entry number.

You should refer to the Aged Trial Balance report when you post payments to ensure that you properly credit client payments.

❑ Type: `1000` in the `Customer no.` field.

❑ Press: [Enter]

The Check number field documents the customer's check number and is an important part of the audit trail. You must complete this field before you can proceed.

❑ Type: `ABC123`

❑ Press: [Enter]

❑ Type: `111098` in the `Date` field.

❑ Press: [Enter]

❑ Type: `339.00` in the `Payment` field.

❑ Press: [Enter]

❑ Press: [Enter] to accept `Account set 1`

If there were a special note that you wanted to record concerning the receipt of the check you could do so in the description field. An example might be the receipt of a check from company A when the billing went to company B if company A was paying company B's bills. In this case, no comment is necessary.

❑ Press: [Enter]

The outstanding invoice for Evans Ltd. will appear in the lower portion of the screen as shown in Figure 16–2.

Figure 16-2

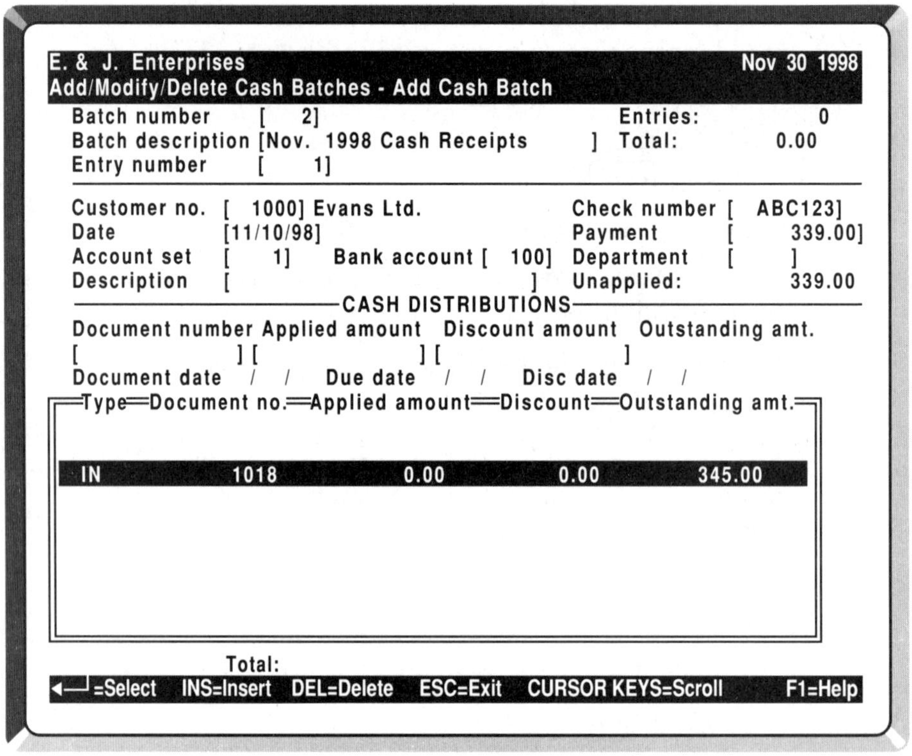

```
┌────────────────────────────────────────────────────────────────────┐
│ E. & J. Enterprises                                     Nov 30 1998  │
│ Add/Modify/Delete Cash Batches - Add Cash Batch                      │
│    Batch number      [    2]                    Entries:         0   │
│    Batch description [Nov. 1998 Cash Receipts    ]  Total:    0.00   │
│    Entry number      [    1]                                         │
│    ─────────────────────────────────────────────────────────────    │
│    Customer no.  [  1000] Evans Ltd.        Check number [  ABC123]  │
│    Date          [11/10/98]                 Payment      [   339.00] │
│    Account set   [   1]   Bank account [  100]  Department  [    ]   │
│    Description   [                        ] Unapplied:      339.00   │
│    ─────────────────────CASH DISTRIBUTIONS────────────────────────   │
│    Document number Applied amount  Discount amount  Outstanding amt. │
│    [          ] [              ] [                     ]              │
│    Document date   /   /   Due date   /   /   Disc date   /   /      │
│  ┌─Type══Document no.══Applied amount══Discount══Outstanding amt.─┐  │
│  │                                                                 │  │
│  │  IN          1018          0.00         0.00         345.00     │  │
│  │                                                                 │  │
│  │                                                                 │  │
│  │                                                                 │  │
│  │                                                                 │  │
│  │                                                                 │  │
│  └─────────────────────────────────────────────────────────────────┘│
│              Total:                                                  │
│  ◄──┘=Select  INS=Insert  DEL=Delete  ESC=Exit  CURSOR KEYS=Scroll  F1=Help │
└────────────────────────────────────────────────────────────────────┘
```

The selector bar will be on the line for invoice number "1018".

❑ Press: [Enter] to indicate that the payment will be applied to invoice 1018.

ACCPAC Plus will show "339.00" in the Applied amount field.

❑ Press: [Enter] to accept the amount.

The cursor will move to the Discount amount field which displays "6.00", the amount calculated by ACCPAC Plus as the discount on this invoice.

❑ Press: [Enter] to accept the discount.

The selector bar will move down to highlight the next item or blank line in the information box. Note that the payment amount in the upper half of the screen was for $339.00 and that the Total at the bottom of the screen also now reads $339.00. This indicates that the payment has been fully allocated.

❑ Press: [Esc]

```
┌─────────────────────────────────────────────────────┐
│                                                       │
│      Save entry    Header    Detail    Cancel         │
│                                                       │
└─────────────────────────────────────────────────────┘
```

You now have the option of saving the entry, cancelling the entry, or changing either the Header or Detail. Review the information displayed on the screen. If you have an error in the upper portion of the screen, select "Header" to make corrections. If there is an error in the lower portion of the screen, select "Detail". Once there are no errors,

❏ Select: `Save entry`

ACCPAC Plus will allow you to exit from the customer's cash distributions portion of the screen when the total applied does not equal the payment amount. You can apply the unapplied amount later, as described in the Reconcile Accounts section later in Chapter 17.

The system will allow you to make partial payments that have an invoice number totally different from the ones your company uses when you cannot identify what is being paid. ACCPAC Plus will also allow you to record an overpayment which results in a credit for that particular invoice number.

RECORDING A MULTIPLE-INVOICE PAYMENT

The second payment you will record is check #H005678 for $2,920 from Hibou Co. received Nov. 16, 1998 in payment for invoices 1016 and 1020.

❏ Type: `1040` in the `Customer no.` field.

❏ Press: [Enter]

❏ Enter the check number, date received, payment amount, and account set in the proper fields.

❏ Press: [Enter] to leave the description blank.

When you have finished, ACCPAC Plus will display the CASH DISTRIBUTIONS screen for Hibou Co. (Figure 16–3).

Figure 16–3

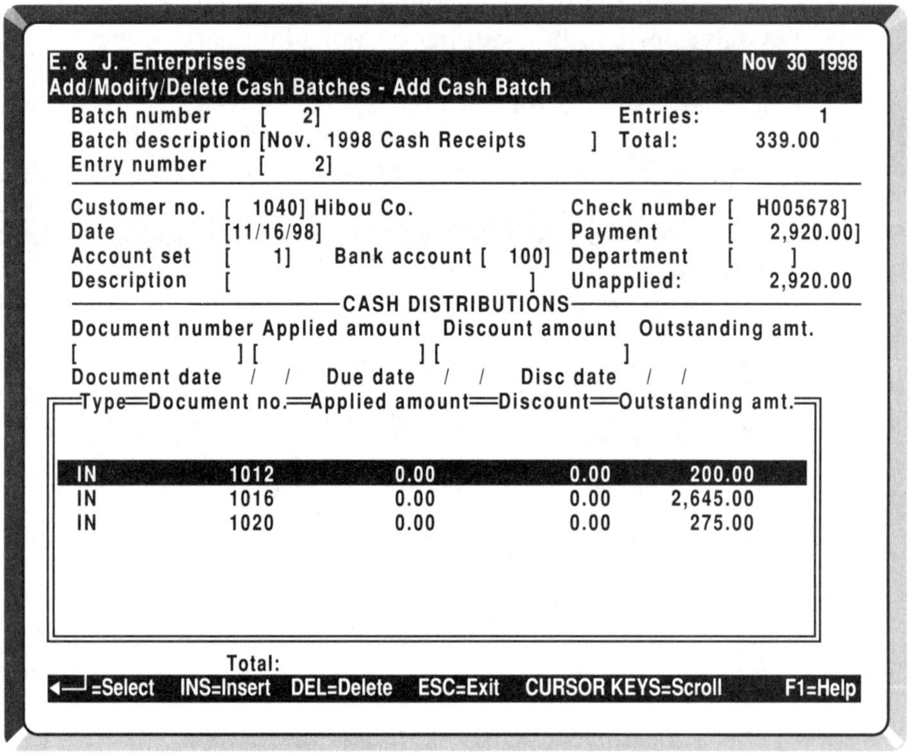

```
┌──────────────────────────────────────────────────────────────────────┐
│ E. & J. Enterprises                                       Nov 30 1998  │
│ Add/Modify/Delete Cash Batches - Add Cash Batch                        │
│   Batch number    [    2]                      Entries:            1   │
│   Batch description [Nov. 1998 Cash Receipts      ]  Total:    339.00  │
│   Entry number    [    2]                                              │
│  ───────────────────────────────────────────────────────────────────  │
│   Customer no.  [  1040] Hibou Co.         Check number [  H005678]    │
│   Date          [11/16/98]                 Payment      [   2,920.00]  │
│   Account set   [    1]   Bank account [  100] Department [    ]       │
│   Description   [                         ] Unapplied:     2,920.00    │
│  ──────────────────────────CASH DISTRIBUTIONS─────────────────────     │
│   Document number Applied amount  Discount amount   Outstanding amt.   │
│   [           ] [                ] [                ]                   │
│   Document date   /  /   Due date   /  /   Disc date   /  /            │
│  ┌═Type═Document no.═Applied amount═Discount═Outstanding amt.═┐        │
│  │                                                            │        │
│  │  IN       1012         0.00         0.00       200.00      │        │
│  │  IN       1016         0.00         0.00     2,645.00      │        │
│  │  IN       1020         0.00         0.00       275.00      │        │
│  │                                                            │        │
│  │                                                            │        │
│  └────────────────────────────────────────────────────────────┘      │
│            Total:                                                      │
│  ◄──┘=Select  INS=Insert  DEL=Delete  ESC=Exit  CURSOR KEYS=Scroll  F1=Help │
└──────────────────────────────────────────────────────────────────────┘
```

❑   Move the selector bar to invoice 1016.

❑   Press: [Enter]

ACCPAC Plus is now ready to apply the payment to invoice number 1016, as indicated by "1016" displayed in the Document number field. The cursor will be in the Applied amount field, which will display the total amount of the invoice ("2645.00") since this amount is less than the total payment.

❑   Press: [Enter] to apply this amount to invoice number 1016.

The cursor will move to the Discount amount field which displays "0.00" as the payment was received later than the discount date of October 31, 1998.

❑   Press: [Enter] to indicate that no discount applies to this invoice.

Note that the total line at the bottom of the screen has been updated to show 2,645.00 in the Applied amount column. The selector bar will have moved to the next invoice listed, invoice 1020. Since invoice 1020 was the other invoice paid,

❑   Press: [Enter]

The cursor will move to the Applied amount field and display the amount $275.00. This is the full amount of invoice 1020 and, in fact, is the correct amount required to complete the transaction.

❑   Press: [Enter] to accept "275.00" as the Applied amount.

❑   Press: [Enter] to accept "0.00" as the Discount amount.

The total of invoices paid, as shown in the Applied amount column, will equal the payment ($2,920).

❏ Press: [Esc] to indicate that the cash distribution is complete.

Figure 16–4

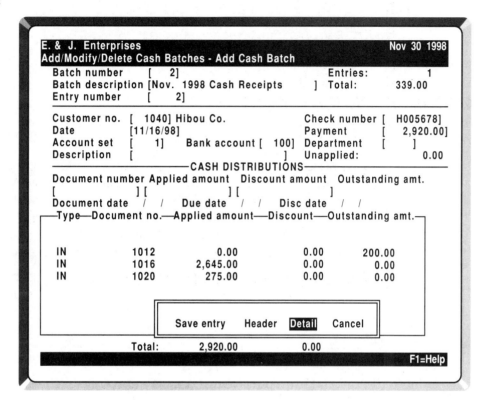

```
E. & J. Enterprises                                         Nov 30 1998
Add/Modify/Delete Cash Batches - Add Cash Batch
   Batch number      [    2]                      Entries:          1
   Batch description [Nov. 1998 Cash Receipts    ] Total:      339.00
   Entry number      [    2]

   Customer no.  [  1040] Hibou Co.         Check number [   H005678]
   Date          [11/16/98]                Payment      [   2,920.00]
   Account set   [    1]   Bank account [   100] Department [    ]
   Description   [                           ] Unapplied:       0.00
   ───────────────────────CASH DISTRIBUTIONS───────────────────
   Document number Applied amount  Discount amount  Outstanding amt.
   [            ] [              ] [                           ]
   Document date   /  /  Due date   /  /  Disc date   /  /
   ┌─Type─Document no.─Applied amount─Discount─Outstanding amt.─┐
   │                                                            │
   │    IN        1012         0.00         0.00      200.00    │
   │    IN        1016     2,645.00         0.00        0.00    │
   │    IN        1020       275.00         0.00        0.00    │
   │                                                            │
   │              ┌──────────────────────────────────────┐     │
   │              │ Save entry   Header   Detail  Cancel  │     │
   │              └──────────────────────────────────────┘     │
   └────────────────────────────────────────────────────────────┘
          Total:       2,920.00              0.00
                                                         F1=Help
```

If the information on your screen does not agree with Figure 16–4, now is the time to make corrections. You would select "Header" if the error is in the upper portion of the screen or "Detail" if the error is in the Cash Distributions. If there are no errors,

❏ Select: Save entry

RECORDING A PARTIAL PAYMENT

For some reason, Mukrob Industries Inc. sent E. & J. Enterprises only a partial payment (check #981 for $2,500) for invoice 1022. The check arrived on November 28, 1998.

❏ Enter the appropriate information in the Header portion of the screen typing "Partial payment" in the description field.

❏ Select: Invoice 1022

❏ Press: [Enter] to accept the automatic allocation of ''2500.00'' in the Applied amount field.

The cursor will move to the zero in the Discount field.

❏ Press: [Enter]

❏ Press: [Esc] to accept the cash application.

❏ Select: Save entry

RECORDING PREPAYMENTS

NorWest Export Co. has decided to purchase a specialized software package with a retail price of $4,000 plus $200 sales tax and $400 value added tax. Since the software is extremely specialized, E. & J. Enterprises will probably not be able to sell it to another client should NorWest Export Co. fail to complete the purchase. Furthermore, NorWest Export Co. has a credit limit of only $2,000. To eliminate the risk of loss, Erin asked NorWest Export Co. to pay $3,000 when it orders the software. NorWest Export Co. agreed. On November 19, 1998, E. & J. Enterprises received the purchase order (NWE 621) with a check for $3,000.

❏ Enter the following information for entry 4: NorWest Export Co., customer number 1020, check number NWE6581 $3,000, received November 19, 1999, Account set 1.

❏ Type: Prepayment re P.O. NWE621 in the Description field.

❏ Press: [Enter]

To indicate that the amount being paid is not to be applied to an invoice displayed in the information box,

❏ Press: [INSERT]

If an invoice number is assigned for this transaction, you could enter that invoice number in the document number field. When the invoice batch is entered and posted later, ACCPAC Plus will automatically apply the prepayment to the outstanding amount of the invoice but will not calculate and apply any discounts.

If the invoice number is not known, a control number should be entered in the document number field. After both the invoice and the check have been posted you would then use the Cash Processing Menu to reconcile the posted prepayment to the posted invoice as described in Chapter 17.

In this example, you do not know what the invoice number will be so you must enter a control number. Use NorWest Export Co.'s purchase order number as the control number.

❏ Type: NWE621

❏ Press: [Enter]

The cursor will move to the Applied amount field and the amount $3,000.00 will appear.

- ❑ Press: Enter

- ❑ Press: Enter again to accept "0.00" as the amount of the discount.

Note that the document type displayed is "UP", unallocated payment. The prepayment amount of $3,000.00 now appears with a minus sign after indicating that the amount is a credit.

- ❑ Press: Esc

Figure 16–5

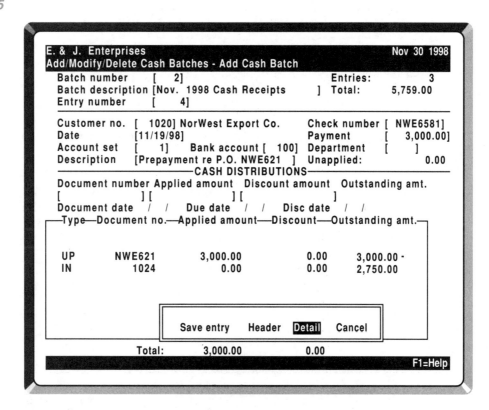

```
E. & J. Enterprises                                          Nov 30 1998
Add/Modify/Delete Cash Batches - Add Cash Batch
  Batch number      [    2]                    Entries:         3
  Batch description [Nov. 1998 Cash Receipts  ] Total:     5,759.00
  Entry number      [    4]
  ─────────────────────────────────────────────────────────────────
  Customer no.  [  1020] NorWest Export Co.   Check number [ NWE6581]
  Date          [11/19/98]                    Payment      [  3,000.00]
  Account set   [   1]   Bank account [  100]  Department   [    ]
  Description   [Prepayment re P.O. NWE621  ]  Unapplied:       0.00
  ─────────────────────────CASH DISTRIBUTIONS───────────────────────
  Document number Applied amount  Discount amount  Outstanding amt.
  [          ] [              ] [                ]
  Document date   /  /   Due date   /  /   Disc date   /  /
  ─Type─Document no.─Applied amount──Discount──Outstanding amt.─┐

   UP      NWE621        3,000.00        0.00     3,000.00 -
   IN        1024            0.00        0.00     2,750.00


           ┌─────────────────────────────────────────────┐
           │  Save entry    Header   Detail    Cancel     │
           └─────────────────────────────────────────────┘
         Total:     3,000.00                0.00
  ─────────────────────────────────────────────────────────────────
                                                          F1=Help
```

Compare your screen with that shown in Figure 16–5. If there is an error, select "Header" or "Detail" as required and then edit the prepayment.

When you are sure that you have made no errors,

- ❑ Select: Save entry

RECORDING BALANCE-FORWARD ACCOUNTS

PerCorp Inc. is the only customer with a balance-forward account. On Nov. 30, 1998, E. & J. Enterprises received check #00126 for $2,000 from PerCorp Inc.

- ❑ Enter the information for this transaction in the top half of the data-entry screen.

After you enter the description, the cursor will move to the Invoice number field in the BALANCE FORWARD ACCOUNTS section of the screen. If you wished to apply the payment to a specific invoice, you would look up the invoice number and enter it in this field. If the invoice number field is left blank, ACCPAC Plus will apply the amount of the payment starting with the oldest outstanding invoice or debit note.

❑ Press: [Enter] to leave the Invoice number field blank.

ACCPAC Plus will display the amount of the payment, and the cursor will move to the Discount field. Since no discounts apply to the outstanding invoices, this field will contain "0.00".

❑ Press: [Enter]

❑ Select: Save entry

RECORDING A MISCELLANEOUS CASH RECEIPT

E. & J. Enterprises has decided to use the Accounts Receivable to document all cash receipts. Occasionally, a company receives cash that is not related to an invoice sent to a customer and must document this. On November 26, Erin and Joan received a letter from their insurance agent informing them that they had been overcharged $37.50. The agent's check, INS0093, accompanied the letter.

❑ Use [SPACEBAR] or [DELETE] to erase the contents of the Customer no. field.

❑ Press: [Enter]

Figure 16–6

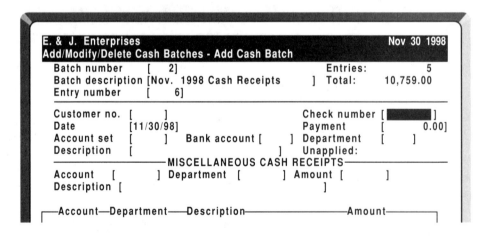

The display in the lower portion of the screen will change as shown in Figure 16–6. The "Header" portion of the screen will not be changed.

❑ Type: INS0093 in the Check number field.

❑ Press: [Enter]

❑ Type: `112698` in the `Date` field.

❑ Press: [Enter]

❑ Type: `37.50` in the `Payment` field.

❑ Press: [Enter]

❑ Press: [Enter] to leave the `Account set` field blank.

You must enter the General Ledger account number that is to be debited.

❑ Type: `100` in the `Bank account` field.

❑ Press: [Enter]

❑ Type: `Insurance rebate` in the `Description` field.

❑ Press: [Enter]

The MISCELLANEOUS CASH RECEIPTS portion of the screen is used to record the credit portion of the transaction. In this example, the credit would be made to General Ledger account number 300, Prepaid Expenses.

❑ Type: `300` in the `Account` field.

❑ Press: [Enter]

The cursor will move to the Amount field to allow you to record the amount to be distributed to this account.

❑ Type: `37.50`

❑ Press: [Enter]

❑ Press: [Enter] again to leave the `Description` field blank.

❑ Press: [Esc] to indicate that the distribution is complete.

❑ Select: `Save entry`

❑ Press: [Esc] three times to return to the Cash Processing Menu.

PRINTING THE CASH BATCH LISTING

You have now finished recording the cash receipts. Before you can post these entries to the Accounts Receivable, you must print the Cash Batch Listing.

❑ Select: `4. Print cash batches` from the Cash Processing Menu.

ACCPAC Plus will display the Print Cash Batches screen.

❑ Select: `Print`

Compare your printout with the one shown in Table 16–1. The Cash Batch Listing arranges the transactions by entry number. It shows the check number, bank account number, account set, date, customer number and name, type of transaction, document number, discount, and check amount for each entry. It also gives the totals for the Discount and Amount columns.

For entry 4, note the "UP" in the type column to indicate that the transaction was an unallocated payment. For entry 5, both the type and document number columns are blank as this is a balance forward customer. In entry 6, the "300" in the Account column identifies the account to be credited in this miscellaneous cash receipt.

If your printout shows an error, use the "Add/modify/delete cash batches" option to make corrections. Then, print the Cash Batch again.

Table 16–1

```
Date: Nov 30 98    4:39pm              E. & J. Enterprises                        Page:   1
A/R Cash Batches

Batch number      :    2
Batch description :  Nov. 1998 Cash Receipts

Entry     Check   Bank  Bank  Acct            Cust.       Doc. No./    Job/          Discount
 No.        No.   Acct  Dept  Set  Date        No.  Tp   Acct  Dept Description                        Amount

  1       ABC123   100         1 Nov 10 98    1000  IN   1018                          6.00          339.00
          Customer Name : Evans Ltd.
          Description   :                                           Total :           6.00          339.00 *

  2       H005678  100         1 Nov 16 98    1040  IN   1016                          0.00        2,645.00
                                                    IN   1020                          0.00          275.00
          Customer Name : Hibou Co.
          Description   :                                           Total :           0.00        2,920.00 *

  3          981   100         1 Nov 28 98    1030  IN   1022                          0.00        2,500.00
          Customer Name : Mukrob Industries
          Description   : Partial Payment                           Total :           0.00        2,500.00 *

  4       NWE6581  100         1 Nov 19 98    1020  UP   NWE621                        0.00        3,000.00
          Customer Name : NorWest Export Co.
          Description   : Prepayment re P.O. NWE621                  Total :           0.00        3,000.00 *

  5        00126   100         1 Nov 30 98    1010                                     0.00        2,000.00
          Customer Name : PerCorp Inc.
          Description   : R. O. A.                                   Total :           0.00        2,000.00 *

  6       INS0093  100           Nov 26 98          300                                               37.50
          Customer Name :
          Description   : Insurance Rebate                           Total :           0.00           37.50 *


                                                                   Batch Total :      6.00       10,796.50
                                                                              ================   ================

6 transaction(s) printed.
```

POSTING TO THE ACCOUNTS RECEIVABLE LEDGER

Once the Cash Batch Listing has been printed, ACCPAC Plus will return to the Cash Processing Menu.

❑ Select: `5. Post cash batches`

The Post Cash Batches screen will appear displaying the following warning:

```
┌─────────────────────────────────────────────────────────────┐
│ ┌───────────────────────────────────────────────────────────┐ │
│ │          Warning! Back up data before proceeding.          │ │
│ │ This function will post entries in the selected range of batches. │ │
│ │                                                           │ │
│ │            Post        Edit        Cancel                 │ │
│ └───────────────────────────────────────────────────────────┘ │
└─────────────────────────────────────────────────────────────┘
```

❑ Back up your data files.

❑ Enter the commands to return to the Post Cash Batches Menu.

Since you now have a backup copy of your data, you may proceed with posting.

❑ Select: `Post`

❑ Press: [Enter] to continue when posting is complete.

ACCPAC Plus will return to the Cash Processing Menu.

PRINTING THE CASH POSTING JOURNAL

The Cash Posting Journal is very similar to the Cash Batch Listing you printed earlier (Table 16–1). However, you can choose to list information sequentially by customer number or check date or check number. This journal also includes a General Ledger Summary section.

❑ Select: `6. Print cash posting journal`

The defaults displayed on the screen will print a journal for posting sequences "1" and "2". Posting sequence "1" was automatically performed by ACCPAC Plus when you posted the invoice batch that included entries with cash payments. The journal will be sorted by customer number.

❑ Select: `Print`

After printing is complete, the following message will appear at the bottom of the screen:

```
┌─────────────────────────────────────────────────────────────┐
│ ┌───────────────────────────────────────────────────────────┐ │
│ │         Do you want to clear all posting journals          │ │
│ │                 within the specified range?                │ │
│ │                                                           │ │
│ │               Yes             No                          │ │
│ └───────────────────────────────────────────────────────────┘ │
└─────────────────────────────────────────────────────────────┘
```

❑ Type: `Y` to clear the journals and return to the Cash Processing Menu.

- ❑ Press: [Esc] twice to return to the ACCPAC Accounts Receivable Master Menu.

PRINTING THE AGED TRIAL BALANCE

- ❑ Select: `4. Reports`
- ❑ Select: `3. Analysis reports`
- ❑ Select: `2. Aged trial balance`
- ❑ Press: [Enter] to accept "11/30/98" as the date to use in calculating balances.
- ❑ Select: `Print` to print the default report.

Compare your printout of the Aged Trial Balance with that printed in Chapter 15. Note that three different codes now appear in the Type column: "IN" denotes an invoice that has been posted, "CA" refers to a cash entry, and "DS" refers to discounts. A minus sign following amounts with "CA" or "DS" in the TP field indicates that the amounts are credits. You would normally keep a copy of this version of the Aged Trial Balance report in your office, since it constitutes an excellent audit trail of invoice payments.

- ❑ Exit from ACCPAC Plus.
- ❑ Back up your data files.

REVIEW QUESTIONS

1. Describe the options available from the Cash Processing Menu.
2. When would you use the Invoice Processing Menu rather than the Cash Processing Menu to record cash receipts?
3. Describe the steps that you would take to record a prepayment.
4. When you enter payment information for an open item customer, how do you identify which invoices are being paid?
5. What are the differences between recording payments to balance forward and open item customers?
6. Describe how you would use Accounts Receivable to record a cash receipt that does not affect the Accounts Receivable control account.
7. What would happen if you attempted to post cash batches before you had printed the Cash Batch Listings?
8. Why should you keep a printout of the Aged Trial Balance?

EXERCISE

Select your company from the Start Menu, using November 30, 1998 as the New date. During the month, your company has received payment on various accounts. To save time, you are recording cash receipts at month-end from the bank deposit book instead of recording them when you receive them. Your bank deposit book lists the following transactions:

Table 16–2

```
November 10, 1998    Barilak & Assoc ck B552 re invoice A008, amount $1,130.
November 15, 1998    Dillingham ck DL1437 re A007 & A009, amount $2,997.50.
November 24, 1998    Graves & Dawn ck GD665 re invoice A011, amount $350.
November 25, 1998    Graves & Dawn ck GD669 re prepayment, amount $3420.
November 26, 1998    Foster Ins. ck FI887 re rebate on premium, amount $77.85
November 27, 1998    Dillingham ck DL1501 re A012, amount $565.
```

1. Enter the information to record these transactions. The prepayment from Graves & Dawn was for software that you ordered specially for them.
2. Print the Cash Batch Listing and review it for errors.
3. Post the batch to the Accounts Receivable ledger.
4. Print and clear the Cash Posting Journal.
5. Print the Aged Trial Balance.
6. Quit ACCPAC Plus.
7. Back up your data.

17 Adjustments & Reconciliation

You may have to adjust entries for cash receipts to change amounts or other information. If the Invoice batch or Cash batch containing the entry to be changed has not been posted, you can modify the batch. If the entry has been posted, ACCPAC Plus will allow you to enter these changes using either the Invoice Processing Menu or the Adjustments Processing Menu. If you use the Invoice Processing Menu, the customer statistics will be updated when the batch is posted. If you use the Adjustments Processing Menu, the customer statistics will not be updated when the batch is posted.

As part of a company's internal control policy, only managers who do not handle cash or record Accounts Receivable should be allowed to authorize adjustments to Accounts Receivable. This policy reduces the potential for fraudulent write-offs of bona fide Accounts Receivable. It also protects employees from being falsely accused of prematurely writing off accounts.

❑   Using November 30, 1998 as the New date, enter the commands necessary to display the ACCPAC Accounts Receivable Master Menu for E. & J. Enterprises.

INVOICE PROCESSING METHOD

The Invoice Processing Menu should be used to enter changes when the change is related to an invoice already posted to the Accounts Receivable and when the customer statistics should be updated to reflect the change. In this chapter, you will look at two common situations: an invoice that was posted to the wrong customer and an invoice for an incorrect amount.

The Wrong Customer Invoiced

When going through the overdue accounts, Erin Gogetter discovered that invoice number 1012, sent to Hibou Co., had not been paid. She suspected that this invoice should have been sent to Evans Ltd. When she telephoned Evans Ltd., she was informed that Evans was waiting for the invoice. Invoice number 1012 had indeed been sent to the wrong customer by mistake. You must make an adjustment to remove invoice number 1012 from the files of account 1040, Hibou Co., and add it to account 1000, Evans Ltd.

☐ Select: `3. Transaction processing` from the ACCPAC Accounts Receivable Master Menu.

☐ Select: `1. Invoice processing`

☐ Select: `1. Add/modify/delete invoice batches`

☐ Press: [Enter] in the blank `Batch number` field.

☐ Select: `Yes` to create a new batch.

☐ Type: `Nov. 1998 Credit & Debit Notes` in the `Batch descrip-tion` field.

☐ Press: [Enter]

☐ Press: [Enter] to accept `Entry number 1`

Figure 17–1

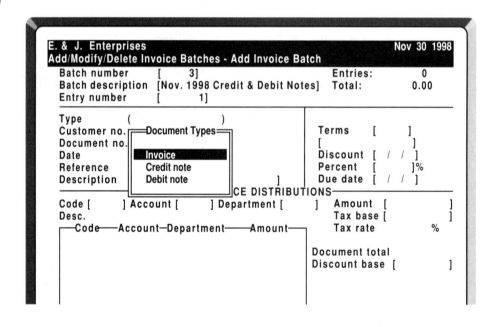

Credit notes

As shown in Figure 17–1, you can choose one of three different Document types: Invoices, Credit notes, or Debit notes. Credit note CN-001, authorized by Erin, will be used to remove invoice 1012 for $200 from Hibou Co.'s account.

❑ Select: Credit note

Figure 17–2

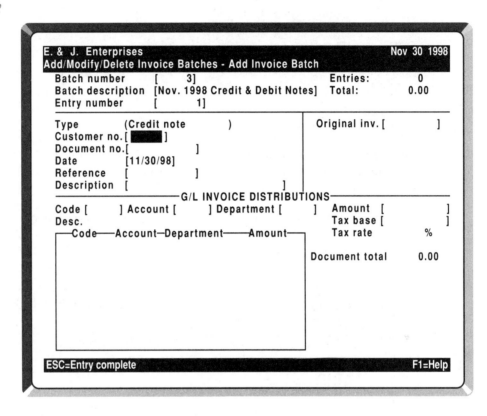

The section displaying fields for terms and discount information will be replaced by a single field for the original invoice number as shown in Figure 17–2.

❑ Type: 1040 in the Customer no. field.

❑ Press: [Enter]

A unique Credit Note or Debit Note number should be used as the Document number. If duplicate document numbers are used, ACCPAC Plus will transfer the entry with the duplicate number to an error batch during posting.

❑ Type: CN-001 in the Document no. field.

❑ Press: [Enter]

When you reallocate an invoice, you should enter the original date of the invoice so that the date the adjustment was entered does not appear on the Accounts Receivable reports as the invoice date. You should use the original date of the invoice so the customer's payment statistics will be updated correctly.

❏ Type: 090598 the date of the original invoice, in the `Date` field.

❏ Press: [Enter]

For control purposes, each adjustment should be documented by a memo. Each memo may be given a unique number followed by the initials of the person authorizing the adjustment. This information should be entered in the Reference field. The documentation for this adjustment is a memo AM001EG, written by Erin.

❏ Type: AM001EG in the `Reference` field.

❏ Press: [Enter]

❏ Type: `Invoice should be in A/C 1000` in the `Description` field.

❏ Press: [Enter]

If the credit note applies to one invoice, you should enter that invoice number in the original invoice number field. ACCPAC Plus will automatically apply the credit note to the proper invoice when both the credit note and the invoice have been posted to the Accounts Receivable.

If the credit note applies to several invoices, or is issued on account, or for some reason you cannot identify the invoice number, the original invoice field can be left blank. If the original invoice number field is left blank, ACCPAC Plus does not automatically apply the credit note for open item accounts. In this case you must reconcile the credit note to the invoice(s) using the Cash Processing Menu described later in this chapter. If the account is a balance forward account, ACCPAC Plus will automatically apply the note to the oldest outstanding transactions.

❏ Type: 1012 in the `Original inv.` field.

❏ Press: [Enter]

The cursor will move to the Code field in the G/L INVOICE DISTRIBUTIONS section in the lower half of the screen.

Credit notes will always result in a credit entry to the Accounts Receivable control account and a debit entry to one or more other accounts. You must choose the account or accounts to be debited. In this case, the invoice was for accounting services; therefore, the debit will be to accounting fees and no sales tax or value added tax adjustments are necessary.

❏ Type: fees in the `Code` field.

❏ Press: [Enter]

❏ Type: 200.00 in the `Amount` field.

❏ Press: [Enter]

❏ Press: [Esc] to indicate that the distribution of the credit note is complete.

Review the entry. If you have made an error, choose either the "Header" or "Detail" and make the necessary corrections. Once there are no errors,

❑ Select: `Save entry`

When you save this transaction, which reverses the invoice to Hibou Co.'s account, ACCPAC Plus resets the screen to receive the next entry.

Debit notes

The next entry, DN-001, will add the invoice to Evans Ltd.'s record.

❑ Select: `Debit note`

❑ Type: `1000` in the `Customer no.` field.

❑ Press: [Enter]

❑ Type: `DN-001` in the `Document no.` field

❑ Press: [Enter]

❑ Press: [Enter] to accept 09/05/98 as the date of the original invoice.

❑ Type: `AM001EG` in the `Reference` field.

❑ Press: [Enter]

❑ Type: `Transfer invoice from A/C 1040` in the `Description` field.

❑ Press: [Enter]

❑ Type: `1012` in the `Original inv.` field.

❑ Press: [Enter]

You used the code "fees" to clear the invoice from Hibou Co.'s account since the original transaction was an invoice for accounting services. You must use the same code again to distribute the entry to the proper General Ledger account.

❑ Type: `fees` in the `Code` field.

❑ Press: [Enter]

Since a debit note will always result in a debit to accounts receivable, and a credit to another account, the screen will not indicate debit or credit.

❑ Type: `200.00` in the `Amount` field.

❑ Press: [Enter]

❑ Press: [Esc] to indicate that the distribution of this debit note is complete.

Review the entry. If there are any errors, make the necessary corrections. Once there are no errors,

❑ Select: `Save entry`

Invoice Amount Incorrect

Reviewing the invoices, Joan found that PerCorp Inc. had been invoiced $1,900 for a laser printer when they had been quoted $1,800. Invoice 1019, dated November 7, 1998, must be adjusted to reflect the $100 error, and the 5% sales tax and 10% value added tax charged. A credit note, CN-002, was sent to PerCorp Inc. as authorized by Joan in AM002JA.

- ❑ Select: `Credit note`
- ❑ Type: `1010` in the `Customer no.` field.
- ❑ Press: [Enter]
- ❑ Type: `CN-002` in the `Document no.` field.
- ❑ Press: [Enter]

Remember to use the original invoice date so that the customer statistics will be updated correctly.

- ❑ Type: `110798` in the `Date` field.
- ❑ Press: [Enter]
- ❑ Type: `AM002JA` in the `Reference` field.
- ❑ Press: [Enter]
- ❑ Type: `Overcharged $100 on printer` in the `Description` field.
- ❑ Press: [Enter]
- ❑ Type: `1019` in the `Original inv.` field.
- ❑ Press: [Enter]
- ❑ Enter the following G/L Invoice Distributions:

```
sales      100.00
stax         5.00
vat         10.00
```

- ❑ Press: [Esc] to indicate that the distribution is complete.
- ❑ Select: `Save entry`
- ❑ Press: [Esc] three times to return to the Invoice Processing Menu.
- ❑ Print the Invoice Batch.

Table 17–1

```
te: Nov 30 98   6:21pm                  E. & J. Enterprises                                    Page:   1
R Invoice Batches

tch number      :    3
tch description :  Nov. 1998 Credit & Debit Notes

try      Cust.     Document Document              Discount  Disc.   Due      Distr. GL Acct-Dept/
No. Type No.            No. Date    Reference     Date    Percent Date       Code Description            Amount

  1 CN    1040       CN-001 Sep 05 98 AM001EG                                fees Accounting Fe          200.00-
     Customer Name : Hibou Co.                    Original Inv.:     1012                             ——————-
     Description   : Invoice should be in A/C 1000                           Total     :              200.00- *

  2 DN    1000       DN-001 Sep 05 98 AM001EG                                fees Accounting Fe          200.00
     Customer Name : Evans Ltd.                   Original Inv.:     1012                             ——————-
     Description   : Transfer invoice from A/C 1040                          Total     :              200.00  *

  3 CN    1010       CN-002 Nov 07 98 AM002JA                                sales Merchandise S         100.00-
                                                                            stax Sales Tax Pay            5.00-
                                                                             vat Value Added T           10.00-
     Customer Name : PerCorp Inc.                 Original Inv.:     1019                             ——————-
     Description   : Overcharged $100 on printer                             Total     :              115.00- *


                                                                            ——————
                                                                 Total Credit Notes :     315.00-
                                                                 Total Debit Notes  :     200.00

                                                                 Batch Total        :     115.00-
                                                                                        ========

3 transaction(s) printed.
```

Compare your printout to Table 17–1. If there are errors, make the necessary corrections and print the Invoice Batch again.

❑ Post the invoice batch.

❑ Print and clear the posting journal.

❑ Press: [Esc] until the ACCPAC Accounts Receivable Master Menu is displayed on the screen.

ADJUSTMENT PROCESSING METHOD

In this section you will enter the same adjustments that you entered through the Invoice Processing Menu. Changes entered through the Adjustment Processing Menu will not update the customer statistics as they were posted.

In addition to adjusting posted invoice entries, the Adjustments Processing Menu will allow you to make adjustments to the following:

1. Interest invoices generated by ACCPAC Plus during period end or billing cycle procedures.

2. Cash batch entries that have been posted.

3. Debit or Credit notes that have been posted.

4. Adjustments to other adjustments that have been posted.

To prevent duplicate posting, you will delete the Adjustment batch at the end of this section.

❑ Select: 3. Transaction processing
❑ Select: 3. Adjustment processing
❑ Select: 1. Add/modify/delete adjustment batches

Figure 17–3

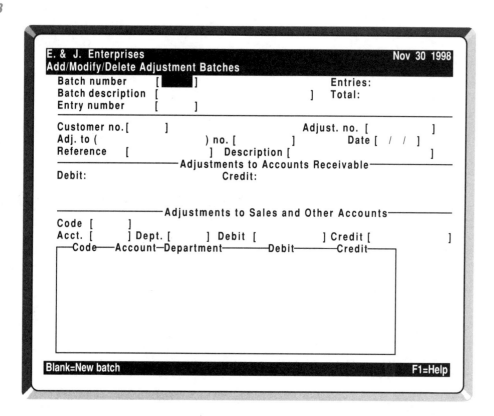

ACCPAC Plus will display the data entry screen for making adjustments (Figure 17–3). Note the following differences between this screen and the invoice screen:

1. The information entry area is reduced.

2. A section has been added to display the total debits and credits of each adjustment to the Accounts Receivable.

3. A fourth section allows you to enter debit or credit adjustments to other General Ledger accounts.

❑ Press: `Enter` in the blank `Batch number` field.

❑ Select: `Yes` to create a new adjustment batch.

The computer will search the files and determine the next batch number in sequence. The number "1" will appear in the Batch number field and the cursor will move to the Batch description field.

❑ Type: `November 1998 Adjustments`

❑ Press: `Enter`

The Wrong Customer Invoiced

The first two entries will remove invoice 1012 from Hibou Co.'s account and transfer it to Evans Ltd.

❑ Press: `Enter` to accept "1" as the `Entry number`

❑ Type: `1040` in the `Customer no.` field.

❑ Press: `Enter`

You must enter a unique adjustment number, a control number used to identify the adjustment for later reference. If you try to enter a blank adjustment number, ACCPAC Plus will display an error message: "Invalid entry. Field cannot be blank." and you would have to press **F2** to clear the error message and enter an adjustment number. If the adjustment number is duplicated, the entry with the duplicate will be transferred to an error batch during posting of the adjustment batch.

❑ Type: `CN-001` in the `Adjust. no.` field.

❑ Press: `Enter`

A selection box will appear on the screen.

```
Adjustment to
Invoice
Interest invoice
Cash
Credit note
Debit note
Adjustment
```

You must identify the type of document that is being corrected. ACCPAC Plus uses this information to identify the debits and credits necessary to make the corrections.

❑ Select: `Invoice`

You must identify the specific document number that the adjustment is to be made to. ACCPAC Plus will not accept a blank field. If you did not know the correct document number, you should enter a unique dummy number and reconcile the adjustment as described later in this chapter. In this case, you know that the invoice number is 1012.

❑ Type: `1012` in the `no.` field.

❑ Press: Enter

When you reallocate an invoice to a customer, you should enter the original date of the invoice so that the adjustment date does not appear on the Accounts Receivable reports as the invoice date. Remember that Adjustment Batch entries do not update the customer statistics.

❑ Type: `090598` the date of the original invoice, in the `Date` field.

❑ Press: Enter

The documentation for this adjustment is memo AM001EG, written by Erin.

❑ Type: `AM001EG` in the `Reference` field.

❑ Press: Enter

❑ Type: `Invoice should be in A/C 1000` in the `Description` field.

❑ Press: Enter

The cursor will move to the "Code" field in the "Adjustments To Sales And Other Accounts" section at the bottom of the screen.

❑ Type: `fees` to indicate that the adjustment is being made to account 720, Accounting Fees.

❑ Press: Enter

❑ Type: `200.00` in the `Debit` field to record the amount of the adjustment.

❑ Press: Enter

The debit to account 720 will be displayed in the information box in the lower portion of the screen. As this is a debit adjustment to an invoice, ACCPAC Plus displays the matching credit of $200.00 in the "Adjustment to Accounts Receivable" portion of the field.

❑ Press: Esc to indicate that the distribution of this entry is complete.

If you have make an error, select either "Header" or "Detail", and then enter the correct information. Once you have determined that the information entered is correct,

❑ Select: `Save entry`

When you save this entry, which reverses invoice 1012 to Hibou Co., ACCPAC Plus resets the screen to receive the next adjusting entry. This next adjusting entry, a debit note, will add invoice 1012 to Evans Ltd.'s account.

- ❑ Type: `1000` in the `Customer no.` field.
- ❑ Press: [Enter]
- ❑ Type: `DN-001` in the `Adjust. no.` field.
- ❑ Press: [Enter]
- ❑ Select: `Invoice`
- ❑ Type: `1012` in the `no.` field.
- ❑ Press: [Enter]
- ❑ Press: [Enter] to accept September 5, 1998 as the `Date.`
- ❑ Type: `AM001EG` in the `Reference` field.
- ❑ Press: [Enter]
- ❑ Type: `Transfer invoice from A/C 1040` in the `Description` field.
- ❑ Press: [Enter]

The cursor will move to the Code field in the "Adjustments to Sales and Other Accounts" portion of the screen.

- ❑ Type: `fees`
- ❑ Press: [Enter]

The cursor moves once again to the Debit field in the "Adjustments to Sales and Other Accounts" section. Note that you are creating a balanced adjustment with neither an increase nor a decrease in the Accounts Receivable. The first entry resulted in a debit to account 720 and a credit to account 200 (A/R). The effect of this was to remove the invoice from account 1040. You must now set up the invoice in Customer account 1000, so the entry must be the reverse of the first.

- ❑ Press: [Enter] or [⇆] to move the cursor to the `Credit` field.
- ❑ Type: `200.00`
- ❑ Press: [Enter]
- ❑ Press: [Esc] to indicate that this entry is complete.
- ❑ Select: `Save entry`

Invoice Amount Incorrect

Joan had found that PerCorp Inc. had been invoiced $1,900 for a laser printer when they had been quoted $1800. Invoice 1019, dated November 7, 1998, must be adjusted to reflect the $100 error, and the 5% sales tax and 10% value added tax charged. A credit note, CN-002, was sent to PerCorp Inc. as authorized by Joan in AM002JA.

- ❏ Type: `1010` in the `Customer no.` field
- ❏ Press: [Enter]
- ❏ Type: `CN-002` in the `Adjust. no.` field.
- ❏ Press: [Enter]
- ❏ Select: `Invoice` from the `Adjustment to` options.
- ❏ Type: `1019` in the `no.` field.
- ❏ Type: `110798` in the `Date` field.
- ❏ Type: `AM002JA` in the `Reference` field.
- ❏ Press: [Enter]
- ❏ Type: `Overcharged $100 on printer` in the `Description` field.
- ❏ Press: [Enter]
- ❏ Enter the following "Adjustments to Sales and Other Accounts".

```
sales      debit      100.00
stax       debit        5.00
vat        debit       10.00
```

ACCPAC Plus will display the matching credit to Accounts Receivable in the "Adjustments to Accounts Receivable" portion of the screen.

- ❏ Press: [Esc] to indicate that the distribution is complete.
- ❏ Select: `Save entry`
- ❏ Press: [Esc] three times to return to the Adjustment Processing Menu.
- ❏ Print the Adjustment Batch listing.

Table 17-2

```
te: Nov 30 98    6:40pm              E. & J. Enterprises                              Page:   1
R Adjustment Batches

tch number    :    1
tch description :  November 1998 Adjustments

try  Cust.  Adjustment                     Adjustment to  Distr.
No.   No.         No. Date    Reference    Type      No.  Code  Acct  Dept      Debit        Credit

 1   1040     CN-001 Sep 05 98 AM001EG      IN       1012       200                          200.00
                                                         fees  720            200.00
     Customer Name : Hibou Co.                                                _____      _____
     Description   : Incoice should be in A/C 1000            Total :         200.00         200.00 *

 2   1000     DN-001 Sep 05 98 AM001EG      IN       1012       200           200.00
                                                         fees  720                           200.00
     Customer Name : Evans Ltd.                                               _____      _____
     Description   : Transfer invoice from A/C 1040           Total :         200.00         200.00 *

 3   1010     CN-002 Nov 07 98 AM002JA      IN       1019       200                          115.00
                                                        sales  700            100.00
                                                         stax  520              5.00
                                                          vat  540             10.00
     Customer Name : PerCorp Inc.                                             _____      _____
     Description   : Overcharged $100 on printer                Total :       115.00         115.00 *


                                                             Batch Total :    515.00         515.00
                                                                          ================ ================

3 transaction(s) printed.
```

Compare your printout to Table 17–2. If there are errors, make the necessary corrections and print the Invoice Batch Listing again.

Compare the Adjustment Batch listing to the Invoice Batch listing printed earlier in this chapter. Note that the Adjustment Batch listing provides more detailed distribution information than the Invoice Batch listing for the credit and debit notes.

The data entered in this Adjustment Batch is identical to that entered by the Invoice Processing Method earlier in this chapter. If you wished to record this information in the Accounts Receivable you would post the Adjustment Batch, and then print and clear the Posting Journal. As the information in this Adjustment Batch is identical to that posted by the Invoice Processing method, you will now delete this Adjustment Batch.

- ❑ Select: `1. Add/modify/delete adjustment batches` from the Adjustment Processing Menu.
- ❑ Type: `1` in the `Batch number` field.
- ❑ Press: [Enter]
- ❑ Select: `Delete batch`

☐ Select: `Yes` to confirm that you want to delete this batch.

☐ Press: `[Esc]` twice to return to the Transaction Processing Menu.

RECONCILIATION

For open item accounts you may not always be able to allocate a payment or a credit note to an invoice immediately. After a period of time you receive additional information and are able to apply the payment or credit note. The following examples illustrate this situation:

1. A check is received from a customer as a prepayment and recorded as an unallocated payment. When the goods are delivered or the services are performed, an invoice is issued and then the payment is applied to the invoice.

2. A check is received from a customer but you cannot identify which invoices it should be applied to. As the accounts age and further information is received from the customer, you are able to apply the payment to the proper invoices.

3. A credit note applies to several invoices and cannot be automatically allocated by ACCPAC Plus.

4. You have issued a credit note against an invoice that is no longer receivable. You should then apply the credit note against the remaining invoices in the customer's account.

5. A debit note has been issued to a customer whose account contains an unallocated payment.

You can reconcile these payments or notes to the appropriate invoices using the Cash Processing Menu.

In Chapter 16 you recorded a prepayment of $3,000 from NorWest Export Co. Before you can reconcile the prepayment and the invoice, you must post invoice 1030 to Norwest Export Co.'s account.

☐ Create a new invoice batch and record entry number 1 as shown in Figure 17–4.

Figure 17–4

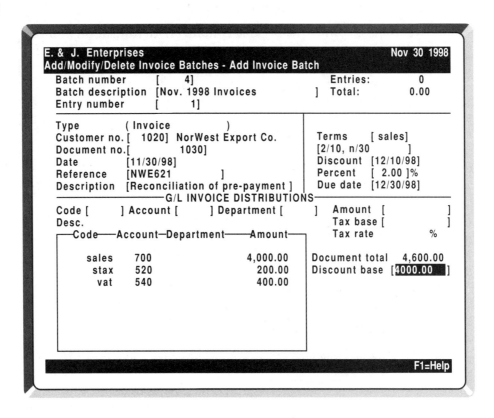

```
E. & J. Enterprises                                    Nov 30 1998
Add/Modify/Delete Invoice Batches - Add Invoice Batch
     Batch number     [    4]              Entries:        0
     Batch description [Nov. 1998 Invoices    ]  Total:      0.00
     Entry number      [    1]

     Type       ( Invoice            )
     Customer no. [  1020]  NorWest Export Co.    Terms   [ sales]
     Document no.[        1030]                   [2/10, n/30    ]
     Date        [11/30/98]                       Discount [12/10/98]
     Reference   [NWE621        ]                 Percent  [ 2.00 ]%
     Description [Reconciliation of pre-payment ] Due date [12/30/98]
     ─────────────────G/L INVOICE DISTRIBUTIONS─────────────
     Code [    ] Account [      ] Department [     ]  Amount  [           ]
     Desc.                                            Tax base [          ]
     ┌─Code──Account─Department──────Amount─┐         Tax rate        %
     │                                       │
     │   sales    700            4,000.00    │   Document total   4,600.00
     │   stax     520              200.00    │   Discount base [4000.00   ]
     │   vat      540              400.00    │
     │                                       │
     │                                       │
     │                                       │
     └───────────────────────────────────────┘

                                                              F1=Help
```

❏ Print the Invoice Batch listing.

❏ Post the Invoice Batch.

❏ Print and clear the Invoice Posting Journal.

You can now reconcile the account for NorWest Export Co. as there is a valid invoice to apply the prepayment to.

❏ Press: [Esc] twice to return to the ACCPAC Accounts Receivable Master Menu.

❏ Select: 3. Transaction processing from the ACCPAC Accounts Receivable Master Menu.

❏ Select: 2. Cash Processing

❏ Select: 1. Add/modify/delete cash batches

❏ Press: [Enter] in the blank Batch number field.

❏ Select: Yes to create a new batch.

❏ Type: November A/C Reconciliation in the Description field.

❏ Press: [Enter]

❏ Press: [Enter] to accept Entry number 1

❏ Type: 1020 in the Customer number field.

❑ Press: [Enter]

The check number field must contain an identification number. If you were reconciling a credit note you could enter the credit note number plus "rec" to indicate that this is a reconciliation of the posted credit note. To reconcile multiple posted credit notes and/or checks, you would enter a control number such as "rec-", to indicate reconciliation, followed by the batch number, a dash, and the entry number. In this case, the prepayment was made with check NWE6581, which has already been posted.

❑ Press: [F5]

ACCPAC Plus will display the posted checks, credit notes, and debit notes in a selection box.

❑ Move the selector bar to NWE6581   CA.

❑ Press: [Enter]

The unapplied amount of the posted check will be displayed. Note that the payment will automatically show a zero amount and that the cursor will bypass the payment field after you enter the date of the reconciliation.

❑ Type: 113098

❑ Press: [Enter]

❑ Press: [Enter] to accept Account set 1

❑ Type: NorWest prepayment on inv1030 in the Description
field.

❑ Press: [Enter]

❑ Move the selector bar to invoice 1030.

❑ Press: [Enter]

The information for invoice 1030 will appear in the Applied amount field of the CASH DISTRIBUTIONS. The outstanding amount of this invoice is $4,600. The "Applied amount" field will display the lessor of the outstanding amount of the invoice ($4,600) or the unapplied amount of the check ($3,000).

❑ Press: [Enter] to apply the prepayment amount of $3,000 to the invoice.

ACCPAC Plus will calculate the discount amount ($80.00) based on the $4,000 discount base recorded when the invoice was entered. The discount earned by the prepayment of $3,000 should be $60.

❑ Type: 60.00 in the Discount amount field.

❑ Press: [Enter]

The cash distribution information will be transferred to the information box in the lower portion of the screen. If there was an unapplied amount remaining, you could apply that amount to another invoice.

❑ Press: [Esc] to indicate the cash distribution is complete.

❑ Select: Save entry

Any further reconciliations of payments or credit notes could now be entered using these same steps.

❑ Press: [Esc] three times to return to the Cash Processing Menu.

❑ Print the Cash Batch.

❑ Post the Cash Batch.

❑ Print and clear the Cash Posting Journal.

❑ Print the Aged Trial Balance.

Review this report to confirm that invoice 1012 has been transferred from Hibou Co. to Evans Ltd. and that NorWest Export Co.'s prepayment has been applied to invoice 1030.

Quit ACCPAC Plus and back up your data files.

REVIEW QUESTIONS

1. Describe the options available on the Adjustment Entry Menu.
2. Why must any adjustments to Accounts Receivable be authorized by a senior manager?
3. Why is it preferable to use the original invoice date when making an adjustment?
4. Describe three circumstances in which you may have to adjust an invoice.
5. When would you use the Invoice Processing Method rather than the Adjustment Processing Method?
6. Describe the steps to be taken to reconcile a prepayment after the customer has been invoiced.
7. What is the difference between the processing of open item and balance forward accounts?

EXERCISE

If necessary, refer to the reports printed in the previous exercises.

1. At your company, you have noticed that invoice A001 to Barilak & Associates is long overdue. You believe that this invoice was mistakenly posted to Barilak & Associates rather than to Dillingham & Co. When you phone Bruce Dillingham to confirm this, you learn that the company is still waiting for the invoice. Remove invoice number A001 from Barilak & Associates' account and add it to Dillingham & Co.'s account, entering the original date of the invoice. Use account 700, Sales, as the clearing account.

2. After investigating why invoice number A010 to H. Bazelton has not been paid, you discover that the amount charged was $250 more than the price quoted. Adjust the invoice amount. Remember that you must also adjust both the sales tax and value added tax charged to the customer.

3. On November 30, 1998 invoice A014 was issued to Graves & Dawn. This invoice was for a special purpose software that you had to collect a prepayment for. The selling price of the computer was $5,500 plus 5% sales tax and 10% value added tax. Record the invoice and reconcile the prepayment. Record the Discount amount at $59.50.

4. Print all Batch Listings.

5. Post all batches.

6. Print and clear the Posting Journals.

7. Print the Aged Trial Balance.

8. Back up your data files.

18 Period End Procedures

In this chapter you will perform the following period end procedures.

1. Process recurring charges.

2. Process interest charges.

3. Post unposted batches for the period.

4. Print customer statements.

5. Transfer Accounts Receivable information to the General Ledger.

6. Run the Period End Function

❑ Enter the commands necessary to display the ACCPAC Accounts Receivable Master Menu for E. & J. Enterprises using "November 30, 1998" as the new date.

The ACCPAC Plus Accounts Receivable module can automatically generate invoices for two types of charges: interest on overdue customer accounts and recurring charges, such as monthly fees.

❑ Select: `5. Periodic processing` from the ACCPAC Accounts Receivable Master Menu.

The Periodic Processing Menu (Figure 18–1) will appear.

Figure 18–1

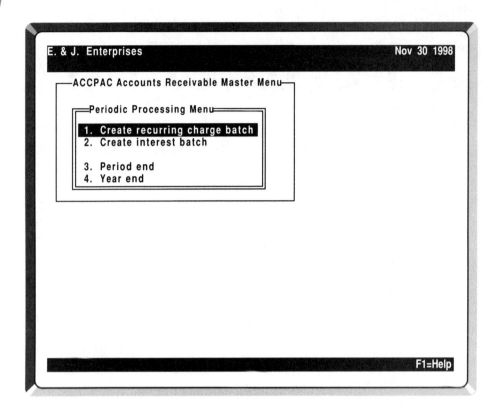

PROCESSING RECURRING CHARGES

The "Create recurring charge batch" option is available only if you selected "Process Recurring Charges" in the company profile. An invoice batch is created crediting all recurring charges to the General Ledger account specified in the Company Profile. Monthly recurring charges could include club fees, rent, insurance fees, and, as for E. & J. Enterprises, accounting fees.

❑ Select: `1. Create recurring charge batch` from the Periodic Processing Menu.

The Create Recurring Charge Batch screen (Figure 18–2) will appear.

The cursor will be in the "Recurring charge" field. The square cursor indicates that the Finder (**F5**) may be used to display information for this field.

❑ Press: F5

The Recurring Charge options will appear in the center of the screen. In Chapter 12 you created one recurring charge code, "fees", for monthly accounting fees. This code specifies net 30 day terms and distribution to General Ledger account 720.

❑ Select: `fees`

Figure 18–2

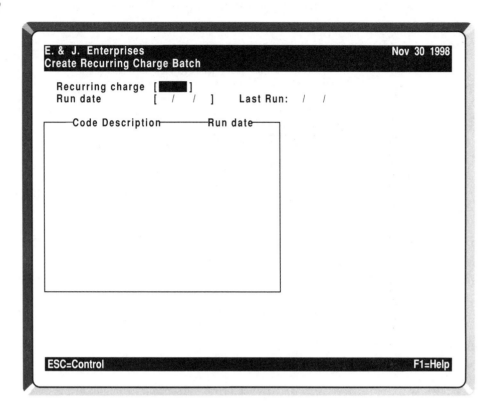

```
E. & J. Enterprises                                    Nov 30 1998
Create Recurring Charge Batch

     Recurring charge  [        ]
     Run date          [  /  /  ]     Last Run:  /  /

         Code Description          Run date
```

```
ESC=Control                                            F1=Help
```

The date entered in the "Run date" field is recorded as the invoice date for each recurring charge generated. The run date shown is calculated by ACCPAC Plus by adding the frequency of the recurring charge to the last run date. You can edit this date for months with less than 30 days (February) or for those months with 31 days.

❑ Press: [Enter] to accept 11/30/98 as the run date.

The cursor will return to the "Recurring charge" field to allow you to specify additional charges to be processed.

❑ Press: [Esc] to indicate that you have finished setting the recurring charge options.

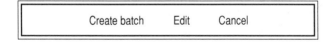

```
Create batch     Edit     Cancel
```

❑ Select: Create batch

ACCPAC Plus will process each customer for which you have specified a recurring charge. Each invoice generated will be entered in the next available Invoice Batch.

Once the Recurring charges batch has been created, the following message will appear:

```
┌─────────────────────────────────────────────────────┐
│                                                       │
│     Recurring charges have been written to batch 5.   │
│                                                       │
│                      Continue                         │
│                                                       │
└─────────────────────────────────────────────────────┘
```

The batch number displayed on your screen may be different.

❏ Press: [Enter] to return to the Periodic Processing Menu.

❏ Press: [Esc] twice to return to the ACCPAC Accounts Receivable Master Menu.

❏ Print the Invoice Batch, using the Invoice Processing Menu.

Compare your printout to that shown in Table 18–1. Note the Batch Description "Recurring charges   Nov 30 98" and the sequentially numbered document numbers. If there are errors in your printout, use the "Add/modify/delete invoice batches" option to make corrections and print the batch again.

Table 18–1

```
Date: Nov 30 98   10:08am              E. & J. Enterprises                              Page:  1
A/R Invoice Batches

Batch number      :    5
Batch description : Recurring charges     Nov 30 98

Entry      Cust.     Document Document              Discount Disc.   Due     Distr. GL Acct-Dept/
 No. Type No.           No. Date      Reference     Date     Percent Date     Code Description      Amount

  1 IN    1000      MAF-0001 Nov 30 98 EV-6943               0.00  Dec 30 98   fees Accounting Fe    225.00
    Customer Name : Evans Ltd.                                                                      ───────
    Description   : Monthly Payroll Processing     Discount Base: 0.00           Total      :       225.00  *

  2 IN    1040      MAF-0002 Nov 30 98 H325                  0.00  Dec 30 98   fees Accounting Fe    250.00
    Customer Name : Hibou Co.                                                                       ───────
    Description   : Monthly Payroll               Discount Base: 0.00           Total      :       250.00  *
                                                                                                    ───────

                                                                             Total Invoices :       475.00
                                                                                                    ────────-
                                                                             Batch Total    :       475.00
                                                                                                   ===========

  2 transaction(s) printed.
```

❑ Post the invoice batch.

❑ Print and clear the posting journal.

❑ Press: [Esc] twice to return to the ACCPAC Accounts Receivable Master Menu.

PROCESSING AUTOMATIC INTEREST CHARGES

❑ Select: 5. Periodic processing

The "Create interest batch" option calculates the interest due on overdue accounts using the information you entered on the System Options and Interest Charges screen in Chapter 12. Each invoice generated will be entered in the next available Invoice Batch.

❑ Select: 2. Create interest batch

The Create Interest Batch screen (Figure 18–3) will appear.

Figure 18–3

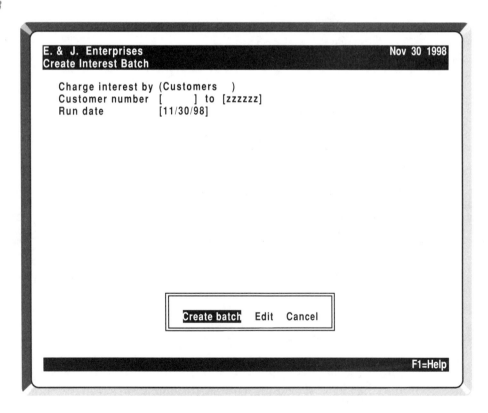

```
 E. & J. Enterprises                                   Nov 30 1998
 Create Interest Batch

    Charge interest by (Customers  )
    Customer number   [      ] to [zzzzzz]
    Run date          [11/30/98]
```

```
                    Create batch   Edit   Cancel
```

```
                                                       F1=Help
```

You may charge interest by "Customers" or "Billing cycles". The selection you make depends upon the Clear Transaction Detail option that you recorded in the Company Profile in Chapter 12. If you had chosen to clear transactions at the period end, you may enter a range of either customer numbers or billing cycles.

If you had set the profile to clear transactions by billing cycle, you must enter a range of billing cycles. For E. & J. Enterprises you set the Clear Transaction Detail option to Period End.

The default settings for the calculation of interest, as shown in Figure 18–3, are acceptable. Interest is to be charged by customers, the full range of customers is identified, and the run date of November 30, 1998 is correct. If you wished to make changes in the default settings, you would select "Edit".

ACCPAC Plus uses the run date you specify (usually the period end) as a base for its calculations. For open item accounts, it compares this run date to the original date of each outstanding item and applies interest if the invoice has been outstanding for more than the specified amount of time. You specified the interest rate in the Company Profile. You may change the interest rate according to market rates, but the rate must be the same for all customers.

ACCPAC Plus treats balance forward accounts differently from open item accounts. The program calculates the mid-point of each aging category, which becomes the number of days overdue for that category. For example, overdue "0 to 30" days becomes "15 days overdue". This averaged time period becomes the basis for calculating interest charges.

❑ Select: `Create batch`

After checking each customer, ACCPAC Plus will display the following message:

```
No interest charges are due.

Continue
```

❑ Press: [Enter] to continue.

If interest charges were due, ACCPAC Plus would have created an invoice for each charge and entered these invoices in the next available invoice batch. You would then print and post the batch, and print and clear the posting journal as you did for recurring charges.

❑ Press: [Esc] to return to the ACCPAC Accounts Receivable Master Menu.

DISPLAY BATCH STATUS

Before printing customer statements or posting the Accounts Receivable transaction to the General Ledger, you should make sure that all relevant batches have been posted to the Accounts Receivable.

❑ Select: `2. Inquiries` from the ACCPAC Accounts Receivable Master Menu.

❑ Select: `3. Display batch status`

❑ Select: `Invoice Batches`

Figure 18–4

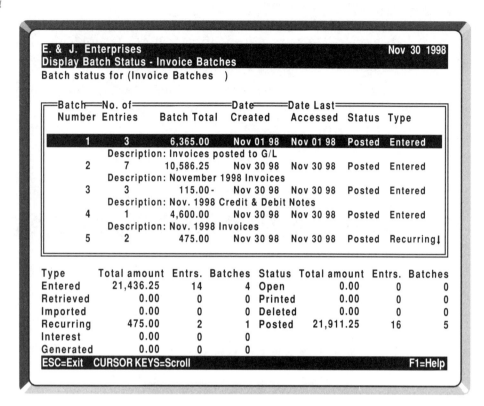

```
E. & J. Enterprises                                    Nov 30 1998
Display Batch Status - Invoice Batches
Batch status for (Invoice Batches   )

╔═Batch══No. of══════════════Date══════Date Last═══
  Number  Entries    Batch Total   Created     Accessed   Status  Type

      1        3       6,365.00    Nov 01 98   Nov 01 98   Posted  Entered
      Description: Invoices posted to G/L
      2        7      10,586.25    Nov 30 98   Nov 30 98   Posted  Entered
      Description: November 1998 Invoices
      3        3         115.00-   Nov 30 98   Nov 30 98   Posted  Entered
      Description: Nov. 1998 Credit & Debit Notes
      4        1       4,600.00    Nov 30 98   Nov 30 98   Posted  Entered
      Description: Nov. 1998 Invoices
      5        2         475.00    Nov 30 98   Nov 30 98   Posted  Recurring↓


Type       Total amount  Entrs.  Batches  Status  Total amount  Entrs.  Batches
Entered      21,436.25      14       4     Open         0.00       0        0
Retrieved         0.00       0       0     Printed      0.00       0        0
Imported          0.00       0       0     Deleted      0.00       0        0
Recurring       475.00       2       1     Posted  21,911.25      16        5
Interest          0.00       0       0
Generated         0.00       0       0
ESC=Exit   CURSOR KEYS=Scroll                                    F1=Help
```

The display of batch status information is in three sections as shown in
Figure 18–4. The upper section is a scroll box containing information on each
batch. You can use the arrow keys to scroll the display up or down to show additional batches.

The lower portion of the screen displays summarized information for all batches.
On the left, batches are summarized by batch type. On the right, batches are summarized by status. Note any open or printed batches. You should print or delete
any open batches and then post or delete the printed batches. Be sure to print
and clear the posting journals before continuing.

❑ Press: [Esc]

❑ Display the Batch Status for Cash Batches and then Adjustment Batches.

❑ Delete or post any unposted batches.

❑ Press: [Esc] until the ACCPAC Accounts Receivable Master Menu is displayed.

PRINTING CUSTOMER STATEMENTS

❑ Select: 4. Reports from the ACCPAC Accounts Receivable Master Menu.

❑ Select: 1. Statements/letters/labels

Review the default settings shown in Figure 18–5. You change these default settings by selecting "Edit" and entering the desired changes.

❑ Select: Edit

Figure 18–5

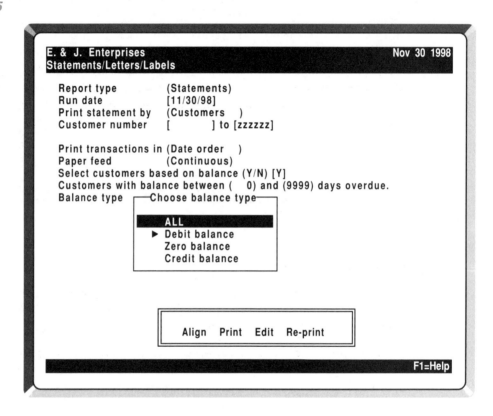

Document Type

The default is to print Customer statements using a standard statement specification in the ACCPAC Plus Accounts Receivable module. This specification prints statements on standard pre-printed forms that are available through printers and stationery stores. In Chapter 19 you will see how to customize statement specifications for other pre-printed forms. You also could choose to print either customer letters or mailing labels.

❑ Select: Statements

Run Date

The "Run date" is required for calculating the number of days an account is outstanding. It is also used by ACCPAC Plus to determine if recurring charges or interest charges should have been processed before printing the statements. For E. & J. Enterprises the "Run date" should be the end of the month; in this case, November 30, 1998.

❑ Type: `113098`

❑ Press: Enter

Print Statement By

This option determines the order in which statements are printed. In the company profile, E. & J. Enterprises chose to process receivables by period end rather than by billing cycles and specified only a monthly billing cycle. For E. & J. Enterprises you can select to print statements either by customer number or by billing cycle. The default setting will print the statements in order of customer number.

If E. & J. Enterprises had chosen to process receivables by billing cycles, you could select to print statements only by billing cycles. You would then have to enter the range of billing cycle codes that you wanted to print in the next field.

❑ Select: `Customers`

Customer Number

The "Customer number" fields allow you to specify a group of customers by entering the beginning and ending customer numbers of the group. The default prints statements for all customers.

❑ Press: Enter twice to accept the default customer numbers.

Transaction Order

If you are using Version 6.0A, this field will not appear on your screen.

This field allows you to control the order that transactions are printed in for the customer statements. You would select `Document order` if you wished the transactions to be grouped by transaction type and printed in order of document number within each type of transaction. If you select `Date order`, transactions will be listed by their document dates. When more than one transaction has the same document date, these transactions will then be sorted by document type and, if necessary, document number.

❑ Select: `Date order`

Paper Feed

The pre-printed statement forms are usually supplied in "Continuous" format. If your statement forms (or letterhead for customer letters) have been supplied as individual forms, you would select the "Sheet" option. When you select the "sheet" option, ACCPAC Plus will pause after printing a page to allow the next sheet to be fed into the printer.

❑ Select the proper setting for your printer.

Select Customers

If you entered "N" in the "Select customers based on balance" field, ACCPAC Plus would print all customers regardless of their account balances. The default "Y" allows you to choose customers with accounts within a certain range of days overdue or by the type of balance in their account.

❑ Press: [Enter] to accept the default "Y".

Days Overdue

The range between "0" and "9999" days overdue will select all customers for printing. If you wished to send special statements (or letters) to customers more than 60 days overdue you would type 60 in the first field.

❑ Press: [Enter] twice to accept the default days overdue.

Balance Type

This option allows you to choose customers based on their account balance. If you had a large customer base, you might select to print only those customers with a debit balance account in order to reduce your printing and postage costs. E. & J. Enterprises has decided to print statements for all of its customers.

❑ Move the selector bar to All

❑ Press: [SPACEBAR] to select All

Triangular pointers will then be displayed beside each balance type.

❑ Press: [Enter]

Align

Before printing the actual customer statements, you should print an alignment test form to verify that the specification prints the data in the correct location on your pre-printed forms.

❑ Select: Align

The alignment test form shows **X**'s where ACCPAC Plus will print text and **9**'s where it will print numbers. If you were using pre-printed standard forms, you would check that the printing did not overlap that on the pre-printed form. If necessary, you could adjust the position of the forms in the printer and print another alignment test form.

Print

The print function will print the actual statements. If you had chosen to process receivables by billing cycle, it also would clear the paid transactions and transfer them to the history file.

❑ Select: `Print`

Once the forms have been printed, the following message will appear:

```
Are the printed statements satisfactory?

        Yes        No
```

If the printout were unsatisfactory for any reason (broken printer ribbon or jammed form) you could select "No", correct the problem, and print the statements again.

❑ Select: `Yes`

Re-print

ACCPAC Plus saves the information for the last batch of statements, letters, or labels that were printed. If you discover that your last printing was not satisfactory, you can use this option to re-print.

POSTING TO THE GENERAL LEDGER

Once you have posted all invoices, cash receipts, and adjustments to the Accounts Receivable ledger and have processed all the automatic interest and recurring charges, you can post these transactions to the General Ledger. In the General Ledger Summary section of each Posting Journal printout, ACCPAC Plus shows that the totals entered in the General Ledger Receivable control account and the Accounts Receivable ledger are equal.

If these totals are out of balance after posting the Accounts Receivable transactions to the General Ledger, look at the General Ledger Accounts Receivable account for postings from a source other than the ACCPAC Plus Accounts Receivable module. Someone likely made an error in typing an account number when entering General Journal adjustments or else made Accounts Receivable adjustments directly to the General Ledger.

Print/Consolidate the G/L Transactions

The G/L Transactions report must be printed and cleared before proceeding with the month-end procedures. This report is the audit trail of all transactions generated by the Accounts Receivable for posting to the General Ledger. The report contains all the transactions posted since the last time the report was printed and cleared.

❑ Select: `2. Print/consolidate G/L transactions` from the Reports Menu.

The transactions reported can be sorted by General Ledger account number, by transaction or document date, or by journal entry. The default is to sort by account number. If you wish to change this setting, you would select "Edit" and then choose either "Journal entry" or "Transaction date".

❑ Select: `Print` to print the report sorted by General Ledger account number.

When printing is complete the following message will appear:

```
Do you want to consolidate the G/L transactions?

           Yes          No
```

If you do not consolidate the General Ledger transactions, each line on the report will be transferred to the General Ledger as a separate line. As the printed G/L Transactions report is a detailed audit trail document you do not have to duplicate all the details in the General Ledger.

❑ Select: `Yes`

The following choices will appear in an option box:

```
Consolidate by
Date/source code/account code
Date/account code
```

If you select "Date/source code/account code", for each date there will be one debit and/or one credit entry for each source code within an account. The reference for each entry is the source code shown in the G/L Transactions report, and the description for each entry is "Consol. by AR" on the date.

If you select "Date/account code", for each date there will be one debit and/or one credit entry for each account. Both the source code and reference will be ARCO. This choice reduces the amount of detail transferred to the General Ledger.

❑ Select: `Date/account code`

After the ACCPAC Plus sorts and consolidates the file, the Reports Menu will appear on the screen.

You cannot proceed with the period end without clearing the G/L Transactions report. This must be done through the General Ledger when the General Ledger and Accounts Receivable are integrated. If you were using only the Accounts Receivable, ACCPAC Plus would display a message allowing you to clear G/L Transaction report.

Review the G/L Transaction report. Each transaction posted to the Accounts Receivable is printed in this report. Within General Ledger accounts the transactions are sorted by date and then an entry number, which is determined by the posting sequence, batch, and batch entry numbers. The source code is "AR" for Accounts Receivable followed by two letters that represent the original type of entry to the Accounts Receivable. Debits and credits are totalled for each General Ledger account and for the complete report.

❑ Press: [Esc] to return to the ACCPAC Accounts Receivable Master Menu.

❑ Press: Q to return to the Start Menu.

Retrieving Subledger Batches

You should post Account Receivable batches to the General Ledger through the General Ledger and Financial Reporter module.

❑ Select: G/L E. & J. Enterprises from the Start Menu.

If necessary, add this selection to the Start Menu. Refer to Chapter 2 if you need detailed instructions.

The Last access date field shows the last date that you used the General Ledger and Financial Reporter for E. & J. Enterprises.

❑ Type: 113098 in the New date field for the period end, November 30, 1998.

❑ Press: [Enter]

If the new date is eight or more days later than the last access date, ACCPAC Plus will display the following prompt in the lower portion of the screen:

```
New date is more than one week later than old date.

        Accept        Edit
```

❑ Select: Accept

The information message will appear:

```
There are outstanding subledger batches to be retrieved

                    Continue
```

❏ Press: [Enter]

❏ Select: 3. Transaction processing

❏ Select: 1. Batch processing

❏ Select: 2. Retrieve subledger batches

The Retrieve Subledger Batches screen (Figure 18–6) will be displayed.

Figure 18–6

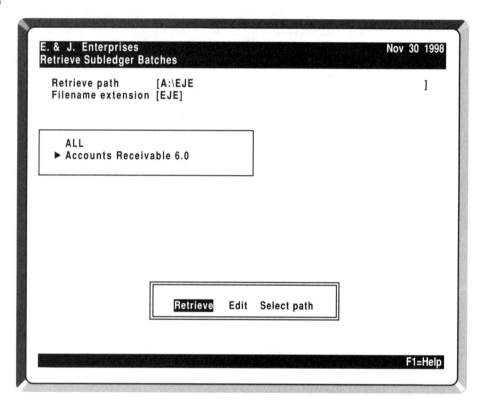

The "Retrieve path" field describes the source from which ACCPAC Plus will retrieve the subledger batch file. The default is determined by the Start Menu line that specifies the subdirectory **EJE** in the root directory of Drive **A**. The Filename extension identifies files with **EJE** as the extension. If your Accounts Receivable data files were stored on a different disk drive, or in a different subdirectory of drive A, or with a different extension, you could select "Select path" and enter the proper information.

The option box in the upper portion of the screen displays the subledger batches found in the location specified by the retrieve path and filename extension. "Accounts Receivable 6.0" should be the only outstanding subledger batch. The default is to retrieve "ALL" subledger batches.

❏ Select: `Retrieve`

As ACCPAC Plus is retrieving the batch, it will display and update a "Totals" information box at the right of the screen. Once the batch has been brought into the General Ledger, the following message will be displayed:

```
┌─────────────────────────────────────────────────────────┐
│                                                           │
│    Retrieval completed. Entries have been written to batch X.   │
│                                                           │
│                        Continue                          │
│                                                           │
└─────────────────────────────────────────────────────────┘
```

The batch number indicated by the X is the General Ledger batch to which the consolidated transaction information has been transferred.

❏ Press: [Enter] to continue.

The General Ledger will automatically clear the G/L Transactions report and then display the Batch Processing Menu.

❏ Press: [Esc] to return to the Transaction Processing Menu.

❏ Select: `2. Print batches`

❏ Select: `Print`

Review the printed Batch Listing. Each entry consists of the consolidated transaction information for one date. For the first entry "99" has been assigned as the period number because the date, Sep 05 98, is before the start of the current fiscal year. This is an invalid fiscal period as indicated by the error code 2. If you did not change the status of period 1 to "open" after running the Change Fiscal Year function in Chapter 9, this same error code would be printed beside each line. Before posting the batch to the current year in the General Ledger you would have to edit the Company Profile to change the status of period 1 to "open" (Chapter 3). During posting ACCPAC Plus would transfer entry 1 to another batch which you could modify to change the fiscal period (Chapters 5 and 6) and then post to the previous fiscal year (Chapter 9).

❏ Select: `1. Batch processing`

❏ Select: `1. Add/modify/delete batches`

❏ Enter the batch number for the batch retrieved from the Accounts Receivable.

❏ Modify the batch, changing the fiscal period for entry 1 from "99" to "1".

❏ Save the changes and print the batch again.

❏ Post the batch to current year in the General Ledger.

❏ Print and clear the posting journal.

❏ Press: [Esc] to return to the ACCPAC General Ledger Master Menu.

❏ Press: Q to return to the Start Menu.

PERIOD END

Before continuing with the period end processing, you should back up your data files.

❑ Select: A/R E. & J. Enterprises

❑ Press: [Enter] to accept November 30, 1998 as the New date

❑ Select: 5. Periodic processing

❑ Select: 3. Period end

The "Transaction clearing date" is the date up to which fully paid transactions will be cleared from the current Accounts Receivable data and transferred to historical data. This date is also used to calculate the date up to which historical information should be deleted.

❑ Press: [Enter] to accept the Transaction clearing date of 11/30/98.

ACCPAC Plus will display the warning message shown in Figure 18–7.

Figure 18–7

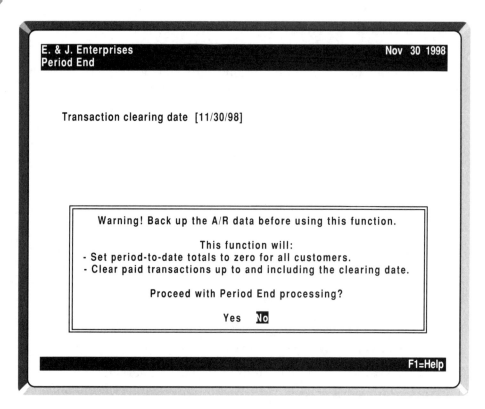

E. & J. Enterprises   Nov 30 1998
Period End

    Transaction clearing date [11/30/98]

        Warning! Back up the A/R data before using this function.

                        This function will:
        - Set period-to-date totals to zero for all customers.
        - Clear paid transactions up to and including the clearing date.

                Proceed with Period End processing?
                            Yes   No

                                                            F1=Help

If you have not backed up your data files you should choose "No" and then return to the Start Menu to back up these files.

❑ Select: Yes

The following message will appear:

```
┌──────────────────────────────────────────────┐
│                                                │
│      Clear customer history up to Oct 31 98?   │
│                                                │
│                Yes        No                   │
│                                                │
└──────────────────────────────────────────────┘
```

This function allows you to clear the fully paid transaction in formation from the historical file used by the Inquiries Menu. If you wished to keep this information for reference you would select "No".

❑ Select: Yes

The next message displayed allows you to clear the batch status information for all batches except "open" batches. It does not reset the batch numbers to zero.

```
┌──────────────────────────────────────────────┐
│                                                │
│          Clear batch status information?       │
│                                                │
│                Yes        No                   │
│                                                │
└──────────────────────────────────────────────┘
```

❑ Select: Yes

ACCPAC Plus will move the fully paid transactions to the history file and then delete those transactions that are dated before October 31, 1998 from the history file. Once the batch status has been cleared, the Periodic Processing Menu will reappear.

❑ Press: [Esc] to return to the ACCPAC Accounts Receivable Master Menu.

❑ Select: Q to return to the Start Menu.

❑ Back up your data files for use in Chapter 19.

YEAR END

Do not attempt this function now. The following material is for your reference after you have completed processing a full year's entries to Accounts Receivable.

The purpose of this function is to transfer customer sales totals for the current year to the previous year's total in preparation for a new fiscal year. The function also resets batch numbers, posting sequence numbers, and clears the batch status information. The recurring charges year-to-date totals are reset to zero. Year-to-date statistics are moved to last-year statistics and the current-year statistics are reset to zero.

This function is used only once each year, after the Period End function is completed at the end of the last fiscal period. You must not run this function twice, or you will reset the customer statistics to zero for both the current year and the previous year.

When you have completed the period end procedures for the final period of the fiscal year, you would complete the following steps to prepare for a new fiscal year:

1. Back up your data files to two disks. These back-up disks should be write-protected and stored in a safe location.

2. Enter the last day of the fiscal year as the "New date".

3. Select: `5. Periodic Processing`

4. Select: `4. Year end`

5. Verify that the "Transaction clearing date" displays the last day of the fiscal year and press **Enter**.

6. You would then receive a warning about backing up your data. If you had not backed up your data files, you would select "No" and do so before proceeding to select "Yes".

7. Clear the customer history file.

8. Return to the Start Menu and back up your data files again.

After completing these steps you would be prepared to enter Accounts Receivable information for the new fiscal year.

REVIEW QUESTIONS

1. Describe the sequence of operations that should be completed at period end.
2. What are recurring charges and how are they processed?
3. Why should you print Customer Statements before transferring the Accounts Receivable information to the General Ledger or running the Period End Function?
4. Describe the steps necessary to transfer the Accounts Receivable information to the General Ledger.
5. What does the Period End Function do?
6. Why must you be sure to run the Year End Function only once?

EXERCISE

The end of the first period is November 30, 1998.

1. Charge interest on all overdue accounts. Post the batch. Print and clear the Invoice Posting Journal for these interest charges.
2. Process the recurring charges. Post the batch. Print and clear the Invoice Posting Journal for these recurring charges.
3. Print the Detailed Aged Trial Balance.
4. Print and consolidate the G/L transactions.
5. Retrieve the Accounts Receivable subledger batch in the General Ledger and print the transaction batch.
6. If necessary, edit the transaction batch and post it to the General Ledger.
7. Print and clear the Posting Journal.
8. Return to the Accounts Receivable and complete the period end procedures.
9. Print the Aged Trial Balance and the Tax Tracking report.
10. Back up your files and exit ACCPAC Plus.

CHAPTER

19 Statements, Letters & Labels

Most companies send period end statements to their customers summarizing the invoices that are still due. A company may also wish to send letters to those customers whose accounts are more than 60 days overdue or to all customers, announcing new products, services, or location. The company may also wish to produce labels for customer mailings. In this chapter, you will customize the printing of customer statements, letters, and labels.

❑ Enter the commands necessary to activate the ACCPAC Plus Accounts Receivable module and to display the ACCPAC Accounts Receivable Master Menu for E. & J. Enterprises. Enter December 30, 1998 as the new date.

GETTING READY

❑ Create Recurring Charges and Interest Charges invoice batches as you did in Chapter 18.

❑ Print the Invoice Batch Listings.

❑ Post the batches.

❑ Print and clear the Posting Journal.

❑ Press: ⌊Esc⌋ to return to the ACCPAC Accounts Receivable Master Menu.

CREATING A STATEMENT SPECIFICATION

In Chapter 18 you printed customer statements using a default statement specification (STMT) for printing on standardized pre-printed forms. If your company does not want to use these standard pre-printed forms, it can design its own forms and have them printed commercially. You must set up a specification file to print the information on your customized forms. A specification file stores the codes required to produce the format that you desire, the codes that transfer information from the Accounts Receivable data files to the printed statements, and the text that you want to print. In this section you will create a specification to fit E. & J. Enterprises' needs.

When modifying or creating a new specification for a customer statement, you should incorporate space for the following information:

1. your company's name, address, and telephone number;
2. the customer's name, address, and account number;
3. the statement date and page number;
4. the transaction dates, invoice numbers, and amounts;
5. the total amount due;
6. the aging totals;
7. and any text that you wish to print.

E. & J. Enterprises has decided to print its statements on 8.5 x 11 inch paper rather than on the shorter paper required by the default specification.

❑ Select: 6. Housekeeping   from the ACCPAC Accounts Receivable Master Menu.

❑ Select: 2. Maintain specifications

The Maintain Specifications screen (Figure 19–1) will appear.

The options available on the menu bar at the bottom of the screen are described below:

Make active	tells ACCPAC Plus which specification you want to use.
Edit	is used to create new specifications and to alter existing ones.
Copy	allows you to copy a specification.
Delete	removes a specification from the data files. Once a specification has been deleted, it cannot be recovered.
Align	tests the column alignment and layout of specifications in other ACCPAC Plus modules.
Print	prints the specifications of the document selected.
Retrieve	moves specifications created in the Easywriter II wordprocessing module to the Accounts Receivable module.
Import	brings specification files from other software packages into the Accounts Receivable module.

Changes to a specification should be made to a copy of the working specification and then tested to ensure that the new statement works. A duplicate specification must be given a different name from the original specification.

Figure 19–1

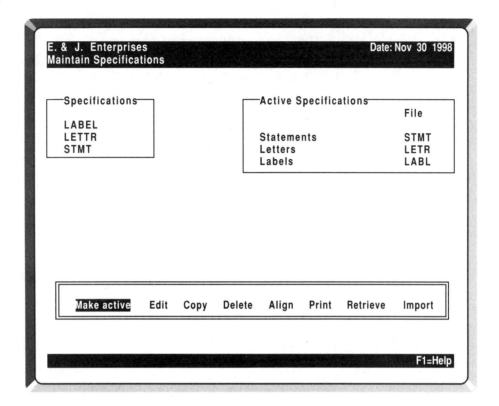

E. & J. Enterprises   Date: Nov 30 1998
Maintain Specifications

```
┌─Specifications─┐              ┌─Active Specifications─┐
│                │              │                  File │
│  LABEL         │              │                       │
│  LETTR         │              │  Statements      STMT │
│  STMT          │              │  Letters         LETR │
│                │              │  Labels          LABL │
└────────────────┘              └───────────────────────┘


        ┌────────────────────────────────────────────────────────────┐
        │  Make active   Edit   Copy   Delete   Align   Print   Retrieve   Import  │
        └────────────────────────────────────────────────────────────┘

                                                              F1=Help
```

❑ Select: `Edit`

The option box at the bottom of the screen will disappear and the specifications box will become active as indicated by the data entry field and the enhanced double line on the display.

❑ Type: `ST-1` in the blank `Edit` field to assign the name "ST–1" to the new specification.

❑ Press: Enter

The display will then change to a blinking cursor in the first row and 19 rows of plus signs. This is the ACCPAC Plus equivalent of a blank screen for entering specifications.

Form Control Specifications

Form control specifications determine how the customer statements will be printed. The four different types of form control specifications are described below.

Comment Specifications

Comment specifications are not used in calculations or printed as part of the statement itself. They are simply comments that are used to describe the specification or a section of the specification. The text of a comment will appear when you "Edit" or "Print" a specification but will not be printed when you use the specification to print a document. Each comment specification must begin with two periods (..) at the left margin, followed by the text of the comment.

The first three lines on your specification document will be comments identifying the statement, its author, and the date it was created.

❑ Type: `.. CUSTOMER STATEMENT SPECIFICATION NUMBER ONE`
❑ Press: [Enter] to move the cursor to the second line.
❑ Type: `.. BY JOAN AND ERIN`
❑ Press: [Enter]
❑ Type: `.. ON TODAY'S DATE`
❑ Press: [Enter]

Detail Length Specification

The detail length specification tells ACCPAC Plus how many lines are available on the form for printing the customer transaction details. Standard computer paper (8.5 x 11 inches) has a total of 66 lines so the detail size specification will be 66 less the number of lines allowed for the header and footer. The number of lines available must be entered at the left margin in the first line immediately following the comment lines.

Your specification will have 22 lines for the header and 9 lines for the footer, leaving 35 lines for the customer information. No period precedes the detail length specification, which must be on the first line following the comments.

❑ Type: `35`
❑ Press: [Enter]

Dollar Size Specification

All statement specifications must include a dollar size specification on the line following the detail length specification. The dollar size specification identifies the number of characters (from one to fifteen) allowed for printing currency amounts. You must count numbers, decimal points, commas, and a trailing plus or minus sign. For example, "1,000.00" would require at least nine spaces. You should allow more space than you expect to use. The number of characters is entered at the left margin on the line below the detail size specification.

To allow 13 characters for the dollar size specification,

❑ Type: `13`
❑ Press: [Enter]

Pitch Specification

The pitch specification is optional. It is used to alter the number of characters per inch that will be printed on the statement. If you do not insert this specification, ACCPAC Plus will use your printer's default setting or the last setting sent to the printer. It is good practice to include a pitch specification in each specification.

The pitch specification uses the form **.Pn,** where **n** stands for the number of characters per inch that you require. (The condensed print specification for most printers is **.P17.**) It should be entered at the left margin of the line immediately following the dollar size specification.

You can change the pitch within a document by entering a different pitch specification immediately before the first line you want to change. All subsequent lines will be printed in that type size until the pitch specification is changed again.

To set the pitch specification at 10 characters per inch,

❑ Type: `.P10`

❑ Press: [Enter]

The Header

The header is the upper section of the customer statement. Each line in the header specification must begin with **.H,** even if you want a blank line. You have allowed 22 lines for the header.

❑ Type: `.H`   to specify that the first line in the header is blank.

❑ Press: [Enter]

Indent

@nn controls the size of the indent, **nn** being the number of spaces from the left margin. Standard computer paper is 80 characters wide at a pitch specification of **.P10**.

.H @35STATEMENT prints the text "STATEMENT" 35 spaces from the left side of the page.

❑ Type: `.H @35STATEMENT`   on the second line of the header.

❑ Press: [Enter]

❑ Type: `.H`   to leave the third line of the header blank.

❑ Press: [Enter]

Information codes

Information codes tell ACCPAC Plus which information you wish to retrieve from the Accounts Receivable data files for printing. You can combine text and information codes on the same line. A percentage sign, %, at the beginning of an information code instructs ACCPAC Plus to print a piece of information stored in its memory.

@31DATE : prints "DATE : " starting 31 spaces from the left of the page.
%M1.M   %M1.D   %M1.Y prints the date of the statement. Each part of the date must start with a percentage sign.

> **%M1.M** prints the first three letters of the name of the month.
> **%M1.D** prints the day of the month.
> **%M1.Y** prints the year.

❑ Type: `.H @31Date : %M1.M %M1.D %M1.Y` on the fourth line of the header.

❑ Press: [Enter]

%M2 prints the page number.

❑ Type: `.H @60Page %M2` on line five of the header to print the page number starting 60 spaces from the left margin.

❑ Press: [Enter]

%M3 prints the company's name from the Company Profile.

❑ Type: `.H @12%M3` on line 6 of the header.

❑ Press: [Enter]

%M4, %M5, %M6, and **%M9''** print the four address lines from the Company Profile. **%M7** prints the zip or postal code.

❑ Enter the specifications to print the four address lines and the zip code or postal code 12 spaces from the left margin on the next five lines.

❑ Type: `.H` to leave header line 12 blank.

❑ Press: [Enter]

%C1 prints the customer number.

❑ Type: `.H @35Customer Number %C1` on line 13 of the header.

❑ Press: [Enter]

%C2 prints the customer name.

❑ Type: `.H @12%C2` on line 14 of the header.

❑ Press: [Enter]

%C3, %C4, %C5, and **%C13** print the four address lines from the customer information and **%C6** prints the customer's zip or postal code.

❑ Enter the specifications to print the four address lines and the zip code starting 12 spaces from the left margin.

- ❑ Type: `.H` to leave line 20 of the header specification blank.
- ❑ Press: [Enter]
- ❑ Type: `.H @12Invoice @22Date @32Code @42Reference @62Amount` to print the column headings on line 21.
- ❑ Press: [Enter]
- ❑ Type: `.H` to leave line 22 blank.
- ❑ Press: [Enter]

Detail Specification

The detail specification controls the printing of the detailed invoice and payment information for the customer. You only have to enter one specification line to print all the transactions on the customer statement. Each transaction will appear on a separate line in the format specified. The detail specification line must start with **.L** at the left margin.

%**L2**	prints the invoice number.
%**L1.N**	prints the number of the month of the invoice date.
%**L1.D**	prints the day of the month of the invoice date.
%**L1.Y**	prints the last two digits of the year of the invoice date.
%**L3**	prints the two-character transaction type code (invoice, cash receipt, interest, recurring charge, or adjustment).
%**L4**	prints the eight-character reference, which is usually the customer's purchase order number or the name of the person authorizing the charge.
%**L5.1**	prints the invoice amount, with debits and credits in the same column.

- ❑ Type: `.L @12%L2 @22%L1.N/%L1.D/%L1.Y @32%L3 @42%L4 @62%L5.1` on the first line below the header specification.
- ❑ Press: [Enter]

Footer Specification

Each line in the footer must begin with **.F**. You have allowed nine lines for the footer.

%**F1.1**	stands for the statement total.
%**F2.1**	indicates the current total.
%**F3.1**	stands for the net amount overdue in the first aging category, as defined in the Company Profile.
%**F4.1**	refers to the net amount overdue in the second aging category.
%**F5.1**	refers to the net amount overdue in the third aging category.

❑ Enter the following footer specification lines, starting on the line below the detail specification:

```
.F
.F
.F @42Total @62%F1.1
.F
.F @10Current @24 30 Days @39 60 Days @54 90 Days
.F
.F @5%F2.1 @20%F3.1 @35%F4.1 @50%F5.1
.F
.F
```

❑ Press: [Esc] to indicate that you have finished making changes.

❑ Select: Save changes

PRINTING A SPECIFICATION

The Maintain Specifications screen will now show your new specification, ST–1, in the specifications box. Before using ST–1 to print customer statements you should print a copy of the specification and check it for errors.

❑ Select: Print

❑ Move the selector bar to ST-1.

❑ Press: [Enter]

❑ Type: 10 in the With an indent of: field.

❑ Press: [Enter]

ACCPAC Plus will display the following message:

```
┌──────────────────────────────────────────────┐
│                                                │
│       Print file ST–1 with an indent of 10.    │
│                                                │
│              Continue      Exit                │
│                                                │
└──────────────────────────────────────────────┘
```

❑ Select: Continue

Compare your specification with the one shown in Table 19–1. Note any errors that need to be corrected.

Table 19–1

```
.. CUSTOMER STATEMENT SPECIFICATION NUMBER ONE
.. BY JOAN AND ERIN
.. ON TODAY'S DATE
35
13
.P10
.H
.H @35STATEMENT
.H
.H @31 Date : %M1.M %M1.D %M1.L
.H @60Page %M2
.H @12%M3
.H @12%M4
.H @12%M5
.H @12%M6
.H @12%M9
.H @12%M7
.H
.H @35Customer Number %C1
.H @12%C2
.H @12%C3
.H @12%C4
.H @12%C5
.H @12%C13
.H @12%C6
.H
.H @12Invoice @22Date @32Code @42Reference @62Amount
.H
.L @12%L2 @22%L1.N/%L1.D/%L1.Y @32%L3 @42%L4 @62%L5.1
.F
.F
.F @42 Total @62%F1.1
.F
.F @10Current @24 30 Days @39 60 Days @54 90 Days
.F
.F @5%F2.1 @20%F3.1 @35%F4.1 @50%F5.1
.F
.F
```

EDITING A SPECIFICATION

❑ Select: Edit

❑ Move the selector bar to ST-1 in the Edit box.

❑ Press: [Enter]

The screen will display the first 20 lines of the specification. You can move the cursor using the directional keys. To correct an error you would move the cursor to the error and type the correct information. You can insert a character by pressing **Insert** and typing the character. To delete a character you move the cursor to the character and press **Delete**. To insert a line you move the cursor to the first space in the line above where you want the line to be inserted and press **Enter**. A line can be deleted by pressing **F6**.

❑ Move the cursor to the beginning of the first comment line.

❑ Press: [Enter]

❑ Type: `..FOR USE WITH 8.5 X 11 PAPER`

❑ Move the cursor to the `J` in `JOAN` on line three.

❑ Type: `your name.`

If necessary, use the **Delete** or **Spacebar** to erase extra characters.

❑ Make any other corrections necessary.

❑ Press: [Esc] when all corrections have been made.

❑ Select: `Save changes`

PRINTING STATEMENTS

Before you can print statements with the new specification, you must make that specification active.

❑ Select: `Make active` from the menu bar.

The "Active Specifications" box in the upper right of the screen will become highlighted. Three specification types, Statements, Letters, and Labels, are displayed to the left of the box, with the selected specification file names to their right.

❑ Select: `Statements      STMT`

The highlighted bar will move to the Specifications box on the left.

❑ Select: `ST-1`

A message box will appear at the bottom of the screen.

```
┌─────────────────────────────────────────┐
│                                           │
│      Make ST-1 active for Statements?     │
│                                           │
│            Yes        No                  │
│                                           │
└─────────────────────────────────────────┘
```

❑ Select: `Yes`

❑ Press: [Esc] twice to return to the ACCPAC Accounts Receivable Master Menu.

❑ Select: `4. Reports`

❑ Select: `1. Statements/letters/labels`

❑ Enter the information to print statements as of December 30, 1998 for all customers on continuous form paper.

- ☐ Print the Alignment form. If necessary, edit the specification again and reprint the Alignment form.
- ☐ Print the customer statements.

A message box will appear at the bottom of the screen.

```
┌─────────────────────────────────────────────┐
│                                               │
│        Are the printed statements satisfactory? │
│                                               │
│              Yes        No                    │
│                                               │
└─────────────────────────────────────────────┘
```

- ☐ Select: `Yes`

Review the statements. The main reason for the new statements being unsatisfactory would be an error that you missed in the specification. If necessary, review your printed specification again, edit the specification, and print the statements again.

- ☐ Press: [Esc] to return to the ACCPAC Accounts Receivable Master Menu.

CUSTOMER LETTERS

ACCPAC Plus can be used to print letters to be sent to customers. The specification "LETTR", included with the Accounts Receivable module, prints a collection letter to customers with a portion of their account more than 90 days overdue. Erin and Joan have decided to change this letter and send the revised letter to customers with a portion of their account more than 60 days overdue.

- ☐ Select: `6. Housekeeping`
- ☐ Select: `2. Maintain specifications`

Copying A Specification

Rather than changing the original specification, you should edit a copy of the specification in case your changes do not work.

- ☐ Select: `Copy`

The screen display will change and the "Copy from" box will be highlighted.

- ☐ Select: `LETTR`

A "Copy to" box will appear on the screen.

- ☐ Type: `LTR60`
- ☐ Press: [Enter]

Letter Specifications

The specification guidelines for letters and labels are the same.

❑ Select: `Edit`

❑ Select: `LTR60`

The screen will display the first 20 lines of the specification shown in Figure 19–2.

Figure 19–2

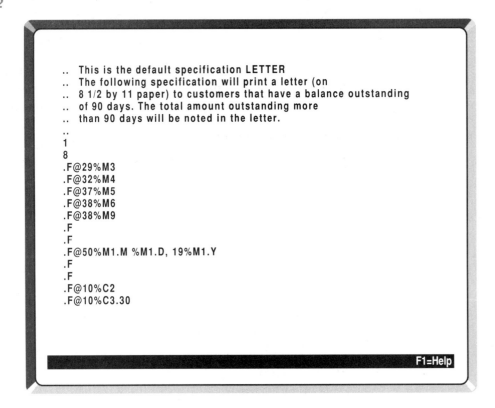

```
..   This is the default specification LETTER
..   The following specification will print a letter (on
..   8 1/2 by 11 paper) to customers that have a balance outstanding
..   of 90 days. The total amount outstanding more
..   than 90 days will be noted in the letter.
..
1
8
.F@29%M3
.F@32%M4
.F@37%M5
.F@38%M6
.F@38%M9
.F
.F
.F@50%M1.M %M1.D, 19%M1.Y
.F
.F
.F@10%C2
.F@10%C3.30
```

F1=Help

❑ Type: `LTR60`   over the specification name   `LETTER`

❑ Delete any excess characters with the spacebar or delete key.

❑ Type: `60`   over the   `90`   on the last two comment lines.

For letters (or labels) you must enter a detail length specification of "1" in the first line after the comments. This will produce a single blank line at the top of the page. You must then include one information specification for each line available on the page. If you are using 11-inch paper you must enter 65 information specification lines.

The second specification must be a dollar-width specification. If the letter (or label) does not contain dollar amounts, you would enter "0".

Each specification line must begin with **.F**.

❏ Move the cursor to the last line of the first paragraph of the letter portion of this specification.

You must change this line to print the amount more than 60 days overdue.

❏ Type: `%F4.1` over the `%F5.1` information specification.

❏ Type: `60` over `90`.

❏ Move the cursor to the first letter of the last line of the second paragraph.

Erin and Joan have decided not to extend credit to customers with accounts more than 60 days overdue.

❏ Type: `not be able to extend additional credit`

❏ Replace Mrs. M. Smith with your name.

❏ Press: [Esc] to indicate that there are no further changes.

❏ Select: `Save changes`

❏ Enter the commands to make `LTR60` the active specification for letters.

❏ Press: [Esc] twice to return to the ACCPAC Accounts Receivable Master Menu.

Printing Letters

❏ Select: `4. Reports`

❏ Select: `1. Statements/letters/labels`

❏ Select: `Edit`

❏ Select: `Letters` from the `Document type` box.

You must now change the defaults displayed to print letters to customers with accounts 60 to 89 days overdue.

❏ Press: [Enter] to move the cursor to the `CUSTOMERS with balance between` field.

❏ Type: `60`

❏ Press: [Enter]

❏ Type: `89` in the second days overdue field.

❏ Delete any excess characters.

❏ Press: [Enter]

❏ Press: [Esc] to indicate that there are no more changes.

❏ Select: `Align`

Review the alignment form. The run date has been printed and text that would be added from the ACCPAC Plus date files is indicated by **X**'s. The space for the amount outstanding is indicated by **9**'s.

If you were to select "Print", there should be no customers to print. Erin and Joan will use this letter in the future.

LABELS

You can also print labels.

☐ Select: Edit

☐ Select: Labels

☐ Move the cursor to the Select customers based on balance (Y/N) field.

☐ Type: N

☐ Press: Enter

☐ Select: Print

The customer information printed fits on standard one-inch labels available in continuous form from your stationery supplier.

☐ Quit ACCPAC.

☐ Back up your data files.

REVIEW QUESTIONS

1. Why would a company decide to create its own customer statement specifications rather than use the default specification in the ACCPAC Plus Accounts Receivable module?
2. What information should be included on all customer statements? Why?
3. Describe the function of each of the four form control specifications.
4. Name the three sections of a statement and describe the information included in each.

EXERCISE

1. Using the "Edit" option, create a statement specification (called "STTWO") for your company. The specification should print a complete statement on blank 8.5 x 11 inch computer paper. You may use the "ST–1" specification created for E. & J. Enterprises as a model.
2. Print the statement specifications and an alignment printout. Make any corrections necessary and use the specifications to print customer statements.
3. Back up your data files.

20 Macavity & Co. Case

This case continues from the General Ledger case presented in Chapter 11. After Macavity & Co.'s first month of operations, Rum Tum Tugger decided to add the ACCPAC Plus Accounts Receivable module to the computerized accounting system. The ACCPAC Plus Accounts Payable module will be added later.

After completing this case, organize and submit Macavity & Co.'s printouts. Each printout *must* contain your initials following the company name. Save the data files for your instructor to evaluate.

1. ADDING TO THE START MENU

Using the same data disk that you used for Chapter 11, create a line on the Start Menu using the following information:

Start Name	Macavity A/R
Program	Accounts Receivable
Drive	A:
Data Directory	Cat
Data Extension	Cat

2. CREATING THE ACCOUNTS RECEIVABLE

Create the Accounts Receivable files using the following data.

Company Data

Company Name	Macavity & Co. (and your initials)
Address	1313 Fishbone Alley
	Alleycat Junction
	Meowville
	KIT-KAT
Telephone	111-555-9999
Fax	111-555-9998
Company Number	9
Contact	Rum Tum Tugger

System Options and Interest Charges

System options

Process recurring charges	N
Keep transaction history for	30 days
Allow edit of retrieved/imported batches	Y
Allow edit of customer statistics	Y
Clear transaction detail by	Period end

Interest charges

Charge interest on	Overdue invoices
Charge interest on accounts	1 day(s) overdue
Compound interest	N
Minimum interest charge	0.00
Round up to minimum	N
Annual interest rate	12.00
Invoice - Prefix	INT-
Invoice - Sequence number	1

Customer Defaults and Statement Options

Customer defaults

Account type	Open item
Credit limit	5000.00
Statements	Y
Interest	Y

Statement Options

Aging
Accept the default aging periods of 1-30, 31-60, and 61-90.

Dunning Messages

Current	Thanks for keeping your account current
1 to 30 days	Please keep your account current
31 to 60 days	Account overdue. Please pay!
60 to 91 days	Payment required on overdue invoices!
Over 90 days	Please pay account immediately!
Print zero balance statements	N
Print blanks instead of zeros	Y

ACCPAC Plus Integration

G/L departments	N
Send to G/L reference field	Customer name
Send to G/L description field	Document description
Integrate with Job Costing	N
Retainage Accounting	N

Start the program using August 1, 1997 as the date.

3. HOUSEKEEPING

Adding the Control Account Set

Add the following control account set:

Account set code	1
Description	Accounts Receivable - General
Receivable control	1201
Bank	1101
Payment discounts	4115
Interest income	5300

Adding the Billing Cycle

Add the following billing cycle:

Billing cycle code	1
Description	Monthly
Frequency	30

Adding the Terms

There are two terms codes. The first, terms code "sales", has as a description "2/10, n/30". The second terms code is "cash" with the description "Cash sales". Complete the fields with the appropriate information to create these codes.

Adding the Distributions

Distribution code	sales
Description	Merchandise sales
G/L account	4101
Tax tracking	N

Add the following distributions: "stax" - Sales Tax Payable, G/L account number 2105. Tax tracking is to be recorded at 5%.

The third distribution code is "vat", Value Added Tax Payable, G/L account number 2110. Tax tracking is to be recorded at 10%.

Print the company profile.

4. CREATING THE CUSTOMER ACCOUNTS

During July, you posted credit sales to two customers, Mistoffelees and Skimbleshanks. As well, three other customers have been approved for credit. The full profiles for all five customers follow. All of the customers will be open accounts, except for Mistoffelees, which will be a balance forward account.

Create these five customer accounts.

a) Customer Number 1000

Name	Bustopher Jones
Short name	Busto
Address	1 James Street
	Fatcat Place
	Meowville
	KIT-KAT

Salesperson	Kitty
Terms	sales
Credit Limit	5000
Billing cycle	1
Account set	1
Start	07/01/97
Telephone	111-555-9997
Fax	111-555-9996
Contact	B. Jones
Account type	Open item
Interest	Yes
Statements	Yes
Report group	goods
Customer Type	Base
Ship via	Pick up
Territory	9
Tax group, status, and exemption	press [ENTER] in each field

b) Customer Number   1020

Name	Old Deuteronomy
Short name	Deute
Address	17 High Street
	Market Square
	Meowville
	KIT-KAT
Salesperson	Kitty
Terms	sales
Credit Limit	5000
Billing cycle	1
Account set	1
Start	07/01/97
Telephone	111-555-9995
Fax	111-555-9994
Contact	O. Deuteronomy
Account type	Open item
Interest	Yes
Statements	Yes
Report group	goods
Customer Type	Base
Ship via	Pick up
Territory	9
Tax group, status, and exemption	press [ENTER] in each field

c) Customer Number   1040

Name	Growltiger
Short name	Growl
Address	The Old Barge
	The Docks
	Meowville
	KIT-KAT
Salesperson	Dewi
Terms	sales
Credit Limit	5000
Billing cycle	1
Account set	1
Start	07/01/97
Telephone	111-555-9993
Fax	111-555-9992
Contact	Growltiger
Account type	Open item
Interest	Yes
Statements	Yes
Report group	goods
Customer Type	Base
Ship via	Pick up
Territory	9
Tax group, status, and exemption	press [ENTER] in each field

d) Customer Number   1060

Name	Mistoffelees
Short name	Misto
Address	72 Magic Way
	Conjuring St.
	Meowville
	KIT-KAT
Salesperson	Dewi
Terms	sales
Credit Limit	5000
Billing cycle	1
Account set	1
Start	07/01/97
Telephone	111-555-9991
Fax	111-555-9990
Contact	Mistoffelees
Account type	Balance forward
Interest	Yes
Statements	Yes
Report group	goods
Customer Type	Base
Ship via	Pick up
Territory	9
Tax group, status, and exemption	press [ENTER] in each field

e) *Customer Number   1080*

Name	Skimbleshanks
Short name	Skimb
Address	25 Luggage Van
	Train Station
	Meowville
	KIT-KAT
Salesperson	Dewi
Terms	sales
Credit Limit	5000
Billing cycle	1
Account set	1
Start	07/01/97
Telephone	111-555-9989
Fax	111-555-9988
Contact	Skimbleshanks
Account type	Open item
Interest	Yes
Statements	Yes
Report group	goods
Customer Type	Base
Ship via	Pick up
Territory	9
Tax group, status, and exemption	press [ENTER] in each field

Print the Customer list and statistics report and review it for errors. Make any necessary corrections.

5.   ENTERING THE JULY TRANSACTIONS

You must now post the July transactions (posted to the General Ledger in Chapter 11) for credit sales to the Accounts Receivable Ledger. The balance in the General Ledger Accounts Receivable control account must equal the total of the Accounts Receivable subsidiary ledger accounts.

Exit from the Accounts Receivable module and start it again using July 31, 1997 as the New date.

Create a batch to post the July credit sales transactions to the Accounts Receivable ledger. The transactions were as follows:

a)   Mistoffelees: $100 (plus 5% sales tax and 10% value added tax), invoice number 001, reference Mist-1, dated July 13, 1997. The invoice was for 1,000 fishbone toothpicks.

b)   Skimbleshanks: $150 (plus 5% sales tax and 10% value added tax), invoice number 002, reference Skim-1, July 27, 1997. The invoice was for 150 fishbone toothpicks.

Print the invoice batch and review it for errors. Post the invoice batch and print the Invoice Posting Journal sorted first by Customer number, then by Document number. Clear the posting journal after the second Invoice Posting Journal has been printed. Print a copy of the Aged Trial Balance in Detail and compare it to the Accounts Receivable, Trade control account in the General Ledger Trial Balance that you printed in Chapter 11.

Exit from the Accounts Receivable module and start the General Ledger module using July 31, 1997 as the New date.

Retrieve the Accounts Receivable batch into the General Ledger, print the batch, then delete it so that a duplicate posting is avoided.

6. ENTERING THE AUGUST INVOICES

Exit from the ACCPAC General Ledger module. Restart ACCPAC Accounts Receivable for Macavity & Co. and reset the date to August 31, 1997. Enter the following invoices in the second invoice batch:

a) August 5: Bustopher Jones purchased fishbone toothpicks on credit for $175, invoice number 003, reference Jone-1. You will charge 10% Value Added Tax and 5% Sales Tax on the $175.00 purchase. The total invoice including tax will be $201.25.

b) August 7: Old Deuteronomy purchased fishbone toothpicks for $200, invoice number 004, reference Deut-1. Include the Value Added Tax and Sales Tax. Total invoice, $230.00.

c) August 17: Growltiger purchased fishbone toothpicks for $150, invoice number 005, reference Grow-1. Include VAT and Sales Tax on the $150.00.

d) August 27: Mistoffelees purchased another load of toothpicks for $200, invoice number 006, reference Mist-2. Add Value Added Tax and Sales Tax on to the invoice.

e) August 30: Growltiger purchased some more toothpicks for $250 for his pirate friends, invoice number 007, reference Grow-2. (Includes the sales tax and value added tax.)

Print the Invoice Batch List and review it for errors. Post the batch to the Accounts Receivable Ledger. Print the Invoice Posting Journal sorted by Customer number then by Document number. Clear the posting journal after you print the second version of the Invoice Posting Journal. Print the Aged Trial Balance in detail.

7. ENTERING THE AUGUST CASH RECEIPTS

Enter the following cash receipts.

a) August 1: Check number 246 for $115 in payment of invoice number 001 received from Mistoffelees.

b) August 22: Bustopher Jones made a partial payment of $100 on invoice number 003 using check number 731.

Print the Cash Batch List and review it for errors. Post the cash batch to the Accounts Receivable Ledger. Print the Cash Posting Journal sorted by Customer number, then clear the posting journal. Print the updated Aged Trial Balance in detail.

8. MAKING THE AUGUST ADJUSTMENTS

It has come to your attention that one of the transactions was incorrect. Invoice number 006 was recorded as a sale to Mistoffelees; it should have been recorded as a sale to Old Deuteronomy. Make the necessary adjustments, print the Adjustment Batch, post it to the Accounts Receivable Ledger, and print the Adjustment Posting Journal sorted by Customer number. Clear the posting journal after you have finished. Print the updated Aged Trial Balance in detail.

9. PROCESSING INTEREST CHARGES

Process interest charges on August 31 and then print a copy of the Aged Trial Balance in detail.

10. PRINTING/CONSOLIDATING THE TRANSACTIONS

Print the G/L transactions by account. Consolidate the G/L transactions by Date/account code in preparation for posting to the General Ledger.

11. TRANSFER THE INFORMATION TO THE GENERAL LEDGER

Exit from the Accounts Receivable module and start the General Ledger module using August 31, 1997 as the date. Retrieve the A/R subledger batch into the General Ledger. Print and post the batch. Print and clear the batch posting journal. Print an updated copy of the General Ledger listing. Compare the Accounts

Receivable control account to the total of the Accounts Receivable on the Aged Trial Balance. Exit from the General Ledger module and start the Accounts Receivable module using August 31, 1997 as the Start date.

12. *MONTH END PROCESSING*

Clear the paid and adjusted Accounts Receivable transactions. Print a final version of the Aged Trial Balance in detail.

Exit from ACCPAC Plus.

IV ACCOUNTS PAYABLE

CHAPTER

21 Accounts Payable Data Creation

In Unit IV, you will add the ACCPAC Plus Accounts Payable module for E. & J. Enterprises. This company is already using the General Ledger and Financial Reporter and Accounts Receivable modules. You would follow similar procedures to use the Accounts Payable module with a manual or non-ACCPAC General Ledger. Each chapter will guide you through one step in setting up and operating the ACCPAC Plus Accounts Payable module.

If you have not completed Unit I, Introduction, and Unit II, General Ledger and Financial Reporter, you should read Chapter 1, Using ACCPAC Plus, and work through Chapter 2, The System Manager. If you have not completed the General Ledger Unit, you will not be able to import Accounts Payable transactions into the General Ledger, nor will you be able to use the Finder to identify General Ledger account codes.

Erin and Joan have decided that it is now time to prepare the ACCPAC Plus Accounts Payable module for use on the computer.

GETTING READY

If ACCPAC Plus has not been installed on your computer system, you must install both the System Manager and the Accounts Payable module. If your Accounts Payable module was supplied with a later version of the System Manager than is installed on your computer system, you must install the new System Manager and the Accounts Payable module.

❑ Install the System Manager and the Accounts Payable module.

If necessary, turn to Chapter 2, The System Manager, for step-by-step instructions for installing the System Manager and your Accounts Payable module.

Before you can work with Accounts Payable you must add a line to the Start Menu. This line should read `A/P E. & J. Enterprises`. You should select Accounts Payable from the Program Menu, Drive A:, Directory A:\EJE and Extension EJE so that the Accounts Payable can integrate with the General Ledger data files created in Unit II.

❑ Add this line to the Start Menu.

If necessary, turn to Chapter 2, The System Manager, for step-by-step instructions for adding to the Start Menu.

CREATING ACCOUNTS PAYABLE DATA

❑ Select: `A/P E. & J. Enterprises` from the Start Menu.

The title screen (Figure 21–1) will appear.

Figure 21–1

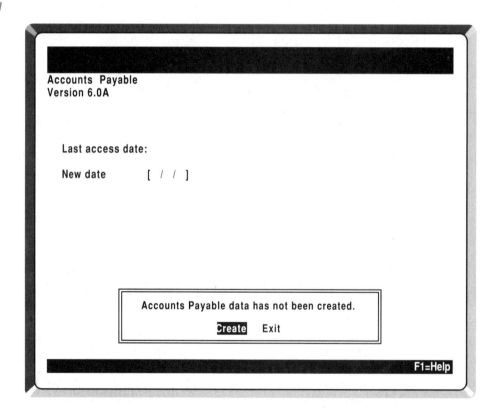

❑ Select: `Create`

ACCPAC Plus will present a series of data entry screens that allow you to create Accounts Payable data files for a company.

Company Data

The next screen records basic information about the company.

❑ Enter the information about E. & J. Enterprises, as shown in Figure 21–2.

This information is the same as that entered in the General Ledger and Financial Reporter Unit and the Accounts Receivable Unit, except for the `Identity num-ber` field. This new field can be used to record the company's identification number for 1099 reporting or the company's value added tax licence number.

You must use an identity number in conjunction with the 1099 report requirements in the United States. If your company reports payments to vendors who are subject to 1099 reporting you must enter a company identification number. If the company is a sole proprietorship, you should enter the owner's social security number as the company identification number.

Figure 21–2

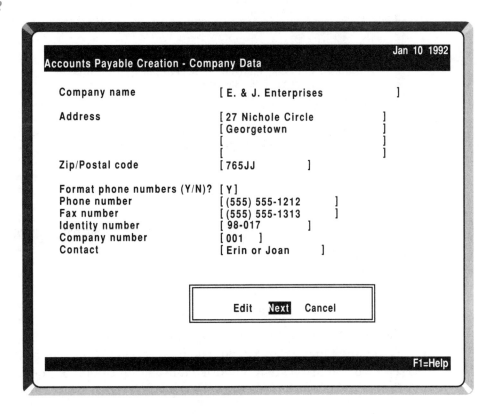

When you have finished, review the screen. If you have made an error, select `Edit` to loop back through the fields and make the necessary corrections. Once you have made the corrections and are ready to proceed,

❑ Select: `Next`

System Options and Defaults

The System Options and Defaults screen (Figure 21–3) lets you specify how ACCPAC Plus will handle vendor accounts. To simplify the adding of new vendor accounts, you should select the options that will apply to most of your vendors. You can change these defaults if you add new vendors who require other arrangements.

Figure 21–3

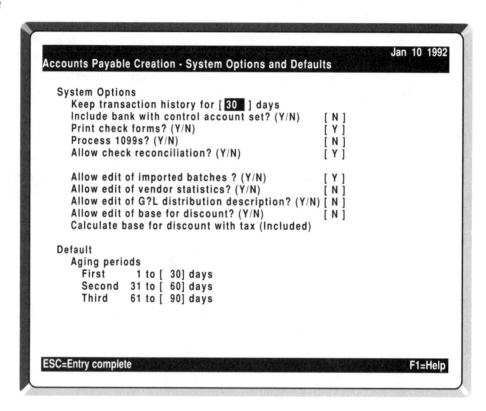

```
                                                          Jan 10 1992
Accounts Payable Creation - System Options and Defaults

    System Options
       Keep transaction history for [ 30  ] days
       Include bank with control account set? (Y/N)      [ N ]
       Print check forms? (Y/N)                          [ Y ]
       Process 1099s? (Y/N)                              [ N ]
       Allow check reconciliation? (Y/N)                 [ Y ]

       Allow edit of imported batches ? (Y/N)            [ Y ]
       Allow edit of vendor statistics? (Y/N)            [ N ]
       Allow edit of G?L distribution description? (Y/N) [ N ]
       Allow edit of base for discount? (Y/N)            [ N ]
       Calculate base for discount with tax (Included)

    Default
       Aging periods
          First     1 to [  30] days
          Second   31 to [  60] days
          Third    61 to [  90] days




ESC=Entry complete                                       F1=Help
```

Keep transaction history for [ ] days

This option allows you to control the number of days that fully paid transactions will be retained in the history file. The transaction history can be displayed on the screen using the Display Vendor Transactions option on the Inquiries Menu or printed in the Vendor Transactions report.

❏ Press: [Enter] to accept the default of 30 days.

Include bank with control account set

This option allows you to include General Ledger bank (cash) accounts in the control account sets that you will define later in this chapter. Including a cash account in a control account set that you assign to a vendor specifies the bank account to be used when you produce checks for that vendor.

You cannot change your choice for this option after the Accounts Payable data files have been created, without deleting all the data files and then creating them again.

E. & J. Enterprises has only one cash account in the chart of accounts, but may wish to add others (e.g. payroll, or foreign currency) in the future. These bank accounts would be assigned to the appropriate control account sets.

❑ Type: Y
❑ Press: [Enter]

Print check forms

This option allows you to print both manual and computer-generated checks. You must select this option to be able to print either type of check. If you do not select this option, ACCPAC Plus prints only the advices and will not print checks. E. & J. Enterprises wants to be able to print both checks and advices.

❑ Type: Y
❑ Press: [Enter]

Process 1099s

This option is used in the United States, where companies must report payments to vendors subject to "1099" reporting. Even if your company does not produce 1099 forms, you can use this option to accumulate payments to vendors during selected time periods.

❑ Type: N
❑ Press: [Enter]

Allow check reconciliation

Selecting this option allows you to use ACCPAC Plus to reconcile checks produced by the Accounts Payable module to your company's bank statement. If this option is chosen ACCPAC Plus keeps a record of the status of each posted check. You can then change the status of each check and print a Check Reconciliation Report.

If you do not choose this option, you must manually reconcile the checks with your company's bank statement. Erin and Joan have decided to use ACCPAC Plus to reconcile E. & J. Enterprises' bank statements.

❑ Type: Y
❑ Press: [Enter]

Allow edit of imported batches

This controls whether you can edit invoice and check batches retrieved from other ACCPAC Plus modules or imported from another program. If you select this option and then edit a retrieved or imported batch, the audit trail reports printed by the program will not be accurate. If you add another ACCPAC Plus module or integrate your system with another program, you can change your selection. E. & J. Enterprises does not plan to use additional ACCPAC Plus modules.

❑ Type: N
❑ Press: [Enter]

Allow edit of vendor statistics

This option enables you to view and edit statistics for each vendor. You can revise period-to-date, year-to-date, and last-year statistics for the vendors. This option is useful when you are converting to ACCPAC Plus from another accounting system. If you do not choose this option, you can view the statistics using the Display Vendor Transactions option on the Inquiries Menu, but you cannot edit them using this function.

❑ Type: Y
❑ Press: [Enter]

Allow edit of G/L distribution description

This option allows you to enter a separate description for each line of an entry, rather than only one description per entry.

❑ Type: Y
❑ Press: [Enter]

Allow edit of base for discount

Selecting this option allows you to change the discount base calculated by ACCPAC Plus for each transaction entry. The method used to calculate the discount base will be specified in the next step. You should choose this option to allow flexibility in case one of your suppliers offers partial discounts in the future.

❑ Type: Y
❑ Press: [Enter]

Calculate base for discount with tax

This determines whether the program will include or exclude the tax amount of the invoice when calculating the base for discount. If you select Included, it will be the total amount payable. If you select Excluded, ACCPAC Plus will calculate the default base for discount as the total amount payable less the total tax.

❑ Select: Excluded

Default - Aging periods

You can specify the length of the Default Aging periods that ACCPAC Plus uses to group transactions for reporting on the Aged Overdue Payables, Aged Cash Requirements, and Aged Retainage reports. You may change the aging periods as required when you print the individual reports.

❑ Press: Enter three times to accept the default settings of 1 to 30, 31 to 60, and 61 to 90 days for the Accounts Payable aging periods.

Your computer should now display the completed System Options and Defaults screen as shown in Figure 21–4. Compare the entries to those displayed on your screen. If there are errors, select "Edit" and make the necessary corrections.

Figure 21–4

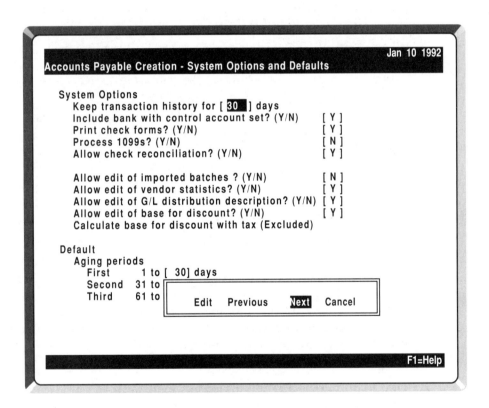

❑ Select: Next to display the next data entry screen.

ACCPAC Plus Integration

The choices entered on this screen enable you to integrate your Accounts Payable data with the ACCPAC Plus General Ledger and Job Cost modules, and to use retainage accounting. E. & J. Enterprises will integrate the Accounts Payable module with the General Ledger module, but will not use the Job Cost or retainage accounting.

G/L departments

E. & J. Enterprises wants to integrate the Accounts Payable module with the General Ledger module. E. & J. Enterprises did not use departments in the Chart of Accounts in the General Ledger module.

❑ Type: `N` in the `G/L departments` field.

❑ Press: Enter

Send to G/L reference field

When Accounts Payable transactions are retrieved by the General Ledger module you may determine the type of information that appears in the Reference field on the G/L Transactions report. The "Send to G/L reference field" allows you to select additional information that you want to have appear in the reference field for the transactions when they are retrieved by the General Ledger. The choices are: Vendor name, Document description, Document number, and Document reference.

❑ Select: `Document reference`

Send to G/L description field

The first part of the description field for transactions retrieved by the General Ledger module consists of a posting sequence number, a batch number and an entry number which are assigned by ACCPAC Plus. The "Send to G/L description field" allows you to control the information that appears as the last 13 characters of the description field for transactions when they are retrieved by the General Ledger. The choices are: Vendor name, Document description, Document number, and Document reference.

❑ Select: `Document description`

Post system checks in detail

If you select "no" for this option ACCPAC Plus will create a single General Ledger entry for each batch of system checks rather than producing a separate entry for each system check. If you use the check reconciliation function to keep track of the checks issued you do not need this option. E. & J. Enterprises has decided that they will not post the system checks in detail.

❑ Type: `N`

❑ Press: [Enter]

Integrate with Job Costing

Erin and Joan have decided not to use the Job Costing module. If the Job Cost module is required in the future, you can activate the Job Costing option when required.

❑ Type: N

❑ Press: [Enter]

Retainage accounting

You would use the "Retainage accounting" option if you withhold part of the payment for goods or services for an agreed period of time. This is a common practice in the construction industry or in the sale of complex computer installations. E. & J. Enterprises will not use this option. If you require it in the future, you can activate it as long as there are no unposted transactions in the accounts payable.

❑ Type: N

❑ Press: [Enter]

General Ledger

In this portion of the screen ACCPAC Plus requires that you enter General Ledger account codes that will become the default account codes in the Control Account sets. When you define the control account sets you can change these defaults.

The Chart of Accounts for E. & J. Enterprises is described in Chapter 4, Table 4-2. This information is also available when you use the Finder.

As E. & J. Enterprises is not using either the Job Cost module or retainage accounting, the cursor will move to the `Payable control` field.

❑ Type: 500

❑ Press: [Enter]

The cursor will move to the `Bank` field.

❑ Type: 100

❑ Press: [Enter]

In the `Purchase discount` field,

❑ Type: 754

❑ Press: [Enter]

An options bar will appear at the bottom of the screen as shown in Figure 21–5. If you have made any errors, select `Edit` and make the necessary corrections.

Figure 21–5

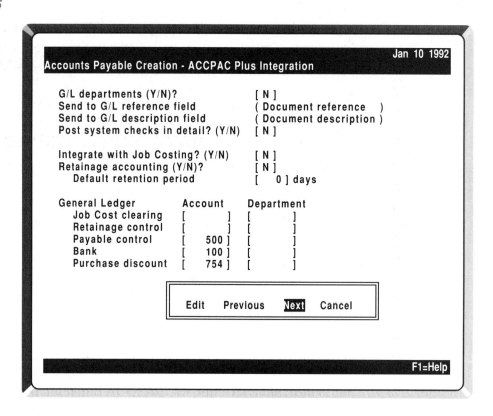

❑ Select: Next

Tax Information

At this point the Tax Information screen will appear as shown in Figure 21–6. You use this screen to enter tax codes, their descriptions, and the names of the taxes. You may also use this screen to specify the information you want reported on the Tax Tracking report for Value Added Tax (VAT) reporting.

Remember that each jurisdiction has its own laws and regulations for the collection of sales tax and value added tax. In this tax model, no sales taxes are collected on the sale of services. As a provider of services, E. & J. Enterprises must pay sales tax (5%) and value added tax (10%) on equipment and supplies used in providing these services. These taxes are considered to be part of the cost of the equipment and supplies.

No sales taxes are collected on the purchase of goods for resale. Value added tax must be paid on all purchases of goods but not services. Any purchase of goods made by E. & J. Enterprises is subject to the 10% value added tax. If a purchase is for equipment or supplies used by E. & J. Enterprises, the sales tax and the value added tax are considered to be part of the cost of the equipment or supplies. If

Figure 21–6

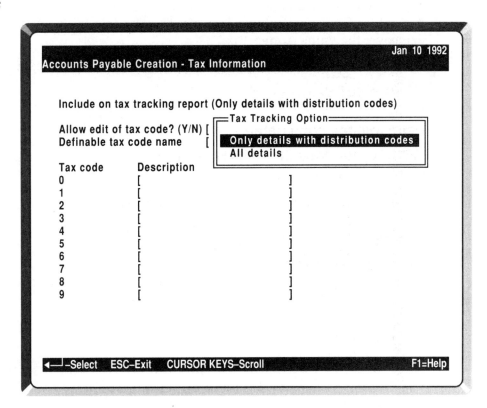

the purchase is for items that will be re-sold, the value added tax paid on the purchase is deductible from the value added tax payable to the government when the items are re-sold.

Include on tax tracking report

This option determines if "Only details with distribution codes" or "All details" are reported on the Tax Tracking report. If you selected "Only details with distribution codes", only those details which include a tax tracking distribution code would be included on the report. If you choose the "All details" option, all purchase, retainage, and job cost details entered for invoices, credit notes, debit notes, and adjustments are totalled on the Tax Tracking report. E. & J. Enterprises must report value added tax paid only on goods purchased for resale.

❑ Select: `Only details with distribution codes.`

Allow edit of tax code

This option is used to determine whether you will be allowed to make changes to the Tax Code field when you enter invoices, credit notes, debit notes, and adjustments. The tax codes are most often used in VAT reporting to classify transactions into VAT categories. In Canada, Value Added Tax is known under the name of the Goods and Services Tax, or GST. If you record purchases from vendors who are not regular suppliers, you must be able to edit the tax code in order to recover the Value Added Tax.

☐ Type: Y

☐ Press: [Enter]

Definable tax code name

You may enter a specific eight-character name for the tax code field to identify the type of tax.

☐ Press: [Enter] to accept "Tax code".

Description

The highlighted bar will move to the "Description" field beside Tax code 0.

☐ Press: [Enter] to move the cursor down so that it rests beside number 1.

☐ Type: VAT Recoverable

☐ Press: [Enter]

☐ Press: [Esc] to indicate that you have finished adding the codes.

You do not have to add a line for Sales Tax since sales tax will be charged on goods only at the retail level in this simulation. If items are purchased for use in the business, and not for resale, sales tax is part of the integral cost and is not accounted for separately.

The options bar will be displayed at the bottom of the screen. If you have made any errors, select Edit and make the necessary corrections.

☐ Select: Create

The computer will work for several moments creating the files and will then display the title screen.

INITIALIZATION

November 1, 1998 is the date that Erin and Joan have decided upon to add the Accounts Payable module to their ACCPAC Plus accounting system.

☐ Type: 110198 in the New date field.

☐ Press: [Enter]

A warning will appear on the screen.

```
┌─────────────────────────────────────────────────┐
│                                                   │
│    New date is more than one week later than old date.  │
│                                                   │
│              Accept        Edit                   │
│                                                   │
└─────────────────────────────────────────────────┘
```

If you had entered a date earlier than the Last access date a similar warning would be displayed.

```
┌─────────────────────────────────────────────────┐
│                                                   │
│         New date is earlier than old date.        │
│                                                   │
│              Accept        Edit                   │
│                                                   │
└─────────────────────────────────────────────────┘
```

These warnings help prevent errors in the recording or processing dates printed on ACCPAC Plus reports that become part of the audit trail. Verify that 11/01/98 is displayed in the New date field.

❑ Type: A to accept 11/01/98 as the New date.

After several moments the ACCPAC Accounts Payable Master Menu will be displayed. As you work through this simulation you will use each of the options on this menu.

PRINTING THE COMPANY PROFILE

To verify the information you have just entered, you can print a Company Profile. It will specify all the options you have selected.

❑ Select: 5. Reports from the ACCPAC Accounts Payable Master Menu.

❑ Select: 4. General reports

❑ Select: 2. Company profile

❑ Press: [Enter] to print the Company Profile.

The first sections of this report show the information that you entered as you created the Accounts Payable data files. The final section, Batch Status, is generated by ACCPAC Plus to show the status of the invoice, adjustment, and check batches.

❑ Press: [Esc] twice to display the ACCPAC Accounts Payable Master Menu.

EDITING THE COMPANY PROFILE

When the company profile was reviewed, it was decided that your name should be put in as the contact person.

❑ Select: 7. Housekeeping from the ACCPAC Accounts Payable Master Menu.

Figure 21–7

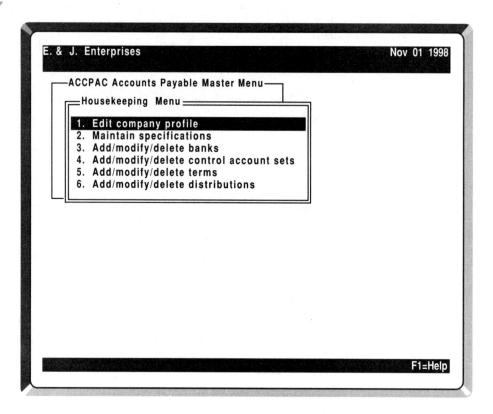

You will work through each of the options shown on the Housekeeping Menu (Figure 21–7) at the appropriate time. Now you will change the name of the contact person in the company profile. You can use these same procedures to correct any errors that may be in the company profile.

❏ Select: 1. Edit company profile

This screen is identical to that displayed during the creation of the Accounts Payable data.

❏ Select: Edit

❏ Press: [Enter] to move the cursor to the Contact field.

❏ Type: YOUR NAME

❏ Use [SPACEBAR] or [DELETE] to erase any excess characters.

❏ Press: [Enter] to indicate that data entry is complete for the contact field.

The following option bar will appear at the bottom of the screen.

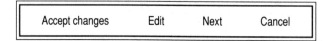

If you wished to make additional changes you would select "Next" until the screen requiring the change was displayed and then "Edit" that screen. When all changes have been made:

❑ Select: `Accept changes`

BANKS

This function allows you to identify the Cash control account in the General Ledger that will be credited when you make payments. To set up the bank accounts that your company uses, you will create a code and name, identify the number of the next check, and enter the General Ledger account code for the bank account. You may set up a number of bank accounts (for example, each branch may have their own bank account to pay suppliers, or you might have bank accounts in different currencies for payment of foreign suppliers). Erin and Joan have only one bank account.

❑ Select: `3.Add/modify/delete banks`

❑ Type: `cash` in the `Bank code` field.

❑ Press: Enter

❑ Type: `Working Funds` in the `Description` field.

❑ Press: Enter

All of the checks written to date have been manually prepared. Since there have not been any automated checks issued, the first system check will be number 1.

❑ Press: Enter to accept the default for check number `1`.

The screen will display the General Ledger Bank account number you added earlier during the creation of the company profile.

❑ Press: Enter to accept the default code.

You now have the option to choose the types of payment formats that will attach to the specifications. A specifications box appears in the lower center of the screen (Figure 21–8). `CHECK` is a check alone with no payment advice. `ADVIC` is a payment advice alone, with no check attached, and `CH-AD` represents a format in which the check is printed with an advice attached. You chose to not prepare 1099 forms when you created the company profile.

You will select `CHECK` for the Check specification; you will select `ADVIC` for the Advice specification; and for the Check and advice, select `CH-AD`.

❑ Move the cursor down one space so that it rests on `CHECK`.

❑ Press: Enter

❑ Move the cursor down two spaces so that it rests on `ADVIC`.

❑ Press: Enter

❑ Move the cursor down three spaces so that it rests on `CH-AD`.

Figure 21–8

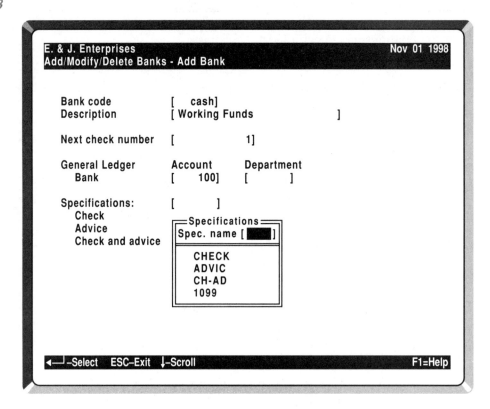

□ Press: [Enter]

The option bar will appear at the bottom of the screen. If you have made any errors, select Edit and make the necessary corrections.

□ Select: Add

□ Press: [Esc] to return to the Housekeeping Menu.

CONTROL ACCOUNT SETS

This function allows you to specify the General Ledger accounts to be used when Accounts Payable transaction information is posted to the General Ledger. You must define at least one control account set before any vendors are added to the vendor list. Each control account set consists of a payable control account, a purchase discounts account, and (if you had selected the Retainage Accounting option) a retainage account.

Erin and Joan have a simple set of books and will need to create only one Control Account Set.

□ Select: 4. Add/modify/delete control account sets from the Housekeeping Menu.

Figure 21–9

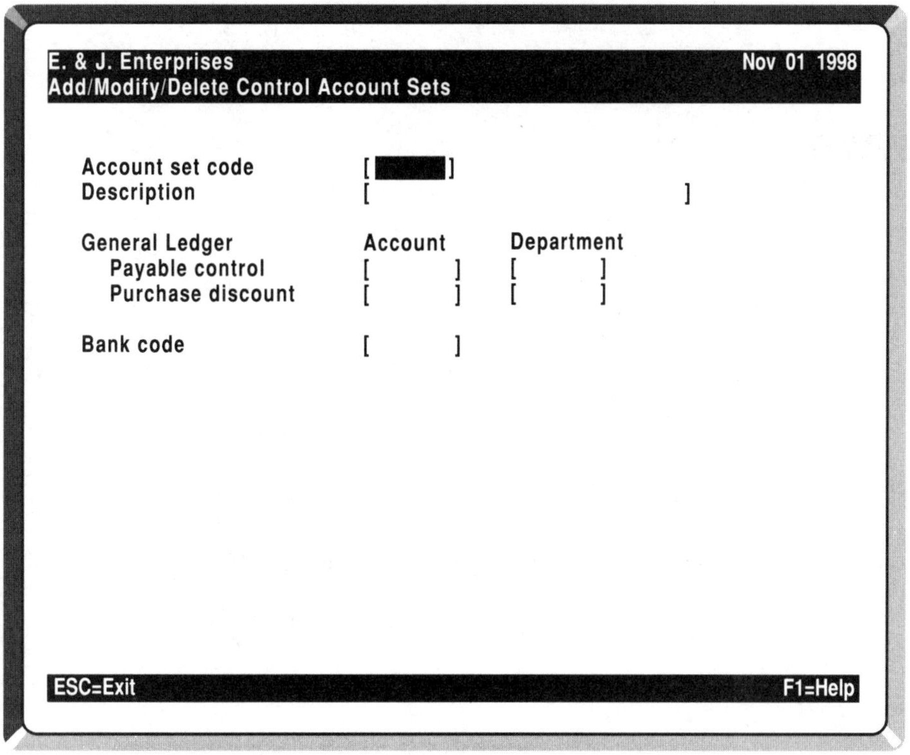

```
┌─────────────────────────────────────────────────────────────────┐
│ E. & J. Enterprises                                  Nov 01 1998  │
│ Add/Modify/Delete Control Account Sets                            │
│                                                                   │
│                                                                   │
│       Account set code          [▇▇▇▇▇▇]                          │
│       Description               [                             ]   │
│                                                                   │
│       General Ledger            Account     Department            │
│          Payable control        [       ]   [       ]             │
│          Purchase discount      [       ]   [       ]             │
│                                                                   │
│       Bank code                 [       ]                         │
│                                                                   │
│                                                                   │
│                                                                   │
│                                                                   │
│                                                                   │
│                                                                   │
│ ESC=Exit                                               F1=Help    │
└─────────────────────────────────────────────────────────────────┘
```

The cursor will be resting in the `Account set code` field as shown in Figure 21–9. You must enter a name or number for each Control Account Set.

❑ Type: `1`

❑ Press: [Enter]

❑ Type: `Accounts Payable - General` in the `Description` field.

❑ Press: [Enter]

The cursor will move to the `Payable control` field in the General Ledger section of the screen. You must enter the Accounts Payable Control account code from the General Ledger so that the information which is accumulated for posting will be charged to the proper account. The Accounts Payable General Ledger code you entered on the company profile will be displayed.

❑ Press: [Enter]

If the code was not displayed, you would have to enter it. If ACCPAC Plus cannot find the General Ledger account code that you entered, it will display the Finder window in the lower right portion of the screen. You would then move the selector bar to the proper account and press Enter.

❑ Press: [Enter] to select `754` in the `Purchase discount` field.

❑ Type: `cash` in the `Bank code` field.

❑ Press: [Enter]

❑ Select: Add

❑ Press: [Esc] to return to the Housekeeping Menu.

TERMS

This function allows you to set up payment terms to use in calculating invoice due dates, discount dates, and discount amounts. At least one set of terms must be defined before vendor accounts can be added.

The invoice due dates and discount dates can be set up in a number of different ways. They can be due in a certain number of days, at the end of the next month, on a specific day of next month, or within a certain number of days from a specific day of the month. Most of E. & J.'s accounts offer terms of Net 30. Since some of E. & J.'s vendors offer terms of 2/10, n/30, a second term will be created.

❑ Select: 5. Add/modify/delete terms from the Housekeeping Menu to display the data entry screen shown in Figure 21–10. Each of the terms codes that you will enter are in lower case. The use of lower case will reduce the number of keystrokes required when entering transaction data.

Figure 21–10

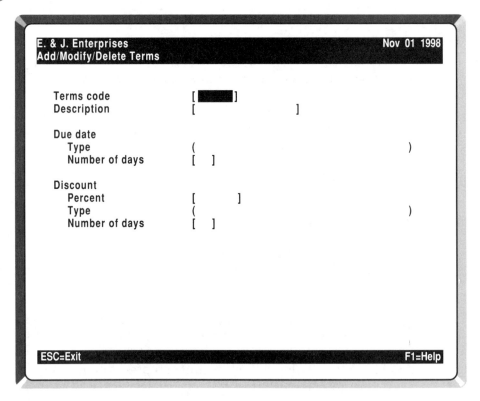

❑ Type: n/30 in the Terms code field.

❑ Press: [Enter]

❑ Type: `Net 30` in the `Description` field.

❑ Press: [Enter]

The Terms Type option box will appear.

❑ Select: `Specific number of days`

❑ Type: `30` in the `Number of days` field.

❑ Press: [Enter]

The cursor will move to the Percent field in the Discount section of the screen. You enter zero as the discount percent if you do not receive early payment discounts.

❑ Press: [Enter] to accept 0.00

❑ Select: `Add`

You will repeat the process now, adding the terms "2/10, n/30".

❑ Type: `2%disc` in the `Terms code` field.

❑ Press: [Enter]

❑ Type: `2/10,n/30` in the `Description` field.

❑ Press: [Enter]

The Terms Type option box will appear.

❑ Select: `Specific number of days`

❑ Type: `30` in the `Number of days` field.

❑ Press: [Enter]

The cursor will move to the Percent field in the Discount section of the screen.

❑ Type: `2.0` in the `Percent` field.

❑ Press: [Enter]

The `Discount Type` box will appear on the screen.

❑ Select: `Specific number of days.`

❑ Type: `10` in the `Number of days` field.

❑ Press: [Enter]

❑ Select: `Add`

A third terms code will now be added for the rent check that is due on the first of each month.

❑ Type: `rent` in the `Terms code` field.

❑ Press: [Enter]

❑ Type: `Monthly rent` in the `Description` field.

❑ Press: [Enter]

The `Terms Type` option box will appear.

❑ Select: `Specific number of days`

❑ Press: Enter to select `0` in the `Number of days` field.

The cursor will move to the Percent field in the Discount section of the screen.

❑ Press: Enter to accept a discount of 0.00.

Review your choices. Once you are satisfied there are no errors,

❑ Select: `Add`

❑ Press: Esc to return to the Housekeeping Menu.

DISTRIBUTIONS

This function allows you to enter and maintain General Ledger distribution codes to speed up the entry of vendor transactions. You can also store and print information on any distribution code using the Tax Tracking feature. When creating the distribution code you should use a name or short form that is easy to remember. This distribution code can be up to six characters long. You can also enter the General Ledger account code.

E. & J. Enterprises will use the following distribution codes:

1. A distribution to be used in recording invoices that contain only purchases for resale. The total amount of the invoice, including value added tax, would be recorded. Tax tracking will apply to this distribution.

    code = pv
    description = Purchase price including VAT
    G/L account = 752
    tax code = 1
    tax tracking = Y
    track type = tax included with purchase

2. A distribution to record purchases of goods for resale, the price of which does not include value added tax. Tax tracking will apply to this distribution.

    code = p
    description = Purchase prices excluding VAT
    G/L account = 752
    tax code = 1
    tax tracking = Y
    track type = purchase

3. A distribution to record the value added tax on the above. Tax tracking will apply to the distribution.

    code = v
    description = VAT recoverable on code p

G/L account = 542
tax code = 1
tax tracking = Y
track type = tax

4. A distribution for a regularly occurring expense on which tax is not applicable, in this case rental expenses for office space and equipment. Tax tracking will not apply to this distribution.

code = r
description = Rental expenses
G/L account = 920
tax code = 0
tax tracking = N

Note that each of the Distributions codes is only one or two lower case letters making data entry more efficient.

❏ Select: 6. Add/modify/delete distributions from the Housekeeping Menu to display the screen shown in Figure 21–11.

Figure 21–11

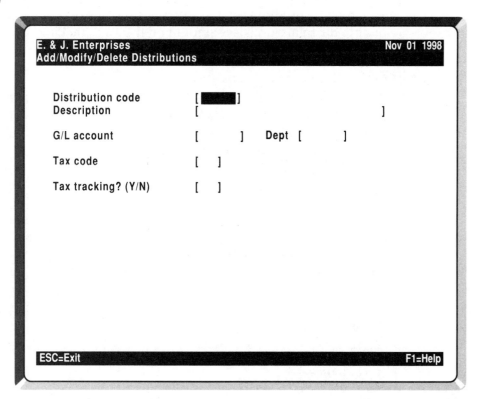

```
E. & J. Enterprises                                        Nov 01 1998
Add/Modify/Delete Distributions

        Distribution code        [       ]
        Description              [                              ]

        G/L account             [       ]   Dept  [        ]

        Tax code                [   ]

        Tax tracking? (Y/N)     [   ]




ESC=Exit                                                      F1=Help
```

❏ Type: pv in the Distribution code field.
❏ Press: [Enter]

❑ Type: `Purchase price includes VAT` in the `Description` field.

❑ Press: [Enter]

❑ Type: `752` in the `G/L account` field.

❑ Press: [Enter]

If ACCPAC Plus cannot find the General Ledger account code that you have entered, it will display the Finder window in the lower right portion of the screen. You would then move the selector bar to the proper account and press Enter.

❑ Type: `1` in the `Tax code` field.

❑ Press: [Enter]

❑ Type: `Y` in the `Tax tracking? Y/N` field.

❑ Press: [Enter]

The Tax tracking `Type` option box will appear on the screen. There are three options, as follows:

Purchase

`Purchase` is used to keep track of amounts that do not include tax. It adds the amount to the total purchases amount on the Tax Tracking report.

Tax

This keeps track of the tax paid and the tax base, and reports the total tax paid and the total tax base on the Tax Tracking report. You would use Tax distribution codes to enter detail lines that are strictly tax amounts and that appear on the document separately from item prices.

Tax included purchase

This option allows you to enter the total amount of a purchase that includes tax. When you select this option, you will enter the tax rate and specify a General Ledger account for the tax amount.

❑ Select: `Tax included purchase`

❑ Type: `10.0` in the `Tax rate` field.

❑ Press: [Enter]

❑ Type: `542` in the `G/L tax account` field.

❑ Press: [Enter]

Review the data entry screen. If there are errors, select "Edit", and then make the necessary corrections.

❑ Select: `Add`

The second distribution code is for purchases where the purchase price does not include the value added tax.

❑ Type: p in the Distribution code field.

❑ Press: [Enter]

❑ Type: Purchase price excludes VAT in the Description field.

❑ Press: [Enter]

❑ Type: 752 in the G/L account field.

❑ Press: [Enter]

❑ Type: 1 in the Tax code field.

❑ Press: [Enter]

❑ Type: Y in the Tax tracking? Y/N field.

❑ Press: [Enter]

❑ Select: Purchase.

If the information displayed on the screen is correct,

❑ Select: Add

Next you will add the Distribution code for the value added tax on purchases recorded using the Distribution code p.

❑ Type: v in the Distribution code field.

❑ Press: [Enter]

❑ Type: VAT recoverable on code p in the Description field.

❑ Press: [Enter]

❑ Type: 542 in the G/L account field.

❑ Press: [Enter]

❑ Type: 1 in the Tax code field.

❑ Press: [Enter]

❑ Type: Y in the Tax tracking? (Y/N) field.

❑ Press: [Enter]

❑ Select: Tax

The screen will now display a new data entry field on the screen for the Tax rate. The rate entered in this field will be used to calculate the tax base during transaction entry. The rate for value added tax is 10%.

❑ Type: 10.0

❑ Press: [Enter]

❑ Select: Add

❑ Add the last Distribution code using the letter r. Remember to enter `920` in the `G/L account` field and select `Tax code 0`. This distribution will not track taxes.

After you have finished adding the Distributions,

❑ Press: Esc twice to return to the ACCPAC Accounts Payable Master Menu.

PRINTING GENERAL REPORTS

Can you remember all the codes and information that you have entered for banks, control account sets, terms, and distributions? ACCPAC Plus can supply this information in two ways.

1. You can use the Finder by pressing the F5 key when the square cursor is displayed in a data entry field and then you can select the appropriate information.

2. You can print the information using the "Reports" option on the ACCPAC Accounts Payable Master Menu. To document and verify the codes and information you will now print a series of reports.

❑ Select: `5. Reports` from the ACCPAC Accounts Payable Master Menu.

❑ Select: `4. General reports`

❑ Select: `4. Control account sets`

The default settings displayed on the screen will print the information for all control account sets.

❑ Select: `Print`

❑ Print the reports for Banks, Terms, and Distributions.

❑ Press: Esc twice to display the ACCPAC Accounts Payable Master Menu.

If necessary use the Housekeeping option of the ACCPAC Accounts Payable Master Menu to correct any errors and print the reports again.

EXITING FROM ACCPAC PLUS

If necessary, press **Esc** until only the ACCPAC Accounts Payable Master Menu is displayed.

❑ Select: `Q. Quit` from the ACCPAC Accounts Payable Master Menu.

❑ Press: Esc at the Start Menu.

ACCPAC Plus will ask,

```
┌──────────────────────────────────────────────────────┐
│                                                        │
│          Do you really want to exit the system?        │
│                                                        │
│                  Yes        No                         │
│                                                        │
└──────────────────────────────────────────────────────┘
```

☐ Select: `Yes`

☐ Back up your data files.

REVIEW QUESTIONS

1. What is a data extension? Why must each company have a unique data extension on all its files?
2. Describe the procedure to create a start line for a company.
3. Describe the purpose of the following options on the Systems Options and Defaults screen: "Allow check reconciliation?", "Allow edit of imported batches?", "Allow edit of base for discount?".
4. Describe the purpose of the following options on the ACCPAC Plus Integration screen:"G/L Departments", "Integrate with job costing", "Retainage accounting".
5. List the options available on the Housekeeping Menu and describe the purpose of each.
6. When editing the "Contact" field in the company profile, how do you remove excess characters?
7. What happens if you enter an account code that does not exist on the ACCPAC Plus Integration screen?
8. What is the function of the F5 key?

EXERCISE

1. Add a new line called "A/P" and your name to the Start Menu. Use the Accounts Payable module. The data files will be stored in the subdirectory "EXERCISE" in the root directory of drive A. Use your initials as the data extension.
2. Select your company's Accounts Payable module from the Start Menu. Use November 1, 1998 as the date.
3. Create the Accounts Payable ledger files using the information found in Table 21–1.
4. Using the Housekeeping function, create the Banks, Control account sets, Terms, and General Ledger distributions codes. Use the same codes used by E. & J. Enterprises.
5. Print the Banks, Control account sets, Terms, and Distribution reports.
6. Print a copy of the company profile.
7. Exit from ACCPAC Plus.
8. Back up your data files.

Table 21–1

```
Company Data
    Name      Your Name Co. Ltd.
    Address   123 Accounting St.
              Anytown
              456MAIL
    Phone     777-555-1212
    Fax       777-555-1313
    Identity number 001
    Company number 001
    Contact   Your Name

System Options and Defaults
    Keep transaction history for 30 days
    Include bank with control account set ``Y''
    Print check forms ``Y''
    Process 1099s ``N''
    Allow check reconciliation ``Y''
    Allow edit of imported batches ``N''
    Allow edit of vendor statistics ``Y''
    Allow edit of G/L distribution description ``Y''
    Allow edit of base for discount ``Y''
    Calculate base for discount with tax ``Excluded''
    Aging periods, 1-30, 31-60, 61-90

ACCPAC Plus Integration
    G/L departments ``N''
    Send to G/L reference field ``Document reference''
    Send to G/L description field ``Vendor name''
    Post system checks in detail ``N''
    Integrate with Job Costing ``N''
    Retainage accounting ``N''
    Payable control ``500''
    Bank ``100''
    Purchase discount ``754''

Tax Information
    Include on tax tracking report ``All details''
    Allow edit of tax code (Y)
    Definable tax code name ``Tax code''
    Tax code 1; VAT Recoverable
```

22 Vendor Data

Now that you have created the Accounts Payable ledger files, you must add vendor account information. Since vendor information changes, you will also modify the vendor account information.

❑ Enter the commands necessary to display the ACCPAC Plus Start Menu.

❑ Select: A/P E. & J. Enterprises from the Start Menu.

The title screen (Figure 22–1) will appear.

Figure 22–1

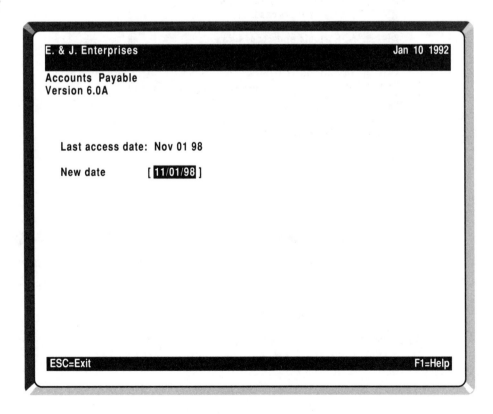

```
E. & J. Enterprises                                    Jan 10 1992

Accounts  Payable
Version 6.0A


   Last access date:  Nov 01 98

   New date           [ 11/01/98 ]
```
ESC=Exit   F1=Help

If your computer does not display this title screen, press **Esc** to return to the Start Menu. Use the information in Chapter 2 to edit the Start Menu line and try again.

ACCPAC Plus should display "Nov 01 98" as the Last access date and "11/01/98" in the New date field. If the New date is incorrect, type "110198" and press **Enter** to change the date. If the New date is correct:

❑ Press: Enter

ACCPAC ACCOUNTS PAYABLE MASTER MENU

ACCPAC Plus will display the ACCPAC Accounts Payable Master Menu. (Figure 22–2). Each of the numbered entries in this menu is described below.

Figure 22–2

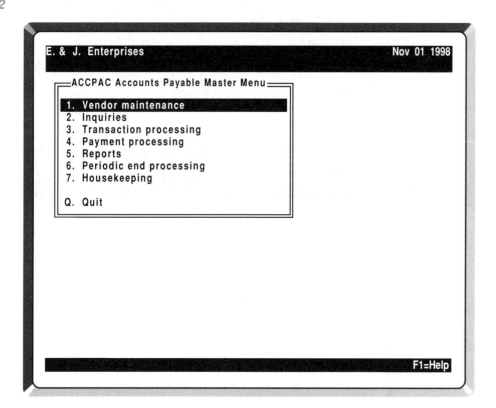

1. Vendor maintenance

This option allows you to add, modify, and delete vendor accounts. You can also import and export vendor records between ACCPAC Plus and other programs.

2. Inquiries

This choice enables you to display vendor information, current and historical transactions, and the status of Invoice, Adjustment, or Manual Check batches.

3. Transaction processing

This function allows you to add, modify or delete invoice and adjustment batches. You can create, archive and delete recurring batches. It also includes functions for retrieving or importing transaction batches. You can then print the batches, post them to the Accounts Payable ledger, and print the posting journal.

4. Payment processing

This function allows you to add, modify, or delete manual check batches, import manual check batches, control the payment of invoices, process system checks, prepare check audit lists, and reconcile outstanding checks. It also allows you to print the batches you have created, to print the manual or system checks and advices, and then to post them to the Accounts Payable ledger.

5. Reports

This option enables you to print and consolidate the G/L transactions for posting to the General Ledger. You can also print analysis reports based on the posted transactions and general reports such as you printed in Chapter 21.

6. Period end processing

This function allows you to clear fully paid transactions for the current month and transfer them to the history file, to clear transactions from the history file, to clear batch status information, and to reset period-to-date statistics to zero.

7. Housekeeping

You have already worked extensively with this menu. It allows you to edit the company profile, to maintain the specifications that make the checks and advices work, and to add/modify/delete banks, control account sets, terms, and distributions.

THE VENDOR MAINTENANCE MENU

❑ Select: 1. Vendor maintenance from the ACCPAC Accounts Payable Master Menu.

The Vendor Maintenance Menu (Figure 22–3) will appear. By using the options from this menu, you will be able to maintain the data on E. & J. Enterprises' vendors.

Figure 22–3

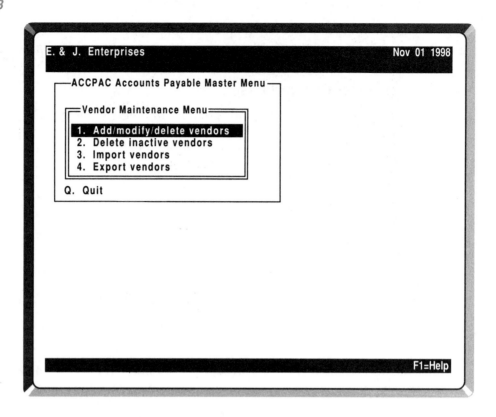

ADDING NEW VENDORS

Now you will record data for several of E. & J. Enterprises' vendors.

❏ Select: 1. Add/modify/delete vendors to display the data entry screen (Figure 22–4) used for adding new vendors to the Accounts Payable data files.

The first vendor you will add to the system is Home Realty.

Vendor number

You can choose any combination of up to six characters or digits as a vendor number. You should use at least four characters to allow for an increase in the number of vendors. The vendor number can be used to determine the order in which records will be printed on many reports. You cannot change vendor numbers after you have created the vendor data record. E. & J. Enterprises will use a simple sequential numbering system. Vendor numbers for the Accounts Payable will start with "99" to differentiate them from the four-digit Accounts Receivable numbers. To avoid problems with upper-and lower-case letters, the company will use only numbers.

❏ Type: 990005 in the Vendor number field.

❏ Press: Enter

Figure 22–4

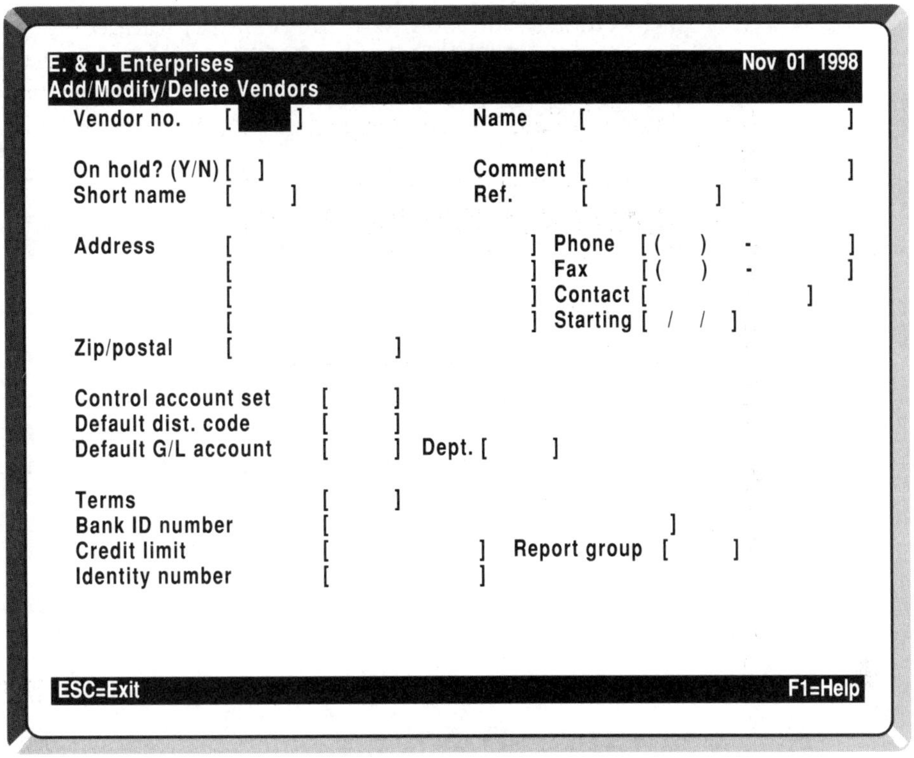

```
┌─────────────────────────────────────────────────────────────────┐
│ E. & J. Enterprises                                  Nov 01 1998  │
│ Add/Modify/Delete Vendors                                         │
│      Vendor no.    [    ]              Name    [              ]   │
│                                                                   │
│      On hold? (Y/N) [  ]               Comment [             ]    │
│      Short name    [    ]              Ref.    [         ]         │
│                                                                   │
│      Address     [              ] Phone  [( )  -      ]            │
│                  [              ] Fax    [( )  -      ]            │
│                  [              ] Contact [         ]             │
│                  [              ] Starting [ / / ]                │
│      Zip/postal  [          ]                                     │
│                                                                   │
│      Control account set   [    ]                                 │
│      Default dist. code    [    ]                                 │
│      Default G/L account   [    ] Dept. [    ]                    │
│                                                                   │
│      Terms                 [    ]                                 │
│      Bank ID number        [              ]                       │
│      Credit limit          [        ] Report group [    ]         │
│      Identity number       [        ]                             │
│                                                                   │
│                                                                   │
│ ESC=Exit                                            F1=Help       │
└─────────────────────────────────────────────────────────────────┘
```

Name

The vendor name may have up to 30 letters and/or digits. You must enter it exactly as you want it to appear on checks and reports.

❏ Type: `Home Realty` in the `Name` field.

❏ Press: Enter

On hold

If a vendor is put "on hold", invoices are not paid during a check run unless you force payment using the Control Payments function.

❏ Press: Enter to accept the "N" default indicating that payments to this vendor are not to be held back.

Comment

The Comment field allows you to store short, important reminders or notes about a vendor. Comments can be printed on the Vendor List and Statistics report.

At this time E. & J. Enterprises does not want to add any comments.

❏ Press: Enter in the blank `Comment` field.

Short name

ACCPAC Plus creates a nickname for the vendor, composed of the first five letters of the name entered in the Name field. For several reports you can sort the vendor accounts according to this short name. If you wished to change the default short name, you would type the new name over the default name and press **Enter**.

- ❏ Type: `HomeR`
- ❏ Press: Enter

Reference

The Ref. field refers to the customer number that the vendor uses to identify your company. You may enter up to sixteen characters. The usual reference to enter would be the vendor's Accounts Receivable code for your company. You are not required to fill this field.

- ❏ Press: Enter to leave the field blank.

Address

ACCPAC Plus provides four fields for entering the vendor's address.

- ❏ Type: `119 North West Cres.`
- ❏ Press: Enter
- ❏ Type: `Hillsboro`
- ❏ Press: Enter
- ❏ Press: Enter twice more to leave the last two lines of the address blank.

Zip/postal

The `Zip/postal` field has room for up to fifteen characters.

- ❏ Type: `OR9NW`
- ❏ Press: Enter

Phone

The Phone field holds up to sixteen digits as a telephone number. If you use telephone numbers from other countries that require international access codes, you should use a consistent format.

- ❏ Type: `5675551212`
- ❏ Press: Enter

Fax

The Fax number data entry field is similar to the Phone data entry field.

❏ Type: 5675551313

❏ Press: [Enter]

Contact

You may want to keep a record of the name of the person to be contacted regarding a vendor account. The name of the contact person may have up to 18 characters.

❏ Type: Kevin Williams in the Contact field.

❏ Press: [Enter]

Starting

This field allows you to enter the date on which you started doing business with this vendor. The default should display "11/01/98", the date you entered as the New date on the title screen. Home Realty is E. & J. Enterprises' landlord. E. & J. Enterprises rented the office space starting on October 1, 1997.

❏ Type: 100197 in the Starting field.

❏ Press: [Enter]

Control account set

You must enter a Control account set code for each vendor record, specifying the Bank, Payable Control and the Purchase Discount accounts used for the vendor's transactions. You have already created the control account set in the Add/Modify/Delete function. If you do not remember the control account set code, use the finder key to obtain a listing.

❏ Press: [F5]

As you can see, only one control account set (Control code 1) has been created.

❏ Press: [Enter] to select number 1.

Default distribution code

You can assign a distribution code to a vendor record to represent the General Ledger account used for the vendor's transactions. Use the finder to obtain a listing of the Distributions created earlier.

❏ Press: [F5]

The code "r" was created for monthly rent.

❏ Select: r

Note that the Default G/L account (920) is inserted in the Default G/L account field. You will normally select either the Default dist. code or the Default G/L account. The Default G/L account would be used when the vendor supplies a unique product or service — for example, telephone expense.

Terms

You have already identified three terms codes using the Housekeeping function. You can use the Finder to display these codes on the screen and then select the appropriate code. Home Realty rents the office space to E. & J. Enterprises.

❑ Press: F5

❑ Move the selector bar to rent.

❑ Press: Enter

Bank ID number

You can assign a specific bank identification code for payments made to a vendor. E. & J. Enterprises has only one bank account, so a bank ID number is not necessary.

❑ Press: Enter

Credit limit

ACCPAC Plus will display the credit limit of 0.00. The credit limit field would be used if the vendor sets a credit limit for your company. This field does not have to be completed.

❑ Press: Enter

Report group

The report group field is a code that groups vendors for reporting purposes. The Report group may have up to 6 letters and/or digits. To add a group, you must type a code into the vendor record. This Report group code has not been previously created. All records that you assign to this code will be in the same group. For example, you could assign all vendors for a particular product type or a region to the same report group. When you sort data for analysis reports by report group, all vendors with the specified code will be included. The report group can be printed on the Vendor List and Statistics report.

Erin & Joan have decided to assign vendors to either "goods" for goods in trade, or "admin" for administrative expenses. Home Realty supplies office space which represents an administrative expense.

❑ Type: admin

❑ Press: Enter

Identity number

The Identity number field will accept up to 15 characters. You can use this field to record the vendor identity number for 1099 reporting in the U.S. or for the vendor's Value Added Tax licence number. The number that you enter in this field is printed with the vendor number on the Tax Tracking report. Home Realty's identity number is 77-76859.

❏ Type: 77-76859
❏ Press: [Enter]

Compare the information you have input for this vendor to the screen shown in Figure 22–5. If there are errors, you should select the "Edit" option and make the necessary corrections. If there are no errors:

❏ Select: Next

Figure 22–5

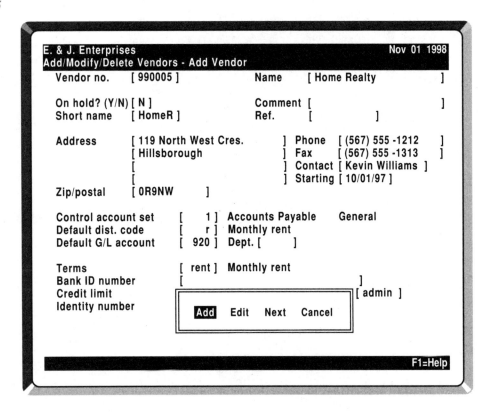

Historical Data

The second data entry screen as shown in Figure 22–6 allows you to enter information about the vendor's previous history with the company. Office space was rented from Home Realty for the entire previous year at the monthly rate of $1100. Since November is the first month of the fiscal year, there is no Period-to-date or Year-to-date information to be added.

❏ Press: [Enter] or [TAB] to move the cursor to the Last-Year section in the lower half of the screen until it rests in the Amount column beside "Invoices".

❏ Type: 13200.00 in the Amount field.

❏ Press: [Enter]

Figure 22–6

```
┌─────────────────────────────────────────────────────────────────────┐
│ E. & J. Enterprises                                     Nov 01 1998   │
│ Add/Modify/Delete Vendors - Add Vendor                                │
│   Vendor number:  990005              Name:    Home Realty            │
│                                                                       │
│                  ──────Period-To-Date──────   ──────Year-To-Date──────│
│                   Amount        Number          Amount        Number  │
│   Invoices     [ 0.00      ]  [      0 ]  [      0.00 ]  [        0 ]  │
│   Payments     [      0.00 ]  [      0 ]  [      0.00 ]  [        0 ]  │
│   Disc. taken  [      0.00 ]  [      0 ]  [      0.00 ]  [        0 ]  │
│   Disc. missed [      0.00 ]  [      0 ]  [      0.00 ]  [        0 ]  │
│   Credit notes [      0.00 ]  [      0 ]  [      0.00 ]  [        0 ]  │
│   Debit notes  [      0.00 ]  [      0 ]  [      0.00 ]  [        0 ]  │
│                                                                       │
│                  ──────────Last-Year──────────                        │
│                   Amount        Number                                │
│   Invoices     [      0.00 ]  [      0 ]  Total days to pay  [    0 ]  │
│   Payments     [      0.00 ]  [      0 ]  No. of paid inv.   [    0 ]  │
│   Disc. taken  [      0.00 ]  [      0 ]                               │
│   Disc. missed [      0.00 ]  [      0 ]                               │
│   Credit notes [      0.00 ]  [      0 ]                               │
│   Debit notes  [      0.00 ]  [      0 ]                               │
│                                                                       │
│ ESC=Entry complete                                          F1=Help   │
└─────────────────────────────────────────────────────────────────────┘
```

Since there were 12 monthly payments, enter the number 12 in the `Number` column to the right.

❑ Type: `12` in the `Number` field.

❑ Press: [Enter]

❑ Type: `13200.00` in the `Payments` field.

❑ Press: [Enter]

❑ Type: `12` in the `Number` field.

❑ Press: [Enter]

If E. & J. Enterprises had taken or missed any discounts, or been issued credit or debit notes, this information could be added in the appropriate fields.

❑ Press: [Enter] eight times to advance the cursor to the `Total days to pay` field.

The rent check is created and paid on the first day of the month so the number of days of credit is 0.

❑ Press: [Enter] to accept the default 0 as the total days to pay.

❑ Type: `12` in the `No. of paid inv.` field.

❑ Press: [Enter]

The following option bar will appear:

```
┌─────────────────────────────────────────────────┐
│                                                   │
│    Add      Edit      Previous      Cancel         │
│                                                   │
└─────────────────────────────────────────────────┘
```

☐ Select: Add

YOUR TURN

Create records for the five vendors shown in Tables 22–1 (a) and (b). Verify each customer's information before adding it to the files.

E. & J. Enterprises will use Vendor number 999999 to record the purchases of goods and services from vendors whose volume of business does not merit individual vendor numbers. Manual checks will be used to pay for these purchases.

Table 22–1 (a)

Customer no.	990015	990025	990035
Name	Pear Computers Inc.	O. K. Furniture	Computer Associates
On hold	No	No	No
Comment			Accpac software
Short name ref.	PearC	OKFur	CompA
Address 1	43 Appleway	19 Franklin Ave.	1240 McKay Dr.
Address 2	Stevensville	Colinsville	San Jose
Address 3			
Address 4			
Postal code	992345	654321	31951
Phone	890-555-1212	777-555-1212	408-555-1212
Fax	890-555-1313	777-555-1313	408-555-1313
Contact	Ian Sacha	Brenda Jane	Mgr. A/R
Starting	01/01/98	11/01/98	11/01/98
Control account set	1	1	1
Default dist. code	pv		pv
Default G/L account		406	
Terms	2%disc	2%disc	n/30
Bank ID number			
Credit Limit			
Report group	goods	admin	goods
Identity number	56-00876	34-94380	23-75709
Last Year Invoices	$2,475.00	$13,480.00	
Last year number	2	4	
Last year payments	0	$10,814.30	
Last year number	0	2	
Disc. taken	0	$220.70	
Disc. taken number		2	
Total days to pay		10	
No. of paid inv.		2	

Table 22–1 (b)

```
Customer no.           990045              999999
Name                   Dubai Software Co.  Miscellaneous
On hold                No                  No
Comment
Short name             Dubai               Misc.
ref.
Address 1              67 N. Gray Cres.
Address 2              Sand City
Address 3
Address 4
Postal code            EAU 011
Phone                  403-555-1212
Fax                    403-555-1313
Contact                Don Roleman
Starting               09/15/97
Control account set    1                   1
Default dist. code     pv
Default G/L account
Terms                  n/30                n/30
Bank ID number
Credit Limit
Report group           goods
Identity number        12-74163
Last Year Invoices     $2,965.00
Last year number       2
Last year payments     $1,315.00
Last year number       1
Disc. taken
Disc. taken number
Total days to pay      31
No. of paid inv.       1
```

Once you have finished entering the vendors,

❏ Press: [Esc] to return to the Vendor Maintenance Menu.

MODIFYING A VENDOR RECORD

When information about a vendor changes, you will have to modify the existing vendor record. You have discovered that some information for vendor number 990035, Computer Associates, must be changed. The company has moved and you entered the address from an old invoice. The correct street address is 836 Bedford St., Vancouver, V5C 2X2. The telephone number is 614-555-1212, the fax number is 614-555-1313, and the new contact is Mr. Ed Dennis.

❏ Select: 1. Add/modify/delete vendors from the Vendor Maintenance Menu.

❏ Type: 990035 in the Vendor number field.

❏ Press: [Enter]

After a few seconds, the information for vendor number 990035 will appear and an option bar will be displayed in the lower portion of the screen.

```
┌─────────────────────────────────────────────────────┐
│ ║                                                   │
│ ║         Modify        Delete                      │
│ ║                                                   │
└─────────────────────────────────────────────────────┘
```

❏ Select: `Modify`

The option bar will change.

```
┌─────────────────────────────────────────────────────┐
│ ║                                                   │
│ ║         Edit      Next      Cancel                │
│ ║                                                   │
└─────────────────────────────────────────────────────┘
```

❏ Select: `Edit`

❏ Press: [Enter] or [TAB] to move the cursor to the Address field.

❏ Type: `836 Bedford St.`

❏ Press: [Enter]

❏ Type: `Vancouver`

❏ Press: [Enter]

❏ Press: [Enter] twice

❏ Type: `V5C 2X2` in the Zip/postal field.

❏ Press: [Enter]

❏ Type: `6145551212` in the `Phone` field.

❏ Press: [Enter]

❏ Type: `6145551313` in the `Fax number` field.

❏ Press: [Enter]

❏ Type: `Mr. Ed Dennis` in the `Contact` field.

❏ Press: [Enter]

❏ Press: [Esc] to indicate that the entry is complete. The following message
   will appear:

```
┌─────────────────────────────────────────────────────┐
│ ║                                                   │
│ ║   Accept changes    Edit     Next     Cancel      │
│ ║                                                   │
└─────────────────────────────────────────────────────┘
```

If you wished to edit the historical data for this vendor you would select "Next"
to display the appropriate screen and then select "Edit" to enter the changes.

❏ Select: `Accept changes`

DELETING A VENDOR RECORD

As companies merge, go out of business, or change product lines, you may delete individual vendor records from the Accounts Payable records. You can use the Add/Modify/Delete Vendors function to delete a vendor if there are no current, retainage, or historical transactions for that vendor. Vendors for which you have added statistics can be deleted. This function only deletes one record at a time.

❑ Type: `990035` in the `Vendor number` field.

❑ Press: Enter

ACCPAC Plus will display the information for Computer Associates and the following option bar.

```
┌─────────────────────────────────────────────────────┐
│                                                       │
│              Modify        Delete                     │
│                                                       │
└─────────────────────────────────────────────────────┘
```

❑ Select: `Delete`

ACCPAC Plus will display a second option bar.

```
┌─────────────────────────────────────────────────────┐
│          Do you really want to delete this vendor?    │
│                    Yes        No                      │
└─────────────────────────────────────────────────────┘
```

This prompt, with the highlight on the "No" option, is a precaution to prevent the accidental deletion of vendor data. If you wanted to delete the vendor you must specify "Yes". If you just press Enter, the vendor will not be deleted. This time you will keep the vendor record since if you delete the record for Computer Associates, you will have to add the vendor record again.

❑ Press: Enter

❑ Press: Esc to return to the Vendor Maintenance Menu.

DELETE INACTIVE VENDORS

You can use the `Delete Inactive Vendors` function to display a list of vendors with zero balances and no activity since a specified date. You can then choose the vendors from this list to be deleted. When the vendors are deleted their historical data is automatically cleared. The `Delete inactive vendors` function will clear all vendors meeting the date specification, whereas the delete part of the `Add/modify/delete vendors` option will delete only one vendor at a time.

❑ Select: `2. Delete inactive vendors` from the Vendor Maintenance Menu. The following screen (Figure 22–7) will appear.

❑ Type: `110198` in the `Last activity date` field.

Figure 22–7

❏ Press: [Enter]

The following option bar will appear:

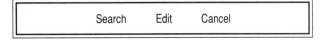

❏ Select: Search

Since you have not entered and posted any transactions for the vendors, the following prompt will appear:

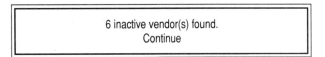

❏ Press: [Enter]

The following prompt will appear:

```
┌─────────────────────────────────────────────┐
│ ┌─────────────────────────────────────────┐ │
│ │       Do you want to delete all inactive  │ │
│ │       vendors or modify the selection?    │ │
│ │                                           │ │
│ │    Delete all    Select vendors    Cancel │ │
│ └─────────────────────────────────────────┘ │
└─────────────────────────────────────────────┘
```

❏ Select: `Select vendors`

If you *do not* want to delete a vendor you would move the selector bar to that vendor and press the spacebar to turn the pointer off.

❏ Press: [Esc]

The final prompt for this function is a safety device. The selector bar is on `Cancel`.

❏ Select: `Cancel` to cancel the `Delete Inactive Vendors` function.

IMPORT VENDORS AND EXPORT VENDORS

The `Import vendors` function allows you to import files containing vendor information into ACCPAC Accounts Payable from other ACCPAC programs and from non-ACCPAC Plus programs. The `Export vendors` function allows you to export the vendor data to external files for spreadsheet or database use in analyzing statistics.

In Unit II, General Ledger and Financial Reporter, you created a set of files for Fred's company and exported a chart of accounts from E. & J. Enterprises. You then imported the chart into Fred's company. The procedure for exporting and importing the vendor information is similar.

❏ Press: [Esc] to return to the ACCPAC Accounts Payable Master Menu.

VENDOR DATA INQUIRY

Sometimes, you may wish to display vendor records on the screen to get information, such as vendors' telephone numbers or credit limits.

❏ Select: `2. Inquiries` from the ACCPAC Accounts Payable Master Menu.

The Inquiries Menu, Figure 22–8, will appear.

The three options on the Inquiries Menu enable you to display information that has been recorded in the ACCPAC Plus Accounts Payable. Up to now, E. & J. Enterprises has recorded only vendor information. Transaction batches will be added in the following chapters.

❏ Select: `1. Display vendor information`

Figure 22–8

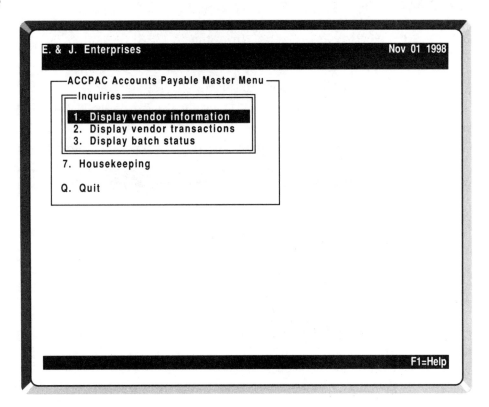

❑ Type: 990005 in the Vendor number field.

❑ Press: [Enter]

ACCPAC Plus will display the vendor profile for Home Realty with an option bar in the lower portion of the screen.

❑ Select: View to clear the option bar from the screen so that you can see the full display.

❑ Press: [Esc] to display the option bar again.

You can view vendor profiles in sequential order by selecting either "Previous vendor" or "Next vendor". If you choose "Select", you must type in a specific vendor number and press Enter.

❑ Press: [Esc] twice to return to the Inquiries Menu.

❑ Press: [Esc] again to display the ACCPAC Accounts Payable Master Menu.

PRINTING THE VENDOR LIST AND STATISTICS

❑ Select: 5. Reports from the ACCPAC Accounts Payable Master Menu.

❑ Select: 1. Analysis reports

The Analysis Reports Menu (Figure 22–9) will appear.
Note that 5. Aged retainage is not available as indicated by the lower in-

Figure 22–9

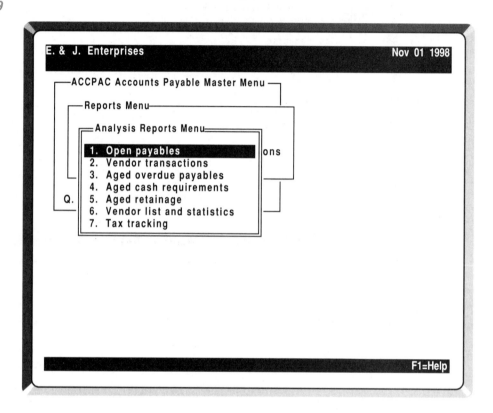

tensity of the display. E. & J. Enterprises did not select retainage accounting
when the Accounts Payable data was created.

❑ Select: 6. Vendor list and statistics

The Vendor List and Statistics screen (Figure 22–10) will appear.

The default setting will print a list of vendor addresses, as indicated by the
pointer beside Address only in the Print these items option box,
sorted sequentially by 1 Vendor number, 2 Control account, 3
Report Group. Print the default Vendor list.

❑ Select: Print

After the report has printed the display will return to the Analysis Reports
Menu. The report that you have just printed contains only the address information for each vendor listed in order of the vendor number.

Figure 22–10

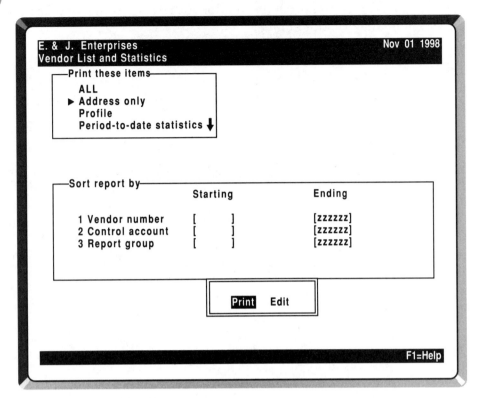

Adding More Detail

ACCPAC Plus allows you to change the information that is printed on the Vendor List and Statistics report. Joan wants a more complete report on each vendor.

❏ Select: `6. Vendor list and statistics` from the Analysis Reports Menu.

❏ Select: `Edit`

The `Print these items` selection box will be made active as indicated by the double outline, the increased brightness of the choices, and the selector bar. You select an item to be included in the report by moving the selector bar to that item and pressing the Spacebar. The selections that you have made will be indicated by a triangular pointer.

You may select the following types of vendor information to include in a report:

Address
Profile — the information entered on the first screen when adding or modifying a vendor record.
Period-to-date statistics
Year-to-date statistics
Last-year statistics
Activity statistics — information recorded by ACCPAC Plus as you record invoices, credit notes, debit notes, and checks during the current fiscal year.

Joan wants a report of the vendor addresses, profiles and last year's statistics sorted by vendor number.

❏ Move the selector bar to `Profile`.

❏ Press: [SPACEBAR]

Note the triangular pointer that now appears to the left of `Profile`.

❏ Move the selector bar to `Last year statistics`

❏ Press: [SPACEBAR]

❏ Press: [Esc] to indicate that you have finished selecting items to be printed.

❏ Select: `Print`

When the report has been printed, compare it to that printed using the default selections. As you can see, one of the advantages of ACCPAC Plus is that you can select the information that you need, then include that information in certain reports.

Sorting the Report

You can also arrange, or sort, the Vendor List and Statistics using different information depending on your needs.

❏ Select: `6. Vendor list and statistics`

The defaults will print the vendor addresses in order of vendor number as printed earlier in this section. Erin would like this information arranged in order of vendor name.

❏ Select: `Edit`

❏ Press: [Enter] to select the default in the `Print these items` selection box and to move the selector bar to the `Sort report by` selection box.

The default is to sort, or arrange, the vendor information by vendor number. If there were duplicate vendor numbers the information for these duplicate vendor numbers would be sorted by control group and report group. The numbered lines or rows describe the information to be used for sorting the report for printing.

❏ Select: line `1 Vendor number`

The `Choices` selection box that appears on the screen allows you to sequentially sort the report according to the following information for each vendor:

Control account
Posting date
Report group
Start date
Vendor balance
Vendor name
Vendor number

Vendor short name
Vendor status
Zip/postal code

❏ Move the selector bar to `Vendor name`.

❏ Press: [Enter]

The `Starting` and `Ending` data entry fields will now be activated as shown by the double outline on your screen. If you wished to specify a group of vendors alphabetically by name you could enter the first vendor name in the `Starting` field and the last vendor name in the `Ending` field. The default blank `Starting` field and z's in the `Ending` field specifies all vendors. Erin wants to include all vendors in the report.

❏ Press: [Enter] twice.

In case more than one vendor has the same vendor name, Erin has decided to sort those vendors by vendor number.

❏ Select: line 2 `Vendor number`

❏ Move the selector bar to `Vendor number`

❏ Press: [Enter]

❏ Press: [Enter] twice to include all vendor numbers.

❏ Press: [Esc] to indicate that editing is complete.

❏ Select: `Print` to print the sorted Vendor List and Statistics.

The ability to allow the user to select and organize the information in analysis reports is a major advantage of ACCPAC Plus.

❏ Quit ACCPAC Plus.

❏ Back up your data files.

REVIEW QUESTIONS

1. Briefly describe each of the ACCPAC Accounts Payable Master Menu options.
2. Under what circumstances would you delete a vendor record from your files?
3. Describe the differences between a Vendor list and a Customer list. Why should these lists be kept confidential?
4. Why would you place a vendor "On Hold"?
5. What is the Inquiries Menu used for?
6. Describe the information contained in the Vendor List and Statistics Report.
7. How long can the vendor number be?
8. Why should you leave a certain amount of space between the vendor numbers you assign?

9. How long can the vendor name be?
10. Why can you delete a vendor record only if its balance is zero?
11. Describe the difference between deleting a vendor record from the "Add/modify/delete vendors" option of the Vendor Maintenance Menu and the "Delete inactive vendors" option from the same menu.

EXERCISE

1. Enter 11/01/98 as the new date.
2. Add the customers listed in Table 22–2 (a) and (b) to the Accounts Payable files that you created in the last exercise. (They are the same vendors as in the General Ledger and Financial Reporter module.)
3. Once you have entered these vendors, print a Vendor list and statistics report and review it for errors. Make any corrections necessary.
4. Back up your data files.
5. Quit ACCPAC Plus.

Table 22–2 (a)

Customer no.	1000	1050	1100
Name	Astro Realty Holdings	Cardinal Associates	Dominion Supplies
On hold	No	No	No
Comment			
Short name ref.	Astro	Cardi	Domin
Address 1	4262 Maitland St.	229 Princess St.,	6930 Baron Circle
Address 2	Your Town	Your Town	Your Town
Address 3			
Address 4			
Postal code	26249	26251	26271
Phone	864-555-1212	864-555-1112	864-555-1012
Fax	864-555-1313	864-555-1113	864-555-1013
Contact	Dave Tynk	J. Currys	Ann Nowak
Starting	01/01/98	11/01/98	11/01/98
Control account set	1	1	1
Default dist. code	r	pv	pv
Default G/L account			
Terms	First of month	2/10,n/30	n/30
Bank ID number			
Credit limit			
Report group	admin	goods	goods
Identity number	AA001	AA002	AA003
Last Year Invoices			
Last year number			
Last year payments			
Last year number			
Disc. taken			
Disc. taken number			
Total days to pay			
No. of paid inv.			

Table 22–2 (b)

Customer no.	1150	9999
Name	Serene Systems Ltd.	Miscellaneous
On hold	No	No
Comment		
Short name ref.	Seren	Misc.
Address 1	193 Leslie St.	
Address 2	Your Town	
Address 3		
Address 4		
Postal code	26243	
Phone	864-555-1412	
Fax	864-555-1413	
Contact	Larry Clarkson	
Starting	11/01/98	
Control account set	1	1
Default dist. code	pv	
Default G/L account		
Terms	n/30	n/30
Bank ID number		
Credit limit		
Report group	goods	
Identity number	AA004	
Last Year Invoices		
Last year number		
Last year payments		
Last year number		
Disc. taken		
Disc. taken number		
Total days to pay		
No. of paid inv.		

CHAPTER

23 Opening Payables

You are adding the Accounts Payable module to a system that includes the General Ledger module and existing data. The next step is to record outstanding invoices already posted to the Accounts Payable control account in the General Ledger. When recording invoices already posted to the Accounts Payable account in the General Ledger, you must take special care to ensure that these transactions are not posted a second time to the General Ledger.

❑ Enter the commands necessary to display the ACCPAC Plus Start Menu.

❑ Select: `A/P E. & J. Enterprises`

ACCPAC should display the title screen with "Nov 01 98" as the Last access date and "11/01/98" as the New date. If the New date is incorrect, type 110198.

❑ Press: Enter

INVOICE PROCESSING MENU

❑ Select: `3. Transaction processing` from the ACCPAC Accounts Payable Master Menu.

❑ Select: `1. Invoice processing` from the Transaction Processing Menu.

The Invoice Processing Menu (Figure 23–1) will appear on the screen.

Two functions on this menu are used in special circumstances.

Create/archive/delete recurring batches

The `Create/archive/delete recurring batches` option allows you to create a copy of an unposted batch and save it to be used again later. This function is useful for recurring transactions. You could create a batch of standard amount expenses that you pay each month — for example, rent or maintenance costs. Each month you can retrieve the batch, create a new batch from it, then edit and post it.

Figure 23–1

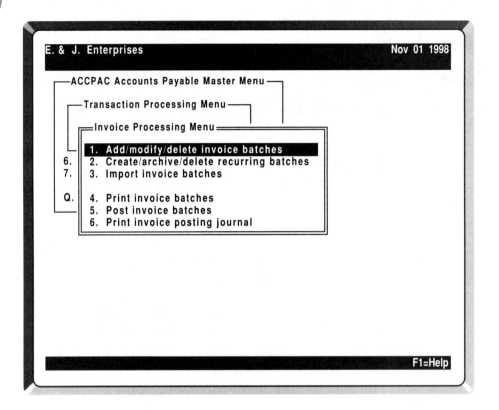

```
┌─────────────────────────────────────────────────────────┐
│ E. & J. Enterprises                          Nov 01 1998 │
│                                                           │
│  ┌─ACCPAC Accounts Payable Master Menu ─┐                 │
│  │                                       │                │
│  │  ┌─Transaction Processing Menu ─┐     │                │
│  │  │                              │     │                │
│  │  │  ┌═Invoice Processing Menu ══════════════┐          │
│  │  │  │ 1. Add/modify/delete invoice batches  │          │
│  │  6.│ 2. Create/archive/delete recurring batches│       │
│  │  7.│ 3. Import invoice batches             │          │
│  │  │  │                                       │          │
│  │  Q.│ 4. Print invoice batches              │          │
│  │  │  │ 5. Post invoice batches               │          │
│  │  │  │ 6. Print invoice posting journal      │          │
│  │  │  └───────────────────────────────────────┘          │
│                                                           │
│                                              F1=Help      │
└─────────────────────────────────────────────────────────┘
```

Import invoice batches

The `Import invoice batches` option allows you to transfer invoice batches from non-ACCPAC Plus programs to the Accounts Payable. You could then modify, print, and post the batch before printing the Posting Journal.

The remaining functions are used to process all invoice batches. You will use each as you enter the opening payables for E. & J. Enterprises.

ENTERING OPENING INVOICES

Now you are ready to enter the outstanding invoices into Accounts Payable. The first invoice is number OK972 from O.K. Furniture, dated September 30, 1998, for office furniture in the amount of $1,800.00. Since the purchase was for furniture to be used in the business and not resold, VAT is not recoverable and will not be accounted for separately.

❏ Select: `1. Add/modify/delete invoice batches`

The Add/Modify/Delete Invoice Batches screen (Figure 23–2) will appear.

Figure 23-2

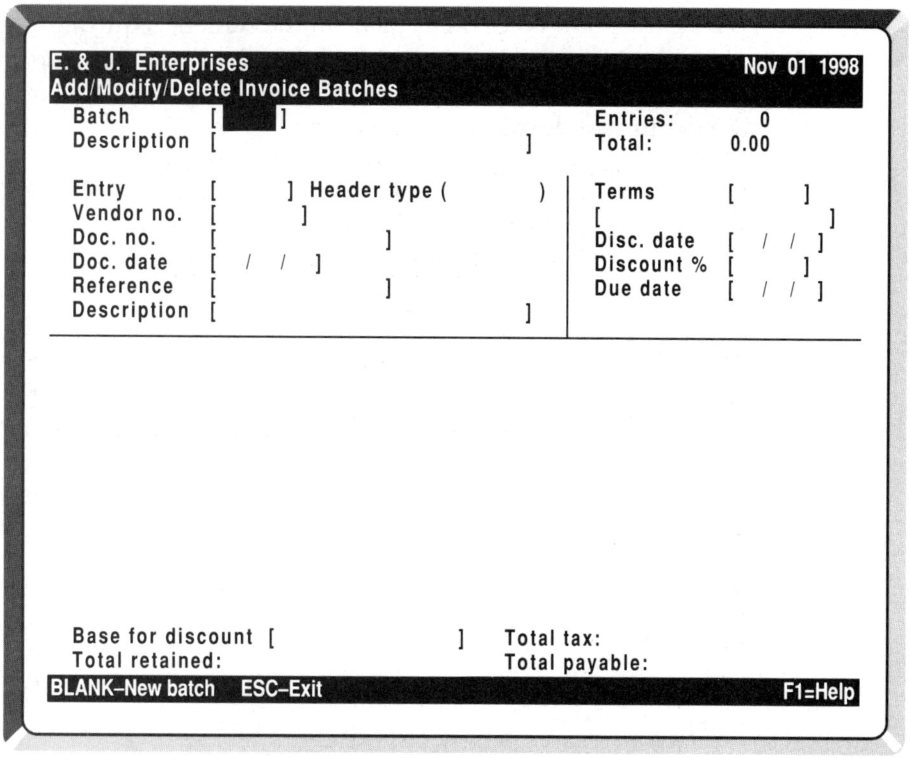

```
┌────────────────────────────────────────────────────────────────┐
│ E. & J. Enterprises                                 Nov 01 1998  │
│ Add/Modify/Delete Invoice Batches                                │
│   Batch       [      ]              Entries:      0              │
│   Description [                   ] Total:        0.00           │
│                                                                  │
│   Entry       [     ] Header type (    )  Terms     [      ]     │
│   Vendor no.  [        ]                  [                 ]    │
│   Doc. no.    [              ]            Disc. date [  /  / ]    │
│   Doc. date   [  /  / ]                   Discount % [      ]     │
│   Reference   [              ]            Due date   [  /  / ]    │
│   Description [                   ]                              │
│                                                                  │
│                                                                  │
│                                                                  │
│                                                                  │
│                                                                  │
│                                                                  │
│   Base for discount  [          ]     Total tax:                 │
│   Total retained:                     Total payable:             │
│ BLANK–New batch   ESC–Exit                              F1=Help  │
└────────────────────────────────────────────────────────────────┘
```

If you make a typing error when entering the invoice information, you can correct it by pressing the backspace key and typing over your mistake. If you have already entered and accepted the information, you can correct it by selecting "Edit" at the final authorization inquiry and correct the invoice then.

❑ Press: [Enter] in the blank `Batch` field.

The following message will appear:

```
┌────────────────────────────────────────────────┐
│                                                  │
│      Are you sure you want to enter a new batch? │
│               Yes         No                     │
│                                                  │
└────────────────────────────────────────────────┘
```

❑ Select: `Yes`

ACCPAC Plus assigns the next available Batch number (number 1) to the new invoice batch file, displays "0" in the Entries field and "0.00" in the Total field at the top right of the screen. The cursor will then move to the batch `Description` field.

❑ Type: `Invoices posted to G/L`

❑ Press: [Enter]

Since this transaction is the first one to be entered, the `Entry` number field will display "1".

❑ Press: [Enter]

A `Header Type` box will appear on the screen, requiring you to identify the type of document that is being entered. Invoices are billings from vendors for goods or services rendered and increase the Accounts Payable. Credit notes are used to document decreases in Accounts Payable that occur for a reason other than making a payment to a vendor. Debit notes signify an increase in the amount owing on the Accounts Payable. Debit and credit notes are discussed in more detail in Chapter 27. This first item is an invoice.

❑ Select: `Invoice`

You must enter the vendor number in the `Vendor no.` field as shown on the Vendor List you printed earlier. If you do not have the list available and cannot remember O.K. Furniture's number, use the Finder. If you enter a vendor number that has not been assigned, the Finder window will appear on the screen with a list of vendor numbers near the one you entered in error. You would then move the selector bar to the correct vendor number and press Enter.

❑ Press: [F5]

❑ Move the selector bar to `990025 O.K. Furniture`.

❑ Press: [Enter]

ACCPAC Plus will display the vendor name and move the cursor to the `Doc. no.` field. ACCPAC Plus will not accept an invoice entry without a document number.

❑ Press: [Enter] to try to enter a blank.

```
                          Error
            Invalid entry. Field cannot be blank.

                         Press F2
```

❑ Press: [F2] to clear the error message from the screen.

❑ Type: `OK972` in the `Document number` field to record the proper invoice number.

❑ Press: [Enter]

The `Doc. date` field automatically displays the date you entered as the New date on the title screen.

❑ Type: `093098` to record the date of the invoice: September 30, 1998.

❑ Press: [Enter]

You would normally use the `Reference` field for your purchase order number or the name of the person ordering the goods or services.

❑ Type: `P0003` to represent E. & J. Enterprises' purchase order number.

❑ Press: [Enter]

The highlighted bar now moves to the `Description` field.

- ❏ Type: `Office furniture`
- ❏ Press: [Enter]

The `Terms` code displayed is the default that you entered when adding the vendor. This code can be changed for a different type of transaction. The invoice had terms of 2/10, n/30. ACCPAC Plus will display the terms code description (2/10, n/30) and the discount percentage (2.00). The Discount date and Due date will also be displayed.

- ❏ Press: [Enter] to accept the terms.

An option bar will appear.

Save entry	Header	Detail	Cancel

- ❏ Select: `Detail`

The Distribution Detail screen (Figure 23–3) will appear.

Figure 23–3

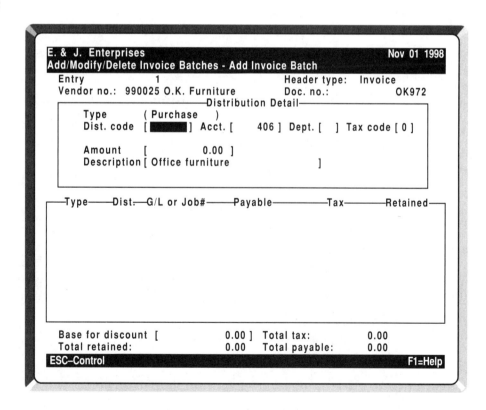

The cursor will move to the "Distribution Detail" portion of the screen.

If you enter a Distribution code that is other than one that you created when setting up the Distributions in Chapter 21, the program will display the G/L account code entered in the vendor record. If the vendor record specifies a Distribution code that does not have a G/L account assigned to it, no account code will be displayed. You will then have to enter the G/L account code.

When you created the vendor file for O.K. Furniture you did not identify a Distribution code, but you did enter an Account code.

☐ Press: [Enter] in the blank `Dist. code` field.

The cursor will move to the `Acct.` field. General Ledger account number 406 (Office Furniture) will be displayed.

☐ Press: [Enter]

The cursor will move to the `Tax code` field, and will display "0". Since VAT is not recoverable on this purchase, you do not record it in Tax code 1.

☐ Press: [Enter] to accept the default `0` in the `Tax code` field.

☐ Type: `1800.00` in the `Amount` field.

☐ Press: [Enter]

The cursor will move to the `Description` field which displays "Office furniture".

☐ Press: [Enter]

The cursor will return to the `Dist. Code` field for further distributions on this invoice.

☐ Press: [Esc] to indicate that the distribution is complete.

The cursor will move to the `Base for discount` field which displays "1800.00". The actual invoice was for $1,636.36 with VAT of $163.64. The discount is to be calculated on the amount of $1,636.36.

☐ Type: `1636.36`

☐ Press: [Enter]

An option bar will appear as shown in Figure 23–4.

Review your data carefully. If there are errors in the invoice information, select "Header" and make the necessary corrections. If there is an error in the General Ledger distribution, select "Detail" to enter corrections. Once you are satisfied that there are no errors,

☐ Select: `Save entry`

The Entries field in the upper right corner will change to "1" and the Total field will change to 1,800.00. The `Entry` number field will display the next entry number in sequence.

Figure 23–4

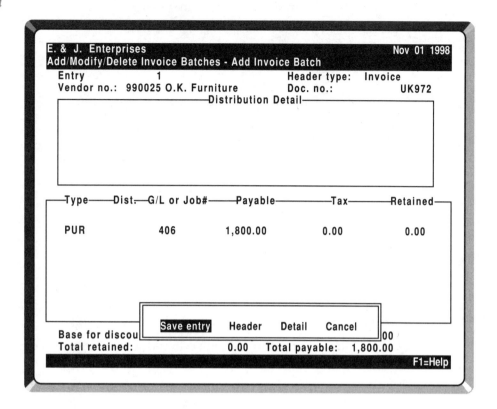

Entering a Purchases Invoice

The next invoice to be entered is number 103109 from Pear Computers Inc., dated October 31, 1998, for the purchase of a computer and printer ($2,250) for inventory. The invoice totalled $2,475 including value added tax of $225. E. & J. Enterprises' purchase order was P0005. This entry will require distribution to two General Ledger accounts, VAT Recoverable, and Purchases.

ACCPAC Plus will display the Vendor number, Date, Reference and Description of the last entry.

❏ Press: [Enter] to accept Entry 2.

The Header Type box will appear.

❏ Select: Invoice

❏ Press: [F5] to activate the Finder.

❏ Select: 990015 Pear Computers Inc.

❏ Type: 103109 in the Doc. no. field.

❏ Press: [Enter]

❏ Type: 103198 in the Doc. date field.

❏ Press: [Enter]

❏ Type: P0005 in the Reference field.

❏ Press: [Enter]

❏ Type: Computer & Printer in the Description field.

❏ Press: [Enter]

❏ Press: [Enter] to accept "2%disc" as the Terms code.

The option bar will appear.

```
┌─────────────────────────────────────────────────────┐
│                                                       │
│     Save entry      Header      Detail      Cancel    │
│                                                       │
└─────────────────────────────────────────────────────┘
```

❏ Select: Detail

❏ Press: [Enter] to accept Dist. code pv.

❏ Press: [Enter] to accept Tax code 1.

❏ Type: 2475.00 in the Amount field.

❏ Press: [Enter]

ACCPAC Plus uses the information entered when you defined the distribution code to calculate the amount of value added tax included in the amount of the invoice.

❏ Press: [Enter] to accept "225.00" as the Tax amount.

❏ Press: [Enter] to accept "Computer & Printer" as the Description.

❏ Press: [Esc] to indicate that distributions on this invoice are complete.

Discounts are not normally extended on sales tax or value added tax. The Discount base field will display the full amount of the invoice less the tax.

❏ Press: [Enter] to accept $2,250.00 as the base for discount.

❏ Select: Save entry

Your Turn

❏ Enter the information for the following invoice.

Invoice number OK1010, dated October 31, 1998, from O.K. Furniture for $745.00. E. & J. Enterprises' purchase order number was P0006. The purchase was for office furniture (G/L account number 406) so the Value Added Tax is not recoverable. The full amount of $745 is to be distributed to the furniture account. The basis for discount will be $677.27. When you have saved the above entry:

❏ Enter the information for the following invoice.

Invoice number 87795, dated October 31, 1998, from Dubai Software Corp. for $1,650.00. E. & J. Enterprises' purchase order number was P0008. This purchase was for software for resale and, therefore, the VAT is recoverable. The purchase of software was for $1,500.00 and the VAT was $150.00. Once the invoice has been recorded,

❏ Press: [Esc] twice to return to the Invoice Processing Menu.

PRINTING AN INVOICE BATCH

The Invoice Batch lists all the invoices you have entered in the batch.

❏ Select: 4. Print invoice batches from the Invoice Processing Menu.

The Print Invoice Batches screen (Figure 23–5) will appear.

Figure 23–5

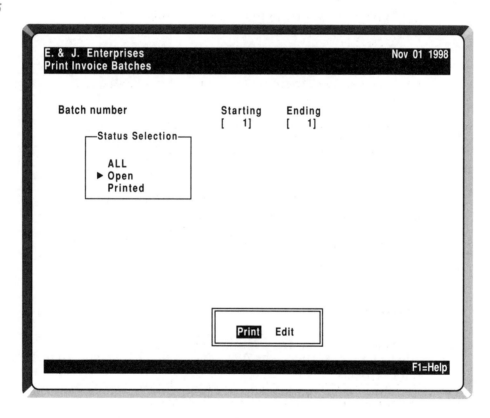

Ensure that the printer is ready and on line to your computer. If you had entered several Invoice batches, you could select "Edit" and enter the range of the batches that you wanted to print in the "Starting" and "Ending" batch number fields.

❏ Press: [Enter] to print the Invoice Batch.

Table 23–1

```
Date: Nov 01 98   12:37am              E. & J. Enterprises                         Page:   1
A/P Invoice Batch List

Batch number          [   1]   to   [   1]
Status(es) selected:  Open

Batch number:    1   Invoices posted to G/L
Creation date: Nov 01 98  Status: Open

Entry    Vendor Vendor                                  Acct.  Dept. Tx
 No. Ty Number Name                  Document No. Ty  Dist.  (Job-Ph-Cat) Cd Tax/Base/Net    Document Amount

  1 IN 990025 O.K. Furniture              OK972 PUR        406          0                          1,800.00
          Date: Sep 30 98       Ref: P0003                                                       ————————
          Due:  Oct 30 98 Terms:2%disc 2/10,n/30                        Total invoice            1,800.00 *
          Desc: Office furniture
          Disc: Oct 10 98 ( 2.00%) Base:      1,636.36

  2 IN 990015 Pear Computers Inc.        103109 PUR    pv  752       1 Net:    2,250.00            2,475.00
          Date: Oct 31 98       Ref: P0005                 Tax:      542       Tax:     225.00
          Due:  Nov 30 98 Terms:2%disc 2/10,n/30                                                 ————————
          Desc: Computer & Printer               Total tax:      225.00  Total invoice           2,475.00 *
          Disc: Nov 10 98 ( 2.00%) Base:      2,250.00

  3 IN 990025 O.K. Furniture             OK1010 PUR        406          0                            745.00
          Date: Oct 31 98       Ref: P0006                                                       ————————
          Due:  Nov 30 98 Terms:2%disc 2/10,n/30                        Total invoice              745.00 *
          Desc: Office furniture
          Disc: Nov 10 98 ( 2.00%) Base:        677.27

  4 IN 990045 Dubai Software Co.          87795 PUR    pv  752       1 Net:    1,500.00            1,650.00
          Date: Oct 31 98       Ref: P0008                 Tax:      542       Tax:     150.00
          Due:  Nov 30 98 Terms:  n/30 Net 30                                                    ————————
          Desc: Software for resale              Total tax:      150.00  Total invoice           1,650.00 *


                                                   Total invoices          6,670.00
                                                   Total debit notes           0.00
                                                   Total credit notes          0.00
                                                                          ————————
                                                   Batch total payable       6,670.00
                                                                          ================
      4 transaction(s) printed.
```

After you have printed the A/P Invoice Batch List (shown in Table 23–1), review it for errors.

EDITING AN INVOICE BATCH

If an invoice batch contains any mistakes, you can edit it using the "Add/modify/delete invoice batches" option on the Invoice Processing Menu. You can edit a batch at any time before it is posted to the Accounts Payable ledger. After it has been posted, you are not permitted to make changes to that batch. The batch total shown on the A/P Invoice Batch List you just printed is

$6,670 but the balance in the General Ledger Accounts Payable account was only $6,570. Someone made an error in recording the amount of invoice number OK972 to O.K. Furniture. The correct amount of the distribution to office furniture is $1,700.00, not $1,800.00 as entered.

❏ Select: `1. Add/modify/delete invoice batches` from the Invoice Processing Menu.

❏ Type: `1` in the `Batch` field.

❏ Press: [Enter]

An option bar will appear at the bottom of the screen.

Modify batch	Delete batch

❏ Select: `Modify batch`

❏ Press: [Enter] to accept the batch `Description`.

The cursor will move to the Entry field. Look at the A/P Invoice Batch List that you have just printed to find the error. You can see that it occurs in batch entry number 1.

❏ Type: `1` in the `Entry` field.

❏ Press: [Enter]

The invoice entry for O.K. Furniture will be displayed, as shown in Figure 23–6.

❏ Select: `Modify entry`

The invoice should have recorded the distribution to "Office furniture" of $1,700, not $1,800.

❏ Select: `Detail`

The selector bar will move to the information box in the lower part of the screen. The highlighted bar will be resting on the only entry for this invoice.

❏ Press: [Enter] to select this entry line for correction.

❏ Press: [Enter] to accept the blank Distribution code.

❏ Press: [Enter] to accept Account 406.

❏ Press: [Enter] to accept Tax code "0".

❏ Type: `1700.00` in the `Amount` field.

❏ Press: [Enter]

❏ Press: [Esc] twice to indicate that you have finished editing the details.

The cursor will move to the Base for discount field which displays 1536.36, the re-calculated base for discount.

❏ Press: [Enter]

Figure 23–6

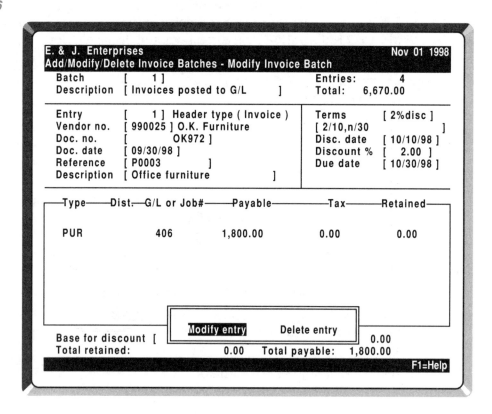

❏ Select: `Save entry`

After you "Save entry" the total amount of the batch should be $6,570.00 as shown at the top right of the screen. If a different amount is displayed on your screen you should review the four entries to locate the error. You can then correct the error using the steps described in this section.

❏ Press: ⌈Esc⌋ twice to return to the Invoice Processing Menu.

❏ Print the Invoice Batch List again to document the changes made.

POSTING TO THE ACCOUNTS PAYABLE LEDGER

After you have printed and reviewed the revised Accounts Payable Invoice Batch List and corrected all the entry errors, you may post the batch to the Accounts Payable ledger.

❏ Select: `5. Post invoice batches` from the Invoice Processing Menu.

The Post Invoice Batches screen (Figure 23–7) will appear.

In case there is a power fluctuation or a computer problem, you should back up your data files before posting this batch.

❏ Select: `Cancel`

Figure 23–7

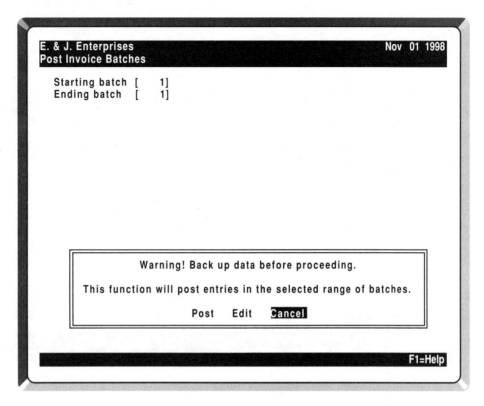

```
E. & J. Enterprises                                    Nov  01 1998
Post Invoice Batches

   Starting batch  [     1]
   Ending batch    [     1]




          ┌─────────────────────────────────────────────┐
          │    Warning! Back up data before proceeding.  │
          │                                              │
          │ This function will post entries in the selected range of batches. │
          │                                              │
          │          Post     Edit     Cancel            │
          └─────────────────────────────────────────────┘


                                                        F1=Help
```

❑ Press: [Esc] twice to display the ACCPAC Plus Accounts Payable Master Menu.

❑ Press: Q   to return to the Start Menu.

❑ Press: [F3] to access the System Manager.

❑ Select: DOS

❑ Enter the DOS commands to back up your data files.

❑ Type: exit   to return to the System Manager.

❑ Press: [Esc] to return to the Start Menu.

❑ Enter the commands necessary to return to the Post Invoice Batches screen.

❑ Select: Post   to proceed with the posting.

Each time you post batches to the Accounts Payable ledger a new posting sequence number will be assigned. ACCPAC Plus will not allow you to post a batch twice.

If the batch that is being posted contains an error that ACCPAC Plus can detect, a warning message will be displayed on the screen and the entry that contains the error will be transferred to the next available batch. You should correct the error and then print and post the new batch.

Once posting is complete, ACCPAC Plus will display the following message.

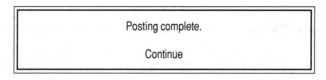

Posting complete.

Continue

❑ Press: ⌊Enter⌋ to continue.

PRINTING THE INVOICE POSTING JOURNAL

❑ Select: 6. Print invoice posting journal

The Print Invoice Posting Journal screen allows you to select the posting journals to be printed by posting sequence number as shown in the Starting and Ending fields in Figure 23–8.

Figure 23–8

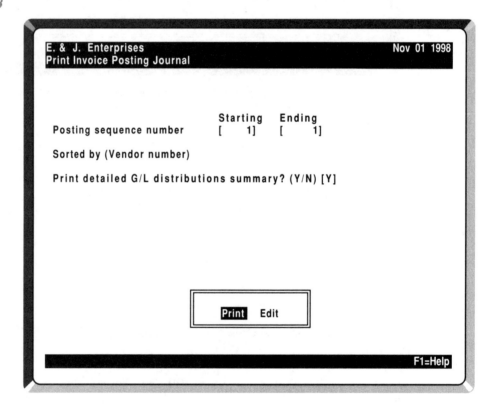

❑ Select: Edit
❑ Press: ⌊Enter⌋ twice to accept the default Starting and Ending posting sequence numbers.

The default setting prints the Invoice Posting Journal sorted by Vendor number. You can also print the posting journals sorted by `Document date` for a chronological printout or by `Document number`.

❏ Press: Enter to accept the default sorting by `Vendor number`.

The `Print detailed G/L distributions summary` field controls the information printed in the last portion of the journal. If you select "N", the General Ledger distributions will be summarized on one line. If you select "Y" the General Ledger distributions will be summarized by distribution code.

❏ Type: `Y`

❏ Press: Enter

❏ Select: `Print`

When the printing has finished, ACCPAC Plus will display the following message:

```
Do you want to clear all posting journals within the specified range?

           Yes           No
```

If you wished to print the Invoice Posting Journal again, you would select "N" and the information would not be erased. You could print the Invoice Posting Journal again and, if necessary, sort it by `Document date` or `Document number`.

❏ Select: `Yes`

Once you have cleared the A/P Invoice Posting Journal, ACCPAC Plus will clear the invoice batch. Clearing does not remove all traces of the posted invoices, since they are now in the Accounts Payable Ledger, however the batch itself no longer exists.

❏ Press: Esc twice to return to the ACCPAC Accounts Payable Master Menu.

Printed copies of the Invoice Posting Journal form the audit trail necessary to verify that posting is accurate. The first part of the report describes each entry that was posted. The second part of the report is the General Ledger Summary. The third part of the report is only printed if ACCPAC Plus detected an error in an entry. The report identifies the batch number and entry number containing the error and the number of the new batch created by ACCPAC Plus. You can use this information to correct the error before posting the new batch.

PRINT/CONSOLIDATE G/L TRANSACTIONS

The next step is to prepare the data for transfer to the General Ledger.

❏ Select: `5. Reports` from the ACCPAC Accounts Payable Master Menu.

❑ Select: `3.Print/consolidate G/L transactions` from the Reports Menu.

Figure 23–9

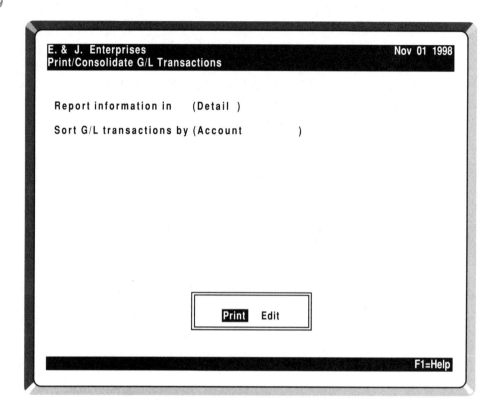

The default setting, as shown in Figure 23–9, will print the report in Detail, and will sort and summarize the General Ledger transactions by General Ledger account numbers. If you wished to print the report in summary form or sort the transaction by `Account`, `Journal entry`, or `Transaction date`, you would select "Edit" and then select the required option.

❑ Select: `Print`

After the report has been printed, ACCPAC Plus will display the following message.

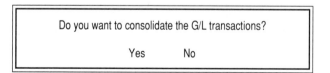

❑ Select: `No`

If the Accounts Payable is not integrated with the General Ledger, a second message would appear:

```
┌─────────────────────────────────────────────────────────┐
│                                                           │
│           Do you want to clear the G/L transactions?      │
│                                                           │
│                     Yes          No                       │
│                                                           │
└─────────────────────────────────────────────────────────┘
```

If the Accounts Payable was not integrated with the General Ledger, you would clear the information now by selecting "Y". Since the Accounts Payable and General Ledger are integrated, ACCPAC Plus will not allow you to clear the General Ledger transactions using the Accounts Payable module. These transactions will be cleared automatically from the Accounts Payable when they are retrieved by the General Ledger.

❑ Press: [Esc] to return to the ACCPAC Accounts Payable Master Menu.

❑ Press: Q to return to the Start Menu.

DELETING THE INVOICE BATCH IN THE GENERAL LEDGER

You have already posted these transactions to the General Ledger when you were working through Unit II, General Ledger and Financial Reporter. If you posted the transactions just completed, it would result in a duplication.

If you were using a manual General Ledger, you would clear the information after running the "Print/consolidate G/L transactions" function. If your Accounts Payable is integrated with the General Ledger module, you must bring the information into the General Ledger and then delete the invoice batch. The following deletion process is used only when initially converting to the ACCPAC Plus Accounts Payable when you are using the ACCPAC Plus General Ledger. It is not used in the processing of invoices that are part of normal ongoing accounting procedures.

If G/L E.& J. Enterprises is not displayed on the Start Menu, refer to Chapter 2 for the necessary steps to create the proper Start Menu line.

❑ Select: G/L E. & J. Enterprises

❑ Type: 110198 in the New date field.

❑ Press: [Enter]

❑ Select: Accept to confirm the date.

ACCPAC Plus will start the General Ledger program and determine if there are any batches to be retrieved.

```
┌─────────────────────────────────────────────────────────┐
│                                                           │
│      There are outstanding subledger batches to be retrieved. │
│                                                           │
│                      Continue                             │
│                                                           │
└─────────────────────────────────────────────────────────┘
```

❑ Press: [Enter] to continue.

❑ Select: 3. `Transaction processing` from the ACCPAC General Ledger Master Menu.

❑ Select: 1. `Batch processing` from the Transaction Processing Menu.

❑ Select: 2. `Retrieve subledger batches`

Figure 23–10

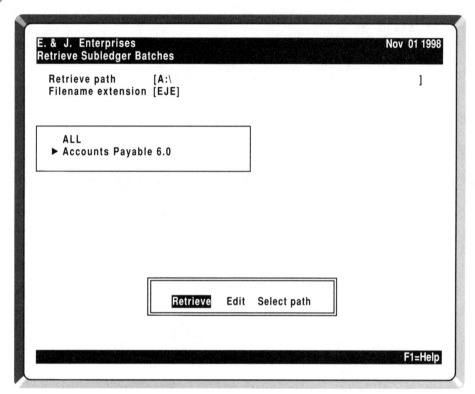

The Retrieve Subledger Batches screen (Figure 23–10) identifies that there are "Accounts Payable 6.0" batches to be retrieved.

❑ Select: `Retrieve`

The next screen display, as shown in Figure 23–11, illustrates that one batch with four entries has been created. The debit and credit totals equal $6,570.00.

❑ Press: [Enter] to continue.

In a few moments the screen will display the `Batch Processing Menu`.

❑ Select: 1. `Add/modify/delete batches`

❑ Press: [F5] in the `Batch` field.

❑ If necessary, move the selector bar to the batch `Retrieved from AP`.

❑ Press: [Enter]

Figure 23–11

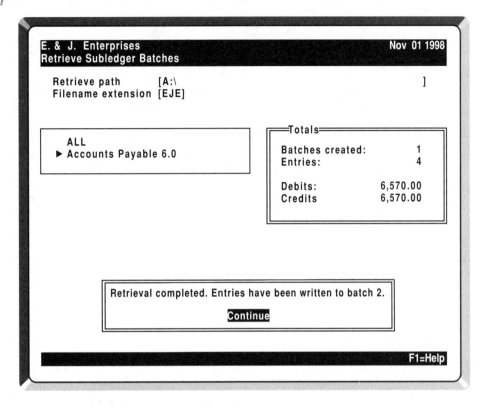

```
E. & J. Enterprises                                    Nov 01 1998
Retrieve Subledger Batches

   Retrieve path        [A:\                                    ]
   Filename extension  [EJE]


   ┌─────────────────────────────┐   ┌─Totals──────────────────────┐
   │   ALL                       │   │ Batches created:        1   │
   │ ► Accounts Payable 6.0      │   │ Entries:                4   │
   │                             │   │                             │
   └─────────────────────────────┘   │ Debits:          6,570.00   │
                                      │ Credits          6,570.00   │
                                      │                             │
                                      └─────────────────────────────┘



         ┌──────────────────────────────────────────────────┐
         │ Retrieval completed. Entries have been written to batch 2. │
         │                      Continue                      │
         └──────────────────────────────────────────────────┘


                                                          F1=Help
```

The general information on the batch (description, number of entries, and debit and credit amounts) will appear in the upper part of the screen. An option bar at the bottom of the screen will display the following choices.

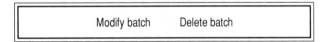

```
      Modify batch      Delete batch
```

❑ Select: `Delete batch`

ACCPAC Plus will ask you to confirm that you wish to delete the batch.

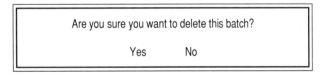

```
   Are you sure you want to delete this batch?

            Yes        No
```

❑ Select: `Yes`

You have now deleted the retrieved Accounts Payable batch so it cannot be posted to the General Ledger.

❑ Press: [Esc] three times to return to the ACCPAC General Ledger Master Menu.

You should confirm that the batch has been deleted in the General Ledger module.

❑ Select: `2. Inquiries`

❑ Select: `2. Display batches`

After a few seconds ACCPAC Plus will present the `Display Batches` screen with the following message in the lower portion of the screen.

```
There are no batches to display.

Continue
```

❑ Press: [Enter]

❑ Press: [Esc] to return to the ACCPAC General Ledger Master Menu.

❑ Quit the ACCPAC Plus General Ledger.

❑ Back up your data files.

REVIEW QUESTIONS

1. What are the differences between the Accounts Payable Invoice Processing Menu and the Accounts Receivable Invoice Processing Menu?
2. Describe how you would make changes to an invoice batch after you have entered it and printed the Invoice Batch Listing.
3. What errors will the computer identify when you are recording invoices? What errors won't it identify?
4. Why is it very important that you back up your data files before you post invoice batches to the Accounts Payable ledger?
5. Why would you want to have the Invoice Posting Journal sorted by Vendor number, Document Number, or Document Date?
6. Why is it an advantage to print the G/L distributions summary on the Invoice Posting Journal?
7. Describe the procedure to transfer information from the Accounts Payable to the General Ledger.
8. When adding Accounts Payable to the General Ledger, what steps must you take to record those transactions that have already been posted to the General Ledger, without duplicating them in the General Ledger?
9. Compare the Detailed Aged Accounts Receivable report and the Open Payables report.

EXERCISE

Select your company from the Start Menu and enter November 1, 1998 as the New date. If you review the closing General Ledger for the company you used in the earlier exercises, you will see that the closing balance of Accounts Payable is $9,300. This closing balance consists of the following invoices and amounts.

1. Create an invoice batch of the unpaid items as of October 31. See Table 23–2.
2. Print the Invoice Batch Listing.
3. Post the batch to Accounts Payable.
4. Print the Invoice Posting Journal and clear the posting data.
5. Transfer the information to the General Ledger. You will set the New date as November 1, 1998.
6. Print the General Ledger batch.
7. Delete the General Ledger batch.
8. Back up your data disk.

Table 23–2

```
       Batch 1
       Description; To record opening invoices
       Entry 1
First invoice
   Vendor: Dominion Supplies
   Doc. no.: 981327
   Document Date: Oct. 1, 1998
   Reference: P.O. 1245
   Description: Computer supplies
   Terms: n/30
   Distribution code: purch
   Tax code 1
   Amount: $1100.00
   Tax amount: $100.00
Second invoice
   Vendor: Cardinal Associates
   Doc. no.: 2318
   Document Date: Oct 14, 1998
   Reference: P.O. 1246
   Description: Computer software
   Terms: 2/10,n/30
   Distribution code: purch
   Tax code 1
   Amount: $2,200.00
   Tax amount: $200.00
   Base for discount: $2,000.00
Third invoice
   Vendor: Serene Systems Ltd.
   Doc. no.: 4550
   Document Date: Oct 14, 1998
   Reference: P.O. 1247
   Description: Computer Hardware
   Terms: n/30
   Distribution code: purch
   Tax code 1
   Amount: $6,000.00
   Tax amount: $500.00
```

24 Regular Invoices

In previous chapters, you created the Accounts Payable data and entered the opening invoices. You are now ready to enter regular invoices that have arisen in the normal course of business since that time.

❑ Enter the commands necessary to display the ACCPAC Plus Start Menu.

❑ Select: `A/P E. & J. Enterprises` from the Start Menu.

❑ Type: `111598` in the ` New date` field.

❑ Press: [Enter]

The screen will indicate that the New date is more than one week later than the Last access date.

```
┌─────────────────────────────────────────────────────────────┐
│ ┌───────────────────────────────────────────────────────┐   │
│ │   New date is more than one week later than old date. │   │
│ │                                                       │   │
│ │              Accept      Edit                         │   │
│ └───────────────────────────────────────────────────────┘   │
└─────────────────────────────────────────────────────────────┘
```

❑ Select: `Accept`

ENTERING INVOICES — SINGLE DISTRIBUTION

The first invoice for you to enter is number 110506 from Pear Computers Inc., dated November 5, 1998, for the purchase of 15 software utility packages intended for resale. The invoice total is $385 with VAT included. The terms are 2/10,n/30 and the purchase order number is P0009.

❑ Select: `3. Transaction processing` from the ACCPAC Accounts Payable Master Menu.

❑ Select: `1. Invoice processing` from the Transaction Processing Menu.

The Invoice Processing Menu (Figure 24–1) will appear on the screen.

❑ Select: `1. Add/modify/delete invoice batches`

Figure 24–1

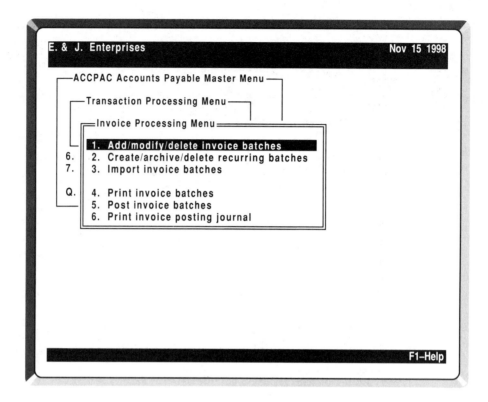

The Add/Modify/Delete Invoice Batches screen (Figure 24–2) will appear.

Remember that if you make a typing error when entering the invoice information, you can correct it by using the backspace or delete key and then typing the correct information. If you have already entered and accepted the information, you can correct it by selecting   Edit   from the option box and correcting the invoice.

❑ Press: [Enter] in the blank   Batch number field to create a new batch.

The following message will appear:

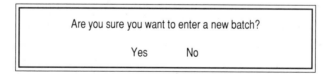

❑ Select: Yes

ACCPAC Plus assigns the next available Batch number, (number 2), to the new invoice batch file, displays "0" in the Entries field and "0.00" in the Total field at the top right of the screen. The cursor will then move to the batch Description field.

❑ Type: November invoices

Figure 24–2

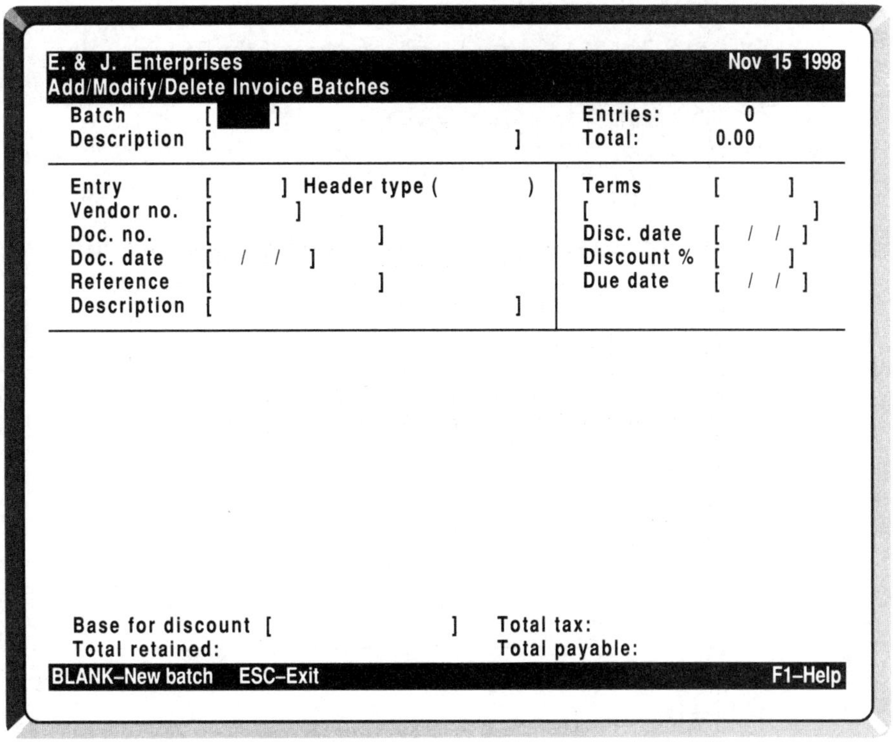

```
┌────────────────────────────────────────────────────────────────┐
│ E. & J. Enterprises                              Nov 15 1998     │
│ Add/Modify/Delete Invoice Batches                               │
│    Batch        [     ]              Entries:        0          │
│    Description  [                 ]  Total:          0.00       │
│   ─────────────────────────────────────────────────────────    │
│    Entry       [     ] Header type (      )   Terms    [    ]   │
│    Vendor no.  [        ]                     [              ]   │
│    Doc. no.    [             ]                Disc. date [ / / ] │
│    Doc. date   [  /  /  ]                      Discount % [    ] │
│    Reference   [             ]                Due date  [ / / ]  │
│    Description [            ]                                    │
│                                                                  │
│                                                                  │
│                                                                  │
│                                                                  │
│                                                                  │
│    Base for discount  [            ]   Total tax:               │
│    Total retained:                     Total payable:           │
│ BLANK–New batch   ESC–Exit                           F1–Help    │
└────────────────────────────────────────────────────────────────┘
```

❏ Press: [Enter]

Since this transaction is the first one to be entered in this batch, the Entry number field will display "1".

❏ Press: [Enter] to accept Entry 1.

A Header Type box will appear on the screen, requiring you to identify the type of document that is being entered.

❏ Select: Invoice

In the Vendor no. field, you must enter the vendor number as shown on the Vendor List you printed earlier. If you do not have the list available and cannot remember Pear Computers Inc.'s number, use the Finder.

❏ Press: [F5]

❏ Move the selector bar to 990015 Pear Computers Inc.

❏ Press: [Enter]

ACCPAC Plus will display the vendor name and move the cursor to the Document number field.

❏ Type: 110506 in the Doc. no. field to record the invoice number.

❏ Press: [Enter]

The `Doc. date` field automatically displays the date you entered as the New date on the title screen.

- ❏ Type: 110598 to record the date of the invoice, November 5, 1998.
- ❏ Press: Enter
- ❏ Type: P0009, E. & J. Enterprises' purchase order number.
- ❏ Press: Enter

The highlighted bar now moves to the Description field.

- ❏ Type: Utility software
- ❏ Press: Enter

ACCPAC Plus will display the Terms code description (2/10,n/30) and the Discount percentage (2.00). The Discount date and Due date will also be displayed.

- ❏ Press: Enter to accept the Terms.

An option bar will appear.

```
┌─────────────────────────────────────────────────────────┐
│   ┌─────────────────────────────────────────────────┐   │
│   │  Save entry      Header      Detail      Cancel  │   │
│   └─────────────────────────────────────────────────┘   │
└─────────────────────────────────────────────────────────┘
```

- ❏ Select: Detail

The cursor will appear in the Distribution Detail portion of the Add Invoice Batch screen (Figure 24–3).

- ❏ Press: Enter to accept pv in the Dist. code field.

General Ledger account number 752 (Purchases) will be displayed in the `Acct.` field. The cursor will be in the `Tax code` field which displays code "1".

- ❏ Press: Enter to accept Tax Code 1.

The cursor will move to the Amount field.

- ❏ Type: 385.00
- ❏ Press: Enter

ACCPAC Plus uses the distribution code information to determine that the amount entered includes Value added tax at a rate of 10%. The amount of value added tax that was paid on the invoice appears then in the Tax amount field.

- ❏ Press: Enter to accept the Tax amount of $35.00. The cursor will move to the Description field which now displays "Utility software".
- ❏ Press: Enter

The cursor will return to the Dist. code field for further distributions on this invoice.

- ❏ Press: Esc to indicate that the distribution is complete.

Figure 24–3

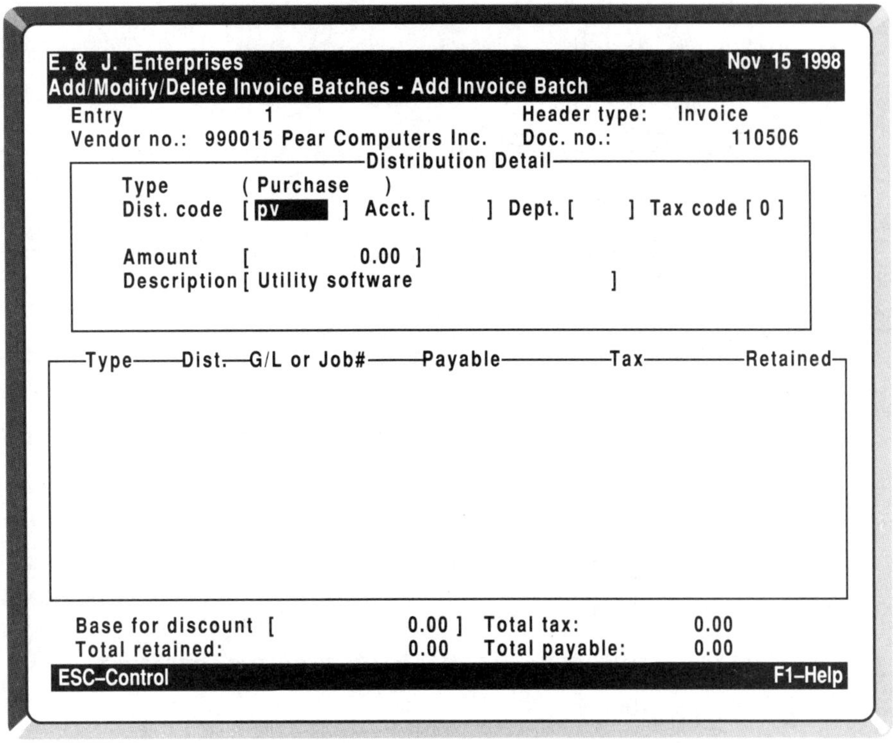

```
┌─────────────────────────────────────────────────────────────────┐
│ E. & J. Enterprises                              Nov 15 1998      │
│ Add/Modify/Delete Invoice Batches - Add Invoice Batch             │
│   Entry          1                  Header type:    Invoice       │
│   Vendor no.:  990015 Pear Computers Inc.   Doc. no.:    110506   │
│ ┌──────────────────────Distribution Detail──────────────────────┐│
│ │   Type      ( Purchase   )                                     ││
│ │   Dist. code [ pv    ]  Acct. [    ] Dept. [    ] Tax code [ 0 ]││
│ │                                                                ││
│ │   Amount    [          0.00  ]                                 ││
│ │   Description [ Utility software              ]                ││
│ │                                                                ││
│ └────────────────────────────────────────────────────────────────┘│
│ ┌─Type──Dist.─G/L or Job#────Payable────────Tax─────────Retained─┐│
│ │                                                                ││
│ │                                                                ││
│ │                                                                ││
│ │                                                                ││
│ │                                                                ││
│ │                                                                ││
│ └────────────────────────────────────────────────────────────────┘│
│   Base for discount  [            0.00 ]  Total tax:      0.00    │
│   Total retained:                  0.00   Total payable:  0.00    │
│ ESC–Control                                            F1–Help    │
└─────────────────────────────────────────────────────────────────┘
```

The cursor will move to the `Base for discount` field which displays "350.00".

❏ Press: [Enter]

Review the data carefully. If there are errors in the invoice information portion, select "Header" and make the necessary corrections. If there is an error in the General Ledger distribution, select "Detail" to enter corrections. Once you are satisfied that there are no errors,

❏ Select: `Save entry`

The Entries field in the upper right corner will change to "1" and the Total field will change to 385.00. The Entry number field will display the next Entry number in sequence.

ENTERING INVOICES – MULTIPLE DISTRIBUTION

Often an invoice has to be distributed to more than one General Ledger account. For example, E. & J. Enterprises rents both office space and office equipment from Home Realty and pays for both on the same check. The office rent of $1,200 must be distributed to General Ledger account 920 and the equipment rent of $75 to account 925.

Record the invoice from Home Realty for November's rent as follows:

❑ Press: [Enter] to accept 2 as the next entry.

❑ Press: [Enter] again to identify the item as an invoice.

❑ Press: [F5]

❑ Move the selector bar to 990005 Home Realty

❑ Press: [Enter]

ACCPAC Plus will display the vendor name and move the cursor to the Doc no. field.

❑ Type: Nov rent in the Doc. no. field.

❑ Press: [Enter]

The Doc. date field displays the date that you entered for the prior transaction.

❑ Type: 110198 to record the date of the invoice, November 1, 1998.

❑ Press: [Enter]

❑ Type: Rent in the Reference field.

If necessary, use the space bar to erase excess characters.

❑ Press: [Enter]

The highlighted bar now moves to the Description field.

❑ Type: Nov. office and equip. rent

Make sure that you delete any excess characters.

❑ Press: [Enter]

❑ Press: [Enter] to accept the Terms code rent.

ACCPAC Plus will display the terms code description Monthly rent and the Discount percentage (0.00). The Discount date will be blank. The Due date (11/01/98) will be displayed. The following option bar will appear:

Save entry	Header	Detail	Cancel

❑ Select: Detail

The Distribution Detail screen (Figure 24–4) will appear.

❑ Press: [Enter] to accept the default "r" in the Dist. code field.

General Ledger account number 920 (Office rent expense) will be displayed in the Acct. field. The cursor will be in the Tax code field.

❑ Press: [Enter] in the Tax code field to accept "0".

The highlighted bar will move to the Amount field.

Figure 24–4

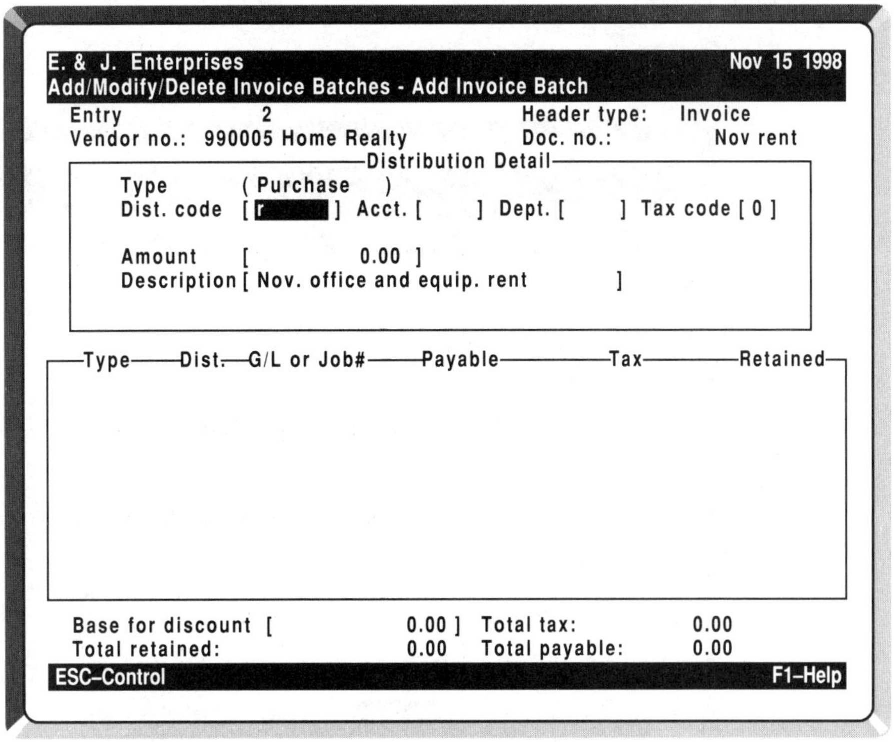

```
┌─────────────────────────────────────────────────────────────────┐
│ E. & J. Enterprises                              Nov 15 1998      │
│ Add/Modify/Delete Invoice Batches - Add Invoice Batch            │
│    Entry           2                 Header type:   Invoice       │
│    Vendor no.:  990005 Home Realty   Doc. no.:      Nov rent      │
│    ─────────────────────Distribution Detail─────────────          │
│ ┌─────────────────────────────────────────────────────────────┐ │
│ │    Type      ( Purchase   )                                   │ │
│ │    Dist. code  [ r      ]  Acct. [     ]  Dept. [    ] Tax code [ 0 ] │ │
│ │                                                               │ │
│ │    Amount    [          0.00 ]                                │ │
│ │    Description [ Nov. office and equip. rent         ]        │ │
│ └─────────────────────────────────────────────────────────────┘ │
│                                                                   │
│ ┌─Type──Dist.─G/L or Job#─────Payable────────Tax────────Retained─┐ │
│ │                                                               │ │
│ │                                                               │ │
│ │                                                               │ │
│ │                                                               │ │
│ │                                                               │ │
│ │                                                               │ │
│ └─────────────────────────────────────────────────────────────┘ │
│    Base for discount  [           0.00 ]  Total tax:      0.00    │
│    Total retained:                0.00    Total payable:  0.00    │
│ ESC–Control                                           F1–Help     │
└─────────────────────────────────────────────────────────────────┘
```

❏ Type: `1200.00`

❏ Press: [Enter]

Since there is no VAT on rent, the cursor will move to the "Description" field.

❏ Press: [Enter] to accept the description displayed.

The cursor will return to the `Dist. code` field for further distributions on this invoice.

❏ Use the space bar to blank out any characters in the `Dist. code` field.

❏ Press: [Enter]

❏ Type: `925` in the `Acct.` field.

❏ Press: [Enter]

❏ Press: [Enter] in the `Tax code` field to accept "0".

❏ Type: `75.00` in the `Amount` field.

❏ Press: [Enter]

The cursor will move to the `Description` field.

❏ Press: [Enter]

❏ Press: [Esc] to indicate that you have finished distributing the expenses.

An option bar will now appear at the bottom of the screen as shown in Figure 24–5.

Figure 24–5

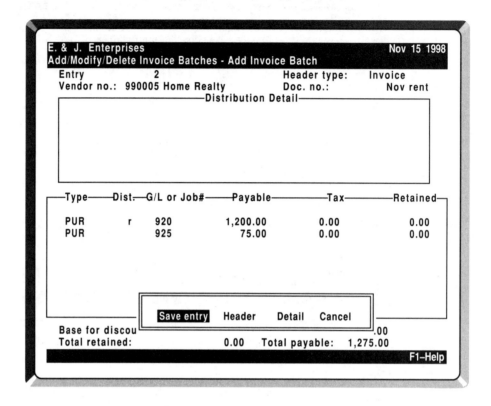

Review the data entered carefully. If there are errors in the invoice information portion, select "Header" and make the necessary corrections. If there is an error in the General Ledger distributions, select "Detail" to enter corrections. Once you are satisfied that there are no errors,

❑ Select: `Save entry`

The Entries field in the upper right corner will change to "2" and the Total field will change to 1,660.00. The Entry number field will display the next entry number in sequence.

❑ Press: `Esc` twice to return to the Invoice Processing Menu.

❑ Select: `4. Print invoice batches` from the Invoice Processing Menu.

❑ Select: `Print`

EDITING AN INVOICE BATCH

While reviewing the invoice entries, Joan noticed that the invoice from Pear Computers Inc. for the Utility software was recorded for $350.00 plus tax. The correct amount should have been $530.00 plus tax. You must edit the transaction to correct this mistake.

☐ Select: `1. Add/modify/delete invoice batches` from the Invoice Processing Menu.

☐ Type: `2` in the `Batch` field.

☐ Press: [Enter]

An option bar will appear at the bottom of the screen.

```
┌──────────────────────────────────────────────────┐
│                                                    │
│        Modify batch        Delete batch            │
│                                                    │
└──────────────────────────────────────────────────┘
```

☐ Select: `Modify batch`

☐ Press: [Enter] to accept the `Batch` description.

The cursor will move to the batch Entry field. Look at the A/P Invoice Batch List that you have just printed to find the error. You can see that it occurs in batch entry number 1.

☐ Type: `1` in the `Entry` field.

☐ Press: [Enter]

The invoice entry for Pear Computers Inc. will be displayed, as shown in Figure 24–6.

☐ Select: `Modify entry`

The total amount of the invoice was $530 plus VAT, not $350 so you must change the detail of the invoice.

☐ Select: `Detail`

The selector bar will move to the information box in the lower part of the screen. The highlighted bar will be resting on the only entry for this invoice.

☐ Press: [Enter] to select this entry line for correction.

☐ Press: [Enter] to accept the Distribution code.

☐ Press: [Enter] to accept the Tax code.

☐ Type: `583.00` ($530 + $53VAT) in the `Amount` field.

☐ Press: [Enter]

☐ Press: [Enter] to accept `53.00` in the `Tax amount` field.

☐ Press: [Esc] to indicate that you have finished editing this detail.

Figure 24–6

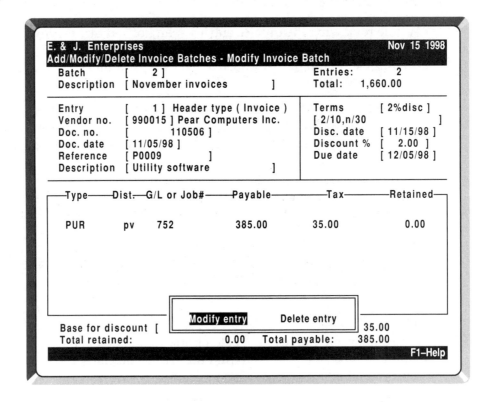

The selector bar will highlight the next detail line which should be blank. If you wished to add another detail or distribution for this invoice you would press Enter.

❏ Press [Esc] to indicate that you have finished editing details.

The cursor will move to the `Base for discount` field which displays 530.00.

❏ Press: [Enter]

❏ Select: `Save entry`

After you "Save entry" the total amount of the batch at the top right of the screen should be $1,858.00. If a different amount is displayed on your screen you should review the entries to locate the error. You can then correct the error using the steps described in this section.

❏ Press: [Esc] twice to return to the Invoice Processing Menu.

❏ Print the Invoice batch again to document the changes made.

YOUR TURN

Now you must record the rest of E. & J. Enterprises' invoices.

Enter the following invoices to a new batch, using the appropriate distribution codes. The discount base should not include value added tax. Verify the vendor numbers using the screen display or the Finder. Confirm the General Ledger account codes by referring to your Chart of Accounts printout.

❏ Enter the following invoices:

1. Invoice number CA55987 from Computer Associates, dated November 6, 1998, for three ACCPAC Plus accounting programs intended for resale (account code 752, amount $750 VAT included). The purchase order number is P0010.

2. Invoice number 110312 from O. K. Furniture, dated November 6, 1998, for a mobile computer table intended for resale. The invoice amount was $110.00 VAT included. The purchase order number is P0011. The Base for discount will be $100.

3. Invoice number 99843 from Dubai Software Co., dated November 7, 1999, for graphics software intended for resale at $356.75, VAT included. The purchase order number is P0012. Payment is due in 30 days.

Once you have finished entering the invoices, you must print an Invoice Batch Listing before posting the transactions.

❏ Press: ⌈Esc⌋ twice to return to the Invoice Processing Menu.

❏ Select: 4. Print invoice batches

Print the Invoice Batch List and compare it to the imformation provided in Tables 24–1.

Table 24–1

```
Date: Nov 15 98   2:00am            E. & J. Enterprises                          Page:   1
A/P Invoice Batch List

Batch number          [   2]   to  [   3]
Status(es) selected:  Open

Batch number:    3   November invoices
Creation date: Nov 15 98  Status: Open

Entry    Vendor Vendor                            Acct.  Dept. Tx
No. Ty  Number Name              Document No. Ty   Dist.  (Job-Ph-Cat) Cd Tax/Base/Net    Document Amount

   1 IN 990035 Computer Associates    CA55987 PUR    pv    752       1 Net:     681.82        750.00
        Date: Nov 06 98      Ref: P0010          Tax:   542         Tax:     68.18
        Due:  Dec 06 98 Terms: n/30 Net 30                                               _____
        Desc: Accounting software          Total tax:      68.18  Total invoice          750.00 *

   2 IN 990025 O.K. Furniture          110312 PUR    pv    752       1 Net:     100.00        110.00
        Date: Nov 06 98      Ref: P0011          Tax:   542         Tax:     10.00
        Due:  Dec 06 98 Terms:2%disc 2/10,n/30                                           _____
        Desc: Furniture inventory purchase Total tax:      10.00  Total invoice          110.00 *
        Disc: Nov 16 98 ( 2.00%) Base:      100.00

   3 IN 990045 Dubai Software Co.       99843 PUR    pv    752       1 Net:     324.32        356.75
        Date: Nov 07 98      Ref: P0012          Tax:   542         Tax:     32.43
        Due:  Dec 07 98 Terms: n/30 Net 30                                               _____
        Desc: Graphics software            Total tax:      32.43  Total invoice          356.75 *


                                                        Total invoices        1,216.75
                                                        Total debit notes          0.00
                                                        Total credit notes         0.00
                                                                               _____
                                                        Batch total payable   1,216.75
                                                                               ================
     3 transaction(s) printed.
```

If you have made any errors, use the `Add/modify/delete invoice batches` option to make corrections. Print the A/P Invoice Batch List again and confirm that the corrections have been recorded. You can edit an invoice batch any time before it is posted to Accounts Payable. After a batch has been posted, you cannot modify the posted batch.

POSTING TO THE ACCOUNTS PAYABLE LEDGER

After you have printed and reviewed the revised A/P Invoice Batch List, you can post the batch to the Accounts Payable ledger.

❑ Back up your data files before continuing.

❑ Select: `5. Post invoice batches` from the Invoice Processing Menu.

To proceed with the posting:

Figure 24–7

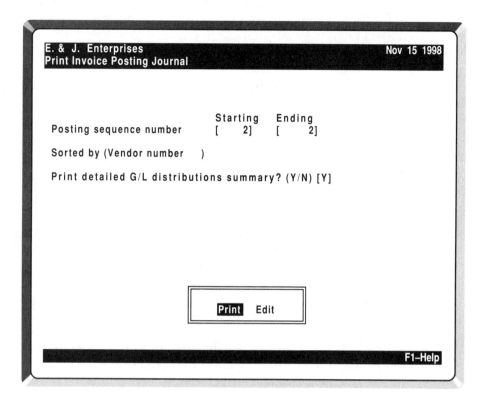

```
E. & J. Enterprises                                    Nov 15 1998
Print Invoice Posting Journal


                              Starting   Ending
    Posting sequence number   [    2]    [    2]

    Sorted by (Vendor number   )

    Print detailed G/L distributions summary? (Y/N) [Y]




                        ┌─────────────────┐
                        │   Print   Edit  │
                        └─────────────────┘


                                                          F1–Help
```

❏ Select: `Post`

If ACCPAC Plus finds an error during posting it will display an error message on the screen. If the error is a duplication of a document number, the entry with the duplication will not be posted but will be transferred to a new Accounts Payable invoice batch generated by ACCPAC Plus. You will have to modify the new batch to correct the error, then print the batch and post it. Once posting is complete the following prompt will appear:

```
Posting complete.
Continue
```

❏ Press: [Enter] to continue.

ACCPAC Plus will return to the Invoice Processing Menu.

PRINTING THE INVOICE POSTING JOURNALS

The Invoice Posting Journals give you a listing of all the transactions that you have posted but not cleared.

❏ Select: `6. Print invoice posting journal`

The defaults displayed, as shown in Figure 24–7, will print the Posting Journal for Posting sequence number 2, sorted by Vendor number, with a detailed General Ledger distributions summary.

❏ Select: `Print`

Once printing is complete, ACCPAC Plus will display the following message.

```
Do you want to clear all posting journals within the specified range?

            Yes          No
```

❏ Select: `No` to retain the Posting Journal data.

Review your printout carefully. The first section lists the entries by vendor order. The second section lists the General Ledger distributions by code and account number and the third section is a Posting Error Report that identifies any error that ACCPAC Plus was not able to transfer to another batch, such as a deleted entry. Errors transferred to a new batch are identified by their original batch and entry numbers.

Erin and Joan also want to see the posting journals sorted by document number as part of their control procedures for invoice numbers.

❏ Select: `6. Print invoice posting journal`

❏ Select: `Edit`

❏ Press: [Enter] twice to accept the Posting sequence numbers.

ACCPAC Plus will display a "Sort journal by" option box.

```
                    Sort journal by
                    Vendor number
                    Document date
                    Document number
```

❏ Move the selector bar to `Document number`.

❏ Press: [Enter]

❏ Press: [Esc] to indicate that the editing is complete.

❏ Select: `Print`

Once the posting journal has been printed, an option box will be displayed again, asking if you want to clear the posting journals.

❏ Select: `Yes`

❏ Press: [Esc] twice to return to the ACCPAC Accounts Payable Master Menu.

VENDOR TRANSACTION INQUIRY

You can display vendor account details on the screen.

- ☐ Select: 2. Inquiries from the ACCPAC Plus Accounts Payable Master Menu.

- ☐ Select: 2. Display vendor transactions from the Inquiries Menu.

- ☐ Type: 990025 in the Vendor number field.

- ☐ Press: [Enter]

To display the details of the transactions starting from a given date you type in the date and press Enter.

- ☐ Type: 090198 in the Starting date field.

- ☐ Press: [Enter]

Figure 24–8

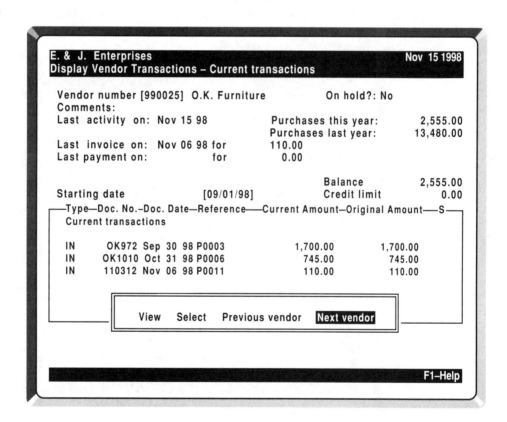

The upper portion of the screen (Figure 24–8) will display summarized information for the account of O.K. Furniture. It shows the last date of activity and the date and amount of the last invoice and payment. It shows the purchases to date for both the current year and the last year. The balance of the account is $2,555.00.

The lower portion of the screen will display a one line summary for each detail posted to the Accounts Payable for O.K. Furniture between September 30, 1998 and November 6, 1998.

The option bar allows you to "Select" another vendor by vendor number or to display information for the "Previous vendor" or the "Next vendor". You can also display more complete details for each transaction.

❏ Select: View

The option box will disappear and the selector bar will highlight the first transaction, invoice OK972.

❏ Press: [Enter]

Figure 24–9

ACCPAC Plus will display all of the information concerning this invoice as shown in Figure 24–9. Since this invoice is unpaid, the "Last activity on" date is September 30, 1998, the date of the original invoice.

❏ Press: [Esc] to return to the "Current transactions" box.

❏ Press: [Esc] to return to the option bar.

- ☐ Select: `Previous vendor`

- ☐ Type: `100198 in the  Starting date` field.

- ☐ Press: [Enter]

The screen will display the information for vendor number 990015, Pear Computers Inc.

- ☐ Press: [Esc] three times to return to the ACCPAC Accounts Payable Master Menu.

VENDOR TRANSACTION REPORT

In addition to displaying the transactions for selected vendors you can also print a Vendor Transactions report.

- ☐ Select: `5. Reports` from the ACCPAC Plus Accounts Payable Master Menu.

- ☐ Select: `1. Analysis reports` from the Reports Menu.

- ☐ Select: `2. Vendor transactions` to display Figure 24–10, the Vendor Transactions screen.

Figure 24–10

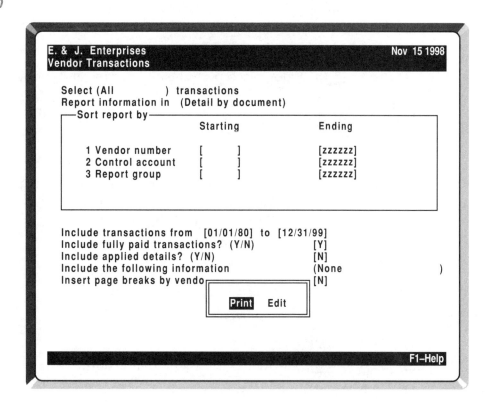

```
E. & J. Enterprises                              Nov 15 1998
Vendor Transactions


    Select (All          )  transactions
    Report information in   (Detail by document)
  ┌─Sort report by──────────────────────────────────────────┐
  │                        Starting         Ending           │
  │                                                          │
  │     1 Vendor number     [      ]        [zzzzzz]         │
  │     2 Control account   [      ]        [zzzzzz]         │
  │     3 Report group      [      ]        [zzzzzz]         │
  │                                                          │
  │                                                          │
  └──────────────────────────────────────────────────────────┘


    Include transactions from  [01/01/80]  to  [12/31/99]
    Include fully paid transactions?  (Y/N)        [Y]
    Include applied details?  (Y/N)                [N]
    Include the following information            (None          )
    Insert page breaks by vendo┌─────────────────┐[N]
                               │ Print   Edit    │
                               └─────────────────┘


                                                       F1-Help
```

❑ Select: Edit

The Select( )transactions field allows you to select the transaction types to be included in the report. You can print the report including "All" types of transactions or you can choose to report only one of the transaction types displayed in the selection box.

❑ Press: [Enter] to accept All.

The Report information in field allows you to choose the order in which the transactions will be printed for each vendor.

❑ Select: Detail by date for a chronological report of activity in each vendor's account.

The Sort report by selection box allows you to choose the order in which vendors are printed in the report. The vendor data base is first sorted by the information specified in line 1. If there are any duplications, the duplicated information is sorted by the information specified in line 2. The same applies for duplications remaining after the sort by line 2; these would then be sorted by the information specified in line 3.

Erin wants a report of vendors sorted alphabetically by name and then number.

❑ Select: line 1

❑ Select: Vendor name from the Choices box.

❑ Press: [Enter] twice to accept the default starting and ending vendor names.

❑ Select: line 2

❑ Select: Vendor number from the Choices box.

❑ Press: [Enter] twice to accept the default starting and ending vendor numbers.

Since each vendor has a unique number, it is impossible to have duplications in this sub-sort.

❑ Press: [Esc] to indicate that you have finished making your choices.

The Include transactions from field displays the default date 01/01/80. This date is a DOS default date that is displayed by ACCPAC Plus to ensure that all transactions are included in the report.

❑ Type: 090198 for September 1, 1998.

❑ Press: [Enter]

The second date field displays 12/31/99.

❑ Type: 113098 for November 30, 1998.

❑ Press: [Enter]

❑ Press: [Enter] to include all fully paid transactions.

❑ Type: Y in the Include applied details field.

❑ Press: [Enter]

You can include extra information in the report.

```
┌─────────────────────────────────────────────┐
│                                               │
│              Additional information           │
│                                               │
│              Phone/contact/purchases          │
│                 Room for comments             │
│                      Both                     │
│                      None                     │
│                                               │
└─────────────────────────────────────────────┘
```

❑ Select: `Phone/contact/purchases`

❑ Press: [Enter] so that the report does not insert page breaks after each vendor.

❑ Select: `Print`

Review your printed report.

PRINTING THE OPEN PAYABLES REPORT

❑ Select: `1. Open payables` from the `Analysis Reports Menu`.

Figure 24–11

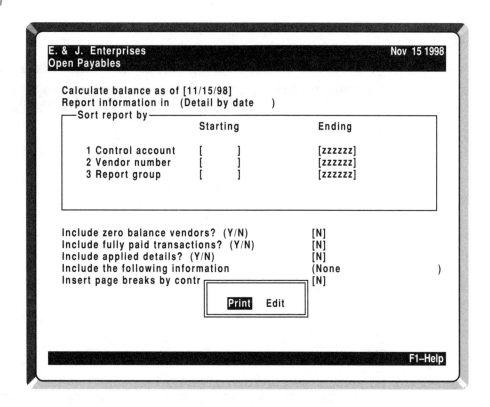

The default settings, as shown in Figure 24–11, will print each vendor's payable information in chronological order (Detail by date) rather than in order of document number or in summary form. As E. & J. Enterprises uses only one control account, vendors will be listed by vendor number. Any vendors with zero balances will not be included in the report. The detailed vendor information will not include any fully paid transactions, credit notes, debit notes, or payments.

❑ Press: [Enter] to print the Open Payables report.

PRINTING THE TAX TRACKING REPORT

The Tax Tracking report provides documentation for the Value Added Tax recoverable that you have paid vendors. When you created the distribution codes you indicated which codes will accumulate information for this report. The report shows all tax information recorded since the last time the report was printed and cleared.

❑ Select: 7. Tax tracking   from the Analysis Reports Menu.

The default settings, as shown in Figure 24–12, will print a report as of November 15, 1998. For each distribution, transactions will be reported in detail rather than in summary form. The report will be sorted by distribution code rather than by vendor number. A tax code summary will not be included in the report.

Figure 24–12

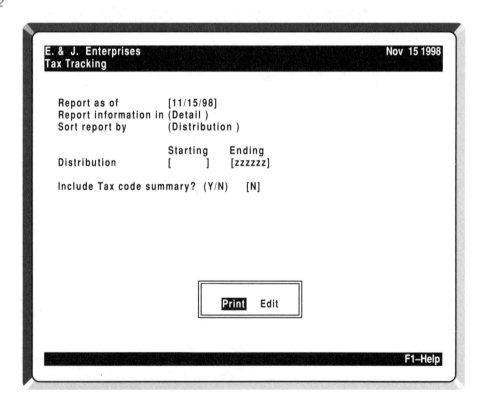

If you wished to change the defaults, you would select "Edit", enter the changes and then press **Esc**.

❏ Select: `Print`

After the report is printed the following message will appear on the screen.

```
┌────────────────────────────────────────────┐
│      Do you want to clear all tax tracking records      │
│              up to the report date?              │
│                                                  │
│           Yes              No                    │
└────────────────────────────────────────────┘
```

Review the Tax Tracking report. If it is clearly printed, you would file it and then clear the records.

❏ Select: `Yes`

❏ Press: [Esc] twice to return to the ACCPAC Accounts Payable Master Menu.

BATCH STATUS INQUIRY

The third option on the Inquiries menu is `Display batch status`. This option displays batch activity since the last time batch status data was cleared.

❏ Select: `2. Inquiries`

❏ Select: `3. Display batch status`

An option box appears allowing you to choose one of Invoice, Adjustment, or Manual Check batches.

❏ Select: `Invoice batches`

Information is displayed in two sections on the screen as shown in Figure 24–13. The lower portion of the screen summarizes batch information by the type of batch and the batch status. For E. & J. Enterprises three invoice batches have been "Posted" and "Entered" with 9 entries totalling $9,644.75.

The upper portion of the screen displays information on each batch.

❏ Press: [Esc] three times to return to the ACCPAC Accounts Payable Master Menu.

❏ Quit ACCPAC Plus.

❏ Back up your data files.

Figure 24–13

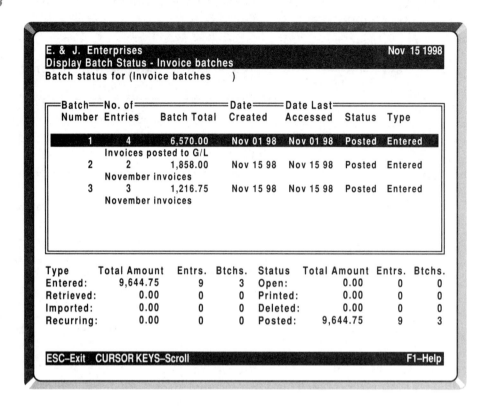

```
E. & J. Enterprises                                    Nov 15 1998
Display Batch Status - Invoice batches
Batch status for (Invoice batches    )

┌─Batch══No. of═════════════════Date══════Date Last═══
  Number Entries      Batch Total  Created    Accessed   Status  Type

     1      4          6,570.00   Nov 01 98  Nov 01 98  Posted  Entered
        Invoices posted to G/L
     2      2          1,858.00   Nov 15 98  Nov 15 98  Posted  Entered
        November invoices
     3      3          1,216.75   Nov 15 98  Nov 15 98  Posted  Entered
        November invoices



Type       Total Amount  Entrs.  Btchs.  Status   Total Amount  Entrs.  Btchs.
Entered:      9,644.75      9       3    Open:         0.00        0       0
Retrieved:        0.00      0       0    Printed:      0.00        0       0
Imported:         0.00      0       0    Deleted:      0.00        0       0
Recurring:        0.00      0       0    Posted:   9,644.75        9       3


ESC-Exit   CURSOR KEYS-Scroll                              F1-Help
```

REVIEW QUESTIONS

1. What happens if you try to enter a vendor number that has not been assigned?
2. What happens if you fail to type a document number when recording an invoice?
3. Why is it important to complete the Reference field when entering an invoice?
4. How do you correct a typing error before you have accepted the information?
5. If you have accepted incorrect information in recording an invoice, how do you correct the error?
6. Why should you print the Invoice Batch Listing before posting it?
7. Describe the procedure used to create a "Recurring batch".
8. What is the purpose of the Open Payables?
9. What is the purpose of the Batch Status Inquiry?
10 Why would you create a "Recurring" batch?

EXERCISE

1. Enter   `11/15/98`   as the new date.
2. Create a new batch to record the following invoices for your company:
   a) Invoice "Nov rent" from Astro Realty Holdings, vendor number 1000 for $1,200, dated November 1, 1998, due November 1, 1998. Purchase order number "Nov rent". The default Distribution code is correct.
   b) Invoice CA246891 from Cardinal Associates for $950.00, dated November 9, 1998. The purchase order number 1260 was for accounting software for resale. The default Distribution code is correct.
   c) Invoice 984673 from vendor number 1100 for $175, dated November 12, 1998. Because the purchase order, number 1261, was for computer supplies to be used by the company, the General Ledger account should be 945 and the tax code is "0".
   d) Invoice number 2756 from vendor number 1150 for $250, dated November 10, 1998. Because the purchase order, number 1263, was for a printer for resale, the Distribution and Tax codes are correct.
2. Print the Invoice Batch Listing and review it for errors. Correct any errors and then print a revised Invoice Batch Listing.
3. Once you are satisfied that the batch reflects the above information exactly, post it to the Accounts Payable ledger.
4. Print the Invoice Posting Journal. Clear the posting data after printing the report.
5. Print the Open Payables report.
6. Back up your data disk.
7. Quit ACCPAC Plus.

25 Processing Manual Checks

ACCPAC Plus Accounts Payable handles two types of checks: manual checks and computer-generated checks. The Accounts Payable module produces, prints, and records computer-generated checks. You should use these checks for all normal payments. In those instances where a check is needed immediately, you can prepare a check manually, or produce a computer-written manual check and then record it in the Accounts Payable. You may have to produce manual checks for C.O.D. purchases, government agencies, purchase deposits, and vendors that the company does not expect to deal with more than once.

❑ Enter the commands necessary to display the ACCPAC Plus Start Menu.

❑ Select: `A/P E. & J. Enterprises`

ACCPAC Plus should display the title screen with "Nov 15 98" as the Last access date and "11/15/98" as the New date. If the New date is incorrect, type 111598.

❑ Press: ⌷Enter⌷

PAYMENT PROCESSING MENU

❑ Select: `4. Payment processing` from the ACCPAC Accounts Payable Master Menu.

The `Payment Processing Menu` (Figure 25–1) will appear.

1. Manual Check Processing

This menu option allows you to Add/modify/delete manual check batches, import and print manual check batches, print and post manual checks, and print a manual check register.

Figure 25–1

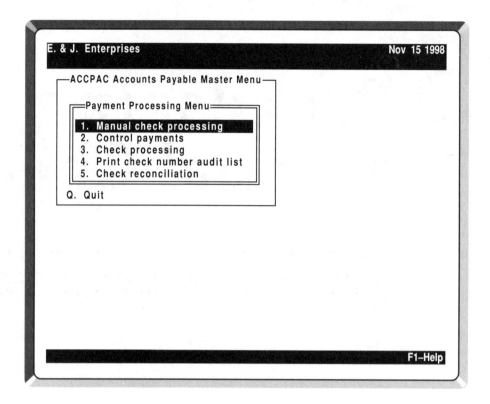

E. & J. Enterprises   Nov 15 1998

┌─ACCPAC Accounts Payable Master Menu─┐

┌═Payment Processing Menu═┐
1. **Manual check processing**
2. Control payments
3. Check processing
4. Print check number audit list
5. Check reconciliation

Q. Quit

F1–Help

2. Control Payments

This option allows you to change the status, due date, discount date and percent, base for discount, prepayment activation date, and maximum payment amount of transactions.

3. Check Processing

This option allows you to print a pre-check register, print and post checks and advices, and print a check register.

4. Print Check Number Audit List

This option allows you to print an audit report of check numbers assigned in check runs. The report lists all system check numbers. It lists only the manual checks that have actually been printed from the program, including posted and unposted direct checks.

5. Check Reconciliation

This option allows you to reconcile checks, print the check reconciliation and print a reversed check audit list.

MANUAL CHECK PROCESSING MENU

❑ Select: 1. Manual check processing from the Payment Processing Menu.

The Manual Check Processing Menu (Figure 25–2) will appear on the screen.

Figure 25–2

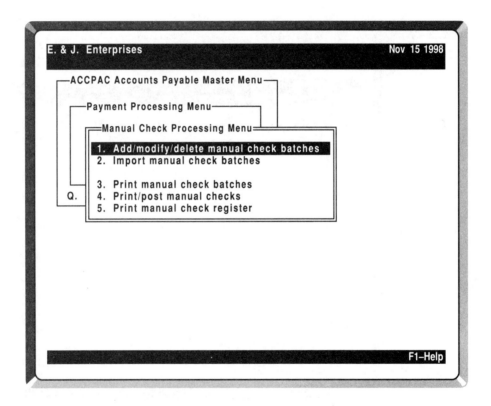

Import Manual Check Batches

You will be using all of the selections from the Manual Check Processing Menu except for 2. Import manual check batches. This option allows you to transfer check batches from non-ACCPAC Plus programs to the Accounts Payable. You could then modify, print and post the batch before printing the check register.

PROCESSING MANUAL CHECKS

You are now ready to record the payment of manual checks. Joan issued a manual check on November 1, 1998 for $1,275.00 to Home Realty to pay the November rent. The manual check number is 14. You must process this manual check before you process the computer-generated checks, otherwise a computer-generated check will be prepared for the invoice when you process them.

Recording a Manual Check Payment

❑ Select: 1. Add/modify/delete manual check batches from the Manual Check Processing Menu.

The Add/Modify/Delete Manual Check Batches screen (Figure 25–3) will appear.

Figure 25–3

```
┌─────────────────────────────────────────────────────────────────────┐
│ E. & J. Enterprises                                      Nov 15 1998  │
│ Add/Modify/Delete Manual Check Batches                                │
│   Batch       [      ]                    Entries:        0           │
│   Description [                        ]  Total:          0.00        │
│   Bank code   [      ]                                                │
│   ───────────────────────────────────────────────────────────────   │
│   Entry       [       ]                                               │
│   Payment type (          )                                           │
│   Print check?  [ ]          Check no. [          ]                   │
│   Vendor no.  [      ]       Name      [                    ]         │
│   Check date  [  /  /  ]                 Reference    [          ]    │
│   Description [                        ]                              │
│   ───────────────────────────────────────────────────────────────   │
│                                                                       │
│                                                                       │
│                                                                       │
│ BLANK–New batch   ESC–Exit                                 F1–Help    │
└─────────────────────────────────────────────────────────────────────┘
```

If you make a typing error when entering the check information, you can correct it by pressing the backspace key and typing over your mistake. If you have already entered and accepted the information, you can correct it by selecting "Edit" from the option box and then make the correction.

❑ Press: [Enter] in the blank Batch field.

The following message will appear:

```
┌─────────────────────────────────────────────────────────────┐
│                                                               │
│           Are you sure you want to enter a new batch?         │
│                                                               │
│                          Yes    No                            │
│                                                               │
└─────────────────────────────────────────────────────────────┘
```

❑ Select: `Yes`

ACCPAC Plus assigns the next available Batch number (number 1) to the new
check batch file, displays "0" in the Entries field and "0.00" in the Total field at
the top right of the screen. The cursor will move to the batch Description field.
You can enter up to 30 characters in the field.

❑ Type: `November manual checks`

❑ Press: [Enter]

You must identify the bank account that the check was drawn on. You identified
the Bank code in Chapter 21. If you cannot remember the code, use the Finder
key.

❑ Press: [F5]

❑ Move the selector bar to `cash Working funds`

❑ Press: [Enter]

ACCPAC Plus will display the bank account description (Working funds) and
move the cursor to the Entry field. Since this transaction is the first one to be
entered, the Entry number field will display `1`.

❑ Press: [Enter]

A `Payment Type` box will appear on the screen, requiring you to identify the
type of payment that is being entered. `Cash invoice` is used to record a
check that has been written, but the liability has not been previously recorded in
the ACCPAC Accounts Payable. `Payment` records the payment if an invoice
has been previously recorded in the ACCPAC Accounts Payable and
`Prepayment` records an advance payment.

❑ Select: `Payment`

The cursor will move to the `Print check` field. This option allows you to indicate whether you will print the check and advice from Accounts Payable, or
whether you are entering a check that has already been issued manually. Since
this manual check has already been written, it is not necessary to print it again. If
you wished to print a computerized "manual" check you must select "Y" and
then select `Print` from the option box that appears once the fields have been
completed.

❑ Type: `N`

❑ Press: [Enter]

The cursor will move to the `Check no.` field. The check number was 14. The
check number may consist only of digits since letters of the alphabet are not accepted.

❑ Type: 14

❑ Press: [Enter]

In the `Vendor no.` field you must enter the Vendor number as shown on the Vendor List. If you do not have the list available and cannot remember Home Realty's number, use the finder. If you enter a vendor number that has not been assigned, the Finder window will appear on the screen, listing vendor numbers near the one you entered in error. You would then move the selector bar to the correct vendor and press Enter.

❑ Press: [F5]

❑ Move the selector bar to `990005 Home Realty`

❑ Press: [Enter]

ACCPAC Plus will display the vendor name in the `Name` field.

❑ Press: [Enter]

The `Check date` field automatically displays the date (November 15, 1998) that you entered as the New date on the Title screen.

❑ Type: `110198` to record the date of the check, November 1, 1998.

❑ Press: [Enter]

You use the `Reference` field to identify the invoice number of the document you are paying.

❑ Type: `Nov rent` to represent the November rent.

❑ Press: [Enter]

The highlighted bar now moves to the `Description` field.

❑ Type: `Nov. office and equip. rent`

❑ Press: [Enter]

An option bar will appear.

```
Save entry   Header   Address   Detail   Print   Cancel
```

The `Address` option is new. It allows you to display the vendor name, number, and address on the screen.

❑ Select: `Detail`

The Invoice Payment screen (Figure 25–4) will appear.

The cursor will move to the `Invoice Listing` box where a description of the outstanding invoices appears. There is only one invoice outstanding for Home Realty.

❑ Press: [Enter] to accept `Nov rent` as number of the Document to be paid.

The cursor will move to the `Payment amount` field which displays "1275.00".

446 · Accounts Payable

Figure 25–4

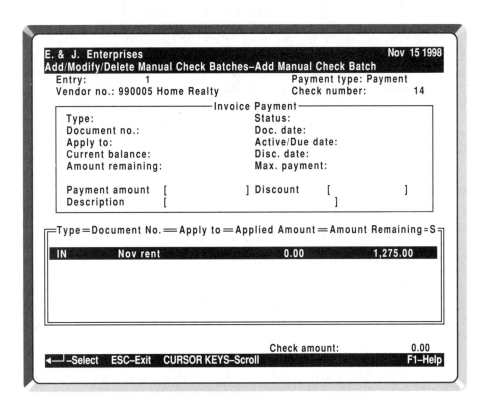

```
┌──────────────────────────────────────────────────────────────────────┐
│ E. & J. Enterprises                                     Nov 15 1998    │
│ Add/Modify/Delete Manual Check Batches–Add Manual Check Batch          │
│    Entry:           1                   Payment type: Payment          │
│    Vendor no.: 990005 Home Realty           Check number:         14   │
│              ──────────────────Invoice Payment──────────────────       │
│    ┌─────────────────────────────────────────────────────────────┐    │
│    │ Type:                          Status:                       │    │
│    │ Document no.:                   Doc. date:                   │    │
│    │ Apply to:                       Active/Due date:             │    │
│    │ Current balance:                Disc. date:                  │    │
│    │ Amount remaining:               Max. payment:                │    │
│    │                                                              │    │
│    │ Payment amount    [          ] Discount     [           ]    │    │
│    │ Description       [                         ]                │    │
│    └─────────────────────────────────────────────────────────────┘    │
│  ┌─Type═Document No.══Apply to═Applied Amount══Amount Remaining═S─┐    │
│  │ IN          Nov rent                 0.00           1,275.00   │    │
│  │                                                                │    │
│  │                                                                │    │
│  │                                                                │    │
│  └────────────────────────────────────────────────────────────────┘   │
│                                        Check amount:          0.00     │
│  ◄──┘–Select   ESC–Exit   CURSOR KEYS–Scroll              F1–Help      │
└──────────────────────────────────────────────────────────────────────┘
```

❑ Press: [Enter]

Home Realty does not offer a discount for prompt payment of the rent.

❑ Press: [Enter] to accept the discount (0.00) shown.

❑ Press: [Enter] to accept the Description.

The cursor will return to the Invoice Listing box to allow you to select another invoice that was paid on the same manual check. Since there was only one invoice paid, you have finished allocating the payment.

❑ Press: [Esc]

Review the data carefully. If you have made errors in the Header, select "Header" and make the necessary corrections. If there is an error in the payment application portion, select "Detail" to enter corrections. Once you are satisfied that there are no errors:

❑ Select: Save entry

The Entries field in the upper right corner will change to "1" and the Total field will change to 1,275.00. The Entry number field will display the next entry number in sequence.

Recording a Cash Invoice Payment

When E. & J. Enterprises ordered the 15 utility packages from Pear Computers, a rush was put on the order and Joan agreed to pay for the courier charges. Since the company delivering the materials did not normally deal with E. & J. Enterprises, they required immediate payment. Check 15 was used to pay the freight charges which amounted to $35.00. The check was paid to Veryquick Delivery Co. on November 4. The invoice number was A133.

❑ Press: `Enter` to accept entry 2.

The Payment Type box will appear.

❑ Select: `Cash invoice`

The cursor will move to the `Print check` field. Since the manual check was written on November 14, 1998, it is not necessary to print it again.

❑ Type: `N`

❑ Press: `Enter`

The cursor will move to the `Check no.` field. The check number was 15.

❑ Press: `Enter` to accept `15`.

Veryquick Delivery Co. is not on the vendor list, and there is no purpose in adding it since Joan does not expect to do business with them again. The miscellaneous vendor account will be used to record the payment.

❑ Type: `999999` in the `Vendor no.` field.

❑ Press: `Enter`

❑ Type: `Veryquick Delivery` in the `Name` field to identify the vendor on the reports.

❑ Press: `Enter`

The `Check date` field automatically displays the date that you entered for the last manual check in this batch.

❑ Type: `110498` to record the date of the check, November 4, 1998.

❑ Press: `Enter`

❑ Type: `110506` (Pear Computers' invoice number) in the `Reference` field.

Ensure that excess characters are blanked out.

❑ Press: `Enter`

The highlighted bar now moves to the `Description` field.

❑ Type: `Delivery cgs. Pear Computers`

❑ Press: `Enter`

The highlighted bar will move to the `Cash invoice no.` field.

❑ Type: `A133`

❑ Press: [Enter]

An option bar will appear.

```
Save entry   Header   Address   Detail   Print   Cancel
```

❑ Select: `Detail`

The Distribution Detail screen (Figure 25–5) will appear.

Figure 25–5

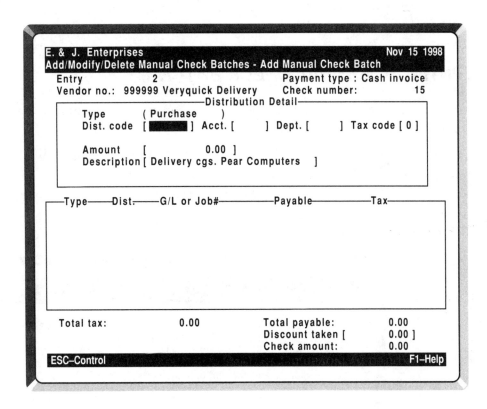

The highlighted bar will appear in the `Dist. code` field. Freight-in has not been set up with a distribution code. Ensure that the field is blank. If necessary, use the space bar to blank out any letters.

❑ Press: [Enter]

❑ Type: `756` in the `Acct.` field.

❑ Press: [Enter]

The highlighted bar will move to the `Tax code` field. Since delivery charges involve payment of salaries to contractors and fees to other carriers, Value Added Tax will be included in the invoice.

❑ Type: `1`

- ❑ Press: [Enter]
- ❑ Type: 35.00 in the Amount field.
- ❑ Press: [Enter]
- ❑ Press: [Enter] to accept the Description "Delivery cgs. Pear Computers".
- ❑ Press: [Esc] to indicate that you have finished entering this payment.
- ❑ Press: [Enter] to accept 0.00 in the Discount taken field.

An option bar will appear.

- ❑ Select: Save entry
- ❑ Press: [Esc] twice to return to the Manual Check Processing Menu.

PRINTING A MANUAL CHECK BATCH

The manual check batch lists all the manual checks you have entered on the batch.

- ❑ Select: 3. Print manual check batches from the Manual Check Processing Menu.

The Print Manual Check Batches screen (Figure 25–6) will appear.

Figure 25–6

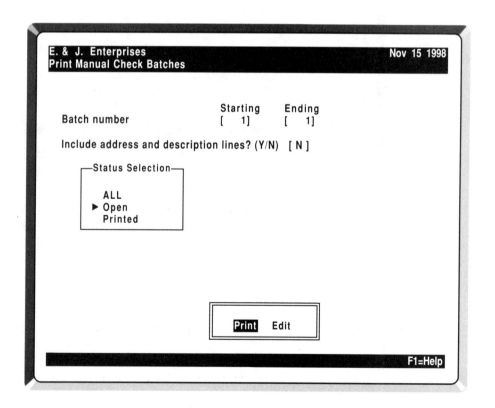

Ensure that your printer is ready and on line to your computer. If you had entered several check batches you could select "Edit" and enter the range of the batches that you wanted to print in the "Starting" and "Ending" Batch number fields.

❑ Press: [Enter] to print the Manual Check Batches shown in Table 25–1.

Table 25–1

```
te: Nov 15 98   12:35am              E. & J. Enterprises                              Page:   1
P Manual Check Batch List

tch number           [   1]    to  [   1]
atus(es) selected:  Open

tch number:     1   November manual checks
eation date: Nov 15 98 Status:  Open
ank Number :   cash   Working Funds

ntry           Check Vendor
  No. Ty      Number Number Vendor Name                         Distribution Detail

                                   Document No.   Apply To No.      Discount Taken            Paid
   1 MC          14 990005 Home Realty       IN     Nov rent                      0.00      1,275.00
        Iss:Nov 01 98 Ref:Nov rent
        Desc:  Nov. office and equip. rent

                                                                  Payment check amount        1,275.00 *

                                   Ty   Dist.  Acct. or Job   Tx Cd                         Amount
   2 MC          15 999999 Veryquick Delivery  PUR      756           1                        35.00
        Iss:Nov 04 98 Ref:110506      Inv:   A133
        Desc:  Delivery cgs. Pear Computers

                                                                  Cash invoice check amount      35.00 *

                                 Total Payables    Total Discounts       Total Checks
               Payments              1,275.00             0.00             1,275.00
               Prepayments               0.00             0.00                 0.00
               Cash invoices            35.00             0.00                35.00
                                   _____      _____        _____
                                      1,310.00             0.00             1,310.00
                                   ============      ============        ============

   2 transaction(s) printed.
```

After you have printed the Manual Check Batch List (shown in Table 25–1), review it for errors.

EDITING A CHECK BATCH

If a check batch contains any mistakes, you can edit it using the `Add/modify/delete manual check batches` option on the Manual Check Processing Menu. You can edit a batch any time before it is posted to the Accounts Payable ledger. After it has been posted, you are not permitted to make changes to that batch.

Someone made an error in the Manual Check Batch you have just printed. The recorded payment to Veryquick for $35.00 failed to include the VAT. The total invoice including VAT came to $38.50.

☐ Select: `1. Add/modify/delete manual check batches` from the Manual Check Processing Menu.

☐ Type: `1` in the `Batch` field.

☐ Press: Enter

An option bar will appear at the bottom of the screen:

```
┌─────────────────────────────────────────────────┐
│                                                   │
│     Modify batch      Delete batch                │
│                                                   │
└─────────────────────────────────────────────────┘
```

☐ Select: `Modify batch`

☐ Press: Enter to accept the batch `Description`

The cursor will move to the `Entry` field. Look at the A/P Manual Check Batch List you just printed to find the error. You will see that it occurs in batch entry number 2.

☐ Type: `2` in the `Entry` field.

☐ Press: Enter

The manual check entry for Veryquick will be displayed, as shown in Figure 25–7.

☐ Select: `Modify entry`

The error occurred in the Detail portion of the check allocation.

☐ Select: `Detail`

The error in this case was the incomplete allocation of all the items on the invoice. The cursor should be highlighting the entry made earlier. This entry is correct. You must add a new line to the distribution.

☐ Use the direction arrow key to move the highlighted bar down one space.

☐ Press: Enter

☐ Press: F5 to view the Distribution code descriptions.

☐ Select: `v  VAT recoverable on code P`

The highlighted bar will move to the `Tax code` field.

☐ Press: Enter to accept `1`

☐ Type: `3.50` in the `Tax amount` field.

☐ Press: Enter

☐ Press: Enter to accept the Tax base of 35.00.

☐ Press: Enter to accept the Description.

☐ Press: Esc to indicate that you have finished entering this allocation.

Figure 25–7

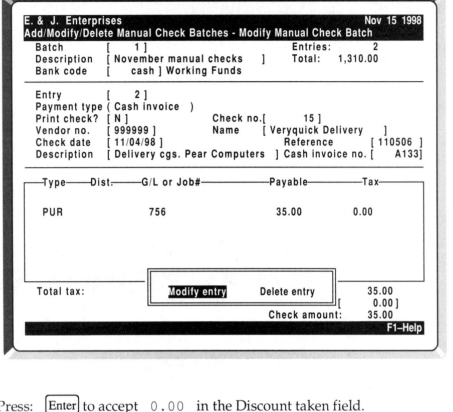

```
E. & J. Enterprises                                    Nov 15 1998
Add/Modify/Delete Manual Check Batches - Modify Manual Check Batch
   Batch        [    1 ]                   Entries:        2
   Description  [ November manual checks  ]  Total:   1,310.00
   Bank code    [    cash ] Working Funds

   Entry        [    2 ]
   Payment type ( Cash invoice  )
   Print check? [ N ]                 Check no.[     15 ]
   Vendor no.   [ 999999 ]            Name     [ Veryquick Delivery   ]
   Check date   [ 11/04/98 ]                   Reference       [ 110506 ]
   Description  [ Delivery cgs. Pear Computers  ] Cash invoice no. [    A133]

   ┌Type────Dist.────G/L or Job#────────Payable────Tax──────
   │
   │ PUR             756                35.00       0.00
   │
   │
   │
   │
   │                        ┌──────────────────────────┐
   Total tax:               │ Modify entry   Delete entry │   35.00
                            └──────────────────────────┘ [  0.00 ]
                                    Check amount:         35.00
                                                          F1–Help
```

❏ Press: [Enter] to accept 0.00 in the Discount taken field.

An option bar will appear.

❏ Select: Save entry

After you save the entry, the total amount of the batch should be $1313.50 as shown at the top right of the screen. If a different amount is displayed on your screen you should review the entries to locate the error. You can then correct the error using the steps described in this section.

❏ Press: [Esc] twice to return to the Manual Check Processing Menu.

❏ Print the Manual Check batch again to document the changes that you have made.

After the A/P Manual Check Batch List has finished printing:

❏ Press: [Esc] twice to return to the ACCPAC Accounts Payable Master Menu.

BATCH STATUS INQUIRY

The third option on the Inquiries menu is Display batch status. This option displays batch activity since the last time the batch status data was cleared.

☐ Ensure that the ACCPAC Accounts Payable Master Menu is displayed on the screen.

☐ Select: `2. Inquiries`

☐ Select: `3. Display batch status`

An option box appears allowing you to choose either Invoice, Adjustment or Manual Check batches.

☐ Select: `Manual Check batches`

Information is displayed in two sections on the screen as shown in Figure 25–8. The lower portion of the screen summarizes batch information by the type of batch and the batch status.

The upper portion of the screen displays information on each batch. If you had

Figure 25–8

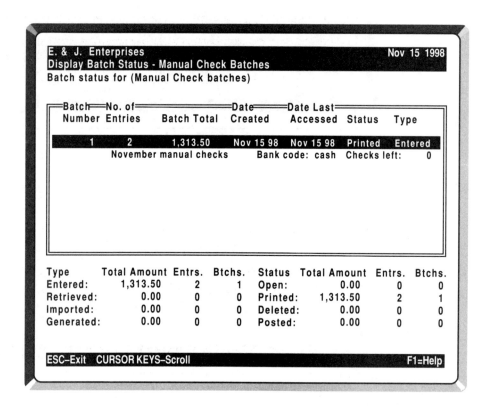

more batches you could move the selector bar down to display the others. One invoice batch has been "Printed" and "Entered" with 2 entries totalling $1,313.50.

☐ Press: [Esc] three times to return to the ACCPAC Accounts Payable Master Menu.

POSTING TO THE ACCOUNTS PAYABLE LEDGER

After you have printed and reviewed the revised Manual Check Batch and corrected all the entry errors, you may post the batch to the Accounts Payable ledger.

❑ Select: `4. Payment processing` from the `ACCPAC Accounts Pay-
able Master Menu.`

❑ Select: `1. Manual check processing` from the `Payment Process-
ing Menu.`

❑ Select: `4. Print/post manual checks` from the Manual Check
Processing Menu.

The Print/Post Manual Checks screen (Figure 25–9) will appear.

Figure 25–9

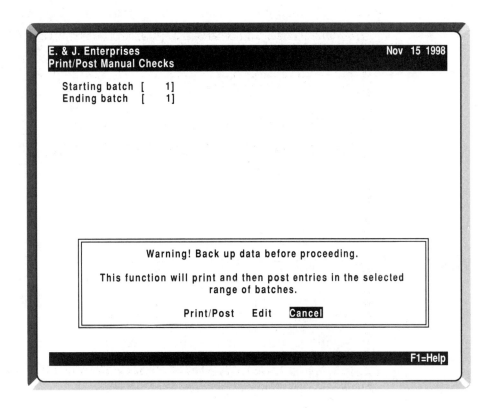

You should back up your data files before posting this batch in case there is a
power fluctuation or a computer problem.

❑ Select: `Cancel`

❑ Press: [Esc] twice to display the ACCPAC Plus Accounts Payable Master
Menu.

❑ Press: `Q` to return to the Start Menu.

❑ Press: [Enter] to access the System Manager.

❑ Select: DOS

❑ Enter the DOS commands to back up your data files.

❑ Type: exit to return to the System Manager.

❑ Press: [Esc] to return to the Start Menu.

❑ Enter the commands necessary to return to the Print/post Manual Checks screen.

❑ Select: Print/Post to proceed with the posting.

Each time you post batches to the Accounts Payable ledger a new posting sequence number will be assigned. ACCPAC Plus will not allow you to post a batch twice.

If the batch that is being posted contains an error that ACCPAC Plus can detect, a warning message will be displayed on the screen. The entry that contains the error will be transferred to the next available batch. You should then correct the error and then print and post the new batch.

Once posting is complete, ACCPAC Plus will display the following message.

```
Posting complete.
Continue
```

❑ Press: [Enter] to continue.

PRINTING THE MANUAL CHECK REGISTER

❑ Select: 5. Print manual check register from the Manual Check Processing Menu.

The Print Manual Check Register screen allows you to select the manual check registers to be printed by posting sequence number as shown in the "Starting" and "Ending" fields in Figure 25–10.

❑ Select: Edit

❑ Press: [Enter] twice to accept the default "Starting" and "Ending" posting sequence numbers.

The default setting prints the Invoice Posting Journal sorted by Bank and check number. You can also print the posting journals sorted by "Vendor number", or by "Check date" for a chronological printout.

❑ Press: [Enter] to accept the default sorting by Bank and check number.

Figure 25–10

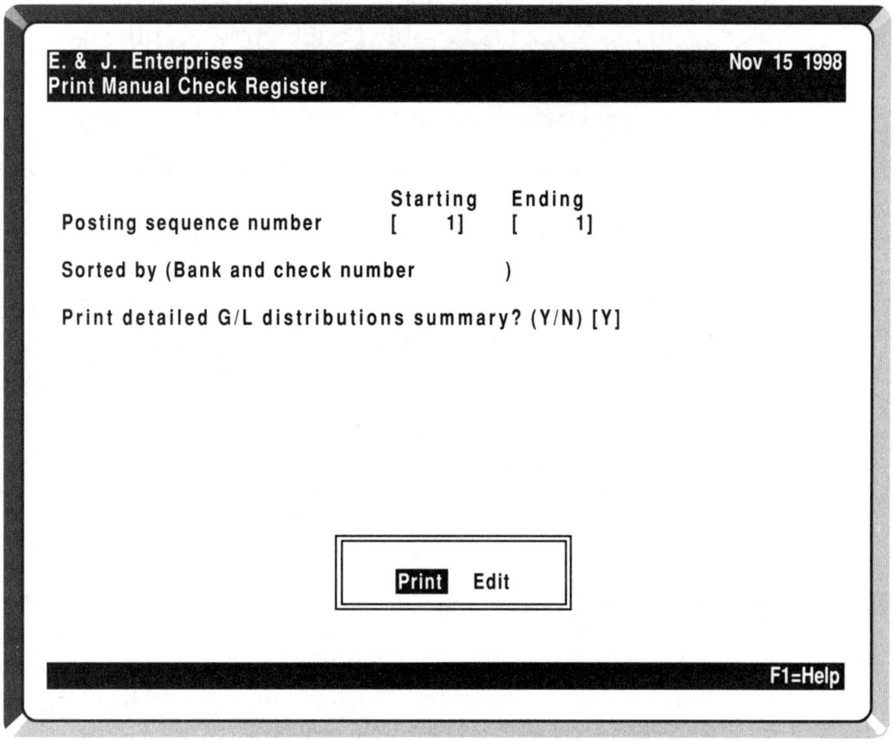

```
E. & J. Enterprises                                    Nov 15 1998
Print Manual Check Register


                                  Starting   Ending
        Posting sequence number   [     1]   [     1]

        Sorted by (Bank and check number        )

        Print detailed G/L distributions summary? (Y/N) [Y]






                            ┌─────────────────────┐
                            │    Print   Edit      │
                            └─────────────────────┘


                                                        F1=Help
```

The `Print detailed G/L distributions summary` field controls the
information printed in the last portion of the journal. If you select "N", the
General Ledger distributions will be summarized on one line. If you select "Y"
the General Ledger distributions will be summarized by distribution code.

❑   Press: [Enter] to accept Y.

❑   Select: `Print`

When the printing is finished, ACCPAC Plus will display the following message:

```
┌──────────────────────────────────────────────────────────────┐
│   Do you want to clear all check registers within the specified range? │
│                                                                │
│                         Yes      No                            │
└──────────────────────────────────────────────────────────────┘
```

If you wish to print the Manual Check Register again, you would select "N" and
the check register information would not be erased. You could then reprint the
manual check register and if necessary, sort it by "Check date" or "Vendor
number".

❑   Select: `Yes`

Once you have cleared the check registers, ACCPAC Plus will clear the manual check batch. Clearing does not remove all traces of the posted checks, since they are now in the Accounts Payable Ledger, however the batch itself no longer exists.

❏ Press: [Esc] twice to return to the ACCPAC Accounts Payable Master Menu.

Printed copies of the A/P Manual Check Register form the audit trail necessary to verify that posting is accurate. The first part of the report describes each entry that was posted. The second part of the report is the General Ledger Summary. The third part of the report is printed only if ACCPAC Plus detected an error in an entry. The report identifies the batch number and entry number containing the error and the number of the new batch created by ACCPAC Plus. You can use this information to correct the error before posting the new batch.

❏ Quit ACCPAC Plus.

❏ Back up your data files.

REVIEW QUESTIONS

1. Under what circumstances would a company issue a manual check?
2. What is the purpose of the "Import invoice batches" function?
3. List and describe the 3 options available from the "Payment Types" box in the "Add/modify/delete manual checks" function.
4. What is the purpose of the "Reference" field when adding a manual check?
5. List the necessary steps to edit a manual check.
6. If you post a batch in which ACCPAC Plus recognizes an error, what does the program do?
7. Why is it necessary to have an "A/P Manual Check Register"?

EXERCISE

1. Enter November 30, 1998 as the New date. Enter the following two invoices using the miscellaneous vendor number, 9999. Your company issued two manual checks during November. Both checks required immediate payment. Neither item had been recorded previously in the Accounts Payable as a liability.

   Check number 102 was for $75 (including VAT) to Rush Delivery Service, invoice number RD304, on November 7. The check paid for delivery service on goods purchased for resale and should be charged to account 756, Freight In. Since VAT is recoverable, the Tax code is "1".

   Check number 103 to Computer Junction was for $2,800 on November 27. Invoice number AA-1873. Your company purchased a new computer to use in the office (account 408, Office Equipment). Terms were C.O.D. VAT is not recoverable.

2. Print the Manual Check Batch Listing.
3. Post the manual check batch to the Accounts Payable ledger.
4. Print and clear the Manual Check Register.
5. Back up your data disk.
6. Quit ACCPAC Plus.

26 Processing System Checks & Reconciling Checks

The great majority of checks that you write will be produced and printed by AC-CPAC Plus Accounts Payable as computer-generated (system) checks. ACCPAC Plus automatically selects the outstanding transactions that will be paid during the next check run and produces a list of those transactions. You will determine the criteria by which transactions are selected for payment.

❑ Enter the commands necessary to display the ACCPAC Plus Start Menu.

❑ Select: `A/P E. & J. Enterprises`

ACCPAC Plus should display the title screen with "Nov 15 98" as the Last access date and "11/15/98" as the New date. If the New date is incorrect, type 111598.

❑ Press: [Enter]

❑ Select: `4. Payment processing` from the ACCPAC Accounts Payable Master Menu.

The following menu, as shown in Figure 26–1, will appear:

Figure 26–1

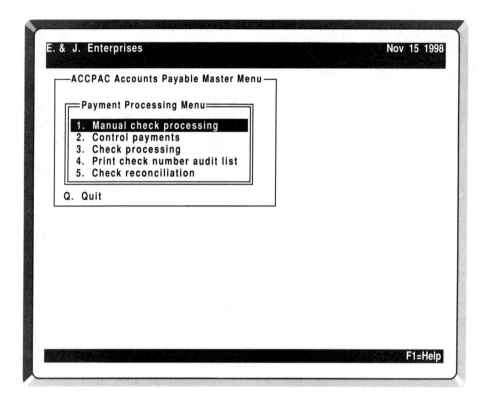

PROCESSING SYSTEM CHECKS

The options available on the `Payment Processing Menu` were discussed in Chapter 25. At that time you were introduced to the manual check functions. Now you are going to learn to generate system checks.

Controlling Payments

The `2. Control payments` option is used to control the timing and amount of payments at both the vendor level and the invoice level. You can set a vendor on hold, meaning that no transactions for that vendor are paid unless you force selective payments. At the invoice level, you can control payment of individual transactions (change the status, due date, discount date and percentage, base for discount, and maximum payment of individual transactions). You can also change the status of a group of selected transactions, thereby controlling their payment.

You use the Control Payments function after printing the Pre-Check Register and reviewing the current payables to select the transactions you want to pay.

❑ Select: `3. Check processing` from the Payment Processing Menu.

The Check Processing Menu (Figure 26–2) will appear.

Figure 26–2

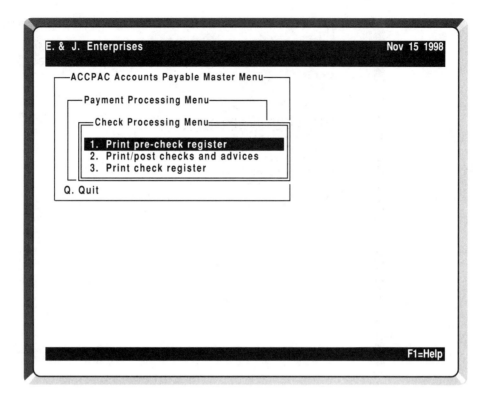

Print Pre-Check Register

Before you process a check run, you should print the `Pre-Check Register` to determine the transactions that will be included. The transactions listed in this register depend upon the due date, discount date, check date, and other options chosen in selecting transactions for payment.

Print/post checks and advices

This function will allow you to print the system checks and advices and post the payment data to vendor accounts.

Print check register

The `Print check register` function allows you to print an audit report of General Ledger transactions generated by a system check run, and to clear the registers after printing.

Printing a Pre-Check Register

❑ Select: `1. Print pre-check register` from the Check Processing Menu.

The Print Pre-Check Register (Figure 26–3) will appear.

Figure 26–3

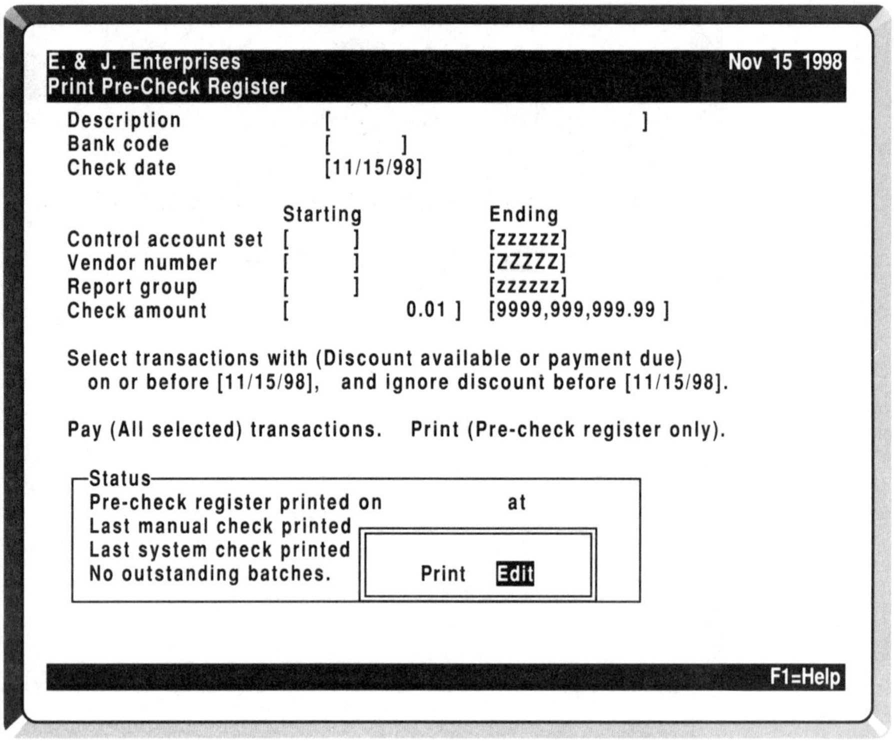

```
┌──────────────────────────────────────────────────────────────┐
│ E. & J. Enterprises                              Nov 15 1998   │
│ Print Pre-Check Register                                       │
│    Description          [                             ]        │
│    Bank code            [      ]                               │
│    Check date           [11/15/98]                             │
│                                                                │
│                      Starting          Ending                  │
│    Control account set  [      ]       [zzzzzz]                │
│    Vendor number        [      ]       [ZZZZZ]                 │
│    Report group         [      ]       [zzzzzz]                │
│    Check amount         [      0.01 ]  [9999,999,999.99 ]      │
│                                                                │
│    Select transactions with (Discount available or payment due)│
│     on or before [11/15/98],   and ignore discount before [11/15/98]. │
│                                                                │
│    Pay (All selected) transactions.   Print (Pre-check register only). │
│                                                                │
│    ┌Status───────────────────────────────────┐                │
│    │ Pre-check register printed on      at    │                │
│    │ Last manual check printed ┌──────────────┐│                │
│    │ Last system check printed │              ││                │
│    │ No outstanding batches.   │ Print  Edit  ││                │
│    │                           └──────────────┘│                │
│    └──────────────────────────────────────────┘                │
│                                                                │
│                                              F1=Help           │
└──────────────────────────────────────────────────────────────┘
```

The default settings will print a pre-check register for all the Control account sets, Vendors, and Report groups. No restriction has been placed on the minimum or maximum amount of the checks to be written. It will print all the transactions with the "Discount available or payment due" on or before November 15, 1998. The checks will be dated November 15, 1998 and ignore any discounts that have expired by November 15, 1998. A check will be prepared for all transactions selected by the pre-check register. The pre-check register will print only the items selected, it will not print those transactions that have had a "hold" put on them.

The `Print Pre-Check Register` screen does not have the Description or Bank code completed. Before you can print a Pre-check register, you must at least identify the bank account on which the checks will be drawn.

❏ Select: `Edit`

❏ Type: `November checks` in the `Description` field.

❏ Press: [Enter]

❏ Type: `cash` in the `Bank code` field.

❏ Press: [Enter]

You will generate a Pre-check register for all invoices that are coming due. You will not restrict the documents to be paid by identifying ranges for the Control account set, Vendor number, or Report group.

❑ Press: [Enter] seven times to move the highlighted bar to the `Check amount` fields. These two "Check amount" fields allow you to specify the range of amounts for which payments can be made in the check run. You will not restrict any payment amounts at this time.

❑ Press: [Enter] twice.

A "Select" option box will appear on the screen as shown.

```
                          Select

                       Payment due
              Discount available or payment due
```

You can choose to print a Pre-check register for only those checks that have reached the end of the credit terms (Payment due), or you can print a Pre-check register to include those transactions where a discount can be taken (Discount available or payment due).

❑ Select: `Discount available or payment due`

❑ Type: `111598` in the `on or before` field to select for payment those transactions that have a discount available, or are due for payment prior to November 15, 1998.

❑ Press: [Enter]

The `ignore discounts before` field allows you to specify the earliest date for which you want to take discounts on the transactions selected for payment. If you do not want to take discounts that have expired, select the date that is displayed. In this case you will ignore any discount that has expired before November 1, 1998.

❑ Type: `110198`

❑ Press: [Enter]

The checks will be dated November 15, 1998.

A "Pay" option box will now appear on the screen as shown.

```
                           Pay

                       All selected
                        Only forced
```

You can choose to pay all the transactions that are selected in the Pre-check register or only pay those that have been forced. E. & J. Enterprises has not forced any payments.

❑ Select: `All selected`

A "Print" option box will appear on the screen as follows:

```
                Print

                Both
          Pre-check register only
          Payables withheld only
```

You can choose to print only the Pre-check register. However, you can also use this option to print a list of only those payables withheld. The "Both" option will print both the Pre-check register and Payables withheld. E. & J. Enterprises has not put a hold on any invoices at this time.

☐ Select: `Pre-check register only`

☐ Select: `Print` to print the Pre-check register.

Compare the printed Pre-check register to Table 26–1 carefully. The report prints the amount currently payable for the listed transactions, the discount available, and the net payment. A Pre-check Register Summary appears at the end of the report, summarizing the amounts of the Pre-check Register. The total currently payable includes payables on hold, and payables not printed on the report if they are less than, or greater than, the specified minimum or maximum check amount. Note the code "S" that appears to the right of the Discount column. The "S" indicates that the transaction has a special discount base (the discount base has altered since the discount is not calculated on the Value Added Tax). The code "D" to the right on the Net Payment column indicates those transactions that have been selected based upon discount availability. The code descriptions are printed above the listing of items chosen for payment.

Table 26–1

```
e: Nov 15 98   12:33am                    E. & J. Enterprises                              Page:   1
-Check Register

ember checks
k:      cash  Working Funds
trol accounts [       ] to [zzzzzz]
dors          [       ] to [zzzzzz]
ort groups    [       ] to [zzzzzz]
cks for [         0.01 ] to [9999,999,999.99 ] dated Nov 15 98.
nsactions are selected if discount available or payment due on or before Nov 15 98.
scounts are not taken if expiring before Nov 01 98.
y all selected transactions.

DES:  P - Maximum payment controlled;  S - Special discount base;  F - Force payment;  D - Transaction selected based on discount

ndor                                Discount  Active /
mber Vendor Name          Document No. Type Date      Due Date   Current Payable       Discount      Net Payment

0015 Pear Computers Inc.      103109 IN  Nov 10 98 Nov 30 98     2,475.00           45.00 S       2,430.00  D
                              110506 IN  Nov 15 98 Dec 05 98       583.00           10.60 S         572.40  D
                                                               _____        _____      _____
                                                                 3,058.00           55.60         3,002.40

0025 O.K. Furniture           OK972 IN  Oct 10 98 Oct 30 98     1,700.00            0.00 S       1,700.00
                             OK1010 IN  Nov 10 98 Nov 30 98       745.00           13.55 S         731.45  D
                                                               _____        _____      _____
                                                                 2,445.00           13.55         2,431.45
                                                               _____        _____      _____
     2 checks to be issued:                                      5,503.00           69.15         5,433.85
                                                               ===========        =========      ==========

                                           — Pre-Check Register Summary —

                                              Current Payable       Discount      Net Payment

                        Total payable:           5,503.00           69.15         5,433.85
                        Less total withheld:         0.00            0.00             0.00
                        Less total unprinted:        0.00            0.00             0.00
                                               _____       _____      _____
                        Total issued:            5,503.00           69.15         5,433.85
                                               ===========       =========      ==========
```

Placing Invoices On Hold

If you decided that an invoice should have payment temporarily withheld, you
can use the "Change payments" option from the Payment Processing Menu and
put the transaction "on hold". Joan decided to hold payment on invoice 110506
from Pear Computers, since one of the software packages had been damaged in
transit.

❏ Press: Esc to return to the Payment Processing Menu.

❏ Select: 2. Control payments from the Payment Processing Menu.

The Control Payments screen will appear as shown in Figure 26–4.

Since there is only one invoice to be placed on hold,

Figure 26–4

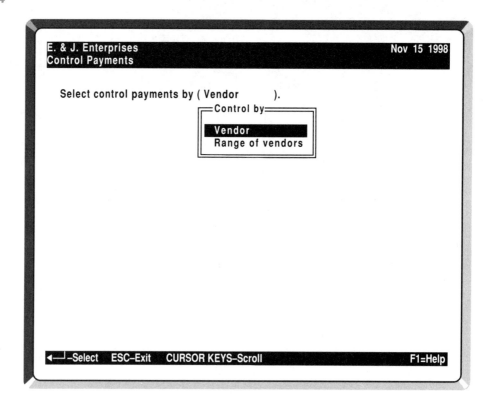

□ Select: Vendor

A second Control Payments screen will appear as shown in Figure 26–5.

□ Type: 990015 in the Vendor number field.

□ Press: [Enter]

□ Select: Invoice from the Types box.

□ Type: 110506 in the Document number field.

□ Press: [Enter]

The screen will display all of the information for invoice 110506. An option bar will appear at the bottom of the screen.

□ Select: Edit.

A Status box will appear, allowing you to force payment (pay the invoice on the next check run even if it is before the due date), or put it on hold (not allow payment to be made on the due date). You can remove a "Forced" or "Hold" status by selecting "None".

□ Select: Hold

Figure 26–5

```
┌──────────────────────────────────────────────────────────────┐
│ E. & J. Enterprises                               Nov 15 1998  │
│ Control Payments                                               │
│                                                                │
│        Vendor number          [███████]                        │
│                                                                │
│                                                                │
│        Document type          (              )                 │
│        Document number        [             ]                  │
│                                                                │
│        Document status        [         ]                      │
│                                                                │
│        Due date               [  /  /  ]    Document date:     │
│        Discount date          [  /  /  ]    Term desc.:        │
│        Discount percent       [         ]                      │
│        Activate prepayment    [  /  /  ]                       │
│                                                                │
│        Base for discount      [          ] Original amount:    │
│        Maximum payment        [          ] Current amount:     │
│                                                                │
│                                                                │
│                                                                │
│                                                                │
│ ESC–Control                                          F1=Help   │
└──────────────────────────────────────────────────────────────┘
```

❑ Press: [Esc] to indicate that you have finished editing this invoice.

A new option bar will appear as follows:

```
┌──────────────────────────────────────────────┐
│                                                │
│      Accept changes     Edit     Cancel        │
│                                                │
└──────────────────────────────────────────────┘
```

❑ Select: `Accept changes`

The following prompt will appear:

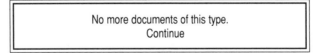

```
┌──────────────────────────────────────────────┐
│                                                │
│          No more documents of this type.       │
│                   Continue                      │
│                                                │
└──────────────────────────────────────────────┘
```

❑ Press [Enter] to continue.

❑ Press: [Esc] three times to indicate that you have finished controlling payments and to return to the Payment Processing Menu.

❑ Select: `3. Check processing` from the Payment Processing Menu.

❑ Print the Pre-check register again.

Compare the new Pre-check register to the one you printed earlier. The total number of checks to be issued remains at 2. The amount currently payable is now $4,920.00 and the net payment will be $4,861.45. The total amount of discounts to be taken is $58.55. The screen will return to the `Check Processing Menu`.

Printing and Posting Checks and Advices

❑ Select: `2. Print/post checks and advices` from the `Check Processing Menu`.

The Print/Post Checks and Advices screen (Figure 26–6) will appear.

Figure 26–6

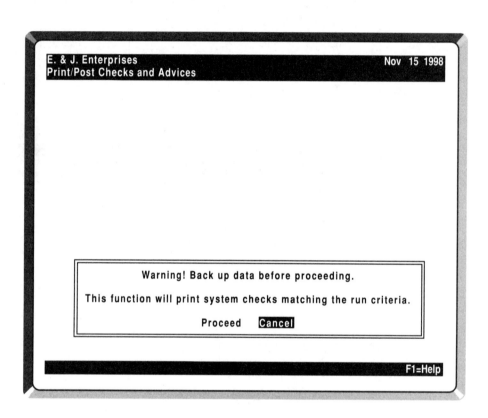

```
E. & J. Enterprises                                        Nov 15 1998
Print/Post Checks and Advices




                    Warning! Back up data before proceeding.

          This function will print system checks matching the run criteria.

                           Proceed    Cancel


                                                              F1=Help
```

In case there is a power fluctuation or a computer problem, you should back up your data files before posting this batch.

❑ Select: `Cancel`

❑ Press: [Esc] twice to display the ACCPAC Plus Accounts Payable Master Menu.

❑ Press: `Q` to return to the Start Menu.

❑ Press: [F3] to access the System Manager.

❑ Select: `DOS`

☐ Enter the DOS commands to back up your data files.

☐ Type: `exit` to return to the System Manager.

☐ Press: ⌈Esc⌉ to return to the Start Menu.

☐ Enter the commands necessary to return to the Print/post Checks and Advices screen.

☐ Select: `Proceed` to proceed with the posting.

A new `Print/Post Checks and Advices` screen will appear. The data on this screen is the same that you saw when you prepared the Pre-Check register. You could change the information for this check run, but it would be unadvisable to do so since the audit trail and control created in printing the Pre-check register would not be consistent with the checks actually printed.

☐ Select: `Proceed`

A third `Print/Post Checks and Advices` screen (Figure 26–7) will appear.

Figure 26–7

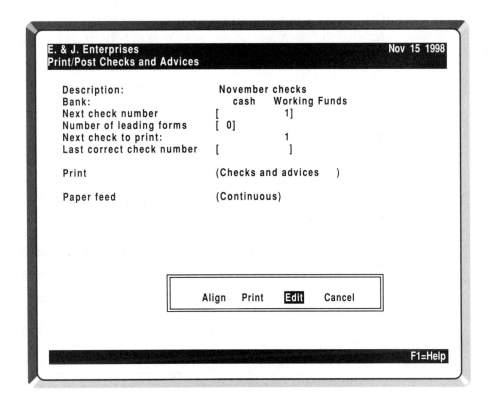

You can change the next check number, number of lead-in blank check forms, the document type (Checks alone, or Checks and Advices), or the type of paper feed used by your printer. E. & J. Enterprises uses a combined Check and Advice.

☐ Select: `Edit`

❑ Press: [Enter] twice to accept the `Next check number` and the `Number of leading forms`

❑ Select: `Checks and advices` from the `Document type` box.

The `Paper feed` option box will appear. E. & J. Enterprises uses Continuous forms.

❑ Select: `Continuous`

An option bar will appear at the bottom of the screen.

```
Align     Print     Edit     Cancel
```

The "Align" option is used to ensure that the printer head is aligned properly on the check. This option should always be run before checks are printed to ensure that you do not waste expensive preprinted check forms. Ensure that your printer is turned on.

❑ Select: `Align`

In an office you would review the check just printed to ensure that the print is properly aligned. In this simulation the checks will be printed on blank paper, so assume that the alignment is correct. Once the alignment form has finished printing,

❑ Select: `Print`

Once the printing has finished, the following message will appear:

```
Were the checks printed correctly?

Yes     No
```

❑ Select: `Yes`

The program will now post the checks to the Accounts Payable ledger without further input. Once the posting is finished, the following message will appear:

```
Posting complete.
Do you want to print advices?

Yes     No
```

You have already printed checks with advices attached. It is not necessary to print advices again.

❑ Select: `No`

A new message will appear,

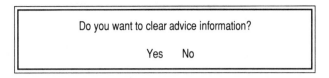

Do you want to clear advice information?

Yes　　No

❑ Select: Yes

The screen will return to the `Check Processing Menu`.

Printing the Check Register

Before continuing, ensure that your printer head is at the top of the page. You may have to reset the printer.

❑ Select: `3. Print check register` from the Check Processing Menu.

The `Print Check Register` screen will appear as shown in Figure 26–8.

Figure 26–8

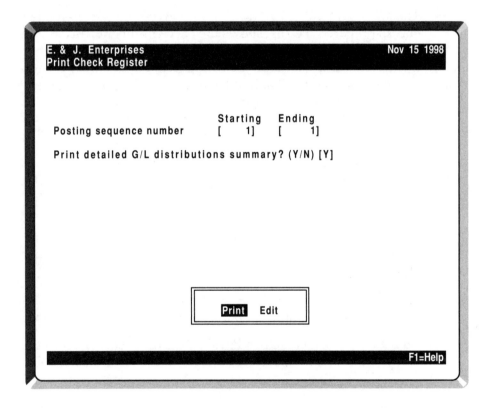

❑ Select: `Print`

After the Check Register has finished printing, the following message will appear.

```
┌──────────────────────────────────────────────────────────────┐
│  Do you want to clear all check registers within the specified range?  │
│                        Yes     No                              │
└──────────────────────────────────────────────────────────────┘
```

❏ Select: `Yes`

❏ Press: Esc to return to the Payment Processing Menu.

Printing the Check Number Audit List

❏ Select: `4. Print check number audit list` from the `Payment Processing Menu`.

The `Check Number Audit List` function will print an audit report of check numbers assigned to check runs. You may select the range of bank codes to be included in the Check Number Audit List. E. & J. Enterprises has only one bank account so you do not have to select bank codes.

❏ Select: `Print`

The `Check Number Audit List` gives you a sequential listing of all system checks prepared. The list shows the check number of any alignment checks and presents the check number, vendor number, vendor name, check date, posting sequence, and amount for all the checks printed. The Check Status is also listed, showing the alignment and outstanding checks. At the bottom, the number of checks issued and outstanding and the total dollar amount ($4,861.45) are shown.

Once the Check Number Audit List has finished printing, the following message will appear on the screen:

```
┌──────────────────────────────────────────────────────────────┐
│         Do you want to clear the Check Number Audit List?       │
│                                                                │
│                        Yes     No                              │
└──────────────────────────────────────────────────────────────┘
```

❏ Select: `Yes`

The screen will return to the Payment Processing Menu.

❏ Press: Esc to return to the ACCPAC Accounts Payable Master Menu.

You will now print an Open Payables report to see the effect that the check run that you have just completed has had on the Accounts Payable.

❏ Select: `5. Reports`

❏ Select: `1. Analysis reports`

❏ Print the Open payables

Verify that the invoices that you have just paid are not listed on the Open Payables. You placed invoice 110506 from Pear Computers Inc. "On Hold". Note the "H" to the right of the invoice's Net Payable amount. This indicates that the invoice is "On Hold". You will have to remove the "Hold" flag before paying the invoice. The total amount of the Accounts Payable should be $3,449.75.

❑ Press ⌊Esc⌋ twice to return to the ACCPAC Accounts Payable Master Menu.

CHECK RECONCILIATION

You must reconcile both manual and system checks with the company's bank statement on a monthly basis.

Reconciling Checks

❑ Select: `4. Payment processing` from the `ACCPAC Accounts Payable Master Menu`.

❑ Select: `5. Check reconciliation` from the `Payment Processing Menu`.

❑ Select: `1. Reconcile checks` from the `Check Reconciliation Menu`.

The following screen (Figure 26–9) will appear.

You must first identify which bank you are reconciling. If you cannot remember the Bank Code, use the Finder key.

❑ Type: `cash` in the `Bank code` field.
❑ Press: ⌊Enter⌋

As part of the audit trail you should enter a `User ID` to identify the individual performing the work.

❑ Type: `Joan`
❑ Press: ⌊Enter⌋

A "Reconcile" option box will appear:

```
┌─────────────────────────────────────────────┐
│                                             │
│              Reconcile                      │
│                                             │
│               Check                         │
│           Range of checks                   │
│                                             │
└─────────────────────────────────────────────┘
```

You use the `Check` option to clear individual checks and to assign a status other than "Cleared" to the checks. You can change the status of any check other than "Reversed", "Alignment", or "Void" checks. You can enter a description for each check you reconcile and print it on the Check Reconciliation report.

Figure 26–9

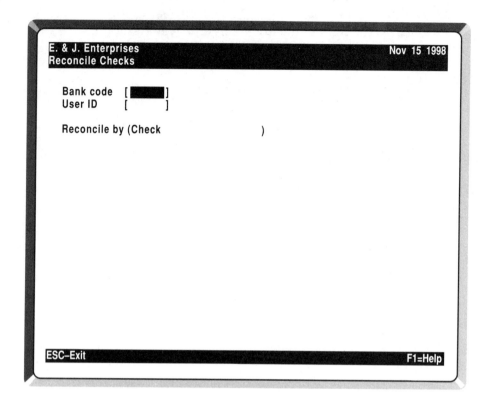

The `Range of checks` option is used to quickly clear large numbers of checks in groups.

If you wanted to clear a large number of checks, but a few of the checks are missing from the range, you would first clear the entire range and then change the missing checks back to outstanding status.

❑ Select: `Check`

The `Reconcile Checks` screen will appear as in Figure 26–10.

There are two ways to proceed with the reconciliation of outstanding checks. The first is by using the `Edit` function. You will reconcile the checks with the second method, `Select check`, later.

Figure 26–10

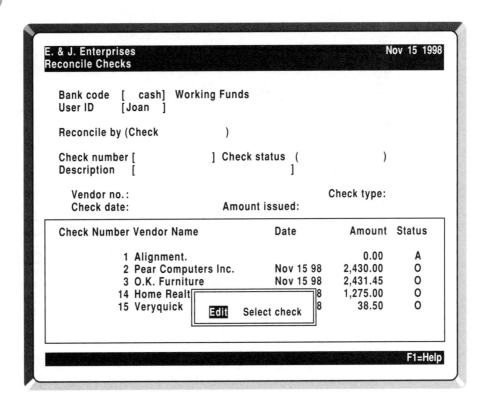

□ Select: `Edit`

A new `Reconcile Checks` screen will appear as shown in Figure 26–11. Review the `Reconcile Checks` screen. It lists all the checks in numerical order. For each check, it gives the Check Number, Vendor Name, Date, Amount, and the Status.

You have received the bank statement just before the end of the month. The two manual checks (14 and 15) have been cleared by the bank.

□ Move the highlighted bar until it rests on check number `14 Home Realty`.

□ Press: Enter

A "Check status" option box will appear to the right.

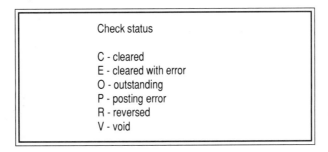

Figure 26–11

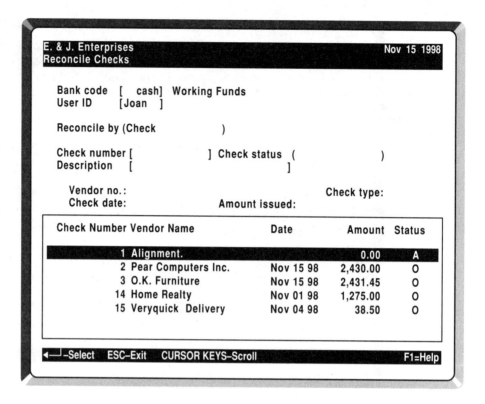

Cleared

This represents a check that has been paid, cleared the bank, and has been returned to your company.

Cleared with error

This represents a check that has been cleared by the bank for an amount that is different from its issued amount. You can enter a description of the source and amount of the error with each check with a "cleared with error" status.

Outstanding

The check has been written, recorded, and sent to the vendor, but has not yet cleared the bank. All posted checks have an initial status of outstanding except for alignment checks or those voided during printing.

Posting error

This is an inaccessible field. ACCPAC Plus assigns this status to checks automatically when there has been a computer error. You cannot alter the "posting error" status.

Reversed

This is a check for which the program has automatically reversed the posted transactions and marked the check "void". When you change a check's status to "reversed", the program reinstates the associated original documents (invoices or credit notes) to their amounts prior to the check being issued.

Void

This is a check that was reprinted during a check run, or one that was reversed by an adjustment entry and then voided.

❑ Select: `C - cleared`

It is normally not necessary to include a comment on cleared checks.

❑ Press: [Enter] in the `Description` field.

The selector bar will return to the Check Information box and will highlight the next check in the sequence. Note the change in status of check number 14.

❑ Select: `15 Veryquick Delivery`

❑ Select: `C - cleared`

❑ Press: [Enter] in the `Description` field.

All of the checks returned by the bank have now had their status changed to "cleared".

❑ Press: [Esc] to indicate that you have finished changing the check status.

The following message will appear:

```
Edit     Select check
```

You could have changed the status of the checks by using `Select check`.

❑ Select: `Select check`

The highlighted bar will move to the `Check number` field.

❑ Type: `14`

❑ Press: [Enter]

The information on the check appears in the upper portion of the screen and the same `Check status` box seen earlier appears to the right.

❑ Type: `C` to accept `Cleared` as the check status.

❑ Press: [Enter] in the Description field.

❑ Press: [Esc] three times to return to the `Check Reconciliation Menu`.

Print Reversed Checks Audit List

If you had reversed any checks you could create an audit trail by printing the "Reversed checks audit list". You would choose selection 3. Print reversed checks audit list from the Check Reconciliation Menu. There are no reversed checks for E. & J. Enterprises.

Printing the Check Reconciliation

❑ Select: 2. Print check reconciliation from the Check Reconciliation Menu.

The Print Check Reconciliation screen will appear as shown in Figure 26–12.

Figure 26–12

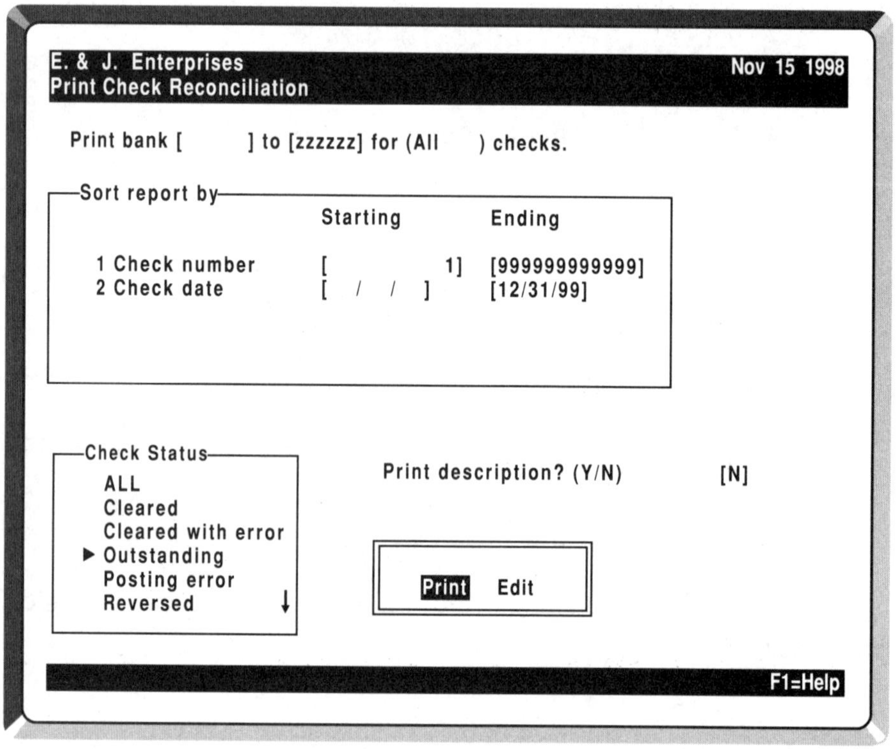

You can control the checks that are included in this report and the order in which they are reported. The settings shown in Figure 26–12 will produce a report of both manual and system checks that are outstanding. Joan wants the information to be listed in order by check number.

❑ Select: Edit

The cursor will move to the Print bank field.

❑ Type: cash

❑ Press: [Enter] twice.

A "Type" option box appears to the right.

```
┌─────────────────────────────────────────┐
│                                           │
│                  Type                     │
│                                           │
│                  All                      │
│                System                     │
│                Manual                     │
│                                           │
└─────────────────────────────────────────┘
```

You can print the Check Reconciliation for all outstanding checks, or you may select only the System or only the Manual outstanding checks for the report.

❑ Select: `All`

The selector bar will move to line 1 in the `Sort report by` option box. ACCPAC Plus will sort the checks by the information that you specify in line 1. If there are any duplications, then these duplicates would be sorted by the information that you select in line 2.

❑ Press: [Enter] to select line `1 Check number`

A "Choices" option box now appears.

```
┌─────────────────────────────────────────┐
│                                           │
│                 Choices                   │
│                                           │
│             Check number                  │
│              Check date                   │
│           Status changed date             │
│                User ID                    │
│                                           │
└─────────────────────────────────────────┘
```

❑ Select: `Check number`

❑ Press: [Enter] twice to accept the full range of check numbers for printing.

Check numbers should not be duplicated but when it happens Joan wants the duplicates to be sorted by check date.

❑ Select: line `2 Check date`

❑ Select: `Check date`

❑ Press: [Enter] twice to accept the Starting and Ending dates.

❑ Press: [Esc] to indicate that you have finished sorting the report.

The "Check Status" box will be highlighted.

```
┌─────────────────────────────────────────────┐
│  ┌───────────────────────────────────────┐  │
│  │                                       │  │
│  │   Check Status                        │  │
│  │   All                                 │  │
│  │   Cleared                             │  │
│  │   Cleared with error                  │  │
│  │   Outstanding                         │  │
│  │   Posting error                       │  │
│  │   Reversed                            │  │
│  │                                       │  │
│  └───────────────────────────────────────┘  │
└─────────────────────────────────────────────┘
```

If you move the highlighted bar down, you will see that there are three more options, "Void, Alignment, and Leading". You use the space bar to turn the options on and off. The pointer on the left indicates that the "Outstanding" checks are to be printed.

❑ Ensure that the highlighted bar is on All.

❑ Press: [SPACEBAR] to turn on the "All" status.

Pointers will appear to the left of all the options.

❑ Press: ⌷Esc⌷ to indicate that you have finished selecting the "Check Status".

❑ Select: Print

Once the report has finished printing, the following message will appear:

```
┌─────────────────────────────────────────────┐
│  ┌───────────────────────────────────────┐  │
│  │                                       │  │
│  │  Do you want to clear checks that are not outstanding?  │  │
│  │                                       │  │
│  │              Yes     No               │  │
│  │                                       │  │
│  └───────────────────────────────────────┘  │
└─────────────────────────────────────────────┘
```

❑ Select: Yes

Review your printout of the Check Reconciliation report. The checks are presented in their numerical order. For each check it gives the Check and Vendor Number, Vendor Name, Reference, Check Date, Amount, and Status. The date that the status was changed, and the ID of the person changing the status are printed to the right of each cleared check. Manual checks are indicated by the letters "MC" between the Amount and Status columns. The summary section at the bottom of the page contains information on the number of the checks issued, cleared, used for alignment, and outstanding.

Once you have cleared the checks that are not outstanding, the following message will appear:

```
┌─────────────────────────────────────────────┐
│  ┌───────────────────────────────────────┐  │
│  │                                       │  │
│  │   Check clearing complete. 3 checks cleared.  │  │
│  │                                       │  │
│  │                Continue               │  │
│  │                                       │  │
│  └───────────────────────────────────────┘  │
└─────────────────────────────────────────────┘
```

ACCPAC Plus has cleared checks 14 and 15 as well as check 1, the alignment check.

❑ Press: [Enter]

The screen will return to the `Check Reconciliation Menu.`

❑ Press: [Esc] twice to return to the ACCPAC Accounts Payable Master Menu.

❑ Back up your data files.

❑ Quit ACCPAC Plus.

REVIEW QUESTIONS

1. Describe the differences between a manual check and a system check.
2. Under what circumstances would a company issue a manual check?
3. Under what circumstances would a company issue a system check?
4. Which type of check, manual or system, has the highest risk of fraud and error?
5. Before generating system checks, you should run the "Pre-Check Register". Why?
6. Describe the purpose of an advice slip.
7. Differentiate between an advice slip and a check.
8. Why must a vendor keep advice slips when it receives payments?
9. Describe the steps to be taken to reconcile the outstanding checks.
10. How frequently should a Bank Reconciliation be prepared?
11. List and describe the options available from the "Check Status" option box in the Reconcile Checks screen.

EXERCISE

1. Enter November 30, 1998 as the new date.
2. Prepare to process the system checks by printing the pre-check register. The Description will be "November system checks" and the Bank code is "cash". The remaining defaults shown on the Pre-Check Register screen are correct.
3. Print and post the checks and advices together on computer paper.
4. Print and clear the Check Register.
5. Print and clear the Check Number Audit List.
6. Print the detailed Open Payables report.
7. Back up your files.
8. Quit ACCPAC Plus.

CHAPTER

27 Processing Adjustments

ACCOUNTS PAYABLE ADJUSTMENTS

You use the adjustment processing option to make corrections to vendor accounts and to correct posting errors that do not affect period-to-date and year-to-date vendor statistics. You can correct posting errors such as distributions to the wrong General Ledger account, or you can change a distribution detail. If the Invoice batch or Check batch containing the entry to be changed has not been posted, you can modify the batch. If the entry has been posted, ACCPAC Plus will allow you to enter changes using either the Invoice Processing Menu or the Adjustments Processing Menu. If you use the Invoice Processing Menu, the vendor statistics will be updated when the batch is posted. If you use the Adjustments Processing Menu, the vendor statistics will not be updated when the batch is posted.

 As part of a company's internal control policy, only managers who do not handle checks or record Accounts Payable should be allowed to authorize adjustments. This policy reduces the potential for the creation and payment of fraudulent liabilities. It also protects employees from being falsely accused of fraud.

❑ Using November 30, 1998 as the New date, enter the commands necessary to display the ACCPAC Accounts Payable Master Menu for E. & J. Enterprises.

The screen will indicate that the New date is more than one week later than the Last access date.

```
┌──────────────────────────────────────────────────┐
│  New date is more than one week later than old date. │
│                                                    │
│              Accept        Edit                    │
└──────────────────────────────────────────────────┘
```

❑ Select: Accept

INVOICE PROCESSING METHOD

The Invoice Processing Menu should be used to enter changes when the change is related to an invoice already posted to the Accounts Payable and when the vendor statistics should be updated to reflect the change. In this chapter, you will look at two common situations: an invoice that was posted to the wrong vendor and an invoice recorded for an incorrect amount.

Invoice Charged to the Wrong Vendor

When going through the accounts payable, Erin discovered that the mobile computer table, purchased from Pear Computers Inc., was recorded as being purchased from O.K. Furniture. You must remove the invoice from the files of O.K. Furniture Co. and add it to the files of Pear Computers Inc.

The use of the term "Debit" or "Credit" does not refer to the Accounts Payable account, but to the other side of the journal entry. You will use a Debit note if you have to increase the liability to a vendor. Likewise, a Credit note is used to reduce the liability to a vendor.

❏ Select: `3. Transaction processing` from the ACCPAC Accounts Payable Master Menu.

❏ Select: `1.Invoice processing` from the Transaction Processing Menu.

❏ Select: `1. Add/modify/delete invoice batches` from the Invoice Processing Menu.

❏ Press: [Enter] in the blank `Batch` number field.

❏ Select: `Yes` to create a new batch.

❏ Type: `Nov. Debit and Credit Notes` in the `Description` field.

❏ Press: [Enter]

❏ Press: [Enter] to accept Entry number `1`.

Credit notes

As shown in Figure 27–1, you can choose one of three different Header types: Invoice, Credit note, or Debit note. Credit note APCN-001, authorized by Erin, will be used to remove invoice 110312 from the O.K. Furniture account.

❏ Select: `Credit note`

The section in the upper right corner of the screen that displays fields for terms and discount information will be replaced by a single field for the original invoice number.

❏ Type: `990025` in the `Vendor no.` field.

❏ Press: [Enter]

Figure 27–1

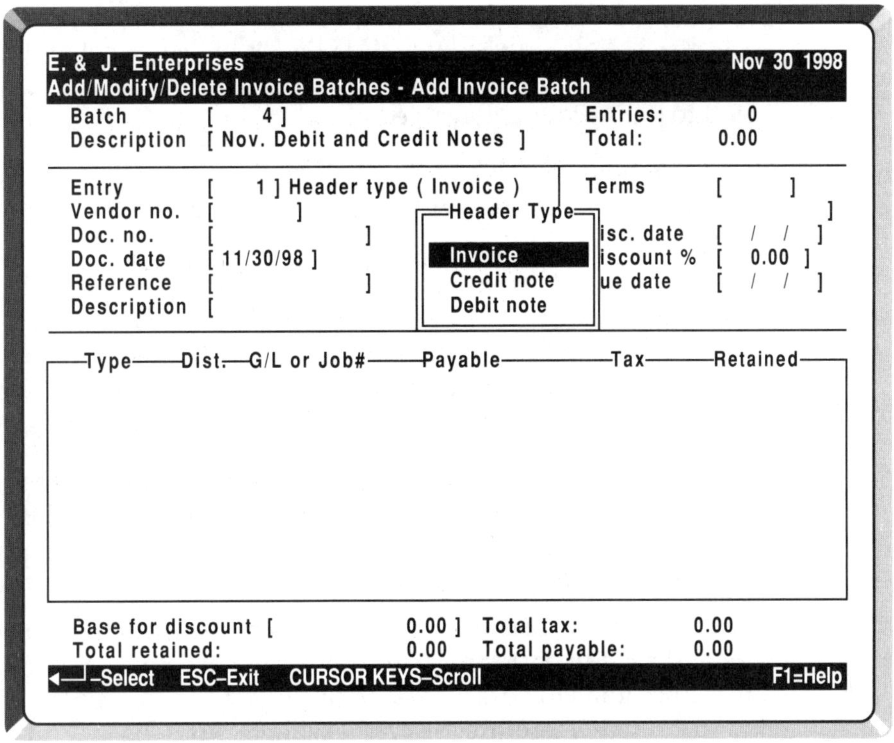

```
┌─────────────────────────────────────────────────────────────────────┐
│ E. & J. Enterprises                                    Nov 30 1998    │
│ Add/Modify/Delete Invoice Batches - Add Invoice Batch                 │
│   Batch       [    4 ]                    Entries:        0            │
│   Description [ Nov. Debit and Credit Notes ]  Total:    0.00         │
│                                                                       │
│   Entry       [    1 ] Header type ( Invoice )  Terms    [      ]     │
│   Vendor no.  [       ]      ┌═Header Type═┐            ]              │
│   Doc. no.    [           ]  │             │ isc. date  [  /  /  ]    │
│   Doc. date   [ 11/30/98 ]   │ Invoice     │ iscount %  [   0.00 ]    │
│   Reference   [           ]  │ Credit note │ ue date    [  /  /  ]    │
│   Description [              │ Debit note  │                          │
│                              └─────────────┘                          │
│  ─Type──Dist.─G/L or Job#──Payable────────Tax────Retained─            │
│                                                                       │
│                                                                       │
│   Base for discount  [          0.00 ]  Total tax:      0.00          │
│   Total retained:               0.00    Total payable:  0.00          │
│ ◄─┘–Select  ESC–Exit  CURSOR KEYS–Scroll              F1=Help         │
└─────────────────────────────────────────────────────────────────────┘
```

A unique Credit Note or Debit Note number must be used as the Document number. If duplicate document numbers are used, ACCPAC Plus will transfer the entry with the duplicated number to an error batch during posting.

❑ Type: APCN-001 in the Doc. no. field.
❑ Press: Enter

When you reallocate an invoice for a vendor, you should enter the original date of the invoice so that the date on which the adjustment was entered does not appear on the Accounts Payable reports as the invoice date. You should use the original date of the invoice so the vendor's statistics will be updated correctly.

❑ Type: 110698, the date of the original invoice, in the Doc. date field.
❑ Press: Enter

For control purposes, each adjustment should be documented by a memo. At E. & J. Enterprises, each memo will be given a unique number followed by the initials of the person authorizing the adjustment. This information will be entered in the Reference field. The documentation for this adjustment is a memo, AP001EG, written by Erin.

❑ Type: AP001EG in the Reference field.
❑ Press: Enter
❑ Type: Inv. should be in A/C 990015 in the Description field.

❑ Press: [Enter]

If the credit note applies to one invoice, you can enter that invoice number in the `Original inv.` field. ACCPAC Plus will then automatically apply the credit note to the proper invoice when both the credit note and the invoice have been posted to the Accounts Payable.

If the credit note applies to several invoices, or is issued on account, or if for some reason you cannot identify an invoice number, the original invoice field can be left blank.

❑ Type: 110312 in the `Orig.invoice` field.

❑ Press: [Enter]

The following option bar will appear:

```
┌─────────────────────────────────────────────────────┐
│   Save entry      Header      Detail      Cancel      │
└─────────────────────────────────────────────────────┘
```

❑ Select: `Detail`

Credit notes always result in a debit entry to the Accounts Payable control account and a credit entry to one or more other accounts. You must choose the account or accounts to be credited. In this case the invoice was for purchases of goods for resale, therefore the credit will be to purchases and value added tax.

❑ Type: `pv` in the `Dist. code` field.

❑ Press: [Enter]

❑ Press: [Enter] to accept Tax code 1.

❑ Type: `110.00` in the `Amount` field.

❑ Press: [Enter]

❑ Press: [Enter] again to accept the Tax amount of $10.00.

❑ Press: [Enter] to accept the Description.

❑ Press: [Esc] to indicate that the distribution of the credit note is complete.

Review the entry. If you have made an error, choose either the "Header" or "Detail" and make the necessary corrections. Once there are no errors,

❑ Select: `Save Entry`

When you save this transaction, which reverses the invoice to O.K. Furniture's account, ACCPAC Plus resets the screen to receive the next entry.

Debit notes

The next entry, APDN-001, will add the liability to Pear Computers Inc.'s records.

❑ Press: [Enter] to accept the next Entry number.

❑ Select: `Debit note`

- ❏ Type: `990015` in the `Vendor no.` field.
- ❏ Press: [Enter]
- ❏ Type: `APDN-001` in the `Doc.no.` field.
- ❏ Press: [Enter]
- ❏ Press: [Enter] to accept 11/06/98 as the date of the original invoice.
- ❏ Press: [Enter] to accept the reference `AP001EG` in the `Reference` field.
- ❏ Type: `Trans. inv. from A/C 990025` in the `Description` field. If necessary, blank out any excess characters.
- ❏ Press: [Enter]
- ❏ Type: `110312` in the `Orig. invoice` field.
- ❏ Press: [Enter]
- ❏ Select: `Detail` from the option bar.

You used the code "pv" to clear the invoice from O.K. Furniture's account. You must use the same code again to distribute the entry to the proper General Ledger account.

- ❏ Press: [Enter] to accept `pv` in the `Dist. code` field.
- ❏ Press: [Enter] to accept Tax code 1.
- ❏ Type: `110.00` in the `Amount` field.
- ❏ Press: [Enter]
- ❏ Press: [Enter] again to accept the `Tax amount` of $10.00.
- ❏ Press: [Enter] to accept the Description.
- ❏ Press: [Esc] to indicate that the distribution of the debit note is complete.

Review the entry. If you have made an error, choose either the "Header" or "Detail" and make the necessary corrections. When there are no errors,

- ❏ Select: `Save Entry`

The screen will not indicate debits or credits since a debit note will always result in a credit to Accounts Payable, and a debit to another account.

Adjusting for the Wrong Invoice Amount

When Erin Gogetter reviewed the Open Payables as of the end of November, she realized that invoice number CA55987 from Computer Associates had been recorded incorrectly. The actual amount was $950.00, not $750.00 as recorded. Rather than create a new invoice, you will put in a debit note to adjust the outstanding amount.

- ❏ Press: [Enter] to accept the next `Entry` number.
- ❏ Select: `Debit note`

❏ Type: 990035 in the Vendor no. field.

❏ Press: [Enter]

❏ Type: APDN-002 in the Doc. no. field.

❏ Press: [Enter]

Remember to use the original invoice date so that the vendor statistics will be updated correctly.

❏ Type: 110698 in the Doc. date field.

❏ Press: [Enter]

❏ Type: AP002EG in the Reference field.

❏ Press: [Enter]

❏ Type: Underallocated $200 on invoice in the Description field.

❏ Press: [Enter]

❏ Type: CA55987 in the Orig. invoice field.

❏ Press: [Enter]

❏ Select: Detail from the option bar.

❏ Press: [Enter] to accept pv in the Dist. code field.

❏ Press: [Enter] to accept Tax code 1.

❏ Type: 200.00 in the Amount field.

❏ Press: [Enter]

❏ Press: [Enter] again to accept the Tax amount of $18.18.

❏ Press: [Enter] to accept the Description.

❏ Press: [Esc] to indicate that the distribution of the debit note is complete.

Review the entry. If you have made an error, choose either the "Header" or "Detail" and make the necessary corrections. Once there are no errors,

❏ Select: Save Entry

❏ Press: [Esc] twice to return to the Invoice Processing Menu.

❏ Print the A/P Invoice Batch List as shown in Table 27–1.

Table 27–1

```
ch number            [    4]    to  [    4]
tus(es) selected:  Open

ch number:    4   Nov. Debit and Credit Notes
ation date: Nov 30 98  Status:  Open

ry    Vendor Vendor                                    Acct. Dept. Tx
o. Ty Number Name                 Document No. Ty   Dist. (Job-Ph-Cat) Cd Tax/Base/Net     Document Amount

  1 CN 990025 O.K. Furniture           APCN-001 PUR     pv    752        1 Net:     100.00-      110.00-
     Date: Nov 06 98      Ref: AP001EG                Tax:    542          Tax:      10.00-
     Original invoice:      110312                                                           _____
     Desc: Inv. should be in A/C 990015        Total tax:     10.00- Total credit note        110.00-*

  2 DN 990015 Pear Computers Inc.       APDN-001 PUR     pv    752        1 Net:     100.00       110.00
     Date: Nov 06 98      Ref: AP001EG                Tax:    542          Tax:      10.00
     Original invoice:      110312                                                           _____
     Desc: Trans. inv. from A/C 990025        Total tax:     10.00  Total debit note         110.00 *
te. Original invoice not found.

  3 DN 990035 Computer Associates       APDN-002 PUR     pv    752        1 Net:     181.82       200.00
     Date: Nov 06 98      Ref: AP002EG                Tax:    542          Tax:      18.18
     Original invoice:      CA55987                                                          _____
     Desc: Underallocated $200 on invoice     Total tax:     18.18  Total debit note         200.00 *


                                                   Total invoices             0.00
                                                   Total debit notes        310.00
                                                   Total credit notes       110.00-
                                                                          _____
                                                   Batch total payable      200.00
                                                                          =============
  3 transaction(s) printed.
```

Compare your printout to Table 27–1. If there are errors, make the necessary corrections and print the A/P Invoice Batch List again.

❑ Post the Invoice batch to the Accounts Payable Ledger.

❑ Print and clear the Invoice Posting Journal.

Once the Invoice Posting Journal has finished printing and has been cleared,

❑ Press: [Esc] twice to return to the ACCPAC Accounts Payable Master Menu.

ADJUSTMENT PROCESSING METHOD

In this section you will enter the same adjustments that you entered through the Invoice Processing Menu. Changes entered through the Adjustment Processing Menu will not update the customer statistics.

To prevent duplicate posting you will delete the Adjustment batch at the end of this section.

❑ Select: 3. Transaction processing from the ACCPAC Accounts Payable Master Menu.

❑ Select: `2. Adjustment processing` from the Transaction Processing Menu.

❑ Select: `1. Add/modify/delete adjustment batches`

ACCPAC Plus will display the Add/Modify/Delete Adjustment Batches screen as shown in Figure 27–2.

❑ Press: Enter in the blank `Batch` field to select the next batch number in sequence.

❑ Select: `Yes` to create a new Adjustment batch.

The computer will search the files and determine the next batch number in se-

Figure 27–2

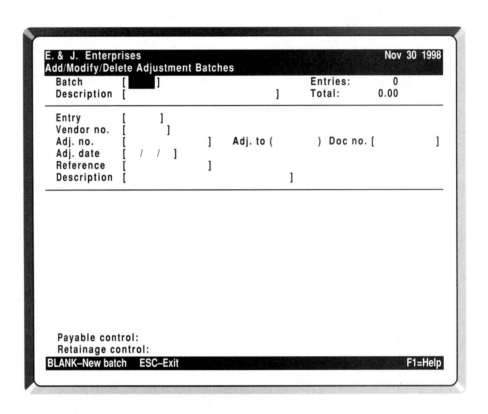

```
E. & J. Enterprises                                    Nov 30 1998
Add/Modify/Delete Adjustment Batches
  Batch        [        ]              Entries:        0
  Description  [                    ]  Total:       0.00
──────────────────────────────────────────────────────────
  Entry        [      ]
  Vendor no.   [        ]
  Adj. no.     [              ]  Adj. to (       ) Doc no. [        ]
  Adj. date    [  /  /  ]
  Reference    [            ]
  Description  [                        ]
──────────────────────────────────────────────────────────




  Payable control:
  Retainage control:
  BLANK–New batch    ESC–Exit                         F1=Help
```

quence. The number "1" will appear in the `Batch` field and the cursor will move to the `Description` field.

❑ Type: `November 1998 Adjustments`

❑ Press: Enter

The Wrong Customer Invoiced

The first two entries will remove invoice 110312 from O.K. Furniture's account and transfer it to Pear Computers Inc.

❏ Press: ⌊Enter⌋ to accept "1" as the `Entry` number.

❏ Type: `990025` in the `Vendor no.` field.

❏ Press: ⌊Enter⌋

You may enter a unique adjustment control number to identify the adjustment for later reference. If the adjustment number is duplicated, the entry with the duplicate will be transferred to an error batch during posting of the adjustment batch. If you leave the `Adj. no.` field blank, the program will generate a unique number using the batch and entry number for the adjustment. For example, if the batch number is 12 and the entry number is 1, the program will assign the adjustment number 12–1.

❏ Type: `APCN-001` in the `Adj. no.` field.

❏ Press: ⌊Enter⌋

An "Adjustment to" selection box will appear on the screen.

```
┌─────────────────────────────────────────────┐
│                                               │
│          Adjustment  to                       │
│                                               │
│          Invoice                              │
│          Credit note                          │
│          Debit note                           │
│          Adjustment                           │
│                                               │
└─────────────────────────────────────────────┘
```

You must identify the type of document that is being corrected. ACCPAC Plus uses this information to identify the debits and credits necessary to make the corrections.

❏ Select: `Invoice`

You should identify, by its number, the specific document that is to be adjusted. In this case you know that the invoice number is 110312.

❏ Type: `110312` in the `Doc. no.` field.

❏ Press: ⌊Enter⌋

When you reallocate an invoice for a vendor, you should enter the original date of the invoice so that the adjustment date does not appear on the Accounts Payable reports as the invoice date. Remember that Adjustment Batch entries do not update the vendor statistics.

❏ Type: `110698`, the date of the original invoice, in the `Adj. date` field.

❏ Press: ⌊Enter⌋

The documentation for this adjustment is memo number AP001EG, written by Erin.

❏ Type: `AP001EG` in the `Reference` field.

❏ Press: ⌊Enter⌋

❏ Type: `Inv. should be in A/C 990015` in the `Description` field.

❏ Press: Enter

The following option bar will appear:

```
┌────────────────────────────────────────────────────────┐
│        Save entry    Header    Detail    Cancel          │
└────────────────────────────────────────────────────────┘
```

❏ Select: Detail

The cursor will move to the Dist. code field in the Distribution Detail section in the upper part of the screen.

❏ Type: pv to indicate that the adjustment is being made to account 752, purchases.

❏ Press: Enter

❏ Press: Enter to accept Tax code 1.

❏ Type: 110.00 in the Credit field to record the amount of the adjustment.

❏ Press: Enter

❏ Press: Enter to accept the Tax amount of $10.00.

❏ Press: Enter to accept the Description.

The credit to account 752 will be displayed in the information box in the lower portion of the screen.

❏ Press: Esc to indicate that the distribution of this entry is complete. If you have made an error, select either "Header" or"Detail", and then enter the correct information. Once you have determined that the information entered is correct,

❏ Select: Save entry

When you save this entry, which reverses invoice 110312 to O.K. Furniture, AC-CPAC Plus resets the screen to receive the next adjusting entry. The next adjusting entry, a debit note, will add invoice 110312 to Pear Computer's account.

The cursor will have moved once again to the Entry number field. You will create a balanced adjustment with neither an increase nor a decrease in the Accounts Payable. The first entry resulted in a debit to account 500 (Accounts Payable). You must now set up the invoice in Customer account 990015, so the entry will be the reverse of the first.

❏ Press: Enter to accept Entry 2.

❏ Type: 990015 in the Vendor no. field.

❏ Press: Enter

❏ Type: APDN-001 in the Adj. no. field.

❏ Press: Enter

❏ Select: Invoice

❏ Type: 110312 in the Doc. no. field.

- ❑ Press: [Enter]
- ❑ Press: [Enter] to accept November 6, 1998 as the `Adj. date`.
- ❑ Press: [Enter] to accept `AP001EG` in the `Reference` field.
- ❑ Type: `Transfer inv. from A/C 990025` in the `Description` field.
- ❑ Press: [Enter]
- ❑ Select: `Detail`

The cursor will move to the `Dist. code` field in the Distribution Detail portion of the screen.

- ❑ Press: [Enter] to accept `pv`.
- ❑ Press: [Enter] to accept Tax code 1.

The cursor will always go first to the Credit field. You must move it to the Debit field to offset the previous entry.

- ❑ Press: [TAB] or [Enter] to move the cursor to the Debit field.
- ❑ Type: `110.00` in the Debit field to record the amount of the adjustment.
- ❑ Press: [Enter]
- ❑ Press: [Enter] to accept the `Tax amount` of $10.00.
- ❑ Press: [Enter] to accept the `Description`

The debit to account 752 will be displayed in the information box in the lower portion of the screen.

- ❑ Press: [Esc] to indicate that the distribution of this entry is complete.

If you have made an error, select either "Header" or "Detail", and then enter the correct information. Once you have determined that the information entered is correct,

- ❑ Select: `Save entry`

When you save this entry, which puts invoice 110312 into Pear Computer's account, ACCPAC Plus resets the screen to receive the next adjusting entry. Since the two entries offset each other, the net change to the General Ledger will be zero.

Invoice Amount Incorrect

Joan had found that Computer Associates had sent an invoice for $950.00 for the three Accounting software packages, however, the invoice was recorded as $750.00. Invoice CA55987, dated November 6, 1998, must be adjusted to reflect the $200 (VAT included) error. An internal debit note, APDN-002, was authorized by Erin in a memo numbered AP002EG.

- ❑ Press: [Enter] to accept Entry 3.
- ❑ Type: `990035` in the `Vendor no.` field.

❏ Press: [Enter]

❏ Type: APDN-002 in the Adj. no. field.

❏ Press: [Enter]

❏ Select: Invoice from the Adjustment to options box.

❏ Type: CA55987 in the Doc. no. field.

❏ Press: [Enter]

❏ Press: [Enter] to accept 11/06/98 in the Adj. date field.

❏ Type: AP002EG in the Reference field.

❏ Press: [Enter]

❏ Type: Underallocated $200 on invoice in the Description field.

❏ Press: [Enter]

❏ Select: Detail

❏ Press: [Enter] to accept the code "pv" shown in the Dist. code field.

❏ Press: [Enter] to accept Tax code 1.

❏ Press: [TAB] or [Enter] to move the cursor to the Debit field.

❏ Type: 200.00 in the Debit field.

❏ Press: [Enter]

❏ Press: [Enter] to accept the Tax amount of $18.18.

❏ Press: [Enter] to accept the Description

❏ Press: [Esc] to indicate that you have finished entering the adjustment.

The screen should now appear as shown in Figure 27–3.

Figure 27–3

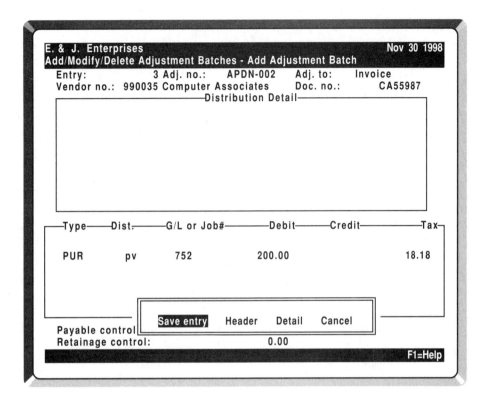

- Select: `Save entry`
- Press: [Esc] twice to return to the Adjustment Processing Menu.
- Print the A/P Adjustment Batch List.

Table 27–2

```
Date: Nov 30 98   12:46am              E. & J. Enterprises                                          Page:   1
A/P Adjustment Batch List

Batch number         [   1]    to  [   1]
Status(es) selected:  Open

Batch number :   1  November 1998 Adjustments
Creation date: Nov 30 98  Status:  Open

Entry Vendor Vendor Name/                              Acct.  Dept. Tx     Retained/Tax/
 No. Number    Adj. No.    Date      Ref. No.   Ty  Dist. (Job-Ph-Cat) Cd  Base/Net/Orig.        Debit        Credit

   1 990025 O.K. Furniture                      PUR    pv   752      1                                         100.00
            APCN-001 Nov 06 98 AP001EG          Tax acct:  542          Base:      100.00-                      10.00
            Adj.to:      110312  Invoice                   500     Payable control        110.00
            Inv. should be in A/C 990015

                                                        Adjustment total              110.00       110.00 *

   2 990015 Pear Computers Inc.                 PUR    pv   752      1                  100.00
            APDN-001 Nov 06 98 AP001EG          Tax acct:  542          Base:      100.00          10.00
            Adj.to:      110312  Invoice                   500     Payable control                            110.00
            Transfer inv. from A/C 990025

                                                        Adjustment total              110.00       110.00 *

   3 990035 Computer Associates                 PUR    pv   752      1                  181.82
            APDN-002 Nov 06 98 AP002EG          Tax acct:  542          Base:      181.82          18.18
            Adj.to:      CA55987  Invoice                  500     Payable control                            200.00
            Underallocated $200 on invoice

                                                        Adjustment total              200.00       200.00 *


                                                            Batch total              420.00       420.00
                                                                                ============  ============

 3 transaction(s) printed.
```

Compare your printout to Table 27–2. If there are errors, make the necessary corrections and print the A/P Adjustment Batch List again.

Deleting an Adjustment Batch

The data entered in this Adjustment Batch is identical to that entered by the Invoice Processing Method earlier in this chapter. If you wished to record this information in the Accounts Payable you would post the Adjustment Batch, and then print and clear the Posting Journal. As the information in this Adjustment Batch is identical to that posted by the Invoice Processing method, you will now delete this Adjustment Batch.

❑ Select: `1. Add/modify/delete adjustment batches` from the `Adjustment Processing Menu`.

❑ Type: `1` in the `Batch` field.

❑ Press: Enter

❑ Select: `Delete batch`

The following prompt will appear:

```
         ┌─────────────────────────────────────────────────────────┐
         │          Do you really want to delete this batch?        │
         │                      Yes    No                           │
         └─────────────────────────────────────────────────────────┘
```

- [ ] Select: `Yes` to confirm that you want to delete this batch.
- [ ] Press: [Esc] three times to return to the ACCPAC Accounts Payable Master Menu.

AGED OVERDUE PAYABLES

The `Aged Overdue Payables` reports on the overdue portion of your Accounts Payable. You would use this function when making decisions about the action and cash required to pay overdue payables.

- [ ] Select: `5. Reports` from the ACCPAC Accounts Payable Master Menu.
- [ ] Select: `1. Analysis reports` from the Reports Menu.
- [ ] Select: `3. Aged overdue payables` from the Analysis Reports Menu.

The following screen (Figure 27–4) will appear:

Figure 27–4

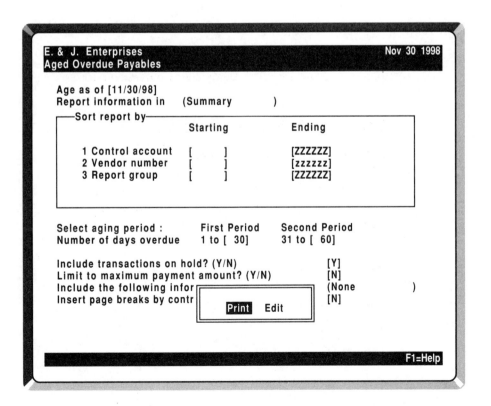

The `Age as of` field shows the New date "11/30/98" from the Start Menu. The default `Number of days overdue` in the first aging period is 1 to 30, and the second aging period is 31 to 60. The default settings will print all amounts payable, including the transactions "On hold". If you wish to change the date, or any other options, you would select "Edit" and make the changes.

❏ Select: `Print`

The `Aged Overdue Payables` report lists the Accounts Payable by Vendor number and Vendor name. It shows every invoice for each vendor on a separate line.

After the report has finished printing, the screen will return to the `Analysis Reports Menu`. Compare your printout with that shown in Table 27–3.

Table 27–3

```
Date: Nov 30 98    12:53am           E. & J. Enterprises                                      Page:   1
Aged Overdue Payables - Summary

Age as of: Nov 30 98
Control account [     ] to [zzzzzz]
Vendor number  [     ] to [zzzzzz]
Report group   [     ] to [zzzzzz]
Include transactions on hold.
```

Vendor No.	Vendor Name/ Doc. Number Doc. Date Due Date Ty	Current/ Unapplied	1 To 30 Days Overdue	31 To 60 Days Overdue	Over 60 Days Overdue	Total Overdue	Total Payables
990015	Pear Computers Inc.	110.00	0.00	0.00	0.00	0.00	110.00
	ON HOLD:	583.00	0.00	0.00	0.00	0.00	583.00
990035	Computer Associates	950.00	0.00	0.00	0.00	0.00	950.00
990045	Dubai Software Co.	2,006.75	0.00	0.00	0.00	0.00	2,006.75
	Control account (1) subtotals:	3,066.75	0.00	0.00	0.00	0.00	3,066.75
	ON HOLD:	583.00	0.00	0.00	0.00	0.00	583.00
		3,066.75	0.00	0.00	0.00	0.00	3,066.75
	ON HOLD:	583.00	0.00	0.00	0.00	0.00	583.00
		3,649.75	0.00	0.00	0.00	0.00	3,649.75
		==========	==========	==========	==========	===========	===========
		100.00 %	0.00 %	0.00 %	0.00 %	0.00 %	100.00 %

```
3 vendor(s) printed.
1 control account(s) printed.
```

AGED CASH REQUIREMENTS REPORT

The `Aged Cash Requirements` reports cash amounts that will be required to meet obligations as they become due. You should use this report when you are analyzing your cash flows and making projections.

☐ Select: `4. Aged cash requirements` from the `Analysis Reports` Menu.

The `Aged Cash Requirements` screen (Figure 27–5) will appear:

Figure 27–5

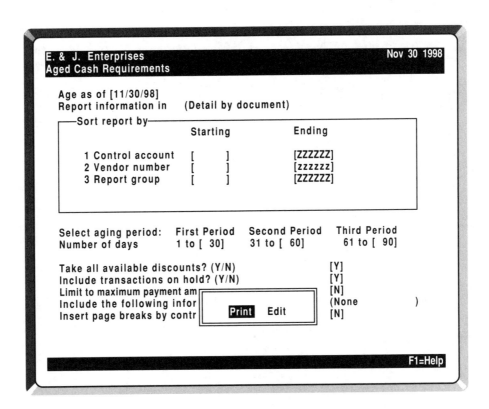

The `Age as of` field shows the New date "11/30/98" as the default date . The report will list the information in detail by date in three aging periods ranging from 1 to 30, 31 to 60, and 61 to 90 days. You can edit the report to fit the needs of your business in the same manner as other reports printed previously.

If you change the `Take all available discounts` to "N", ACCPAC will ignore all discounts. If you accept the default "Y" it will calculate the discounts available during the aging periods. When it prints the report, it will indicate each discounted payable. You can also have the report include all "On hold" transactions and you can limit the maximum amount of a payment to a vendor.

☐ Select: `Print`

The `Aged Cash Requirements` report shows a line for each document. Compare your printout with that shown in Table 27–4.

Table 27–4

```
Date: Nov 30 98   12:57am              E. & J. Enterprises                                    Page:   1
Aged Cash Requirements - Detail by document

Age as of: Nov 30 98
Control account [      ] to [zzzzzz]
Vendor number  [      ] to [zzzzzz]
Report group   [      ] to [zzzzzz]
Take all available discounts.
Include transactions on hold.
```

Vendor No.	Vendor Name/ Doc. Number	Doc. Date	Disc./ Due Date	Ty	Overdue	Current/ Unapplied	31 To 60 Days	61 To 90 Days	Over 90 Days	Total Payables
990015	Pear Computers Inc.									
	APDN-001	Nov 06 98		DN		110.00				
	110506	Nov 05 98	Dec 05 98	IN		583.00 H				
					0.00	110.00	0.00	0.00	0.00	110.00
			ON HOLD:		0.00	583.00	0.00	0.00	0.00	583.00
990035	Computer Associates									
	CA55987	Nov 06 98	Dec 06 98	IN		950.00				
					0.00	950.00	0.00	0.00	0.00	950.00
990045	Dubai Software Co.									
	87795	Oct 31 98	Nov 30 98	IN		1,650.00				
	99843	Nov 07 98	Dec 07 98	IN		356.75				
					0.00	2,006.75	0.00	0.00	0.00	2,006.75
	Control account (1) subtotals:				0.00	3,066.75	0.00	0.00	0.00	3,066.75
			ON HOLD:		0.00	583.00	0.00	0.00	0.00	583.00
					0.00	3,066.75	0.00	0.00	0.00	3,066.75
			ON HOLD:		0.00	583.00	0.00	0.00	0.00	583.00
					0.00	3,649.75	0.00	0.00	0.00	3,649.75
					=========	=========	=========	=========	=========	=========
					0.00 %	100.00 %	0.00 %	0.00 %	0.00 %	100.00 %

```
H: indicates transaction placed on hold.

  3 vendor(s) printed.
  1 control account(s) printed.
```

Once you have reviewed the Aged Cash Requirements Report,

❑ Press: [Esc] twice to return to the ACCPAC Accounts Payable Master Menu.

Back up your data files and quit ACCPAC Plus.

REVIEW QUESTIONS

1. Describe the options available from the Adjustment Processing Menu.
2. Why should any adjustments to Accounts Payable be authorized by a senior manager?
3. Why is it preferable to use the original invoice date when making an adjustment?
4. Describe three circumstances in which you may have to adjust an invoice.
5. When would you use the Invoice Processing Method rather than the Adjustment Processing Method?
6. What is the purpose of the Aged Overdue Payables report?
7. What is the purpose of the Aged Cash Requirements report?

EXERCISE

On November 30, 1998, you discovered that one of the invoices you posted earlier contains a mistake. Vendor 1100, Dominion Supplies, added their invoice incorrectly. The amount of invoice number 984673 should have been $150 instead of $175 (VAT included).

1. Create an adjustment batch to correct the invoice. The adjustment will take the form of a Credit note. Use the same date and General Ledger account from the original posting to adjust the amount.
2. Print the Adjustment Batch.
3. Post the batch to the Accounts Payable ledger.
4. Print then purge the Adjustment Posting Journal.
5. Print the revised Open Payables and confirm that the adjustments have been entered and processed correctly.
6. Back up your data files.
7. Quit ACCPAC Plus.

28 Posting the General Ledger & Period End Procedures

The purposes of the Period end function are to clear paid transactions and transfer them to the history file, to clear transactions in the history file by their last activity date, to clear batch status information, and to reset period-to-date vendor statistics to zero.

Before running the Period end function, you should:

1. Post all the transactions that apply to the period.

2. Print and clear the posting journals.

3. Print the system and manual checks.

4. Print and clear the check registers.

5. Print the G/L Transactions report.

6. Retrieve the transactions into the General Ledger or, if you do not use the AC-CPAC Plus General Ledger, clear the General Ledger data in Accounts Payable.

In this chapter you will perform the following period end procedures.

1. Print and post any unposted batches for the period.

2. Print and clear the posting journals if necessary.

3. Print the G/L Transactions report.

4. Transfer Accounts Payable information to the General Ledger.

5. Run the Period End function.

❑   Enter the commands necessary to display the ACCPAC Accounts Payable Master Menu for E. & J. Enterprises using November 30, 1998 as the New date.

DISPLAY BATCH STATUS

Before continuing, you should make sure that all relevant batches have been posted to the Accounts Payable.

❑   Select: `2. Inquiries` from the ACCPAC Accounts Payable Master Menu.

❑   Select: `3. Display batch status` from the Inquiries Menu.

❑   Select: `Invoice batches`

The display of batch status information is in two sections as shown in Figure 28–1. The upper section is a scroll box containing information on each batch. You can use the arrow keys to scroll the display up or down to show additional batches.

The lower portion of the screen displays summarized information for all batches. On the left, batches are summarized by batch type. On the right batches are summarized by Status. Note if there are any "Open" or "Printed" batches. You must print any open batches and then post the printed batches. Be sure to print and clear the posting journals before continuing.

❑   Press: [Esc]

❑   Display the Batch Status for Adjustment batches and then the Manual Check batches. Note the "Deleted" status of the `Adjustment` batch.

❑   Press: [Esc] until you return to the ACCPAC Accounts Payable Master Menu.

Figure 28–1

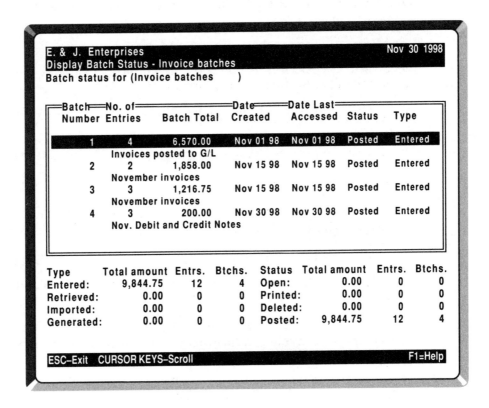

```
┌────────────────────────────────────────────────────────────────────────┐
│ E. & J. Enterprises                                        Nov 30 1998   │
│ Display Batch Status - Invoice batches                                   │
│ Batch status for (Invoice batches      )                                 │
│                                                                          │
│  ┌Batch══No. of════════════════Date══════Date Last═══════════════════┐  │
│  │ Number Entries   Batch Total Created   Accessed   Status   Type    │  │
│  │                                                                    │  │
│  │    1      4        6,570.00  Nov 01 98 Nov 01 98  Posted   Entered │  │
│  │        Invoices posted to G/L                                      │  │
│  │    2      2        1,858.00  Nov 15 98 Nov 15 98  Posted   Entered │  │
│  │        November invoices                                           │  │
│  │    3      3        1,216.75  Nov 15 98 Nov 15 98  Posted   Entered │  │
│  │        November invoices                                           │  │
│  │    4      3          200.00  Nov 30 98 Nov 30 98  Posted   Entered │  │
│  │        Nov. Debit and Credit Notes                                 │  │
│  └────────────────────────────────────────────────────────────────────┘│
│                                                                          │
│  Type       Total amount Entrs. Btchs.  Status  Total amount Entrs. Btchs.│
│  Entered:      9,844.75     12     4     Open:        0.00     0      0   │
│  Retrieved:        0.00      0     0     Printed:     0.00     0      0   │
│  Imported:         0.00      0     0     Deleted:     0.00     0      0   │
│  Generated:        0.00      0     0     Posted:  9,844.75    12      4   │
│                                                                          │
│  ESC–Exit   CURSOR KEYS–Scroll                              F1=Help      │
└────────────────────────────────────────────────────────────────────────┘
```

PRINTING POSTED BATCHES

Once a batch has been printed and posted to the Accounts Payable ledger, it cannot be printed again. The usual way to determine if a batch has been printed and posted is through the `Display Batch Status` option on the Inquiries menu. Trying to print batches is another, less efficient way of determining if there are any entered, but unposted, batches.

❑ Select: `3. Transaction processing` from the ACCPAC Accounts Payable Master Menu.

❑ Select: `1. Invoice processing` from the Transaction Processing Menu.

❑ Select: `4. Print invoice batches` from the Invoice Processing Menu.

Since you have posted all the batches, the following message should appear:

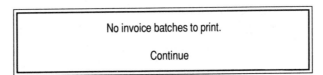

```
┌──────────────────────────────────────────┐
│        No invoice batches to print.        │
│                                            │
│                 Continue                   │
└──────────────────────────────────────────┘
```

❑ Press: [Enter]

If you had not posted all the Invoice batches, you would have to print and post them, then print and clear the Invoice Posting Journal.

❑ Press: ⌷Esc⌷ to return to the `Transaction Processing Menu`

❑ Select: `2. Adjustment processing` from the Transaction Processing Menu

❑ Select: `2. Print adjustment batches` from the Adjustment Processing Menu.

Since you have posted all the batches, the following message should appear:

```
                No adjustment batches to print.

                          Continue
```

❑ Press: ⌷Enter⌷

❑ Press: ⌷Esc⌷ twice to return to the ACCPAC Accounts Payable Master Menu.

❑ Select: `4. Payment processing` and try to print a manual check register and then a system check register.

You should again see messages indicating that there is nothing to print. This confirms that all the invoices, adjustments, and checks have been printed and posted.

❑ Return to the ACCPAC Accounts Payable Master Menu.

POSTING TO THE GENERAL LEDGER

Once you have posted all of the Accounts Payable purchases, adjustments, credit and debit notes to the Accounts Payable Ledger, you can post the transactions to the General Ledger. You have already posted the Invoice Posting Journal to the Accounts Payable Ledger earlier in Chapter 27.

Print/Consolidate G/L Transactions

The next step is to prepare the data for transfer to the General Ledger.

❑ Select: 5. Reports from the ACCPAC Accounts Payable Master Menu.

❑ Select: `3. Print/consolidate G/L transactions` from the Reports Menu.

The default setting, as shown in Figure 26–2, will print the report in detail and will sort and summarize the General Ledger transactions by General Ledger account numbers. If you wished to print the report in summary form, or sort the transaction by "Account", "Journal entry" or "Transaction date", you would select "Edit" and then select the required option.

❑ Select: `Print`

Figure 28–2

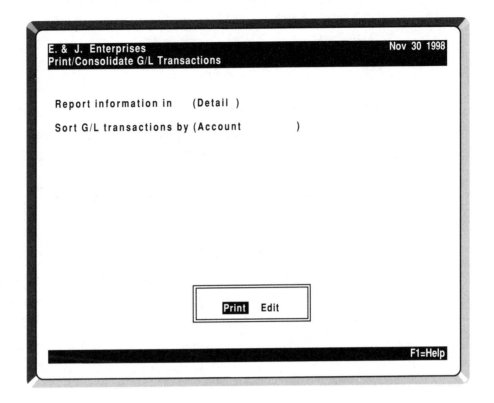

After the report has been printed, ACCPAC Plus will display the following message:

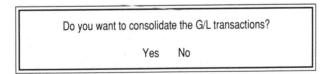

❏ Select: `Yes`

The following prompt will appear:

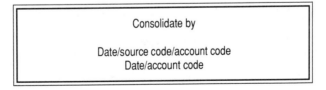

❏ Select: `Date/source code/account code`
❏ Press: [Esc] once to return to the ACCPAC Accounts Payable Master Menu.
❏ Press: `Q` to return to the Start Menu.

If "G/L E.& J. Enterprises" is not displayed on the Start Menu, refer to Chapter 2 for the necessary steps to create the proper Start Menu line.

❑ Select: G/L E. & J. Enterprises

❑ Type: 113098 in the New date field.

❑ Press: [Enter]

❑ Select: Accept to confirm the date.

ACCPAC Plus will start the General Ledger program and determine if there are any batches to be retrieved.

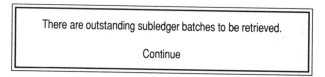

> There are outstanding subledger batches to be retrieved.
>
> Continue

❑ Press: [Enter] to continue.

❑ Select: 3. Transaction processing from the ACCPAC General Ledger Master Menu.

❑ Select: 1. Batch processing from the Transaction Processing Menu.

❑ Select: 2. Retrieve subledger batches from the Batch Processing Menu.

The Retrieve Subledger Batches screen (Figure 28–3) identifies that there are Accounts Payable batches to be retrieved.

Figure 28–3

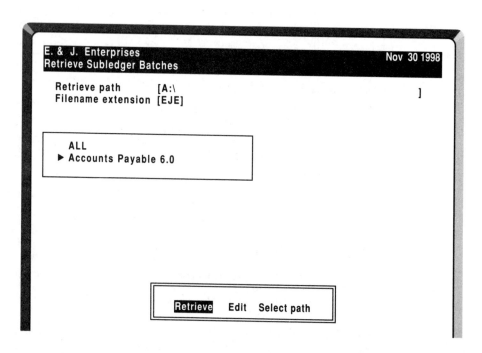

❑ Select: Retrieve

The next screen display, as shown in Figure 28–4, identifies that one batch with 9 entries has been created. The debit and credit totals equal $9,766.75.

Figure 28–4

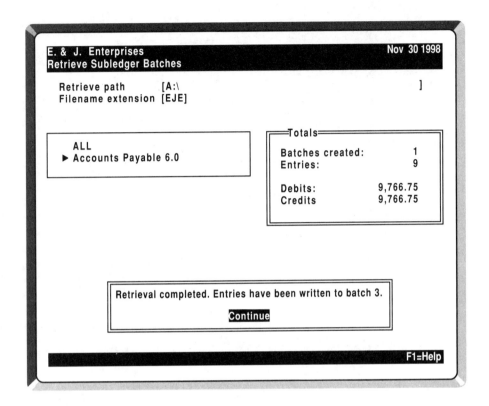

❑ Press: [Enter] to continue.

In a few moments the screen will display the Batch Processing Menu.

❑ Press: [Esc] to return to the Transaction Processing Menu.

❑ Select: 2. Print batches from the Transaction Processing Menu.

❑ Select: Print to print the retrieved Accounts Payable batch.

Once the Batch Listing has finished printing, the screen will return to the Transaction Processing Menu.

❑ Select: 3. Post batches from the Transaction Processing Menu.

The following figure (Figure 28–5) will appear:

❑ Select: 1. Post batches to current year from the Post Batches Menu.

A warning will appear instructing you to back up the data files before proceeding.

❑ Back up your data files.

Figure 28–5

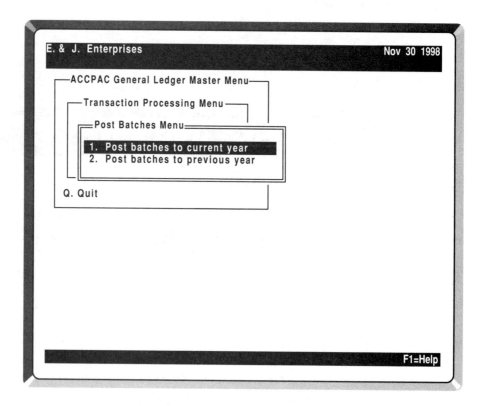

Once you have backed up your data, return to the `Post Batches to Current Year` menu.

❑ Select: `Post`

Once the posting is finished the following message will appear:

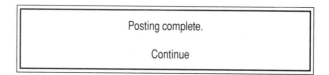

❑ Press: [Enter]
❑ Press: [Esc] twice to return to the ACCPAC General Ledger Master Menu.
❑ Press: `Q` to return to the Start Menu.
❑ Select: `A/P E. & J. Enterprises` from the Start Menu.
❑ Press: [Enter] to accept the `New date` of 11/30/98.

PERIOD END

Before continuing with the period end processing you should back up your data files. Once you have backed up your data files,

❏ Select: 6. Period end processing from the ACCPAC Accounts Payable Master Menu.

❏ Select: 1. Period end from the Period End Processing Menu.

The following "Period End" warning (Figure 28–6) will appear:

Figure 28–6

```
E. & J. Enterprises                                          Nov 30 1998
Period End




          Warning! Back up the A/P data before using this function.

          This function will:
          - Set period-to-date totals to zero for all vendors.
          - Clear paid transactions up to the clearing date.
          - Clear fully invoiced retainage transactions.
          - Remove transactions from history (if selected).

                       Proceed with Period End processing?

                              Yes    No


                                                              F1=Help
```

❏ Select: Yes to continue.

The Transaction clearing date is the date up to which fully paid transactions will be cleared from the current Accounts Payable data and transferred to historical data. This date is also used to calculate the date up to which historical information will be deleted.

❏ Press: [Enter] to accept the Transaction clearing date of 11/30/98.

ACCPAC Plus will display the warning message as shown in Figure 28–7.

If you have not backed up your data files, you should choose "No" and then return to the Start Menu to back up these files.

❏ Select: Yes to clear the batch status information.

Figure 28–7

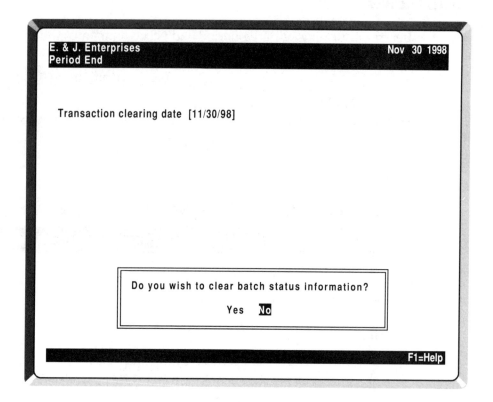

The following option bar will appear:

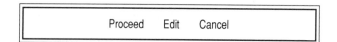

❑ Select: Proceed

This function allows you to clear the fully paid transactions up to the Transaction clearing date. If you keep transaction history, it transfers fully paid transactions to the history file.

ACCPAC Plus will move the fully paid transactions to the history file and then delete those transactions that are dated before October 31, 1998 from the history file. Once the batch status has been cleared, the Period End Processing Menu will reappear.

❑ Press: [Esc] to return to the ACCPAC Accounts Payable Master Menu.

❑ Select: Q to return to the Start Menu.

❑ Back up your data files.

Year End

Do not attempt this function now. The following material is for your reference after you have completed processing a full year of entries to Accounts Payable. The purposes of the Year End function are to transfer vendor transaction totals for the current year to the previous year's total and to set period-to-date and year-to-date totals to zero in preparation for a new fiscal year. It clears paid transactions up to the clearing date. The function also resets batch numbers and posting sequence numbers, and clears the batch status information. Year-to-date statistics are moved to last-year statistics and the current-year statistics are reset to zero.

This function is used only once each year, after the Period end function is completed at the end of the last fiscal period. You must not run this function twice or you will reset the vendor statistics to zero for both the current year and the previous year.

When you have completed the period end procedures for the final period of the fiscal year you would complete the following steps to prepare for a new fiscal year.

1. Back up your data files to two disks. These back-up disks should be write-protected and stored in a safe location should there be any inquiries at some future date. Keep the two disks in different locations.

2. Enter the last day of the fiscal year as the "New date".

3. Select: `6. Period end processing` from the ACCPAC Accounts Payable Master Menu.

4. Select: `2. Year end` from the Period End Processing Menu.

5. You will receive a warning about backing up your data. If you had not backed up your data files you would select "No" and do so before proceeding to select "Yes".

6. Ensure that the `Transaction clearing date` displays the last day of the fiscal year.

    ❑ Press: [Enter]

7. Clear the Vendor History file up to the last day of the fiscal year. The "Clear Vendor History up to" option allows you to choose whether to clear fully paid transactions from the history file. The process clears only those transactions that have been in history for at least the number of days specified on the "Keep Transaction History For" option.

8. Return to the Start Menu and back up your data files to new back-up disks.

After completing these steps you would be prepared to enter Accounts Payable information for the new fiscal year.

❑ Exit from ACCPAC Plus.

REVIEW QUESTIONS

1. Describe the sequence of operations that should be completed at period end.
2. What is the purpose of running the Period end function?
3. Under what circumstances might the Open Payables be out of balance with the G/L Accounts Payable control account?
4. Describe the steps necessary to transfer the Accounts Payable information to the General Ledger.
5. What does the Period end function do?
6. Why must you be sure to run the Year end function only once?
7. What is the purpose of the Print/Consolidate G/L Transactions function?
8. How may the transactions be sorted in the "Print/consolidate G/L transactions" function?
9. Under normal circumstances how often would you post batches to the General Ledger?
10. When would you run the Period end function?
11. When would you run the Year end function?

EXERCISE

The end of the first period is November 30, 1998.
1. Display the Batch status for the Invoice, Adjustment, and Manual Check batches to ensure that they have all been entered and posted to the Accounts Payable ledger.
2. Print and consolidate the G/L transactions. Consolidate the transactions by "Date/source code/account code".
3. Retrieve the transactions into the General Ledger. Use Nov. 30, 1998 as the New date.
4. Print the General Ledger batch.
5. Back up your data files.
6. Post the batch to the General Ledger
7. Return to the Accounts Payable module and proceed with the Period End Processing. The transaction clearing date will be November 30, 1998.
8. Back up your data files again.
9. Quit ACCPAC Plus.

CHAPTER

29 Adjusting Statement Specifications

The Accounts Payable module has three default statement specifications: checks, advice slips, and checks with the advice slips attached. Since all three specifications work in the same manner, you need to learn how to create specifications for only one. You will learn how to create the specifications for the combined check and advice slip. This specification is designed to print statements on standard pre-printed forms, available through commercial printers and stationery stores.

❑ Enter the commands necessary to activate the Accounts Payable module using November 30, 1998 as the New date. Display the ACCPAC Accounts Payable Master Menu for E. & J. Enterprises.

CREATING A SPECIFICATION

If you have old checks that were printed for another accounting program, you may not be able to use the ACCPAC Accounts Payable default specifications to print them since the alignment might be different. Forms suitable for your company's needs and predesigned to fit the configuration of ACCPAC Plus can be purchased from major printing suppliers. You can also design a new specification or change an existing specification to print on your present forms. In this simulation, you will adjust a statement specification so that it prints the combined check and advice slip on 8.5 x 7 inch paper.

The check and advice slip should incorporate the following elements:

1. The company's name and address.

2. The vendor's name and address.

3. The date.

4. The amount of the payment, both in numbers and words.

5. The advice slip.

❏ Select: `7. Housekeeping` from the ACCPAC Accounts Payable Master Menu.

The Housekeeping Menu will appear.

❏ Select: `2. Maintain specifications` from the Housekeeping Menu.

The Maintain Specifications screen (Figure 29–1) will appear.

Figure 29–1

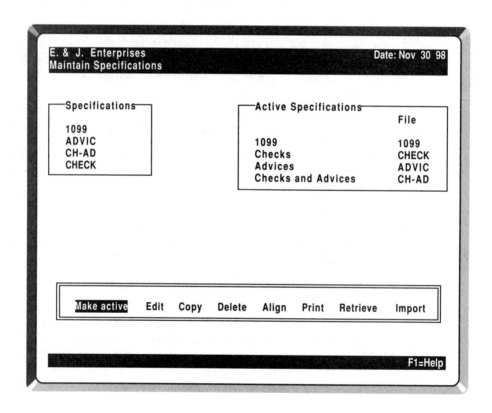

The options listed on the menu bar are described below.

Make active	This menu choice allows you to select the specifications used to print financial statements, checks, forms, and advices.
Edit	allows you to change or create specifications to print a particular financial statement.
Copy	duplicates an existing specification file and allows you to choose a different name for the new file.
Delete	allows you to eliminate a report specification file.
Align	tests column alignment and layout. In the test, printout characters will be replaced with X's and numbers with 9's.
Print	prints the contents of the specification file for the chosen document.
Retrieve	allows you to create statement specifications with the EasyWriter 11 wordprocessing program and bring them into the Accounts Payable.
Import	enables you to import a standard DOS text file (ASC11 text file) to the financial statement of your choice; you could create a title page using wordprocessing software, export it to a DOS file, and then import the DOS file into the Accounts Payable.

From the options bar at the bottom of the Maintain Specifications Menu,

❑ Select: `Edit`

You will assign the name "CHAD1" to this specification document.

❑ Type: `CHAD1` in the `Edit` box.

❑ Press: `Enter`

When creating specifications, you must type the information precisely. A comma in place of a period will cause an error message to appear instead of the printed statement.

The `Maintain Specifications` screen will disappear and your screen will be filled with rows of "+'s". You have not broken the computer! This represents a blank page to allow you to create the specifications.

Before you make any changes, you should be aware of a few keystrokes used to edit the statement specifications:

1. Pressing **Enter** will insert a new line where the cursor is resting. You must avoid pressing **Enter** unless you want to insert a new line.

2. When you wish to scroll up or down, use the directional keys, not **Enter**.

3. Pressing **F6** will delete the line on which the cursor is resting.

4. If you press the **Page-down** or **Page-up** keys on the right side of the keyboard, you will move to the top or bottom of the screen without moving through each line.

5. Holding down **Home** and pressing a directional key will move the cursor as far as it can go in a particular direction.

6. **Del** or **Delete** will delete a single character in the space occupied by the cursor.

7. Pressing **F5** twice will display the Chart of Accounts. Once you have selected the account number, press **Enter** to insert the number in the current specification.

8. Pressing **Esc** will allow you to exit from the file. You may save or cancel your changes when exiting.

Form Control Specifications

Form control specifications determine how the checks and advice slips will be printed. The four different types of form control specifications are described below.

Comment specifications

Comment specifications are not used in calculations or printed on the statement itself. They are simply comments that appear on the specification document. A comments specification line must begin with two periods (..).

The first four lines on your specification document will be comments identifying the statement, its author, and the date it was created.

You may type the following Form Control Specifications in upper- or lower-case, or a combination of the two since these specifications do not control printing. You must be careful to type either upper- or lower-case as shown in the material for the remainder of the chapter.

❑ Type: `..CHECK AND ADVICE SPECIFICATION NUMBER ONE`
❑ Press: [Enter]
❑ Type: `..THE ADVICE PRINTS ABOVE THE CHECK`
❑ Press: [Enter]
❑ Type: `..BY (YOUR NAME)`
❑ Press: [Enter]

❑ Type: ..ON NOVEMBER 30, 1998
❑ Press: [Enter]

Text width specification

The text width specification tells ACCPAC Plus how many characters are available on a line that contains the written currency amount on a check. To ensure that the text amount on a check cannot be altered, the program inserts one or more asterisks before and after the printed text. When defining the text width specifications add four spaces to the number required to allow the program to insert at least one asterisk and one space at each end of the printed amount.

❑ Type: 69 – LENGTH OF THE FIRST TEXTUAL AMOUNT LINE ON CHECK
❑ Press: [Enter]

Body size specification

The standard advice slip portion of the statement is 8.5 inches wide and 3.5 inches, or 21 lines long. The body size specification will be 21 less the number of lines allowed for the header and footer. The number of lines available is entered at the left margin immediately following the Text Width specification. Your specification will have 14 lines for details on the advice slip.

❑ Type: 14 – NUMBER OF DETAIL LINES ON THE ADVICE
❑ Press: [Enter]

Dollar width specification

All specification documents must include a dollar width specification on the line following the body size specification. The dollar width specification identifies the number of characters (from one to fifteen) allowed for printing dollar amounts. You must count numbers, decimal points, commas, and a trailing plus or minus sign. For example, 1,000.00 would require at least nine spaces. You should normally allow more space than you expect to use. The number of characters is entered at the left margin.

Allow 15 characters for the dollar size specification.

❑ Type: 15 – THE WIDTH OF THE COLUMNS ON THE ADVICE
❑ Press: [Enter] twice

Pitch specification

The pitch specification is optional. It is used to alter the number of characters per inch that will be printed on the statement. If you do not insert this specification, ACCPAC Plus will use your printer's default.

The pitch specification uses the form ".Pnn", where "nn" stands for the number of characters per inch that you require. (The condensed print specification for most printers is ".P17".) It should appear at the left margin of the line following the dollar width specification.

A Comment Specification may be entered on the line before the Pitch Specification, identifying the number of letters per inch. Set your pitch specification at 10 characters per inch.

❑ Type: `..SET PITCH TO 10 CHARACTERS PER INCH`

❑ Press: [Enter]

❑ Type: `.P10`

❑ Press: [Enter]

The header specification

The header is the upper section of the advice slip. Each line in the header specification must begin with ".H" even if you want a blank line.

Ensure that the cursor is on the line below the pitch specification, ".P10".

❑ Press: [Enter] to create a blank line.

A percentage sign instructs ACCPAC Plus to print a piece of information stored in its memory. "%V1" stands for the vendor number and "%V2" for the vendor name. "%M1.M %M1.D %M1.Y" prints the month, day, and year of the statement's run date.

❑ Type: `.H @8%V1 @27%V2 @65%M1.M %M1.D %M1.Y` on the first line of the header.

❑ Press: [Enter]

❑ Type: `.H`

❑ Press: [Enter] to leave the next line of the header blank.

The detail specifications

The detail specifications control the detailed invoice and payment information for the vendor. You only have to enter one specification line to print all the transactions on the advice slip. Each transaction will appear on a separate line in the format specified.

The detail specification line must start with ".L" at the left margin."@nn" controls the indent.

"%L2" prints the invoice number.
"%L1.M %L1.D %L1.Y" prints the invoice date.
"%L3" prints the gross amount being paid.
"%L4" prints the discount.
"%L5" prints the net payment.

The numbers before these codes control where the information is printed relative to the left margin.

- ❏ Type: `.L @1%L2 @14%L1.M %L1.D %L1.Y @24%L3 @40%L4 @58%L5`
- ❏ Press: `Enter`

The footer specifications

Each line in the footer must begin with ".F".

"%F1" prints the gross total.
"%F2" prints the discount total.
"%F3" prints the net total.

- ❏ Enter the following footer specification lines, starting on the line below the detail specification:

```
.F
.F @24%F1 @40%F2 @58%F3
.F
.F
.F
```

The Check Specifications

You will enter check specifications identical to the default specifications for checks included in the Accounts Payable module. The specification lines to print the checks must all start with ".C", followed by the indent code.

"%M1.M %M1.D %M1.Y" prints the date in a month/day/year format.
"%A1" prints the amount of the check in numbers, starting with a "$" symbol.
"%A2" writes out the amount of the check in words, with at least one leading and trailing asterisk to delimit the amount.
"%A3" continues printing the amount of the check if the previous line has insufficient space.
"%V2" to "%V6" print the vendor name and address.

- ❏ Enter the following check specification lines, starting on the line below the footer specification:

```
.C
.C
.C
.C
.C @55%M1.M %M1.D %M1.Y
.C
.C @55%A1
.C
.C
.C @8%A2
```

```
.C @8%A3
.C
.C @8%V2
.C @8%V3
.C @8%V4
.C @8%V5
.C
.C
.C
.C
.C
```

Once you have completed editing this specification,

❑ Press: [Esc]

❑ Press: [Enter] to save the changes.

EDITING SPECIFICATIONS

After creating the specifications for the checks, you discover that E. & J. Enterprises has 10,000 pre-printed check forms that Erin wants to use up. Unfortunately, the dollar amount and the date are in the wrong position.

To change the specification, you will first make a copy of it using the "Copy" option from the Maintain Specifications Menu. Call the copy "CHAD2".

❑ Select: `Copy` from the option bar at the bottom of the screen.

❑ Select: `CHAD1` from the `Copy from` option box.

❑ Type: `CHAD2` in the `Copy to` option box.

❑ Press: [Enter]

Remember that you should never make alterations directly to a working statement specification. Always copy it first, then edit the copy.

❑ Select: `Edit` from the option bar.

❑ Select: `CHAD2` from the Edit box.

❑ Locate lines ".C @55%M1.M %M1.D %M1.Y" (the date) and ".C @55%A1" (the dollar amount). On both lines, change the indent positions to 45.

❑ Press: [Esc]

Save your changes when prompted.

You must make a specification active before it can be used to print checks.

❑ Select: `Make active` from the menu bar on the Maintain Specifications screen.

The `Active Specifications` box will be highlighted.

- ❏   Move the selector bar to "Checks and Advices".
- ❏   Press: [Enter]

The selector bar will move to the Specifications box.

- ❏   Select: `CHAD2`

ACCPAC Plus will then ask you to confirm that you want to make "CHAD2" the active specification for Checks and Advices.

- ❏   Select: `Yes`
- ❏   Press: [Esc] twice to return to the Accounts Payable Master Menu.

PAYMENT CONTROL

You will force payment of invoice number 110506 from Pear Computers Inc. which you had earlier placed "On hold" to test the new specification.

- ❏   Select: `4. Payment processing` from the ACCPAC Accounts Payable Master Menu.
- ❏   Select: `2. Control payments` from the Payment Processing Menu.
- ❏   Select: `Vendor` from the Control Payments screen.
- ❏   Type: `990015` in the Vendor number field.
- ❏   Press: [Enter]

ACCPAC Plus will confirm that the vendor is "Pear Computers Inc.".

- ❏   Select: `Invoice` from the Types option box.
- ❏   Type: `110506` in the Document number field.
- ❏   Press: [Enter]
- ❏   Select: `Edit` to change this invoice.
- ❏   Select: `Forced` from the Status box.
- ❏   Press: [Esc] to indicate that you have finished making changes.
- ❏   Select: `Accept changes`

The following figure (Figure 29–2) will appear.

Figure 29–2

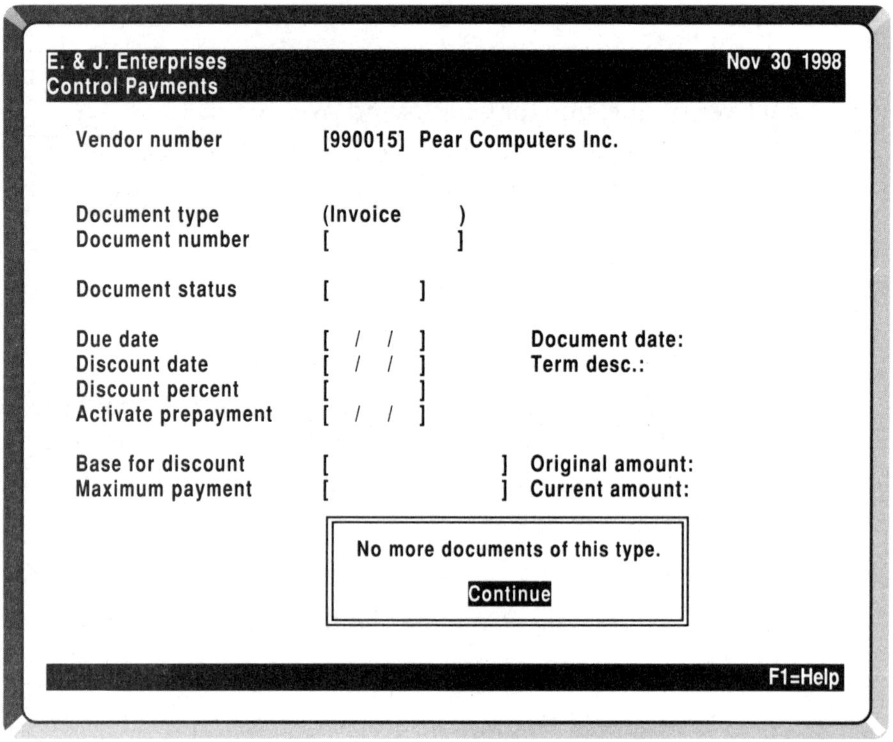

```
 ┌─────────────────────────────────────────────────────────────────┐
 │ E. & J. Enterprises                                  Nov 30 1998  │
 │ Control Payments                                                  │
 │                                                                   │
 │    Vendor number          [990015]  Pear Computers Inc.           │
 │                                                                   │
 │                                                                   │
 │    Document type          (Invoice    )                           │
 │    Document number        [          ]                            │
 │                                                                   │
 │    Document status        [         ]                             │
 │                                                                   │
 │    Due date               [  /  /  ]      Document date:          │
 │    Discount date          [  /  /  ]      Term desc.:             │
 │    Discount percent       [       ]                               │
 │    Activate prepayment    [  /  /  ]                              │
 │                                                                   │
 │    Base for discount      [          ]  Original amount:          │
 │    Maximum payment        [          ]  Current amount:           │
 │                        ┌─────────────────────────────┐            │
 │                        │  No more documents of this type. │       │
 │                        │          Continue              │         │
 │                        └─────────────────────────────┘            │
 │                                                                   │
 │                                                          F1=Help  │
 └─────────────────────────────────────────────────────────────────┘
```

☐ Press: [Enter] to continue.

☐ Press: [Esc] four times to return to the Accounts Payable Master Menu.

PRINTING CHECKS

☐ Select: 4. Payment processing from the ACCPAC Accounts Payable Master Menu.

☐ Select: 3. Check processing from the Payment Processing Menu.

☐ Print the Pre-Check Register for "Only forced" payables. Remember to enter a Description and the Bank code where required.

☐ Print and post the Checks and Advices. Since you have printed a combined check and advice, clear the advices.

☐ Print and clear the check register.

Back up your data files and quit ACCPAC Plus.

REVIEW QUESTIONS

1. For which three statements does the Accounts Payable module include specifications?
2. Give two reasons why it may be necessary to create a new specification.
3. List the four types of form control specifications and describe the function of each.
4. What information must appear on a check?
5. Why is it necessary to keep the advice slip included with a customer's check, even after it has been cashed and the bank statement reconciled?
6. Why is it important to make a copy of a statement specification before modifying it?
7. What is the purpose of the "Print" option found on the Maintain Specifications screen? Can you use it to print checks? If not, how do you print checks?
8. How do you calculate the number of lines on a form available for printing?
9. What do the following specifications print: ".P10", ".H @8%V1", "@40%F2", "@65%V1","%M1.M", and "@58%L5"?

EXERCISE

1. Using the "Edit" option on the Maintain Specifications screen, recreate the statement format, CHAD1, presented in this chapter. Print the statement specifications, and debug them. Make the statement active.
2. Create another check specification "CHCK1", using the specifications given below:

```
..
..Default specification for checks only. This specification
..produces checks that can be printed on the check portion
of
..the Deluxe check form.
..
```
Enter
```
69 — length of the first textual amount line on check
```
Enter
```
..Set printer pitch to 10 characters per inch
.P10
```
Enter
```
.C
.C
.C
.C
.C @55%M1.M %M1.D %M1.Y
.C
.C @55%A1
```

```
.C
.C
.C  @8%A2
.C  @8%A3
.C
.C
.C  @8%V2
.C  @8%V3
.C  @8%V4
.C  @8%V5
.C  @8%V6
.C
.C
.C
```

3. Save and print the new check specifications. Debug the new specification.
4. Make specification "CKCK1" the active specification for the Checks.
5. Use the Control payments function to force payment on invoice number CA246891 from Cardinal Associates.
6. Print a pre-check register for the forced item.
7. Print and post a system check to Cardinal Associates using the new specification. Remember to edit the Print/post Checks and Advices screen to change the print option to "Checks".
8. Print and clear the Check Register.
9. Back up your data files.
10. Quit ACCPAC Plus.

CHAPTER

30 Macavity & Co. Case

Macavity & Co. has decided to include the Accounts Payable on the computer, using the ACCPAC Plus Accounts Payable module. This case continues from the General Ledger and Accounts Receivable cases in Chapters 11 and 20.

After completing this case, organize and submit Macavity & Co.'s printouts. Each printout *must* contain your initials following the company name. Save the data files for your instructor to evaluate.

1. ADDING TO THE START MENU

Using the same data disk that you used for Chapters 11 and 20, create a line on the Start Menu using the following information:

Start Name	Macavity A/P
Program	Accounts Payable
Drive	A:
Data Directory	Cat
Data Extension	Cat

2. CREATING ACCOUNTS PAYABLE

Create the Accounts Payable files using the following data.

Company Data

Company Name	Macavity & Co. (followed by your initials)
Address	1313 Fishbone Alley
	Alleycat Junction
	Meowville
Zip/postal	KIT-KAT
Phone	111-555-9999

Fax	111-555-9998
Identity Number	[ENTER]
Company Number	9
Contact	Rum Tum Tugger

System Options and Defaults

Keep transaction history for	30 days
Include bank with control account set	Y
Print check forms	Y
Process 1099's	N
Allow check reconciliation	Y
Allow edit of imported batches	N
Allow edit of vendor Statistics	Y
Allow edit of G/L distribution description	Y
Allow edit of base for discount	Y
Calculate base for discount with tax	Excluded
Default aging periods	1-30, 31-60, and 61-90.

ACCPAC Plus Integration

G/L departments	N
Send to G/L reference field	Vendor name
Send to G/L description field	Document description
Post system checks in detail	Y
Integrate with Job Costing	N
Retainage Accounting	N
Payable control	2101
Bank	1101
Purchase discount	4520

Tax Information

Include on tax tracking report	All details
Allow edit of tax code	Y
Definable tax code name	Tax code
Tax code 1	VAT recoverable

Start the ACCPAC Accounts Payable module using August 1, 1997 as the New date.

Housekeeping

Add/modify/delete banks

Add the following bank code.

Bank code	cash
Description	Working Funds
Next check number	1
General Ledger Bank	1101
Specifications Check	CHECK
Specifications Advice	ADVIC
Specifications Check and Advice	CH-AD

Add/modify/delete control account sets

Add the following control account sets.

Account set code	1
Description	Accounts Payable-General
G/L Payable control	2101
G/L Purchase discount	4520
Bank code	cash

Add/modify/delete terms

You will set up two sets of terms codes: net 30, and 2/10,n/30.
Enter the following specifications to install terms code n/30.

Terms code	n/30
Description	Net 30
Due date type	Specific number of days
Number of days	30
Discount percent	0.00

Enter the following specifications to install terms code 2/10,n/30.

Terms code	2%disc
Description	2/10,n/30
Due date type	Specific number of days
Number of days	30
Discount percent	2.00
Discount type	Specific number of days
Discount number of days	10

Add/modify/delete distributions

You will create two distribution codes, "VAT" for VAT recoverable, and "PURCH" for purchases. Enter the following to create the distribution for VAT recoverable.

Description code	vat
Description	VAT Recoverable
G/L account	2111
Tax code	1
Tax tracking Tax type	Tax
Tax rate	10.0

Enter the following to create the distribution for Purchases.

Description code	purch
Description	Purchases
G/L account	4510
Tax code	1
Tax tracking Tax type	Tax included purchase
Tax rate	10.0
G/L tax account	2111

Print the company profile for Macavity & Co.

3. Creating Vendor Accounts

During July, you posted purchases from two vendors, Cat Morgen Trading Co. and Tumblebrutus. Purchases were made later from a third vendor, Munkustrap. The full profiles for all three vendors follow. Create the vendor accounts for all three. No comments or references will be added to the vendor profiles.

a) Vendor Number   AP001

Name	Cat Morgen Trading Co.
On hold	No
Short name	CatMo
Address	1 Dory Lane
	Square Rigger Pier
	Meowville
Zip/postal	KIT-KAT
Telephone	111-555-8889
Fax	111-555-8888
Contact	Morgen
Starting date	July 1,1997
Control account set	1
Default dist. code	purch
Terms	n/30
Bank ID number	[ENTER]

Credit limit	[ENTER]
Report group	goods
Identity number	[ENTER]

b) *Vendor Number   AP005*

Name	Munkustrap
On hold	No
Short name	Munku
Address	The Old Fishing Boat
	Old Wharf Way
	Meowville
Zip/postal	KIT-KAT
Telephone	111-555-8887
Fax	111-555-8886
Contact	Munkustrap
Starting date	July 1,1997
Control account set	1
Default dist. code	purch
Terms	n/30
Bank ID number	[ENTER]
Credit limit	[ENTER]
Report group	goods
Identity number	[ENTER]

c) *Vendor Number   AP010*

Name	Tumblebrutus
On hold	No
Short name	Tumbl
Address	95 High Street
	Market Square
	Meowville
Zip/postal	KIT-KAT
Telephone	111-555-8885
Fax	111-555-8884
Contact	Tumblebrutus
Starting date	July 1,1997
Control account set	1
Default dist. code	purch
Terms	2%disc
Bank ID number	[ENTER]
Credit limit	[ENTER]
Report group	goods
Identity number	[ENTER]

Print the Vendor list and statistics report. Review it for errors. Make any necessary corrections using the Add/modify/delete vendors option.

4. POSTING THE JULY TRANSACTIONS

Exit from the Accounts Payable module, then start it again using July 31, 1997 as the New date.

Now you must post the July transactions, which were posted to the General Ledger in Chapter 11. Create a batch to post the July purchases to the Accounts Payable Ledger. The description of the will be: "July Transactions". The transactions were as follows:

a) Tumblebrutus, $410 (VAT included), invoice IN7499, dated July 1, 1997. The terms were 2/10, n/30. The purchase order number is MACAV 002. The purchase was for inventory for resale.

b) Cat Morgen Trading Company, $385 (VAT included), invoice number MORG 001 dated July 31, 1997. The terms were n/30. The Purchase order number is MACAV 003. The purchase was for inventory for resale.

Once you have entered these invoices, print the invoice batch and review it for errors. Post it to the Accounts Payable ledger. Print the Invoice Posting Journal, sorted by Vendor number, then clear the posting journals. Print a copy of the Open Payables report sorted in Detail by date, and compare it to the Accounts Payable, Trade control account in the General Ledger Trial Balance that you printed in Chapter 11.

Exit from the Accounts Payable module, then start the General Ledger module using July 31, 1997 as the New date. Retrieve the Accounts Payable batch into the General Ledger, print the batch, then delete it so that a duplicate posting is avoided.

5. ENTERING THE AUGUST TRANSACTIONS

Exit from the General Ledger module. Re-enter ACCPAC Accounts Payable and set the New date to August 31, 1997. Create a new batch to record the following invoices.

The Description for the batch will be "August Transactions".

a) Vendor   Cat Morgen Trading Co.

Invoice Number	MORG 003
Invoice Date	August 5, 1997
Reference	MACAV 006
Description	Inventory purchases
Terms	[ENTER]
Dist. code	[ENTER]
Tax code	[ENTER]
Amount	50.00
Tax amount	[ENTER]

| Description | [ENTER] |

b) *Vendor Munkustrap*

Doc. No.	MUN 607
Doc. date	August 9, 1997
Reference	MACAV 007
Description	Inventory purchases
Terms	[ENTER]
Dist. code	[ENTER]
Tax code	[ENTER]
Amount	100.00
Tax amount	[ENTER]
Description	[ENTER]

c) *Vendor Tumblebrutus*

Doc. no.	IN7586
Doc. date	August 16, 1997
Reference	MACAV 008
Description	Inventory purchases
Terms	[ENTER]
Dist. code	[ENTER]
Tax code	[ENTER]
Amount	75.00
Tax amount	[ENTER]
Description	[ENTER]
Base for discount	[ENTER]

d) *Vendor Cat Morgen Trading Co.*

Doc. No.	MORG 009
Doc. date	August 20, 1997
Reference	MACAV 009
Description	[ENTER]
Terms	[ENTER]
Dist. code	[ENTER]
Tax code	[ENTER]
Amount	100.00
Tax amount	[ENTER]
Description	[ENTER]

e) Vendor   Munkustrap

Doc. No.	MUN 672
Doc. date	August 25, 1997
Reference	MACAV 010
Description	[ENTER]
Terms	[ENTER]
Dist. code	[ENTER]
Tax code	[ENTER]
Amount	50.00
Tax amount	[ENTER]
Description	[ENTER]

f) Vendor   Cat Morgen Trading Co.

Doc. No.	MORG 017
Doc. date	August 30, 1997
Reference	MACAV 011
Description	[ENTER]
Terms	[ENTER]
Dist. code	[ENTER]
Tax code	[ENTER]
Amount	150.00
Tax amount	[ENTER]
Description	[ENTER]

Print the Invoice Batch List and review it for errors. Post the batch to the Accounts Payable Ledger. Print the Invoice Posting Journal sorted by Vendor number, then clear the posting journal. Print the Open Payables Report in Detail by date.

6. MAKING ADJUSTMENTS

It has come to your attention that the Munkustrap invoice, number MUN 672, was incorrectly recorded for $50. The invoice amount should have been $75.

Create a new invoice batch for Debit note DN-001 dated August 25, 1997. Print the Invoice Batch, post it to the Accounts Payable Ledger, then print the Invoice Posting Journal sorted by Vendor number. Clear the posting journal. Print a copy of the Open Payables in Detail by date.

7. PREPARING MANUAL CHECKS

Macavity & Co. made a special arrangement with Tumblebrutus to pay for the August 16 purchase (invoice number IN7586) upon delivery. You paid the invoice when the goods were received using a manual check, number 105.

Prepare a manual check batch to record the payment of the invoice. Remember to take the discount for early payment. Print the manual check batch, print/post the manual check, and then print the Manual Check Register sorted by Bank and check number. Clear the check register after it has finished printing.

8. PREPARING SYSTEM CHECKS

Print the Pre-Check register. The run date will be August 31. Macavity & Co. wants to take discounts when available. This run will process all the invoices, not only the forced ones. Clear the check register after the printing is finished.

The next step will be to print the checks using option "2. Print/post checks and advices". Accept the check number displayed. You do not have proper check forms, so print the checks on continuous computer paper. Print an alignment test sample, then print the checks. Clear the Advice information. Print a Check Register and then clear the Check Register information. Print the Check Reconciliation.

Print an updated copy of the Open Payables report in Detail by date.

9. PRINTING/CONSOLIDATING THE TRANSACTIONS

Before posting the Accounts Payable transactions to the General Ledger, print the G/L transactions. Consolidate the General Ledger transactions by "Date/account code".

Exit from the Accounts Payable module and start the General Ledger module using August 31, 1997 as the New date. Retrieve the Accounts Payable transactions, print the invoice batch, and post it to the General Ledger. Print and clear the Posting Journal.

Print a new copy of the General Ledger List and compare the total of the Accounts Payable control account to the last copy of the Open Payables Listing.

Exit from ACCPAC Accounts Payable.

Back-up Procedures

DISK OPERATING SYSTEM

DOS is the short form for **D**isk **O**perating **S**ystem. Operating systems act as an interface between the microcomputer, the user, and the application program being used. **MS-DOS**, developed by Microsoft Corporation, is the most widely installed operating system for microcomputers. This appendix will review the basic DOS operations necessary for maintaining your ACCPAC Plus data files.

ACCESSING DOS FROM ACCPAC PLUS

Before entering a DOS command, you should either return to the Start Menu or exit from ACCPAC Plus. If you enter DOS commands when ACCPAC Plus files are open, you may damage these data files. Furthermore, some network software will not let you copy files unless you return to the Start Menu or exit from ACCPAC Plus.

With the Start Menu displayed on the screen, you access DOS through the System Manager.

❑ Enter the commands to display the Start Menu.

❑ Press: F3 to display the System Manager.

❑ Move the selector bar to DOS

❑ Press: Enter

The screen clears and a message is displayed. Depending on the version of DOS and the brand of microcomputer that you are using this message may vary from that shown below.

```
Microsoft(R)  MS-DOS(R)  Version 4.00
(C) Copyright Microsoft Corp. 1981-1982

Type "exit" to return to ACCPAC Plus
```

The last line of the message means that, when you are finished using DOS, you would type exit and press **Enter** to return to the ACCPAC Plus System Manager. You would then press **Escape** to return to the Start Menu.

THE DOS PROMPT

If you access DOS through the System Manager, the DOS prompt will appear just below the message displayed above. This prompt, **C:\DOS>**, has three components.

C: One letter followed by the colon indicates the default drive for your system. In most non-networked systems this letter will be **C** or **D**. If your computer is part of a network, a different letter may be displayed.

\DOS This component indicates the default directory on the default drive. **\DOS** indicates that the system that the authors use defaults to a directory named **DOS** in the root (\), or main directory, of drive C. The system that you are using may default to the root directory of the default drive. This would be indicated on your screen by the backslash (\) without any additional letters.

> The greater-than symbol indicates the MS-DOS operating system.

DOS commands are entered immediately following the DOS prompt. Each command has a structure or syntax that must be followed exactly or the command will not work. After you type a command, check to make sure that the command is spelled properly and that the syntax is right. This includes checking the use of the colon, spaces, and the backslash. You can then press **Enter** to tell DOS to execute the command.

DISK PREPARATION

The magnetic coating on a disk must be prepared, or formatted, for recording information from a computer. The format, or organization of the magnetic material on each side of the disk, depends on the type of disk drive it is to be used in and on the quality of construction of the disk itself.

Disk Types

1. **Double Sided, Double Density (DSDD) 5.25** inch disks have a storage capacity of 360 kilobytes. These disks can be used in either double density or high density 5.25 inch disk drives.

2. **Double Sided, High Density (DSHD) 5.25** inch disks have a storage capacity of 1.2 megabytes. When formatted to their capacity, these disks *can only be used* in a high density 5.25 inch disk drive.

3. **Double Sided, Double Density (DSDD) 3.5** inch disks have a storage capacity of 720 kilobytes. These disks can be used in either double density or high density disk drives.

4. **Double Sided, High Density (DSHD) 3.5** inch disks have a storage capacity of 1.44 megabytes. When formatted to their capacity these disks *can only be used* in high density 3.5 inch disk drives.

Formatting Disks

If you purchase preformatted disks, they are ready for use in your computer system. If the disks are not preformatted you must prepare them for use in your computer by using the **DOS** format command. Disks should be formatted in a disk drive that matches the disk's capacity.

The structure, or syntax, of the DOS format command is as follows. (Always press **Enter** at the end of a DOS command.)

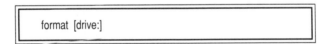

```
format [drive:]
```

This means that you type the DOS command, **format**, press the spacebar once, type the **one** letter for the disk drive that you wish to use for formatting, then type a colon (**:**) and press **Enter** to complete the command. You can enter Dos commands in either UPPER or lower case.

To format a disk in drive A you would enter the following command:

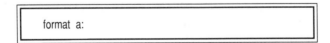

```
format a:
```

After a few seconds the following message would be displayed on the screen.

```
Insert new diskette for drive a:
and strike ENTER when ready
```

After inserting your disk in drive A and closing the drive door, press **Enter**. While the disk is being formatted, DOS will display messages that inform you of the progress of the formatting process.

If you are using DOS version 4.0 or higher, you will be asked to enter a label or name for the disk being formatted. You could then type in up to eleven characters as a name for the disk and press **Enter**. To leave the disk un-named, you could simply press **Enter.**

When formatting is complete, the following message will be displayed for a double sided double density disk.

```
Format complete
362496 bytes total disk space
362496 bytes available on disk

Format another (Y/N)?
```

During the formatting process, DOS will usually identify poor or flawed areas of the disk. These areas are not suitable for storing data. In such a case, DOS will display a line indicating the number of bytes in these "bad sectors" and will mark these areas so that it does not try to store data in them.

If you wish to format another disk, you would type Y in response to the Format another (Y/N)? prompt and press **Enter**. If you did not wish to format another disk, you would type N and press **Enter**.

Your disk is now ready to use in your computer system.

DIRECTORIES

Directories allow you to group your files in convenient categories. Using directories also allows you to store more files on a disk. A double sided double density disk is restricted to 112 files in the main, or **root** directory. A directory in the root directory can contain more than 112 files. If you use the ACCPAC Plus General Ledger, Accounts Receivable, and Accounts Payable modules, you will create more than 112 files. ACCPAC Plus is more efficient when all of the data files for a company are grouped in a single directory that does not contain any other files.

Making Directories

The structure, or syntax, of the DOS command to make a directory is as follows:

```
md  [drive:] path
```

This means that you type the DOS command **md**, press the space bar once, type the **one** letter for the disk drive that your disk is in and then type a colon (:). Path refers to directory names. Remember that you can enter DOS commands in either UPPER or lower case.

To make a directory called **EJE** in the root directory of the disk in drive A, you would enter the following:

```
md  a:\eje
```

The backslash (\) tells DOS that the directory EJE is to be made in the root directory of the disk in drive A.

FILENAMES & PATHNAMES

DOS uses complete **filenames** to identify individual files that are stored on a disk.

A **pathname** identifies the directory in which a file is stored and the complete filename of the stored file. In a pathname, the drive letter, the directory name, and the filename are separated by backslashes (\).

DOS filenames have two parts, the **filename** and the **extension**, separated by a period.

The first part of the filename is the filename itself. This filename can be up to eight characters in length. Each file in a directory must have a unique filename. When you are using ACCPAC Plus, each filename is created by the ACCPAC Plus program to identify a specific file that the program uses. The General Ledger module creates files that start with the letters **GL**.

The extension is separated from the filename by a period and may be up to three characters long. ACCPAC Plus uses extensions to identify the files belonging to a specific company; for example, all the files for E. & J. Enterprises will use the extension **EJE**. ACCPAC Plus allows you to specify the extension in each line on the Start Menu.

COPYING DATA FILES

DOS has three basic commands for copying files, **copy**, **xcopy**, and **diskcopy**. We'll emphasize the use of the first two.

Copy

The **copy** command should be used if your computer system has two disk drives and uses DOS 3.1 or lower. The structure of this command is as follows:

```
copy [drive:] pathname1 [drive:] pathname2
```

[drive:]pathname1 refers to the disk drive, directory and files that you wish to copy and **[drive:]pathname2** refers to the disk drive, directory and files you want to copy to.

If you wish to use the copy command to copy files to a directory, you must make the directory first.

To copy ACCPAC Plus files from the EJE directory in the root directory of a disk in drive A to the EJE directory in the root directory of a disk in drive B, you would enter the following command:

```
copy a:\eje\*.eje  b:\eje\*.eje
```

The * is a wild card, which in this case represents all filenames with the extension EJE in the \EJE directory.

To copy the files with the extension EXT, from the EXERCISE directory of a disk in drive A to the EXERCISE directory of a disk in drive B, you would enter the following command:

```
copy a:\exercise\*.ext  b:\exercise\*.ext
```

Xcopy

The **xcopy** command may be used if you have DOS version 3.2 or higher. This command can be used if your computer system has one or two floppy disk drives. Additional advantages of using **xcopy** are that it is faster than the copy command and it will make directories when necessary. The structure of this command is as follows:

```
xcopy [drive:] pathname1  [drive:] pathname2
```

Two drive systems

Insert your working data disk in drive A and your back-up disk in drive B.

To copy ACCPAC Plus files with the extension EJE from the EJE directory in the root directory of the disk in drive A to the EJE directory in the root directory of the disk in drive B, you would enter the following:

```
xcopy  a:\eje\*.eje  b:\eje
```

If your computer system has two disk drives in addition to a hard drive, DOS will search the target disk for the directory that you wish to copy to. If the directory, EJE in this example, cannot be found on the target disk in drive B, DOS will display the following message:

```
Does EJE specify a filename
or directory name on target
(F = file, D = directory)?
```

To create the directory you would type   D   and press **Enter**. DOS will then read the files from the source disk into your computer's random access memory. Each file will then be written to the target disk.

If you type   F , DOS will copy all or some of the files to a file called EJE and you will lose valuable data.

To copy the files with the extension EXT, from the EXERCISE directory of a disk in drive A to the EXERCISE directory of a disk in drive B, you would enter the following:

```
xcopy  a:\exercise\*.ext  b:\exercise
```

Single drive systems

If your computer system has one disk drive in addition to the hard drive, you may use the **xcopy** command to copy files from one disk to another disk using the same disk drive. DOS will prompt you when it is necessary to insert the source and target disks in the single disk drive.

To copy all the files from the EJE directory of your working disk to the EJE directory of your back-up disk, insert the working disk in drive A and enter the following command:

```
xcopy  a:\eje  b:\eje
```

First DOS will ask you whether eje is a file or a directory. Once you respond that it is a directory, DOS will display a series of instructions directing you to change disks in the disk drive.

Back-up by chapter

If you are using a high density disk, you may wish to back up your data at the end of each chapter to a different directory on your back-up disk. If you make a serious error while working through a chapter, you can delete the files on your working disk and copy the files from the previous chapter on your back-up disk to your working disk. In a business situation you could back up your files after you work with a client's file or at the end of each day.

The **xcopy** command that you would enter must be expanded to include a **sub-directory** for the data files for that chapter or that day's work. For example, if you complete Chapter 4 and wish to back up your working data files from the directory EJE on the disk in drive A to the CH4 subdirectory in the directory EJE on the disk in drive B you would enter the following:

```
xcopy  a:\eje  b:\eje\ch4
```

If the path **\EJE\CH4** is not found on the target disk in drive B, DOS will display the following prompt:

```
Does CH4 specify a filename
or directory name on target
(F = file, D = directory)?
```

If you type   F   DOS will copy all or some of the files to a file called EJE and you will lose valuable data. To create the directory you type   D   and press **Enter**.

DISKCOPY

This command should be used with discretion. **Diskcopy** will erase all files on the target disk as it copies files from the source disk and could result in the loss of valuable data. If you wish to use diskcopy, consult your DOS manual or computer resource person.

DELETING FILES

In some instances it may be necessary to delete files from your disks. This could be necessary if you wish to redo a chapter or if you exceed the capacity of the disk's file allocation table by trying to store General Ledger, Accounts Receivable and Accounts Payable files in the root directory of a double sided double density disk. If you back up each chapter to subdirectories on a high density disk you may also exceed the storage capacity of that disk.
The syntax of the delete command follows:

```
del [drive:] pathname
```

Be very careful when deleting files. It's easy to delete valuable data files, especially when using the wild cards ? and *.

To delete all the files in the root directory of a disk in drive A, you would enter the following command:

```
del a:\*.*
```

The * is a wild card and represents all possible filenames or extensions. DOS will ask you to confirm before deleting the files.

To delete all the files in a subdirectory, you must include the subdirectory in the pathname. For example, to delete all the files in the subdirectory EJE on the disk in drive A, you would enter the following command:

```
del a:\eje
```

DOS will ask you to confirm before deleting the files.

If necessary you can delete only certain files. For example you could delete the Accounts Receivable files in the subdirectory EJE on the disk in drive A by entering the following command.

```
del a:\eje\ar*.*
```

In this case DOS will not ask if you are sure before deleting the files.

REMOVING DIRECTORIES

If you wish to remove a directory from a disk you must first delete all the files in that directory. The syntax of the remove-directory command is as follows:

```
rd [drive:] pathname
```

If you wish to remove the directory FRED from the root directory of a disk in drive A, you would enter the following command, but only after having deleted all of the files in that directory.

```
rd  a:\fred
```

If you are unsure of these DOS commands, the authors recommend that you review any DOS operation with a more experienced user or with your computer-support person.

NOTES

NOTES

NOTES

NOTES

NOTES

NOTES

NOTES

NOTES

NOTES

NOTES